The Legacy of Roman Law in the
German Romantic Era

"Der Fortschritt der Wissenschaft." Sketch by Julius Friedländer and Eduard Philippi. (Reproduced from L. Wickert, *Theodor Mommsen*, vol. 3, facing p. 104.)

The Legacy of Roman Law in the German Romantic Era

HISTORICAL VISION AND LEGAL CHANGE

James Q. Whitman

PRINCETON UNIVERSITY PRESS

PRINCETON, NEW JERSEY

Library of Congress Cataloging-in-Publication Data

Whitman, James Q., 1957–
The legacy of Roman law in the German romantic era :
historical vision and legal change / James Q. Whitman.
Includes bibliographical references.
1. Roman law—Reception—Germany. 2. Civil law—
Germany (West)—History. I. Title.
KK941.W48   1990   340.5'4'0943—dc20   89–48808

ISBN 0-691-05560-2 (alk. paper)

To the memory of Arnaldo Momigliano

CONTENTS

PREFACE

EARLY IN 1849, as the German revolution entered its last months of political failure, two friends of Theodor Mommsen sent him a sketch to commemorate his prominence among the political agitators of Saxony. Mommsen, the great Roman historian and Romanist lawyer, had recently returned to Germany after a quiet scholarly half-decade collecting inscriptions in Italy. Upon taking up his professorship at the University of Leipzig, he had immediately immersed himself in revolutionary activities that would soon lead to his expulsion from Germany for several years of Swiss exile. As Mommsen pursued his academic doom, his friends sketched for him a triptych symbolizing three hundred years of Roman law at Leipzig. In its left wing, under the date 1549, a professor in full medieval academic costume (with the odd addition of a sixteenth-century ruff), leaning at his podium and gazing intently upon his student audience, propounded words taken from the opening of the *Digest* of Justinian: "Justitia est constans et perpetua voluntas ius suum cuique tribuendi," "Justice is the constant and unwavering determination to give unto each his right." In the sketch's central panel, marked 1749 and decorated with rococo flourishes, a corpulent eighteenth-century figure with a relaxed and confident air of enlightenment instructed his students that the king was in all respects absolute: "Rex omnino legibus est solutus." Finally, in the unadorned last panel of the triptych, sat Mommsen himself, gesticulating eagerly, his hat cast to the floor in a moment of exuberance. To *his* students Mommsen proclaimed: "Dominium est furtum!"— "Property is theft." The whole scene was entitled "Progress in Scholarship."[1]

"Progress in scholarship," as these two friends of Theodor Mommsen ironically portrayed it in 1849, is my subject in this study. I wish to describe the aspirations and the beliefs of the so-called Romanist lawyers of nineteenth-century Germany, the specialists in Roman law whose mental world produced this mock triptych. They were lawyers who thought of themselves as revivers of the sixteenth century who had once more given life to the lapsed motto, "Justice is the constant and unwavering determination to give unto each his right." They were lawyers who thought of

---

[1] J[ulius] F[riedländer] and E[duard] P[hilippi], "Der Fortschritt der Wissenschaft." Reproduced in L. Wickert, *Theodor Mommsen*, 4 vols. (Frankfurt a.M., 1969), 3: facing 104; also reproduced above, as the frontispiece. The first passage quoted (from D. 1,1,10) also appears, slightly varied, at the opening of the *Institutes*. For Mommsen's Latin response to this sketch, see ibid., 483f. For Mommsen's political activity in 1849, see ibid., 152–91.

the Enlightenment as an arid and callous betrayal of the proper cultivation of justice. Finally, they were lawyers whose faith wavered in
Mommsen's time, when many of them decided that they themselves were
obliged to betray the principles of the sixteenth century—if not by proclaiming "dominium est furtum," nevertheless by proclaiming doctrines
that seemed almost equally at odds with the German history of Roman
law.

In all these moments of determined advocacy and self-doubt, the Romanist lawyers of early nineteenth-century Germany, the lawyers of the
time of Friedrich Carl von Savigny and his successors, believed themselves
capable of reviving the Roman social order. That, indeed, is what I hope
to demonstrate in this study: that German Romanist lawyers believed
they could, in some measure, revive Rome. To be sure, the Rome that
Savigny and his generation hoped to revive was a distinctively German
one, associated in complex ways with the Holy Roman Empire of the
sixteenth century, under whose aegis Roman law had first entered the
German world. And to be sure, by the time of Mommsen, the hopes of
the generation of Savigny had collapsed. Nevertheless, in the work of Romanist lawyers of both generations, what Paul Koschaker called the "cultural idea of Rome"[2] became a motivating force of unrecognized strength
in German law, and through law, the cultural idea of Rome became a
force in Germany society.

Every German historian knows that Roman law must be somehow important to the understanding of German history. Ancient Roman law remained the basis of the legal order in Germany down until the end of the
nineteenth century. Even during the decades of rapid industrialization at
the end of the century, the study of the *Corpus Iuris Civilis*, a collection
of scraps and fragments of law principally from the first centuries A.D.,
formed the foundation of a German legal education. German judges cited
and pondered ancient texts. Lawyers for the railroads and for industry,
civil servants in the burgeoning German state, and professors of the new
social sciences were all familiar with the reasoning of Paulus and Papinian
and Modestinus, with the conundra of the *Corpus Iuris* about the sale of
slaves and the powers of a Roman *paterfamilias*. Only when the great
German Civil Code came into force in 1900 did the ancient law lose its
pre-eminent place in the German legal order—and the Civil Code itself
was based predominantly on principles of Roman law.

This is a history whose broad outlines are familiar to all German his-

---

[2] Cf. Koschaker, *Europa und das Römische Recht* (Munich/Berlin, 1947), 45, and often
on "die kulturelle Romidee." (Throughout the book, all translations are my own, unless
otherwise indicated. I have not modernized spelling in any original quotations.)

torians. But it is a history whose details have rarely found an audience outside a small community of specialists in technical legal history. These specialists have produced a wealth of fine monographs on the internal doctrinal development of German law.[3] But they have too often shown themselves to be uninterested in exploring the place of Roman legal scholarship in German cultural and political life in general, and have too often neglected the records of legal practice and the importance of the classical tradition. Cultural and political historians, for their part, have (with a notable recent exception[4]) been understandably reluctant to delve much into the details of law. To be sure, even historians with little first-hand experience of the law have been able to absorb some knowledge from the work of two great products of the nineteenth century: Weber and Marx. From Marx, the greatest of the disaffected students of Savigny, historians have learned that Savigny's so-called Historical School of Law was in some way a conservative political force.[5] From Weber, historians have learned to think of the history of German Roman law as a chapter in the history of German bureaucratization and rationalization.[6] But much as one can learn from Marx and Weber, they leave their reader without a full understanding of the Roman legal culture of the nineteenth century. Weber concerned himself with the ultimate, debilitating effect of the use of Roman law on German society; he invested little effort in explaining

---

[3] For works most directly relevant to this study, see, e.g., P. Cappellini, *Systema Iuris*, Per la Storia del Pensiero Moderno Giuridico, vols. 17 and 19 (Milan, 1984–85); J. Rückert, *Idealismus, Jurisprudenz und Politik bei Friedrich Carl von Savigny*, Abhandlungen zur Rechtswissenschaftlichen Grundlagenforschung, Bd. 58 (Ebelsbach, 1984); J. Schröder, *Wissenschaftstheorie und Lehre der "Praktischen Jurisprudenz" auf deutsche Universitäten an der Wende zum neunzehnten Jahrhundert*, Ius Commune Sonderheft 11 (Frankfurt a.M., 1979). Many more such monographs are relied on throughout this study.

[4] M. John, *Politics and the Law in Late Nineteenth Century Germany: The Origins of the Civil Code* (Oxford, 1989).

[5] For Marx's attack (mounted, as scholars occasionally forget, on Hugo and thus only indirectly on Savigny), see "The Philosophical Manifesto of the Historical School of Law," in K. Marx, F. Engels, *Collected Works*, 43 vols. (New York, 1975), 1:203–10. For recent Marx-influenced works, see, e.g., H. Wagner, *Die Politische Pandektistik* (Berlin, 1985); H. Schröder, *Friedrich Karl von Savigny: Geschichte und Rechtsdenken beim Übergang vom Feudalismus zum Kapitalismus in Deutschland* (Frankfurt a.M., 1984); J. Kuczynski, "Savigny—Glanzvolle Jugend eines reaktionaren Gelehrten von einstigem Weltruf," in J. Kuczynski, *Studien zu einer Geschichte der Gesellschaftswissenschaften*, 10 vols. (Berlin, 1977), 6: 125–57, and H. Klenner, "Anmerkungen zu 'Savigny,' " in ibid., 158–73. Needless to say, studies of Savigny's conservatism are not the province of Marx-influenced scholarship alone. For a careful recent statement, see Rückert, *Idealismus, Jurisprudenz und Politik bei Friedrich von Savigny*, pp. 160ff. See also the discussion and citations below, chapter 4.

[6] See esp. Weber, *Economy and Society*, edited by G. Roth and C. Wittich, translated by E. Shils, 2 vols. (Berkeley, 1968), 2:852–55. The immense influence of Weber on the interpretation of German Roman law is noted by Cappellini, *Systema Iuris*, 2:67 and 67 n. 105.

what the Romanist lawyers themselves had hoped to accomplish. Marx and those he influenced, too, have largely misunderstood or caricatured the conservatism of the Romanist lawyers. Thus the concerns of general historians have never been properly wedded to the knowledge of specialists. As a result, we have not fully understood the personalities of the lawyers who produced the great deductive-systematic treatises of the nineteenth century and trained the German bureaucracy; and we have an impoverished understanding of the very subtle and complex legal conservatism that made Antiquity a living political force in the 1820s and 1830s, and that stirred the rebellions of both Marx and Mommsen in the 1840s.

That legal conservatism, I wish to show, was made of an amalgam of classicism and Holy Roman Imperial constitutional tradition, and it had an unexplored impact on German agricultural and commercial life. The Romanist lawyers of the first half of the nineteenth century belonged to a type familiar to the early modern period: the scholar both profoundly learned in the sources of ancient history and deeply committed to the constitutional traditions of his country as he understood them—the type of the antiquarian in politics that could be found throughout Europe in the sixteenth and seventeenth centuries. That type had, for the most part, vanished elsewhere. But it survived in Germany, I hope to show, until as late as 1861.

As a result, classical scholarship and antiquarian constitutionalism retained immense political force in early nineteenth-century Germany. Historians have, indeed, never fully appreciated the political force of German classicism or the lasting strength of Holy Roman Imperial constitutionalism. German love of the classics has, to be sure, been a familiar topic to historians of Germany for a very long time,[7] and occasionally historians have suggested that this love of the classics must have served some political purpose.[8] Legal historians, for their part, have always acknowledged,

[7] E.g., H. Ritter von Srbik, *Geist und Geschichte des deutschen Humanismus*, 2 vols. (Munich, 1950–51).

[8] Most commonly, historians have suggested that knowledge of the classics provided a rising bourgeoisie with a mark that could set them apart from rival classes. E.g., L. O'Boyle, "Klassische Bildung und Soziale Struktur in Deutschland zwischen 1800 und 1848," *HZ* 207 (1968): 584–608; F. Ringer, *Decline of the German Mandarins* (Cambridge, Mass., 1969), 21–22. Recent research has been devoted largely to quantitative analysis on the class diffusion of *Bildung* in German society: e.g., M. Kraul, *Gymnasium und Gesellschaft im Vormärz*, Studien zum Wandel von Gesellschaft und Bildung im Neunzehnten Jahrhundert, vol. 18 (Göttingen, 1980); P. Lundgreen, "Bildung und Besitz," *Geschichte und Gesellschaft* 7 (1981): 262–75; F. Ringer, *Education and Society in Modern Europe* (Bloomington, Ind., 1979), 32–112; idem, "Bestimmung und Messung von Segmentierung: Eine Teilantwort an Lundgreen," *Geschichte und Gesellschaft* 8 (1982): 280–85. For the suggestion that the classics were "neutral ground" in a profoundly divided German polity, see F. Paulsen, *Ge-*

if too often only in passing, that the life of Roman law in Germany formed part of a larger political[9] and cultural life.[10] Nevertheless, no scholar has done enough in tracing the classical tradition in the realm of law, the realm in which love of the classics made its most direct impact on German society. As for the Holy Roman Empire, its significance in German political thought of the late eighteenth century has been the subject of a number of recent historians, most prominent among them the Freiherr von Aretin.[11] But historians have not yet seen how that strength continued into the nineteenth century.

In order to show how the classics and the early modern constitutional tradition entered into nineteenth-century political life, I will take two approaches. First, I will trace the long ideological history of the most powerful subgroup of Romanist lawyers: the professors of Roman law. Second, I will discuss the history of two Romanist attempts to make use of Roman law in order to solve the social problems of the German world between 1815 and 1860: the attempt to engineer agrarian reform through Roman law after 1815, and the attempt to develop a Roman commercial law after 1848.

Of these two themes, I will devote most of my energy to the ideology of the German professors of Roman law. As elsewhere in Europe, the bare text of the *Corpus Iuris* never had the force of law in Germany. From the time that Roman law was introduced into the German world in the sixteenth century, courts and other officials relied on glosses and scholarly literature; by the early nineteenth century a great apparatus of scholarly interpretive work was the main source for Roman law in Germany. Largely as a result, Roman-law professors of the nineteenth century, the era of so-called *Pandektistik*, dominated German legal life: as one early nineteenth-century enemy saw them, they were the "juristic Brahmins, who eternalize their Sanskrit, rule everywhere all silent and still, suck the people's marrow dry, and would like to mark themselves out as the teachers of laws and morals, like the Rabbis of the Jews."[12] Under the leadership of Savigny and numerous brilliant contemporaries and successors, Germany became the land of "scholarly positivism,"[13] of "professorial

---

schichte des Gelehrten Unterrichts in Deutschland, 2d ed., 2 vols. (Berlin, 1921), 2:322. Some of the most interesting work on the political significance of the classics has been done by classicists in recent years, especially by A. Momigliano, K. Christ, and A. Heuss. I will discuss their work below in Chapter 5.

[9] E.g., F. Wieacker, *Privatrechtsgeschichte der Neuzeit,* 2d ed. (Göttingen, 1967), 440ff.

[10] Esp. Koschaker, *Europa und das Römische Recht.*

[11] See the discussion below, Chapter 3.

[12] Quoted by F. C. von Savigny in "Nachträge" to "Vom Beruf unserer Zeit für Gesetzgebung und Rechtswissenschaft" (1828 ed.), in H. Hattenhauer, ed., *Thibaut und Savigny* (Munich, 1973), 245.

[13] R. Stintzing (continued by E. Landsberg), *Geschichte der deutschen Rechtswissen-*

law,"[14] the only region in the West to build its law on academic treatises.[15] Professors succeeded in commanding the confidence of powerful politicians, in controlling the drafting commissions that created the codes of the second half of the century. In the first four chapters of this study, I will trace the tangle of cultural traditions, political accidents, and vacuums of power that made possible this scholarly dominance of German lawmaking, so critical to the maintenance of a Roman legal civilization.

It is my thesis that the political activity of these powerful professors is best understood as a kind of "ancient constitutionalism"—as politics of the revival of pre-absolutist constitutional tradition of the kind whose strength in Britain and elsewhere has been traced by J.G.A. Pocock and others. In order to substantiate this thesis, I must cover a great deal of German history in long strides. I will begin, in chapter 1, with a discussion of the rise of the "ancient constitutional" tradition of the Romanist lawyers, as it developed in the sixteenth century, when links were forged between cultural tradition and legal institutions that continued to govern the possibilities of legal life three centuries later. The experience of the sixteenth century established the idea that Roman law, and Roman-law scholars, were uniquely "impartial"—an idea drawn partly from Roman history, partly from medieval jurisprudence, and partly from the politics of constitutional and religious Reformation in sixteenth-century Germany, where Phillip Melanchthon presided over a German recasting of Roman tradition. This sixteenth-century tradition did not survive the rise of absolutism intact: as I will show in chapter 2, the crucial sixteenth-century idea of Roman "impartiality" fell into decline during the eighteenth century, and the prestige and power of the Roman-law professoriate fell along with it. But the idea of Roman-law "impartiality" retained enough vigor that Roman-law professors of the late eighteenth century could seize on it once again.

In chapters 3 and 4, I will begin the main substance of the study, showing how the sixteenth-century idea of Roman-law "impartiality" revived after 1790, under the new political conditions that helped produce the romantic movement. It was the peculiar political life of the romantic era, which revolved around the ideological revival of the Middle Ages and the Reformation, that made possible a revival of the glory of "impartial" Rome. The absolutist princes began to grow weak in the late 1780s; the French Revolution decisively broke them. As the princes faltered, Germans far and wide began to long for a return to their "ancient constitution," the constitution of the old Holy Roman Empire as it had been re-

schaft, 3 vols. in 5 (Munich/Berlin, 1910), vol. 3, pt. 2: 69ff.; Wieacker, *Privatrechtsgeschichte*, 430ff.

[14] Koschaker, *Europa und das Römische Recht*, e.g., 211.

[15] J. P. Dawson, *The Oracles of the Law* (Ann Arbor, Mich., 1968), 432ff.

formed in the sixteenth century. It was this political revival of the traditions of the Holy Roman Empire, a revival deeply bound up with romantic yearnings for the pre-absolutist past, that allowed the Roman-law professors to reassert their own sixteenth-century corporate tradition, and to present themselves to their countrymen as an "impartial" alternative to the terrors of post-Napoleonic politics. These "impartial" professors lost much of their public prestige during the late 1830s and 1840s. But, as I shall show in chapter 6, they managed to resurrect much of their glorious tradition after 1848, as the long process of codification began.

Alongside this study of the centuries-long ideological tradition of the Roman-law professors, with its intricate roots in Roman history and German constitutional tradition, I will trace two of the great attempts to employ Roman law as a tool of social change in Germany: the attempt to use Roman law to engineer agrarian reform between 1790 and 1848, and the attempt to construct a Roman commercial law in the 1850s. The Romanist lawyers who mounted these two campaigns for social change through law were motivated, I will argue, by the conviction that they could somehow restore Roman social relations through a restoration of Roman law.

In chapter 5, I will discuss agrarian reform, and the hopes of Romanist lawyers like Savigny and Thibaut that Germany could be spared a revolution through the creation of a new Roman property law that would end the tensions and the misery of the largely feudal countryside. As I hope to show, this campaign for a reformist property law was in large measure guided by a vision of Rome espoused by the great Roman historian B. G. Niebuhr. Historians have always concentrated too much on the internal doctrinal history of German jurisprudence, and too little on the details of the practice of law in Germany; I hope that I have remedied this neglect of legal practice by exploiting unused sources for the history of agrarian law in Hannover and Hesse. In Chapter 6, I will discuss, in considerably less detail, the unsuccessful struggles of Rudolf von Jhering and some of his contemporaries to develop commercial principles adequate for nineteenth-century German commerce out of the fragments of the *Corpus Iuris*. These midcentury lawyers, too, had their vision of Rome: it was the Rome of Theodor Mommsen. Both campaigns failed. But both were witness to the strength of Antiquity in German minds, and the hopes of Germans that high culture could be a political force in their society.

One word of caution is in order. This book is not intended as an exhaustive history of German law—though of course I must survey a great deal of that history to make my subject-matter intelligible to an anglophone audience. For exhaustive history, readers must turn to the large learned

literature in German and Italian, much (but hardly all) of which I cite in
the following chapters. My purposes are narrower. I wish, first and foremost, to trace the enduring link between the conception of ancient Rome
and the practice of Roman law in Germany. I also wish to root German
legal historiography in the records of German legal practice, as historians
have to date failed, by and large, to do—though, of course, I can hardly
do more than scratch the surface of the surviving records of practice. And
I wish to record the presence of French and English influences that have
not always been noticed by historians.

Perhaps most importantly, I wish to demonstrate that the history of law
belongs as much to intellectual as to social history. Legal history can
range from high philosophy into wholly forgotten corners of village life;
intellectual, and social (and, indeed, political) history can be integrated in
new ways through the study of law. We have not seen how high culture
and the organization of justice hung together over the centuries; how love
of the classics, learned in the early nineteenth-century universities, could
manifest itself in the work of romantic lawyers in the countryside, so that
the cult of Rome changed the lives of German peasants; how the imperatives of commerce could force fundamental reinterpretations of Roman
history in the mid-nineteenth century. We have not seen how inextricably
high culture and political and social life were bound to one another. By
digging through forgotten doctrinal debates, case reports, provincial legal
journals, and academic treatises, I hope I can show remarkable aspects of
German history where intellectual life converged with political and social
life: in law.

ACKNOWLEDGMENTS

A FELLOWSHIP from the German Academic Exchange Service supported research for this study in Germany. I am grateful to the Handschriften-abteilung of the Niedersächsische Staats- und Universitätsbibliothek Göttingen for permission to quote from the papers of Rudolf von Jhering. Parts of Chapter 6 have appeared previously in my essay, "The Last Generation of Roman Lawyers in Germany," in A. C. Dionisotti, A. Grafton, and J. Kraye, eds., *The Uses of Greek and Latin: Historical Essays* (London: The Warburg Institute, 1988), pp. 211–25. The staffs of Interlibrary Loan Services at Regenstein Library at the University of Chicago, of the International Legal Studies Library and the Langdell Treasure Room of Harvard Law School, and of the Yale Law Library have been very helpful; my thanks. I am grateful to Professors John Boyer and Charles Gray, who served on my doctoral committee at the University of Chicago. Like so many students at the University of Chicago, I benefited from the teaching of Professor Edward Shils, an uncommonly kind teacher.

I have incurred many further debts during the revision of the original dissertation version of this study. Professor Anthony Grafton has done much to guide my career since I entered graduate school, and, like all young Americans interested in the history of scholarship, I have attempted to follow his example. I admired the work of Professor Donald Kelley long before I had the benefit of his comments on my work; I am very glad to be able to acknowledge his help now. I am also very glad to acknowledge the aid of Professor Bruce Frier, whose encouragement was the immediate cause for the publication of this study. Professor Charles Donahue has been unfailingly helpful over several years, not least by making a scholarly life seem attractive in the sometimes inhospitable setting of an American Law School. I am very grateful to him. I am particularly pleased to acknowledge my intellectual debt to Professor Alan Watson, and to thank him for his encouragement and suggestions. I am also obliged to a number of other legal historians for friendly help: in particular, Professors Harold Berman, M. H. Hoeflich, John Langbein, and Joachim Rückert.

My wife knows, though I am sure I have never expressed it to her adequately, how much I owe to her.

I have dedicated this book to the memory of my teacher, Professor Arnaldo Momigliano. I hope it would have satisfied him.

ABBREVIATIONS

ALR	Allgemeines Landrecht
BGB	Bürgerliches Gesetzbuch
C.	Code of Justinian
Coing Handbuch	H. Coing, ed., *Handbuch der Quellen und Literatur der neueren Europäischen Privatrechtsgeschichte*
D.	Digest of Justinian
HZ	*Historische Zeitschrift*
MGH	*Monumenta Germaniae Historica*
Q. Fior.	*Quaderni Fiorentini per la Storia del Pensiero Giuridico Moderno*
ZZS (G)	*Zeitschrift der Savigny Stiftung für Rechtsgeschichte, Germanistische Abteilung*
ZZS (K)	*Zeitschrift der Savigny Stiftung für Rechtsgeschichte, Kanonistische Abteilung*
ZZS (R)	*Zeitschrift der Savigny Stiftung für Rechtsgeschichte, Romanistische Abteilung*

The Legacy of Roman Law in the
German Romantic Era

Chapter I

LAW IN THE FOURTH MONARCHY OF MELANCHTHON

AT THE CLOSE of the 1814 pamphlet that would make him world famous, his *On the Vocation of Our Time for Legislation and Legal Scholarship*, the great early nineteenth-century leader of German law, Friedrich Carl von Savigny, quoted a long passage by Phillip Melanchthon.[1] There is something unexpected in reading this ending to Savigny's pamphlet: Melanchthon's elegant Latin, two-and-three-quarter centuries old, comes as a surprise after pages of German focused on the urgent legal situation of post-Napoleonic Germany. But Savigny was typical of his time in invoking a glorious name from the Reformation. As the national revolutionary armies of the French were driven off, many Germans were persuaded that Luther's reformation had been their own great German revolution, that their own national consciousness had been formed in the sixteenth century decades of religious upheaval. Moreover, the nationalist fascination with the Reformation came particularly easily to Roman lawyers. For the break with the papacy had come just when Roman law penetrated Germany on a large scale, and Roman law had penetrated Germany largely under Melanchthon's intellectual leadership. To Savigny, the founding moment of German religious and national identity had been the founding moment of his own scholarly and political mission.

In this chapter, I wish to show how Roman law took on its political significance during the religious struggles of the sixteenth century, a significance that it still retained in Savigny's time. The powerful sense of tradition among Savigny and his fellow professors, the conviction that they were the continuators of the work of Roman lawyers of the past, made them faithful to a recognizably Melanchthonian conception of Roman civilization, a conception that had, in turn, roots deep in the Middle Ages. Because Roman law in Melanchthon's time was praised as a law of "peace" and "impartiality," Romanist lawyers of the romantic era would be able to proclaim themselves the guardians of peace and impartiality in the decades after Napoleon's expulsion.

---

[1] Friedrich Carl von Savigny, "Vom Beruf unserer Zeit für Gesetzgebung und Rechtswissenschaft," in H. Hattenhauer, ed., *Thibaut und Savigny* (Munich, 1973), 192, quoting Melanchthon, "Oratio de dignitate legum." The passage quoted by Savigny is reproduced in G. Kisch, *Melanchthons Rechts- und Soziallehre* (Berlin, 1967), 238.

German lawyers began using the great collection of Roman legal texts, the *Corpus Iuris Civilis*, on a large scale around 1500, only about twenty years before the upheavals of the Reformation. Roman law thus spread through Germany during a period when the threat of religious civil war was always present. That ever-present threat left its mark on the German—and, in particular, the Lutheran—idea of Roman law. Melanchthon and his many followers, fearful of a destructive conflict with Emperor Charles V, put their hopes in the new Roman law as a force for peace and order, for civilization in its most fundamental sense: a force that could quiet violence. They cultivated and revitalized old medieval associations between Roman law and the peaceful arbitration of disputes. And they worked to associate Rome with a particular Christian vision of peace: in Melanchthon's influential interpretation of world history, Rome was the last of the Four Monarchies of the Book of Daniel, a universal empire embodying a God-given peace. As the sixteenth century progressed, Melanchthon's historical visions and juristic doctrines made him both the pre-eminent interpreter of Roman history and the pre-eminent spokesman for Roman law. His work inspired a flourishing tradition of secular historiography,[2] and his scholarly disciples spread the teaching and study of history all through Germany.[3] At the same time, his orations and pamphlets made him chief among the advocates of Roman law.[4] In this first chapter, I wish to show how Melanchthon's influential political-religious vision of universal empire and his understanding of the practice of law were linked, and how his writings established a vocabulary of praise for Roman law that survived for centuries.

Melanchthon's Rome and Melanchthon's Roman law both had roots deep in the medieval history—in centuries of German efforts to build a state apparatus that could put an end to the private wars that had always afflicted central Europe, and in centuries of belief that the Germans were the heirs of the Roman Empire. Long before Melanchthon's time, Germans had begun to claim that the Holy Roman Empire was the political successor to ancient Rome. Melanchthon adopted this claim as his own. Through a *translatio imperii*, a transfer of political majesty, Germany had become the modern locus of the Fourth Monarchy. As Melanchthon un-

[2] See A. Klempt, *Die Säkularisierung der Universalhistorischen Geschichtsauffassung*, Göttinger Bausteine zur Geschichtswissenschaft, vol. 31 (Göttingen, 1960).

[3] A. Momigliano, "The Introduction of the Teaching of History as an Academic Subject and its Implications," *Minerva* 21, no. 1 (Spring 1983): 11–12; E. C. Scherer, *Geschichte und Kirchengeschichte an den deutschen Universitäten* (Freiburg i.B., 1927), 29–84. Cf. K. Christ, *Römische Geschichte und Deutsche Geschichtswissenschaft* (Munich, 1982), 22. But cf. E. Fueter, *Geschichte der Neueren Historiographie* (Munich/Berlin, 1911), 186–87.

[4] Cf. Kisch, *Melanchthon*, esp. 51–73, and the literature cited there; note also the prominence of Melanchthon among the works cited by O. Stobbe, *Geschichte der deutschen Rechtsquellen*, 2 vols. (Braunschweig, 1864), 2:112 n. 7.

derstood it, this translatio imperii had been achieved largely through Germany's submission to Roman law; accordingly, his understanding of Roman law shaped his understanding of the nature of a Romanized German society. His understanding of Roman law, too, was fundamentally medieval. Like medieval Germans, he thought of a society ruled by Roman law as, first and foremost, a society ruled by written law. And written law, as Melanchthon described it in his "De dignitate legum oratio" of 1538, transformed the world into a place of justice and peace:

> It is fitting to give thanks unto God, for giving to the Empire such law once again. . . . For written law is a firm fortress against tyranny, and the more learned it is, the more justice it gives [quo eruditius est, eo plus continet aequitatis]. . . . Indeed, there would be far more uncertainty, if there were no written law. . . . [T]herefore we must ask the Lord to preserve this learning for the peace of the country.[5]

I will take this passage as my text in tracing Melanchthon's relationship to the traditions of jurisprudence, of medieval state-making and of Reformation peacemaking. Why did Melanchthon believe that the more learned a legal system, the more just? Why did written law bring peace and certainty to the Holy Roman Empire? An intricate tangle of jurisprudential traditions and German constitutional history lay behind Melanchthon's association of writing, justice, and peace. And it was largely because he associated writing, justice, and peace that Melanchthon linked the laws of Rome with the mission of the Holy Roman Empire of the German Nation.

MEDIEVAL BACKGROUND

Roman law was a law of peace. This statement acquired its meaning in the extraordinarily violent world of late medieval Europe—the world of the feuds, private wars, and class persecutions that descended on Europeans unceasingly in the centuries before the rise of modern states. Melanchthon inherited his idea of law from this late medieval society, a society whose primary legal need was for peaceful arbitration of endless and debilitating violent conflict.

The idea that Roman law was suitable for settling the violent conflicts that afflicted European life dates back to the earliest period of the revival of Roman law. Roman law vanished from most of Europe after the fall of the Roman Empire, and, where it survived, it did so only in fragments and abridgments. The modern history of Roman law began only late in the eleventh century, when Italian scholars began systematically studying

---

[5] Melanchthon, "De dignitate legum oratio," in Kisch, Melanchthon, 227.

a copy of the *Digest*, a compilation of texts made by order of the emperor Justinian in the sixth century A.D. The recovery of the *Digest* rapidly stimulated a great revival of learned jurisprudence centered at the University of Bologna.[6] As this revival gathered momentum, northern Italian cities began to seek out scholars trained in Bologna for arbitration of their civic strife. Sometimes they sent their disputes to the new universities for resolution; often, they established institutions of learned justice within the cities themselves.[7] In the twelfth century, this Roman law of peace coalesced with Canon law to form a common learned law used for the arbitration of the violence endemic to Italian cities.[8]

In this medieval tradition of arbitration lie the origins of the idea I wish to trace, the idea of Roman law as a law of peace. Roman-Canon law was applied in peacemaking adjudication by learned arbitrators called, in a somewhat obscure phrase," "arbiter, arbitrator seu amicabilis compositor"—"arbitrator bound by formalities, arbitrator not bound by formalities, or peaceful composer of disputes."[9] Such learned arbitrators appeared everywhere as Roman-Canon law spread northward into the warring countries across the Alps in the twelfth and thirteenth centuries. Indeed, the usefulness of learned law for purposes of peacemaking was one of the major factors in its diffusion: in Switzerland, Austria, and the Rhineland, the medieval records of the use of learned law show a heavy disproportion of appeals to an "arbiter, arbitrator seu amicabilis compositor."[10] Traces of the same reliance on the learned law of peace can also be found in the legal history of the cities of the Midi.[11] Learned law

---

[6] For recent surveys of the literature on the revived study of the *Digest*, see S. Kuttner, "The Revival of Jurisprudence," in R. L. Benson and G. Constable, eds., *Renaissance and Renewal in the Twelfth Century* (Cambridge, 1982), esp. 299–308; C. Radding, *The Origins of Medieval Jurisprudence* (New Haven, Conn., 1988), 1–16.

[7] W. Engelmann, *Die Wiedergeburt der Rechtskultur in Italien* (Leipzig, 1938), 47ff. and esp. 55ff., discusses the growth of these new learned institutions. On the links among new universities, new municipal government, and "neutral" Roman law, see also, K. W. Nörr, "Institutional Foundations of the New Jurisprudence," in Benson and Constable, *Renaissance and Renewal*, 324–38 and J. P. Dawson, *Oracles of the Law* 134ff.

[8] K.-H. Ziegler, "Arbiter, arbitrator, et amicabilis compositor," *ZSS(R)* 84 (1967): 377–78. (Cf. Engelmann, *Wiedergeburt*, 64ff.) It should be remembered that the Church had its own peacemaking tradition: the "God's Peace" was centuries old when the *Corpus Iuris* was rediscovered. See below, p. 10.

[9] The phrase had roots in both Roman and Canon law. Ziegler, "Arbiter, arbitrator," 378–79.

[10] Cf. K. S. Bader, "Arbiter, arbitrator seu amicabilis compositor: Zur Verbreitung einer Canonistischen Formel in Gebieten nördlich der Alpen," *ZSS (K)* 46 (1960): 239–76. Bader's identification of the formula as deriving from canon law, should, however, be revised in light of Ziegler, "Arbiter, arbitrator."

[11] A. Gouron, "Le rôle sociale des juristes dans les villes méridionales au Moyen Age," in *Annales de la Faculté des Lettres des Sciences Humaines de Nice* 9–10 (1969): 56–57. Re-

had many and varied uses. But in medieval Europe Roman-Canon law made its way largely as a peacemaker's law.

A number of features made learned law attractive as a peacemaker's law. First of all, it was written law, and therefore it promised to provide certain and final disposition for disputes: as the Italian commentators on the Roman texts in particular often declared, "ius scriptum" was "certum et finitum."[12] The certainty of written law accounted for much of its attractiveness down into Melanchthon's time and beyond. But if learned law was definite and ascertainable, learned lawyers were also uniquely willing to depart from its strictures when considerations of justice so required. Peculiarly Christian-classical traditions of Canon law had, from an early date, emphasized "equity"—the doing of justice to the parties regardless of the rigor of legal prescriptions.[13] This tradition of considering "equity" made learned jurists particularly suitable for service as arbitrators. Moreover, both Roman and Canon law included provisions for the recusal of judges—something unknown to other available bodies of law.[14] Furthermore, the *Corpus Iuris* included two extensive titles on the law of arbitration.[15] But most important for my purposes was the place of learned law within the complex choice-of-law jurisprudence of the later Middle Ages. Learned law was *ius commune*—an often misunderstood choice-of-law technical term. Out of the technical subtleties of the application of ius commune, I suggest, rose much of Melanchthon's conception of Roman law as the law of peace in a universal empire.

To understand the idea of a "ius commune," and the implied cosmology it carried with it, we must understand how deeply the use of learned law was at odds with settled European views of the legal world. The use of Roman-Canon law conflicted fundamentally with the conceptions medieval Europeans had about their rights. Law in the Middle Ages was generally thought of as local or personal law, embodying local or personal rights. Dwellers of a given medieval city or territory would expect the law of that city or territory to be applied to them in whatever court they might find themselves; they might also expect the law of the nation to which their distant ancestors had belonged—for example the law of the Lombards or the law of the Burgundians—to be applied to them. Such law was

---

printed in idem, *La Science du droit dans le Midi de la France au Moyen Age* (London, 1984).

[12] Cf. W. Wiegand, *Studien zur Rechtsanwendungslehre der Rezeptionszeit*, Abhandlungen zur Rechtswissenschaftlichen Grundlagenforschung, vol. 27 (Ebelsbach, 1977), 51, 94, 99.

[13] See, e.g., U. Wolter, *Ius Canonicum in Iure Civili*, Forschungen zur neueren Privatrechtsgeschichte, vol. 23 (Cologne/Vienna, 1975), 7, and often on *aequitas (canonica)* intended as an antidote to the "rigor iuris romani."

[14] Engelmann, *Wiedergeburt*, 64ff.

[15] D. 4, 8; C. 2, 55 [56]. Cited in Ziegler, "Arbiter, Abitrator," 377.

local law, personal law, "one's own" law. "One's own" law conferred
upon a person rights—grants of special privilege from a monarch, tax
exemptions, marital property rights, rights of reciprocity from other cities
and territories, and so on. None of these local or personal rights could, of
course, be found in the texts of the learned lawyers. Nevertheless, Italian
courts of the later Middle Ages would recognize these rights. In particular, the theory of learned lawyers preserved a priority for local customs
and statutes. But the learned lawyers put the burden on the litigant to
prove that he or she did indeed enjoy the rights he or she claimed. Such
proof could be made by the testimony of witnesses or by the presentation
of written documentation. Only when a litigant could not prove that he
or she had cognizable local or personal rights would courts turn to
learned texts, as sources of a more general body of law, a presumptively
universal "ius commune."

   This "ius commune" was not exclusively Roman-Canon law. Italian
courts used a number of written sources, which they ranked according to
the extent of their territorial application. Roman-Canon law was first in
rank. It was presumed to be universal, in the phrase of the earlier Middle
Ages a "lex omnium generalis," a "general law of all parties." Statutes of
larger territories were less general than Roman-Canon law but more general than local statutes; local customs and local statutes shared a place on
the lowest level of generality. A chart may help illustrate this ranking of
bodies of law:

Roman-Canon Law (Territorially Universal)

Statutes of Larger Territories

Statutes of Smaller Territories/Local Customs

This chart greatly simplifies and stylizes an intricately complex choice-of-
law system, but it gives a generally accurate picture of the medieval
choice-of-law universe. This universe, as first conceived in Italy, was
made up of concentric sovereign circles. As a rule, the innermost circles,
the realms of local customs and local statutes, were realms of local and
personal law, embodying the rights of litigants. Courts would always recognize those rights if their applicability could be proven, sometimes giving local customs priority over local statutes, sometimes giving local statutes priority over local customs. However, if the applicability of local or
personal rights could not be proven, the court would move outward in
the universe of concentric circles—upward on the chart I have shown—
to choose a legal system of a larger territory. (Because proof of rights
could be very difficult, one can say that in practice, local law was sub-
stantively favored, but general law was procedurally favored.) The term
"ius commune" referred to the wider of any two circles, the higher of any

two bodies of law on the chart; that is to say, "ius commune" referred to that body of law in any litigation whose applicability did *not* need to be proven. If a litigant alleged but could not prove that he or she had some right by local custom, and the court applied Roman law, Roman law was the ius commune; by the same token, if a litigant alleged a statute of a smaller territory and the court applied a statute of a larger territory, the statute of the larger territory was the ius commune.[16] Accordingly, the content of "ius commune" fluctuated widely from case to case.[17] Ius commune was not so much the law common to all Europe, as the law common to both litigants in any given proceeding; the phrase might best be translated, not as "common law," but as "shared law." Most often "ius commune" would refer to Roman-Canon law; but the phrase could refer, depending on the litigation, to any written form of law.[18]

This ius commune was perfectly suited to the arbitration of violent conflict, because it was, in the most literal sense, "impartial": whether jurists applied the Roman law, Canon law, or some form of "equity," what they applied was not the personal law of either party, but rather a law common to both parties. It was presumably a reflection of this jurisprudence that Italian learned lawyers acquired, during the Middle Ages, a reputation for being uniquely "impartial."[19] Roman law, in its first European incarnation—submerged as one element of the learned ius commune—thus took on the character of a law of peace from the very beginning. At the same time, it became, in legal minds, the law of an universal empire, an empire of peace.

Two special features marked the diffusion of the ius commune into the violent German periphery of Western Europe. First, the learned law that penetrated Germany during the Middle Ages was primarily Canon law (although to be sure, Roman law had penetrated Germany to some extent by the thirteenth century[20]). In practice only Canon law was taught at the

---

[16] I have simplified here an immensely complex choice-of-law system. For more detailed discussions, see Wiegand, *Rechtsanwendungslehre*; Wiegand, "Zur Herkunft und Ausbreitung der Formel, 'Habere Fundatam Intentionem,' " *Festschrift für Hermann Krause* (Cologne/Vienna, 1975), 126–70. In my account I have relied heavily on Wiegand's works. For the mature conflict-of-laws system as it emerged in the fourteenth century, see also, most recently, J. Canning, *The Political Thought of Baldus de Ubaldis*, Cambridge Studies in Medieval Life and Thought, Fourth Series, vol. 6 (Cambridge, 1987), and the literature cited there.

[17] Wiegand, *Rechtsanwendungslehre*, 158: "[es] wandelt sich der Begriff des ius commune ständig. Das nicht-beweisdürftige Recht ist also ein sich stets verändernder Komplex."

[18] The wide range of the content of the ius commune in medieval Italy is noted by Engelmann, *Wiedergeburt*, 78ff.

[19] Cf. ibid., 62ff.

[20] See H. Coing, *Römisches Recht in Deutschland*, Ius Romanum Medii Aevi pt 5, subpt. 6 (1964), 78, 90; K. Burmeister, *Das Studium der Rechte im Zeitalter des Humanismus in deutschen Sprachbereich* (Wiesbaden, 1974), 12. Cf. esp. W. Trusen, *Anfänge des gelehrten*

German universities; the teaching of Roman law began, for the most part, only at the very end of the fifteenth century.[21] Although courts of arbitration in medieval Germany did apply Roman law, they relied principally on Canon law,[22] and when Germans sought an "arbiter seu arbitrator" it was almost always to clerics that they turned.[23] Only at the very end of the medieval period did the *Corpus Iuris* enter German practice on a large scale.

The second notable characteristic of the ius commune in Germany was its integration into the Public Peace movement. Central government was uniquely weak in Germany in the late Middle Ages; it was the most anarchic of Western Europe's anarchic societies. Private wars were unceasing; roads were the province of Germany's bloody knightly class. In the complete absence of a state with the monopoly of legitimate force, violence flourished. The Public Peace (*Landfriede*) movement, at work with varying degrees of success throughout the Middle Ages, grew up in response to this situation. The idea of the "peace," of the moratorium on violence to be observed in the presence of the king or some other figure of authority, dated well back into the Dark Ages. But the immediate origins of the Public Peace movement lay in the God's Peace movement, begun earlier in the Middle Ages at Cluny. The God's Peace movement was an attempt by church authorities to put periodic temporary halts to violence in the countryside.[24] In later medieval Germany, political authorities began to unite to enforce similar peaces by treaty. By the mid-thirteenth century, the attempt to fashion a Public Peace was a regular element in interterritorial relations among German political units. The Public Peaces were sometimes imposed by kings, sometimes agreed to by

---

Rechts in Deutschland, Recht und Geschichte, vol. 1 (Wiesbaden, 1962); Wolter, *Ius Canonicum*, 4.

[21] This generalization may not be true for a few universities associated with cities—Erfurt, Cologne, Rostock. See Coing, *Römisches Recht in Deutschland*, 69–70. Cited in H. Conrad, *Deutsche Rechtsgeschichte*, 2nd ed., 2 vols. (Karlsruhe, 1966), 2:347. For figures on the attendance of German students at Italian universities, see W. Dotzauer, "Deutsches Studium und deutsche Studenten an europäischen Hochschulen (Frankreich, Italien)," in *Stadt und Universität im Mittelalter und in der früheren Neuzeit*, Stadt in der Geschichte, Veröffentlichungen der Südwestdeutschen Arbeitskreises für Stadtgeschichtsforschung, vol. 3, edited by Maschke and Sydow, (Sigmaringen, 1977), 117–22; cf. also H. de Ridder-Symoens, "Deutsche Studenten an Italienischen Rechtsfakultäten," *Ius Commune* 12 (1984): 287–315.

[22] See, generally, the evaluation of Trusen, *Anfänge*, 148–61; Wolter, *Ius Canonicum*, 4, and the literature cited there.

[23] Bader, "Arbiter, arbitrator," 256ff.

[24] Cf. H. Pirenne, writing of the first great God's Peace of 989: "The prime need of that era, hardly rising above anarchy, was the need of peace, the most fundamental and the most essential of all the needs of society." *Medieval Cities*, translated by F. Halsey (Princeton, N.J., 1952), 78.

signatories to a peace treaty. The peace makers would establish an arbitral tribunal, usually staffed by a captain and several judges, to which they
would agree to submit their disputes. These parties would generally agree
beforehand to have certain types of disputes—principally violent vendet-
tas—adjudicated either according to their personal rights, or according to
general principles of justice.[25] But in time the arbitral tribunals of the
Public Peace grew in power, and parties not signatories to any Public
Peace treaty would be haled before them.[26] Especially after the mid-thirteenth century, Public Peaces were regularly established in those areas of
Germany in which leagues of cities or princes could muster enough common strength to enforce the order declared by treaty in a particular territory (never successfully in the Empire as a whole) for a limited period of
time (often ten years). Signatories to Public Peace treaties were able, at
least for short periods, to monopolize the legitimation of force. Tame as
this regime seems, it did much to bring peace into German lives. Particularly in the Rhineland and in Swabia, German leagues succeeded in establishing lasting and beneficial Public Peaces.[27]

It is possible that Canon law, the principal German ius commune, was
used to arbitrate conflicts under the Public Peace as early as 1254, when
the signatories to the new Rhineland league, attempting to establish some
order in the chaos of the mid-thirteenth century Interregnum, declared
that conflicts were to be settled "by amicable composition or as justice
requires."[28] At any rate, it is clear that in subsequent centuries the ius
commune—among its other uses[29]—regularly served as the law of arbitral peacemaking. Alliances and treaties among cities and princes regularly called for adjudication of disputes according to "justice."[30] This

---

[25] H. Krause, *Die geschichtliche Entwicklung des Schiedsgerichtswesens in Deutschland*
(Berlin, 1930), 33–34.

[26] For an account of the development of the arbitral tribunals as organs of the Public
Peaces, see ibid., 7ff.

[27] See, generally, H. Angermeier, *Konigtum und Landfriede im deutschen Spätmittelalter*
(Munich, 1966). Two recent histories that lay emphasis on the Public Peace movement in
late medieval German history are H. Thomas, *Deutsche Geschichte des Spätmittelalters*
(Stuttgart, 1983), esp. 53ff., 315ff., 423ff.; F.R.H. Du Boulay, *Germany in the Later Middle
Ages* (London, 1983), 76ff. For the connection between the Landfriede and the spread of
the ius commune into Germany, see, most recently, the discussion of S. Rowan, *Ulrich Zasius: A Jurist in the German Renaissance*, Ius Commune Sonderheft 31 (Frankfurt a.M.,
1987), 6–10.

[28] "Confoederatio Pacis Rhenana," §4: "per amicabilem compositionem vel per iusti-
tiam." In *Monumenta Germaniae Historica (MGH) (Constitutiones)* 2:581. Cf. Bader, "Arbiter, arbitrator," 271; Krause, *Schiedsgerichtswesen*, 40ff.

[29] For the variety of the uses of learned law, see generally Trusen, *Anfänge*.

[30] Trusen, *Anfänge*, 153ff. Examples in O. Franklin, *Das Reichshofgericht im Mittelalter*,
2 vols. (Weimar, 1869), 2:23ff. E.g., alliance among Frankfurt, Friedberg, Wetzlar, and
Gelnhausen of 1316: "si inter duas civitates seu inter duarum civitatum cives aliqua discor-

"justice" was characteristically what Canon lawyers dispensed; it was emphatically different from vested local rights. The treaty organizations that established Public Peace in Alsace and the Rhineland directed courts to apply equitable "justice," rather than local or personal law, to all litigants who violated the Public Peace.[31] Thus "justice" entered German political life in response to violence, and when the *Corpus Iuris* entered Germany full force, the Public Peace movement was well established and ready to receive it. Indeed, the full scale introduction of the *Corpus Iuris* was linked from the first with the "Perpetual Public Peace" of 1495.

The *Corpus Iuris* entered Germany on a large scale in the late fifteenth and early sixteenth centuries, as central Europe underwent a governmental revolution. New courts of justice, staffed by jurists trained in Roman law, were widely established by the German princes. Most scholars now agree that the efforts of the princes to base a rational governmental order on the services of learned jurists were instrumental in this so-called Reception of Roman law.[32] At the same time, the German cities made increasing use of the Roman texts beginning in the 1480s.[33] Both in the cities and in the new princely states, the *Corpus Iuris* served the need for some elaborately formed legal system that could provide the basis of government.[34] With the appearance of the new German states—able, in their

dia, questio seu questiones oriuntur, alie due civitates huiusmodi discordiam—decidere debebunt, prout ipse civitates secundum iusticiam viderint expedire." Quoted in ibid., 23n.

[31] "Pax Generalis Rheni Superioris," 1318, *MGH (Constitutiones)* 5:387–88. This partly damaged document, after declaring repeatedly that citizens of signatory cities are to be judged "nach der selben stette rehte und gewonheite," instructs judges of courts of the Public Peace to judge those who violated the peace "nach den schulden. . . . [So] sol dem selben rihter vallen, waz ime billiche vallen sol"—i.e., "secundum iusticiam." The parallel provision in the "Pax Terrae Alsatiae" 1347, *MGH (Constitutiones)* 8:463, after guaranteeing peaceable signatories "ir freyheit, reht und gut gewonheit," declared that violators should be judged "nach der missetät."

[32] See N. Hammerstein, "Zur Geschichte und Bedeutung der Universitäten im Heiligen Römischen Reich," *HZ* 241 (1985): 291–92, and the literature cited there. This article is an excellent introduction to the lively literature on scholarship and society in early modern Germany. I have not been able to see R. Schnur, ed., *Der Beitrag der Juristen für die Ausbildung der frühmodernen Staaten* (Berlin, 1987). Like most interpretations of the Reception, the emphasis on the growth of new princely states has provoked doubt and dissent. See G. Below, *Die Ursachen der Rezeption des Römischen Rechts* (Munich/Berlin, 1905), 52–67; Dawson, *Oracles of the Law*, 183–84; W. Kunkel, "The Reception of Roman Law in Germany," in Strauss, ed., *Pre-Reformation Germany* (New York, 1972), 273. At least some of the debate can perhaps be resolved if we distinguish carefully between the doubtful proposition that the substantive rules of Roman law favored princely power and the more persuasive emphasis on the "Rationalisierungswille" of the early modern states expressed by Wieacker, *Privatrechtsgeschichte*, 175.

[33] The classic study is H. Coing, *Die Rezeption in Frankfurt* (Frankfurt a.M., 1939).

[34] Cf. Wieacker, *Privatrechtsgeschichte*, 124ff. Wieacker's famous thesis, that the Reception of Roman law reflected not so much the attraction of its substantive rules, as the im-

brutal fashion, to suppress most of the violence of previous centuries—
the Public Peace movement was transformed. It became a movement that
embraced the entire Empire, and, for the first time, its ius commune included a large measure of Roman law.

After centuries of vicissitudes, the Public Peace movement culminated
with the Imperial Diet that met at Worms in 1494–95 to negotiate with
the new emperor Maximilian I an unprecedentedly ambitious "Perpetual
Public Peace"—one that would extend over the entire Empire and last
forever.[35] Both princes and emperor were far stronger and more in control of their forces that they had been in the previous centuries; such a
project was no longer impossible. In 1495 the Diet forced Maximilian to
create a new supreme court, the *Reichskammergericht*, intended to serve
as the court of the imperial Landfriede.[36] To ensure its independence of
the emperor, the Reichskammergericht was to have its own fixed seat,
separate from the emperor's court.[37] Moreover, "the common laws of the
Empire" were to be the law of choice in the Reichskammergericht: unless
some applicable local German statute or custom could be proven, "the
common laws of the Empire" would apply.

German lawyers in subsequent centuries traditionally regarded the

---

perative of *Verwissenschaftlichung*, "scholarification," is widely accepted. For a helpful and
circumstantial account of this process, which involved first and foremost the displacement
of the old German lay courts, the *Schöffengerichte*, see G. Dahm, "Roman and Italian Law
in Germany," in Strauss, ed., *Pre-Reformation Germany*, 284ff. The Reception has historically been the most violently controversial topic in all of German scholarship. An account
of the controversy is now conveniently available: P. Bender, *Die Rezeption des Römischen
Rechts im Urteil der Deutschen Rechtswissenschaft*, Rechtshistorische Reihe, vol. 8 (Frankfurt a.M., 1979). An important English-language treatment of the Reception has recently
appeared: G. Strauss, *Law, Resistance and the State: The Opposition to Roman Law in
Reformation Germany* (Princeton, N.J., 1986).

[35] Along with the other literature cited in this section, see esp. the articles of F. Hartung
("Imperial Reform, 1485–1495") and K. S. Bader ("Approaches to Imperial Reform at the
End of the Fifteenth Century") in Strauss, ed., *Pre-Reformation Germany*, 73–135 and
136–61, respectively. For the determination of all parties at the Diet to promote reform, see
H. Angermeier, *Die Reichsreform, 1410–1555: Die Staatsproblematik in Deutschland
zwischen Mittelalter und Gegenwart* (Munich, 1984), 167. See also generally H. Angermeier, "Die Reichsregimenter und ihre Staatsidee," *HZ* 211 (1970): 265–315.

[36] B. Diestelkamp, "Das Reichskammergericht im Rechtsleben des 16. Jht.," in *Rechtsgeschichte als Kulturgeschichte: Festschrift für A. Erler* (Aalen, 1976), 442.

[37] On the political origins of the Reichskammergericht, see H. Angermeier, "Introduction," to idem, ed., *Deutsche Reichstagsakten unter Maximilian I* (Göttingen, 1981), vol. 5,
pt. 1, subpt. 1: 25ff.; Angermeier, *Die Reichsreform, 1410–1555*, 164–84; B. Diestelkamp,
"Zur Krise des Reichsrechts im 16. Jht.," in Angermeier, ed., *Säkulare Aspekte der Reformationszeit* (Munich/Vienna, 1983), 51–52; R. Smend, *Das Reichskammergericht*, pt. 1,
Geschichte und Verfassung (no more appeared). Quellen und Studien zur Verfassungsgeschichte des Deutschen Reiches im Mittelalter und Neuzeit (Weimar, 1911), vol. 1, Heft 3:
1–67; Wieacker, *Privatrechtsgeschichte*, 105, 133.

forced creation of the Reichskammergericht as the court of the Perpetual
Public Peace as the event that marked the formal Reception. Modern
scholars, however, view it as only a "milestone."[38] Yet it was a central
event in the history I trace, for it extended and solidified the association
between Roman law and Public Peace. After 1495, the link between the
living institution of the Reichskammergericht and the luminous historical
tradition of Roman law was fixed. The new court conferred upon Roman
law its meaning as a law of peace in the generation before Melanchthon.
Because the "common laws" were the law of the Reichskammergericht,
Rome could become the realm of the Public Peace, of the new, broadened,
Public Peace that became the political foundation of the Holy Roman
Empire.

THE CULTURAL IDEA OF ROME IN 1495

The "common laws of the Empire" carried with them a cultural idea of
Rome. For "the common laws" were none other than the ius commune,
with its well-developed choice-of-law jurisprudence: the Italian choice-
of-law formula was directly embodied in the oath administered to the
judges of the new court.[39] The new court was to be a court of the widest
of the territorial circles of medieval choice-of-law jurisprudence. As always, the content of the choice-of-law term, and the conception of the
widest circle, fluctuated. The cultural idea of Rome at the Imperial Diet
of 1495 was necessarily as vague and ill-defined as the ius commune itself.
Roman-law principles may have predominated as the common laws were
applied,[40] but the Corpus Iuris Civilis was certainly not their only source.

---

[38] E. Polay, Ursprung, Entwicklung, und Untergang der Pandektistik, Acta Universitatis
Szegediensis. Acta Juridica et Politica, Tomus XXVIII, Fasc. 10 (1981), 10. For the difficulty
in assessing the significance of the Reichskammergericht, see also Rowan, Zasius, 8.

[39] The relevant portion of the oath, with the choice-of-law formula italicized, ran as follows: "Item die alle söllen zuvor Unser Koniglicher oder Kaiserlicher Majestät geloben und
zu den Hailigen swern: Unserm Koniglichen oder Kaiserlichen Camergericht getrewlich und
mit Vleis ob sein und nach des Reichs gemainen Rechten, auch nach redlichen, erbern und
leidlichen Ordnungen, Statuten und Gewohnhaiten der Fürstenthumb, Herrschaften und
Gericht, die für sy pracht werden, dem Hohen und dem Nidern nach seinem besten Ver-
stentnus gleich zu richten." Quoted in Wiegand, Rechtsanwendungslehre, 163 (emphasis in
the original). Alongside Wiegand, " 'Habere fundatam intentionem,' " see F. Ranieri, "Diritto Commune e Diritto Locale nei primi decenni della Giurisprudenza del Reichskammergericht," Diritto Commune e Diritti Locali nella Storia dell'Europa (Atti del Convegno di
Varenna) (Milan, 1980), 71–92. Among earlier authors, see esp. S. Brie, "Die Stellung der
deutschen Rechtsgelehrten der Rezeptionszeit zum Gewohnheitsrecht," Festgabe f. F. Dahn
3 vols. in 1 (Breslau, 1905) 1:129–64. For a general survey of early modern conflict of laws
theory, cf. G. Immel, "Typologie des Privatrechts und Prozeßrechts," in Coing Handbuch,
vol. 2, pt. 2: 61–65.

[40] Stobbe, Rechtsquellen, 2:111.

The common laws included imperial legislation as well as Roman law; they also often included Canon law.[41] Within these fluctuations, it is appropriate to say that the common laws were the law of Rome—but of a Rome that extended over milennia and included popes and modern emperors as well as the ancients. This Rome of many ages gave Germany its law of peace, enforced by the might of the new states, at the end of the Middle Ages. The thickly glossed and commentaried text of the Italian jurists, in which the authority of the Accursian Gloss was formalized in the rule "quidquid non agnoscit glossa, non agnoscit curia"—"what the gloss does not acknowledge [as law], the court does not acknowledge"[42]—embodied innumerable alterations and medieval recastings (as well as discounting all Greek passages); it also included the so-called *Libri feudorum* (texts on feudal law treated as decrees by the modern emperors) as well as sundry other medieval imperial edicts.[43] The use of this italianate *Corpus Iuris* was deeply marked by Canon law: whether or not Canon Law was formally subsumed under the phrase "common laws," Canon law was far better established in Germany and far simpler to apply to contemporary circumstances, and therefore had a tendency to displace the ancient rules: jurists routinely substituted a Canon for a Roman principle if the former seemed more readily applicable.[44] Thus the Rome of the popes was very visible among the sources of the common laws in the generation preceding the Reformation.[45]

These common laws appealed to the princes of the Diet as a law of peaceful adjudication for all the reasons written law had appealed to Germans since the thirteenth century in their effort to make Public Peace. But beyond these familiar attractions, special political factors gave the law of the Rome of many ages an impartial coloring that recommended it to the princes of a German Diet in 1495, hostile as they were to the claims of an emperor who had grown suddenly strong by his burgundian inheritance. Despite the close political identification of the medieval emperors with the Roman tradition, and their use of statements in the *Corpus Iuris* to

[41] For Wiegand's judgment see "Habere Fundatam Intentionem," 167. For a good account, see Rowan, *Zasius*, 6–10. Some later historians have carelessly asserted that "das gemeine Recht" referred solely to Roman law: e.g., Dawson, *Oracles of the Law*, 188; Strauss, *Law, Resistance and the State*, 36, 65 (contrast below n. 45!).

[42] Wieacker, *Privatrechtsgeschichte*, 133ff.; Conrad, *Deutsche Rechtsgeschichte*, 2:342.

[43] See Wieacker, *Privatrechtsgeschichte*, 133–34.

[44] Stobbe, *Rechtsquellen*, 2:135. Canon law procedure was universally used in learned courts.

[45] Cf. Strauss, *Law, Resistance and the State*, 68–69. Elsewhere, Strauss too casually identifies "ius commune" with Roman law. (Cf. above n. 41.) It bears emphasizing that until the seventeenth century "ius commune" did not, strictly speaking, refer to *any* body of substantive law, but was rather a technical choice-of-law term, whose reference varied according to the choice of law in any given case.

justify their claims to power, the Imperial Court had never sponsored the use of Roman law in German courts.[46] The emperors had been too weak to introduce Roman law as in any sense their own.[47] Moreover, by the late fifteenth century, the emperor was losing his sole identification with Roman tradition: the term "Holy Roman Empire of the German Nation"[48] was coming into fashion. Rome belonged to the German nation, to all the estates of the Empire as well as to the emperor; adjudication according to Roman law was therefore adjudication according to impartial common heritage,[49] and the Reichskammergericht could, as one of the surviving documents of the Diet put it, be intended to maintain a "public peace *in the Roman Empire*."[50] As so often before in its history, Roman law could be viewed as impartial, because it was the law of no party and of every party—it was the emperor's law, *and* the law of the princes, *and* indeed the law of the German nation.

With the creation of the Reichskammergericht, Germans had a visible, institutional embodiment of the Roman law of peace. The new court was quickly put to use adjudicating touchy political disputes between lords of various ranks and their subjects as well as between various of the estates of the Empire.[51] The indirect influence of the Reichskammergericht on the many new courts that were the principal arenas of the Reception of Roman law[52] spread the conception of the *Corpus Iuris* as the imperial law of peace making.[53] The *Corpus Iuris*, as the peacemaker's text, was thus

[46] See Coing, *Römisches Recht in Deutschland*, 14; H. Krause, *Kaiserrecht und Rezeption*, Abhandlungen der Heidelberger Akademie der Wissenschaften (Phil.-Hist. Kl.), 1 (Heidelberg, 1952); Kunkel, "Reception of Roman Law," 266–67; R. L. Benson, "Political *Renovatio*: Two Models from Classical Antiquity," in Benson and Giles, eds., *Renaissance and Renewal*, 360ff.; Strauss, *Law, Resistance and the State*, 70–73.

[47] Stintzing, *Geschichte*, 1:58–59.

[48] See K. Zeumer, *Heiliges Römisches Reich Deutscher Nation*, Quellen und Studien zur Verfassungsgeschichte des deutschen Reichs, vol. 4, pt. 2 (Weimar, 1910), 17ff. Cited in N. Hammerstein, "Das Römische am Heiligen Römischen Reich Deutscher Nation," *ZSS* (G) 100 (1983): 121. For the appearance of the phrase "Römisches Reich deutscher Nation" with the *Landfriedensordnung* of 1486, see R. Stadelmann, "Das Zeitalter der Reformation," in L. Just, ed., *Handbuch der deutschen Geschichte*, 6 vols. (Konstanz, 1956), 2:9.

[49] Hammerstein, "Universitäten," 302–3.

[50] Emphasis added. The document is a draft for the procedural rules to be used in disputes between imperial princes. The draft begins: "Wie eyn F. den anderen umb anspruch und vorderung dem landfrid, ym Röm. R. aufgericht, gemessen und nach rechtfertigen sall, wirt aus nachgeschriben artikeln, aus benannten landfrid gezogen, angezeiget and vermarket." In Angermeier, ed., *Deutsche Reichstagsakten*, vol. 5, pt. 1, subpt. 1, 431.

[51] See the examples of the court's early activity in Diestelkamp, "Das Reichskammergericht," 448.

[52] See esp. Stölzel, *Die Entwicklung des gelehrten Richtertums*, 2 vols. (Stuttgart, 1872).

[53] For the case of the Duchy of Jülich-Berg, see Below, *Ursachen der Rezeption*, 34–52; cf. Diestelkamp, "Das Reichskammergericht," 451.

becoming increasingly evident in the daily lives of Germans when Luther and Melanchthon appeared on the scene.

LUTHERANISM AND THE LAW OF PEACE

It was Luther, and above all Melanchthon, who disseminated and cultivated the cultural idea of Rome associated with the ius commune. But neither theologian was a supporter of the ius commune at first. The Lutheran acceptance of the medieval law was slow in coming. In this, they were like many of their contemporaries of the first decades of the sixteenth century. When Luther and Melanchthon appeared on the scene, the ius commune was under violent attack. On the one hand, the introduction of learned law into the German world provoked a widespread and tenacious reaction in favor of older customs—a customary-law reaction similar to reactions in many parts of Europe, but couched in the kind of abusive invective only Germans have ever mastered. This customary-law reaction was bitter and charged with social tensions and resentments that would last for centuries; opponents of Roman law down into the nineteenth century were still invoking that acid literature of opposition that appeared all through the sixteenth century in defense of old rights and customs against the learned law, against lawyers whose tongues Ulrich von Hutten proposed to cut out and whose lips he proposed to sew shut.[54]

But the opposition to the ius commune was not only a customary-law opposition. For by the early sixteenth century, other forms of learned law had appeared alongside the "common laws of the Empire." The same revival of learning that made possible new rational states also stimulated new forms of social agitation, forms founded on the widening knowledge of the Bible and of classical literature. Two new schools began to make fervid converts, as printing and the new learning spread: the ius scripturae, law based somehow on the word of the Bible, which was to replace all other written sources, and all other customary sources as well; and a new humanist Roman law developed by French and Italian humanists and taught in French universities. The new humanist lawyers, opposed to the so-called Mos Italicus, the "Italian style" of commentary on the Corpus Iuris, began developing their own Mos Gallicus, the "French style," aimed at scouring away the accretions of commentaries and glosses on

---

[54] Hutten is quoted in Strauss, Law, Resistance and the State, 28. On the customary-law reaction see Strauss's book generally for a fine treatment. Strauss perhaps neglects too much the extent to which the idea of "customary law" was itself a creation of learned lawyers. For this point, cf. D. R. Kelley, Foundations of Modern Historical Scholarship (New York, 1970), 183ff., and especially A. Watson, The Evolution of Law (Baltimore, 1985), 43–65.

the *Corpus Iuris* in order to return to the pristine law of the ancients.[55]
Early in their careers, the Lutheran leaders were both attracted to one or
the other of these radically new forms of written law. It was not until after
1530, when Melanchthon followed Luther in accepting the ius commune
and the constitutional settlement of 1495, that the medieval tradition I
have traced became integrated into Lutheran theological historiography.
The 1520s, for Melanchthon, were still years of anti-medieval agitation
in the brave new world of ius scripturae and humanist purism.

Throughout Melanchthon's legal development he followed Luther at
more or less of a distance. Luther was an advocate of the ius scripturae
early in the 1520s, but he soon returned to the ius commune. His "An
den christlichen Adel" of 1520 showed a Luther eager to denounce the
ius commune of 1495. Luther exhibited his contempt for the intricacies
of the choice-of-law formula adopted for the Reichskammergericht: "I
could not care less that territorial law and territorial customs have priority over the imperial common laws, and the imperial common laws are
used only in need."[56] The young Luther was full of disdain for the written
law, which was defined in terms of procedural rules—full of disdain, indeed, precisely *because* the ius commune was defined in terms of procedural rules, which seemed to him trivial and remote from God. At this
early stage, Luther—like Johann Eberlin and other agitators of the time—
hinted that he might prefer a legal order founded on the word of scripture.[57] But Luther quickly retreated from this radical scripturalization of
legal life. Indeed, only a year later, he criticized Melanchthon for desiring
some kind of "God's law," a scriptural justice that would not require
lawyers[58]—the *rabulae forenses* ("courthouse pettifoggers"), as Melanch-

---

[55] On the Mos Gallicus of the French humanists, cf. Kelley, *Foundations of Modern Historical Scholarship*, 53–150 (but cf. also D. Osler, "Budaeus and Roman Law," in *Ius Commune* 13 [1985]: 195–212); D. Maffei, *Gli Inizi dell'Umanesimo Giuridico* (Milan, 1956).
One must of course carefully distinguish between humanists like Budé, whose interests extended beyond the field of law, and the lawyers strictly defined of the Mos Gallicus.

[56] "Es dünkt mich gleich, daß Landrecht und Landsitten den kaiserlichen gemeinen
Rechten werden vorgezogen und die kaiserlichen nur zur Noth gebraucht." Quoted in
Stintzing, *Geschichte*, 1:270.

[57] Ibid. On Eberlin's views, see G. Heger, *Johann Eberlin von Günzburg und seine Vorstellungen über Reform in Reich und Kirche*, Schriften zur Rechtsgeschichte, 35 (Berlin,
1985), 94–102. Cf. Strauss, *Law, Resistance and the State*, 22ff. Luther's most notorious
early encounter with law, his public burning of the Canon law texts on December 10, 1520,
has too often made him seem, to scholars of later centuries, an enemy of Canon law *tout
court*. This is not so. The young Luther of 1520 was an enemy of the entire ius commune.
Some of the vast scholarship on the burning of the Canon texts is surveyed by S. Mühlmann,
"Luther und das Corpus Iuris Canonici bis zum Jahre 1530" in *ZSS (K)* 58 (1972): 235–
305.

[58] Cf. Kisch, *Melanchthon*, 114–15.

thon called them.[59] After 1521, Luther generally accepted the common laws, though in a lukewarm and grudging fashion. The common laws became for him the law of the secular authorities of Romans 13, the law of the worldly Reich that from 1522 on he increasingly counterposed to the heavenly Reich, the worldly law to which Christians of this world owed obedience but not enthusiasm.[60] Enthusiasm, for Luther, came only after 1530.

As Luther's rebuke suggests, Melanchthon, too, favored the ius scripturae in the early 1520s, and attacked Canon law.[61] But after Luther chided him, Melanchthon too retreated from his hopes for scriptural justice. He was, however, not yet ready to accept the old ius commune of the secular authorities. True to his early humanist leanings,[62] Melanchthon began to sponsor, not the ius commune, but the humanist idea of a purified Roman law in late 1523 or early 1524.[63] The Melanchthon of the 1520s thus remained, unlike Luther, a consistent anti-medievalist, an opponent of the ius commune, of the Italian commentaries and Italian-trained lawyers—men who, as German humanists liked to say, had "drunk the Accursian absinthe."[64] Melanchthon was not willing even to adopt Luther's attitude of tepid tolerance toward the ius commune.

But why did Melanchthon—and, to some extent, Luther—finally abandon the ius scripturae? As all historians agree,[65] they did so in horror at the growing unrest that exploded in the great breach of the Landfriede,[66] the Peasant War of 1524–25. The exact character of the Peasant War is, and will presumably remain, a point of bitter controversy among histo-

---

[59] See Kisch, Melanchthon, 105. Luther's letter chiding Melanchthon was dated July 13, 1521. Luther's Works, edited by and translated by Krodel (Philadelphia, 1963), 48:258–59.

[60] For Luther's Zwei-Reiche-Lehre, his doctrine of the two empires, see, most recently, the discussion of W. Cargill Thompson, The Political Thought of Martin Luther (Sussex, and Totowa, N.J., 1984), 12ff.

[61] W. Maurer, Der Junge Melanchthon, 2 vols. (Göttingen, 1967), 2:140f., 296, and often.

[62] See generally W. Maurer, Der Junge Melanchthon, 2 vols., Vol 1, Der Humanist (Göttingen, 1967).

[63] Cf. Kisch, Melanchthon, 108, discussing Melanchthon's "Oratio de legibus." This speech was published in 1525, though written in 1523 or 1524. It cannot originally have been precisely the version of the "Oratio" that we possess, for our version includes clear references to the Peasant War. Moreover in the 1523–24 version, Melanchthon refrained from directly criticizing Canon law. Cf. ibid., 108 n. 15.

[64] "Accursianum absynthium bibere." The phrase is Hutten's. Quoted in Stintzing, Geschichte, 1:91.

[65] E.g., S. Ozment, The Reformation in the Cities (New Haven, 1975), 134; Kisch, Melanchthon, 82ff.

[66] For perceptions of the Peasant War as a breach of the Landfriede, see Angermeier, Reichsreform, 1410–1555, 252.

rians. It seems clear enough that the peasant rebels were widely marked
by hostility to the new learned legal institutions.[67] More difficult to determine is what, precisely, peasants proposed as an alternative. Some, at
least, were scriptual law innovators. Witness this 1524 exchange between
the Swabian peasant leader Huldrich Schmid and his social masters.
Schmid's masters suggested that Schmid seek justice in the state's Kammergericht—testimony to the place of the new learned courts in maintaining social peace. But Schmid, like the Luther and Melanchthon of four
years before, desired religious justice without imperial institutions:

> Huldrich Schmid asks: what kind of law did they suggest for him? They an-
> swer "The Camergericht." And thereupon they ask: What law does he want?
> Huldrich answers: "The law of God, which declares unto every estate what
> is proper for it, to do or to leave undone." The lords say with mocking tones:
> "Huldrich, thou askest for God's law. Tell us, who is going to declare this
> law? It will be some time before God comes down from Heaven and holds a
> Judgment Day." Huldrich answers: "My lords, it is hard for me, simple man
> that I am, to name the judge or law-finder [Ussprecher], but I will do this:
> for the next three weeks, I will admonish the priests in every parish to lead a
> common prayer to God, asking Him to send us learned, pious men, who will
> judge and decide this conflict according to the word of Holy Writ."[68]

It is important to recognize that Schmid was not a customary-law reactionary.[69] In the fervor that brought him so close, in his own perception,
to God, he shared the constitutional hopes of the men who stood so much
higher than he on Germany's social scale: he wanted written law adjudi-

[67] See, e.g., G. Franz, ed., *Quellen zur Geschichte des Bauernkrieges* (Munich, 1963), 51
(peasant grievances about "doctores" in local courts as early as 1514 in Württemberg);
ibid., 115 (peasants of Schwarzwald at beginning of war complain of being haled into new
learned princely courts). The fact that the peasants rebelled against the ius commune does
not, of course, mean that they rebelled against Roman law as such. Roman law had no
independent existence apart from written law in general. That is why, as A. Stern pointed
out fifty years ago, no references to Roman law appear in their grievances. (Stern, "Das
Römische Recht und der deutsche Bauernkrieg," in *Zeitschrift für Schweizerische Geschichte* 14 (1934): 20–29. Cf. the "Sachregister" to Franz, *Quellen zur Geschichte des
Bauernkrieges*, s.v. "Recht.") Nevertheless, historians careless in dealing with the complex
history of the ius commune continue to assert or imply otherwise. E.g., P. Zagorin, *Rebels
and Rulers, 1500–1660*, 2 vols. (Cambridge, 1982), 1:187–88; P. Blickle, *The Revolution
of 1525*, translated by Brady and Midelfort (Baltimore, 1982) (implying on one page [p. 86]
that the peasants were rebelling against Roman law while acknowledging the fallacy of the
same assertion in a footnote to another page [218 n. 25]).
[68] Franz, ed., *Quellen zur Geschichte des Bauernkrieges*, 146–47. Schmid's "learned and
pious men" included Melanchthon, Luther, and other leading reformers. Strauss, *Law, Resistance and the State*, 46.
[69] Strauss, ibid., does not give enough weight to the considerable practical differences
between scriptural and customary law.

cation, adjudication by principles of justice between parties rather than of vested rights—though he did not want his justice from a learned Kammergericht. The ius scripturae and the ius scriptum were not wholly different from one another; both were innovative forms of justice. But Schmid was far from being typical of the peasants of this time of conflict.[70] Other peasants were what scholars tend to make all peasants of all times and places out to be: customary-law reactionaries.

At any rate, whatever law German peasants favored, it is clear that many of them opposed learned legal tradition, and that the violence of their opposition tended to impel the Lutheran leadership toward support of learned legal tradition. As the peasants attacked the new justice, Luther defended it, standing firmly by the constitutional principles of 1495, of the empire founded on impartial court adjudication of conflict between the estates. His law was the law of the new state, newly equipped to suppress a violent revolution in the name of Perpetual Peace.[71] But Melanchthon was not yet ready to submit to the Perpetual Public Peace. Rather, he made a public appeal for a humanist Roman law: in 1525 he published his "Oratio de legibus," with an anguished call for an end to "barbarism" and a return to Romanae leges, "Roman laws."[72] He spoke as a humanist, struggling to resurrect the pure Roman tradition: "Opponents [of Roman law] will hiss that it is all darkened and polluted by the contemptible commentaries of the interpreters. But I speak for the Roman laws, not for their modern interpreters."[73] Melanchthon did not show himself to be a complete humanist radical in this oration: he went on to praise the medieval commentators for their effort and enthusiasm—though not for their understanding of ancient texts.[74] But a radical he was in 1525—in a way, as much a legal radical as the peasants, as much a man of the new forms of written law. Humanist Roman law, whatever its intellectual beauty, had never shown itself to be suited to state-making and had no association with the authorities of Melanchthon's time. No doubt Melanchthon believed firmly in Luther's reading of Romans 13, but in his legal thought he had not yet come to a full accommodation with Germany's modern order in the year of the Peasant War.

[70] See the comments on Schmid and his circle of H. Buszello, "Gemeinde, Territorium und Reich in dem politischen Programm des deutschen Bauernkrieges," in Wehler, ed., Der Deutsche Bauernkrieg, 1524–1526, Geschichte und Gesellschaft, Sonderheft 1 (Göttingen, 1975), 118, and Buszello, Der deutsche Bauernkrieg von 1525 als politische Bewegung (Berlin, 1969), 55ff.

[71] Cf. the discussion by W. Günter, Martin Luthers Vorstellung von der Reichsverfassung (Münster, 1976), esp. 74ff. I have found Günter's book particularly helpful.

[72] Cf. Stintzing, Geschichte, 1:272. The "Oratio de legibus" is reproduced by Kisch, in Melanchthon, 189–209.

[73] Melanchthon, "Oratio de legibus," in Kisch, Melanchthon, 205.

[74] Ibid.

This is an important point, for the Peasant War is too often treated as the only formative event in Melanchthon's embrace of Roman law.[75] The Melanchthon of 1525 was not yet the Melanchthon who tied together the medieval jurisprudence of the ius commune with the idea of the translatio imperii. Humanism was not easy to reconcile with the medieval vision of the translatio imperii. For the translatio imperii implied that Roman tradition had been continuous since Antiquity, whereas humanist thought was founded, at least in some measure, on the belief that Rome had fallen in the fifth century A.D., and had vanished from the lives of men until the time of Petrarch. The humanist Melanchthon of the 1520s entertained a cultural idea of Rome that was fundamentally incompatible with notions of the Fourth Monarchy. Not until Melanchthon returned to the Mos Italicus after 1530 did it make sense for him to speak of a continuous medieval Roman tradition. Not until after 1530 could Melanchthon return the old conception of the peacemaker's ius commune and integrate it anew into the vision of universal empire.

Guido Kisch has shown that it was only sometime after 1530 that Melanchthon at last embraced the medieval law.[76] But Kisch and other Melanchthon scholars have not devoted enough effort to identifying the political events that led Melanchthon to alter his thinking when he did, nor to showing how his embrace of the Mos Italicus fit his new faith, after 1530, in the translatio imperii.

The great shift in Melanchthon's thought came, I suggest, not because he feared the peasants would escape state suppression, but because he feared the Empire would suppress the Lutherans themselves. It was when Luther and Melanchthon directly faced imperial power in 1529 and 1530 that they began to speak eagerly for the first time about the value of the ius commune as a guardian of imperial peace. Only when war threatened to obliterate the Reform movement did the Lutherans seize upon the tradition of 1495.

As is well known, Charles V's hostility toward the Reformation brought the Lutheran movement to a new state of precariousness in the late 1520s. The sponsorship of some of the leading German princes gave the Lutherans a kind of security—but it was a security they were likely to have only as long as the emperor was tied down by his wars with the French and the Turks. The Imperial Diet that met at Speyer in March and April of 1529 made declarations that the Lutherans regarded as harsh and threatening. The future fortunes of the movement depended on the course of events at the next year's Diet in Augsburg.[77] It was during the Augs-

---

[75] Most recently, Strauss, *Law, Resistance and the State*, 226–27.

[76] Kisch, *Melanchthon*, esp. 127ff.

[77] See H. Virck, "Melanchthons Politische Stellung auf dem Reichstag zu Augsburg 1530," *Zeitschrift für Kirchengeschichte* 9 (1888): 68.

burg Diet that Melanchthon and Luther adopted a new stance toward the Empire and toward the place of law within it.

By the end of the 1520s Charles V, hard pressed at home and abroad, had a new willingness to accept an imperial peace.[78] In December 1529 Phillip of Hesse, the political mastermind of the movement, suggested to Luther that they make their support for the Habsburgs conditional on the guarantee of a Public Peace in which they could freely propagate the gospel. Luther was wary of this proposal, which seemed to tread too close to resistance to the secular authorities forbidden by Romans 13.[79] Nevertheless, as the Diet proceeded in the summer months of 1530, Luther—who was not himself permitted to attend—came over to Phillip's hope for peace, founded on imperial law, under cover of which they could spread the word of God[80]; by October Luther had been persuaded that safety from an emperor who was a "violator of the Peace"[81] lay in the Roman-Canon law of the ius commune.[82] These summer months, in which Luther came to see the virtue of a neutral peace with a hostile emperor, were the formative moment in the development of Lutheran legal thought.

As the Lutherans, fearful of a civil war that would require more strength than they had, turned back to the old idea of Public Peace in the Empire, they also turned back to the old idea of the ius commune that had been linked with the Public Peace for two-and-a-half centuries. The transformation of Luther's legal thought in 1530 was startling. Luther denounced lawyers regularly throughout his life, often repeating the popular peasant slogan, "Juristen böse Christen"—jurists are bad Christians.[83] But in the critical year of 1530, as he saw the need for a revived Public Peace, he declared that jurists were "Angels of the Empire," "Apostles of the Kaiser"[84]—bizarre words from Martin Luther, a measure of the political pressure he felt. He had tolerated the ius commune as a necessary, but emphatically unreligious, element of secular government

---

[78] See, e.g., Virck, "Melanchthons Politische Stellung," 322ff.

[79] I rely largely on the discussion by G. Müller, "Luthers Beziehungen zu Rom," in H. Junghans, ed., Leben und Werk Martin Luthers, 2 vols. (Göttingen, 1983), 1:374ff., esp. 378–80.

[80] Ibid., 385–86; cf. Virck, "Melanchthons Politische Stellung," 297, on Luther's desire for "die Erhaltung des politischen Friedens."

[81] Müller, "Luthers Beziehungen," 385.

[82] Cargill Thompson, Political Thought of Luther, 104–5; also idem, 90. Cargill Thompson does not, however, recognize the significance of the association of Roman-Canon law with the Landfriede.

[83] Cf. Wieacker, Privatrechtsgeschichte, 142–43.

[84] Luther, "Predigt, daß man Kinder zur Schule halten solle," Werke, vol. 30, pt. 2, 560. Cf. Günter, Luthers Vorstellung, 79. Strauss notes this sermon as unusually favorable to lawyers, within Luther's oeuvre. Strauss, Law, Resistance and the State, 5.

for a decade. But in 1530, for the first time, he spoke actively in favor of secular law.

The degree to which imperial politics could transform Luther's thinking on private law was most evident in his writings on marriage law. Luther had been struggling with his Wittenberg colleagues over marriage law for some years, attempting to draw them onto a common platform for the rejection of the Canon law of marriage. His colleagues, however, viewed the elimination of Canon law as an impractical scheme.[85] The great shift of 1530 spurred Luther to fashion a new marriage-law project, one in which Luther would for the first time accept Roman law as a "specifically Protestant church law."[86] In 1530 Luther adopted an approach first suggested by his follower Johannes Brenz,[87] and declared himself in favor of an "imperial" law of marriage for Germany.[88] Such active sponsorship of secular law would never have been possible for Luther before this year. Indeed, Luther did not embrace only Roman law. Rather, he embraced the entire ius commune, including Canon law, of which he was careful, in his marriage-law essay, to speak well[89]—something he had never done before this year of political crisis. That summer he published an introduction to a work on Canon law in which he emphasized the consonance between Canon law and Lutheran doctrine.[90] This was a strangely altered Luther, who would not only tolerate but actively admire the old written laws of the ius commune. Ius scriptum and Public Peace went hand in hand, and Luther would not accept the one without accepting the other.

As Luther accepted the ius commune, he accepted the translatio imperii. Since 1495 Public Peace and ius commune had been tightly bound up with the idea of the Holy Roman Empire as the universal empire of the old choice of law system. Thus it is no surprise that Luther's ideas on the translatio imperii were also transformed in 1530. A year earlier, when

[85] Stintzing, *Geschichte*, 1:275 and 273–83, generally, on "der Kampf um das kanonische Recht." Three hundred fifty years later, Luther's wedding remained so resonant in the German mind that Wagner contemplated a drama on the subject. Cf., e.g., R. Gutman, *Richard Wagner: The Man, His Mind, and his Music* (New York, 1968), 283. Canon law was deeply ingrained in the German legal system; even Luther could not have simply abandoned Canon law. Cf. W. Maurer, "Reste des kanonischen Rechts im Frühprotestantismus," *ZSS (K)* 51 (1965): 190–253.

[86] The phrase comes from A. Sprengler-Ruppenthal, "Zur Rezeption des Römischen Rechts im Eherecht der Reformatoren," *ZSS (K)* 68 (1982): 395.

[87] Sprengler-Ruppenthal, "Zur Rezeption," 369ff.

[88] Luther, "Von Ehesachen," in *Werke*, vol. 30, pt. 3, 245f. Cf. Sprengler-Ruppenthal, "Zur Rezeption," 372–74; Günter, *Luthers Vorstellung*, 41 n. 65.

[89] Luther, "Von Ehesachen," 248.

[90] Luther, "Vorrede zu Spenglers Auszug aus den päpstlichen Rechten," in *Werke*, vol. 30, pt. 2, 215ff. See generally the discussion of A. Stein, "Luther über Eherecht und Juristen," in Junghans, ed., *Leben und Werk*, 1:182.

Luther delivered his "Field Sermon against the Turks," challenging the pope's claim to have inherited the dignity of the Roman emperors, he was unwilling to declare that the German Empire was the successor to the Roman. The Roman heritage, Luther declared in 1529, had not passed to the popes—but it had not passed to the Germans alone either. Rather, it belonged to all the secular rulers of the formerly Roman world, including the Turks.[91] This was a position he would maintain again in the future, but in his imperial year of 1530 Luther was an advocate of the German claim. He took for the first time a great interest in the details of the imperial constitution and declared for the first time that the Holy Roman Empire of the German Nation was the modern representative of the Roman imperium.[92] Here again, the special problems of marriage law figured prominently in the shift in his thought. Luther's conviction that the rule of the secular authorities should remain inviolate was at war with his hatred of the Canon law of marriage, which the emperor specifically endorsed. Now Luther deduced the necessity of a Roman law of marriage from the German translatio imperii. Christians, Luther argued, must ignore the emperor's deference to the pope on the subject of marriage law, for such deference was in derogation of the universality of the Roman imperium.[93] This argument had political punch: Luther was in effect declaring that the emperor was himself bound by imperial tradition, a tradition emphatically not papal, and a tradition in which the rule of ius scriptum protected all Germans against arbitrary violence in the pursuit of conflicting and ill-defined rights.

Luther's great constitutional and legal reversal was also Melanchthon's. When Luther embraced the German imperial tradition, he was influenced by a new publication of Melanchthon's, a 1530 commentary on Aristotle's *Politics*, in which Melanchthon revived the constitutionalist language of 1495. Melanchthon, too, had been swept up in the new imperial Lutheran movement. Citing the *Corpus Iuris*, he declared that political salvation could only lie in written law; if judges sought to give justice according to their own lights, they would wreak havoc.[94] Melanchthon had returned to the old faith in written law broadly conceived, putting aside the humanist pure Roman law for which he had pleaded in 1525. It is significant that Melanchthon announced his return

[91] Günter, *Luthers Vorstellung*, 47.

[92] Ibid., 41 n. 65, 53.

[93] See Sprengler-Ruppenthal, "Zur Rezeption," 373.

[94] Melanchthon, "Estne iudicandum iuxta scriptum ius an secundum aequitatem," in *Opera* 16:78–81, drawing on Aristotle, *Politics*, III, 16, 1287a. Cited and discussed in Kisch, *Melanchthon*, 175–77. For the probable influence of Melanchthon's 1530 commentary on this Aristotelean passage on Luther's new imperial philosophy, see Günter, *Luthers Vorstellung*, 132.

to the ius commune tradition in reliance on Aristotle, the great scholastic philosopher. In 1525 he had denounced Aristotelean legal thought, which was so inextricably bound up with Catholic thought. Now he became an Aristotelean,[95] working to reinterpret the old idea of the ius commune, in light of Aristotle's characteristic theory of equity, as a law of *iustitia*, a new scholastic justice like that of the medieval Landfriede.[96] Melanchthon had come to the same turning point as Luther, under the same political pressures of the Diet of Augsburg.

And, like Luther, Melanchthon came around to the translatio imperii: in 1531, Melanchthon received the manuscript that became the basis of his own new German-Roman imperial historiography: the "Chronica," a Danielian universal history with an anti-Papist and anti-French tinge sent to him by the astrologer Johannes Carion.[97] It remains uncertain how much of this handbook on the history of the Four Monarchies, published that year under Melanchthon's sponsorship, was written by Melanchthon himself.[98] But whatever his contribution to this first German version of Carion's work, Melanchthon made this immensely influential book[99] his own in subsequent decades, publishing an expanded Latin version in 1558, two years before his death. The *Chronicon Carionis* became the basis of German historiography for a century. It also served as Melanchthon's inspiration as he walked his own road toward a Lutheran theologization of Roman law as the law of state peace in the Empire.

Melanchthon's turn to the translatio imperii went hand in hand with his acceptance of the Mos Italicus: not only did the italianate *Corpus Iuris* include the enactments of the modern emperors, but the Accursian Gloss also explicitly endorsed the belief that there had been a translatio imperii from the French to the Germans.[100] Moreover, in Carion's manuscript, the discovery of the *Digest* in medieval Italy was a pivotal event in the

[95] Cf. Stintzing, *Geschichte*, 1:285, on the contrast between Melanchthon's 1525 attitude to Aristotle and his later attitude.

[96] Melanchthon's debt to Aristotle's conception of *epieikeia* is the principal point of Kisch's interpretation. *Melanchthon*, esp. 168–83. For a more general discussion of *epieikeia* in humanist legal thought, see G. Kisch, *Erasmus und die Jurisprudenz seiner Zeit: Studien zum humanistischen Rechtsdenken*, Basler Studien zur Rechtswissenschaft, Heft 56 (Basel, 1960). For further discussion, see below, pp. 36–37.

[97] W. Goez, *Translatio Imperii* (Tübingen, 1958), 258ff., 270.

[98] See ibid., 259. Carion died in 1538 and never again worked on the manuscript. See C. G. Bretschneider, Preface to Melanchthon, ed., *Chronicon Carionis*, in Melanchthon, *Opera*, 12:707.

[99] The Europe-wide popularity of Carion's book is described by Goez, *Translatio Imperii*, 281ff. Carion, of course, was neither the first European nor the first German to espouse a Danielian historiography. For the earlier history in Europe, see ibid. For the history in the immediately preceding decades in Germany, see Scherer, *Geschichte und Kirchengeschichte*, 11–29.

[100] See Goez, *Translatio Imperii*, 252.

last translatio imperii. As Carion told it, "Werner"—Carion called the early Bolognese jurist Irnerius by his German name—had discovered the *Digest* in the time of the German emperor Lothar: "a learned man named Werner, whom Accursius often calls 'Irnerius' . . . found the Roman legal books in libraries and brought them to light. Lothar ordered that they be read in schools and once again be used in imperial courts."[101] The operative words were "once again": the introduction of Roman law into the courts represented a restoration of the Roman Empire. A year after publishing Carion's book, Melanchthon himself gave a lecture praising Irnerius.[102] In 1537 he gave another, entitled "De Irnerio et Bartolo Jurisconsultis." This oration was an extraordinary departure for an old humanist: it was in praise of Bartolus, the archcommentator and easily the lawyer most detested by the humanist community. "De Irnerio et Bartolo" repeated and embellished the "Lothar-legend" of Carion's *Chronica*. As Melanchthon now communicated the story of the rediscovery of the *Digest*, Irnerius had personally persuaded the emperor to restore the *Romanae leges* to a Germany wracked by war.[103] Melanchthon drew for his audience the historical moral: jurists, Luther's "Angels of the Empire," were necessary agents of peace. Princes must be "the guardians of law and justice," but they could not perform their function without the advice of scholars.[104] Thus scholars took their place along with learned law in the theologian's political vision. By 1550 Melanchthon could declare quite simply that the *Corpus Iuris* was a divinely inspired project.[105] The constitutional settlement of 1495 became part of a divine pax romana,

---

[101] "Ein gelart man genannt Wernherus / den Accursius offt nennet Irnerium / . . . der hat die Römische recht Bücher jnn Bibliotheken gefunden / vnd widder an das liecht bracht / Die hat Lotharius befolen jnn Schulen zu lesen / vnd widderumb darnach zu sprechen jnn Keisarlichen gerichten," Carion, *Chronica durch Magistrum Johan Carion/ Vleissig zusammen gezogen / meniglich nützlich zu lesen* (Wittenberg, 1532), 138–39.

[102] Melanchthon, "De scripto iure et de dignitate veterum interpretum iuris," in Kisch, *Melanchthon*, 228–33. The probable date of 1532 is given in Kisch, *Melanchthon*, 135.

[103] Melanchthon, "Oratio de Inerio et Bartolo," reprinted in ibid., 216. "Fuerat Italia graviter afflicta bellis Henrici Quarti; multorum patrimonia varie, ut fit bellis civilibus, translata fuerant. Ergo cum opus esset gubernatore praedito magna sapientia et aequitate, Italia non nihil recreata est prudentia et moderatione Irnerii, qui cum posteritati etiam consulendum putaret, cupiebat autoritate imperatoria rursus proferri ius Romanum, et certae leges et erudite scriptae extarent; nam incertum ius aeternas discordias parit. Sed in Germania incidit in bella civilia. Postea Irnerius, cum perspecta eius virtus in gubernatione tam longa, et grandior aetas auxisset eius autoritatem, nactus Imperatorem Lotharium Saxonem, non impeditum civilibus bellis, et qui plurima in Italia ad muniendam tranquillitatem constituit, fuit huic hortator, ut curaret Romae et Bononiae rursus enarrari ius Romanum, et ut controversiae ex Romanis legibus diiudicarentur. Ita rursus celebrari et coli studium Romani iuris coepit."

[104] Quoted in ibid., 139.

[105] Ibid., 116–17.

occulted for centuries but slowly reappearing since Irnerius had conveyed to Emperor Lothar the law of peace.[106]

I hope the resonances of the phrases of the 1538 oration I began by quoting can now be clearly heard: it was "fitting to give thanks to God that He has returned law to the Empire;"[107] because the Romanae leges were written law, they were the law of *aequitas*, of justice, and they brought with them peace for Germany; Roman law, because most learned, was most just.[108] Ius scriptum was ius certum, standing above the conflict of claimed rights and the arbitrary impulses of princes. Peace was an urgent need for Melanchthon after 1530, and he sought solutions forged by Europeans for whom peace had been an urgent need for centuries. Learned law was just because it was the law of the widest of the concentric circles of the medieval choice-of-law universe. As such it brought peace, for it was impartial, the law of no party. In a Germany in which no party could act violently against another, the faith could grow. Thus did the ius commune of the Perpetual Public Peace take on its visionary character.

THE CONSCIOUSNESS OF THE JURISTS IN THE MELANCHTHONIAN ORDER

Melanchthon's conversion to the ius commune and the translatio imperii had centuries of consequences. For his writings in large measure shaped the self-image of all later German civil lawyers. How, indeed, could the Lutheran vision not enthrall the "Angels of the Empire," the "Apostles of the Kaiser"? In subsequent decades, Melanchthonianism grew as the Roman-law jurists acquired new duties and new powers in the states of the new Empire, as they spread Melanchthon's teaching, worked to promote the universities, and built new organs of justice. In this section I wish to trace the institutionalization of a proud and powerful Roman-law professoriate in the sixteenth century, the ancestors of Savigny whose status in Germany society was built on the glory of the Roman law that Melanch-

---

[106] For another remarkable Melanchthonian treatment of the *Lotherlegende*, see the *Isagoge per Dialogum in Quatuor Libros Institutionum* of Johannes Apel (Bratislava, 1540). In this dialogue, Apel attempted to demonstrate that the *Brachylogus Juris Civilis*, a systematic introductory epitome which he had discovered in Königsberg, had been compiled by order of the emperor Lothar (esp. p. C [5] verso)—a notable effort at reconciling Humanism with the Lothar legend. Cf. Stintzing, *Geschichte*, 1:292–93. If Wieacker is right in concluding that the relevant passage in Apel's *Isagoge* was added to the text after 1530, the work constitutes yet more evidence of the crucial shift in legal thought at that time. See F. Wieacker, "Einflüsse des Humanismus auf die Rezeption: Eine Studie zu Johann Apels 'Dialogus,' " in *Zeitschrift für die gesamte Staatswissenschaft* 100 (1939): 435.

[107] Melanchthon, "Oratio de dignitate legum," reprinted in Kisch, *Melanchthon*, 227. Cf. ibid., 121.

[108] Ibid., 227.

thon sponsored. Over the course of the century, a new body of institutions grew up as the vessels of Melanchthonian thought. Melanchthon's vision of Rome and the German constitution melded together, in some measure, as the professors of Roman law grew in social stature.

Roman law lent itself to the rise to prominence of the sixteenth-century professoriate: scholars had enjoyed special distinction both in the ancient and in the medieval Roman-law worlds; German professors of Roman law could regard themselves as the heirs of a very great scholarly tradition. Every German professor of Roman law could base his pride on the image of ancient Roman society, the society that held jurists in supremely high esteem. The surviving evidence of ancient legal life provided a picture uncertain in all its details, but clear enough in broad outline to justify high social status for the modern jurists who had been pronounced *ex cathedra lutherana* to be "Angels of the Empire." Latin literature as early modern Europe possessed it was rich in testimony to the high dignity of the ancient lawyers—from the dramatic anecdote communicated by the biographer of Alexander Severus, who reported that the emperor had been accustomed to shield the jurist Ulpian under his own purple cloak,[109] through the bitter satire of Seneca, who charged Claudius with disregard for the traditional prerogatives of the learned jurists.[110] The political program of every Romanist derived immeasurable force and conviction from this literature, from the knowledge that the aristocrats of republican Rome had devoted themselves to law, that the great Roman system had been the work of professional jurists, the best among them leading ministers of the most eminent emperors. The belief that Rome provided the model for the mission of German jurists remained constant from the Renaissance down into the middle of the nineteenth century.

Legal sources testified to the power of the ancient jurists just as literary sources did—and the legal sources were particularly important, for by the sixteenth century they had assumed undoubted force of law in the German-speaking world. The *Corpus Iuris* seemed to show that some Roman jurists possessed a right to give legal opinions by which judges were somehow bound—the so-called *ius respondendi*, "the right to give legal opinions." The significance of the ius respondendi in the ancient world is uncertain. But it was unquestionably the most important legal doctrine behind the growth of professorial power in Germany; accordingly, it will

---

[109] "Ulpianum pro tutore habuit, primum repugnante matre deinde gratias agente, quem saepe a militum ira obiectu purpurae suae defendit, atque ideo summus imperator fuit quod eius consiliis praecipue rem publicam rexit." *Scriptores Historiae Augustae*, "Severus Alexander," LI, 4. The Loeb Library (Cambridge, Mass., 1982), 2:280.

[110] Seneca, *Apocolocyntosis* 12. The Loeb Library (Cambridge, Mass., 1975), 470, describing the reaction of the jurists to Claudius's death: "Iurisconsulti e tenebris procedebant, pallidi, graciles, vix animam habentes, tanquam qui tum maxime reviviscerent."

play a central part in this study. The surviving passages on the ius respondendi are, unfortunately, quite unclear: it is difficult to say which ancient jurists were honored with the ius respondendi, and exactly what force their legal opinons had. The ius respondendi was originally the creation of the emperor Augustus. It is possible that under Hadrian and his immediate successors, a given legal interpretation had the force of law if the leading jurists unanimously agreed to it. The requirement of unanimity was, however, abandoned in late antiquity: in 426 the number of canonical jurists was reduced to five, all of which had been active two or more centuries earlier; legal doctrine was decided by reference to the writings of these five. If a majority of the five favored a given doctrine, it had legal force. Failing a majority, one of the five was considered more authoritative than the others.[111] The *Corpus Iuris* embodied this old tradition of respect for juristic authority: it was a sixth-century compilation of authoritative scholarly opinions of centuries earlier. This ancient scholarly legal authority became the basis for the institutional heart of professorial lawmaking: adjudication of cases by law-faculty committees called *Spruchkollegien*, which I will describe shortly.

German professors of Roman law could also regard themselves as heirs of the great and powerful medieval Italian jurists. The Bolognese lawyers had developed an elaborate jurisprudence based on the legal authority of the Roman lawyers, encapsulated in the famous formula of Baldus: *communis opinio doctorum habet vim consuetudinis*—"the shared opinion of the scholars has the force of custom." This formula established the medieval and early modern equivalent of the ius respondendi and provided the direct model for professorial authority in Germany. As communis opinio, the dense medieval commentaries on the *Corpus Iuris* attained their legal authority: the works of the professors had the legal status of testimony about custom by knowledgeable witnesses. This was, perhaps, not so exalted ·a legal authority as the classical jurists had had. But it was a very considerable authority indeed. Italy was the model for Germany's professorial Roman law, but the practice of professorial law, as Germans adapted it, became wholly German.

Despite the majesty of these models, however, the German ius respondendi could not grow without the aid of another development: the institutionalization of lawyers in the universities. Before the mid-1530s, it would have been difficult for scholars to exercise power on any regular basis, or to form any lasting sense of corporate tradition. For the humanist scholars, who were the natural advocates of Roman law, had not fully established themselves in the German universities, the only institutions

[111] See M. Kaser, *Römische Rechtsgeschichte*, 2d ed. (Göttingen, 1982), 178–79, 229ff.; F. Schulz, *Geschichte der Römischen Rechtswissenschaft* (Weimar, 1961), 132ff., 357ff.

that could have provided them with a settled base. But the decades after 1530 saw the successful integration of the new scholars into the old schools.[112] This was the indispensable first step in the growth of political Melanchthonianism.

To be sure, the university tradition was old in Germany.[113] Roman law had been a scholars' law for centuries, and, as the new learned justice was established in the service of the new states, scholars had appeared in positions of power. Some of the most prominent scholars in early sixteenth-century Germany, Reuchlin and Valentin Forster among them, joined the Reichskammergericht for a time and then returned to the universities[114]; the new court established a fixed point of entry into an imperial center of power for learned men. Nevertheless, these men remained independent humanists more than academics, *poetae* as much as *doctores*. There was little sense that learned men should belong to formally organized political bodies before they exercised formal political power. So, at least, we may conclude from the document most often cited as the great first triumph of legal scholars: the *Carolina*, the great new criminal code of Charles V of 1532. By its terms, the *Carolina* was a triumph of *scholars* rather than of *academics*. It made special mention of scholars, to whom courts were to defer in doubtful cases.[115] But university professors did not yet have a monopoly on this consultative legal function: the *Carolina* directed courts to draw their information from "a nearby academy, city or town, or from other learned scholars."[116] There were scholars in the "Academiae," but in 1532 they were not yet alone. In the subsequent decades, however, the academic monopoly took hold. By 1600, when Georg Remus wrote a commentary on the *Carolina*, the prestige of the professors had so grown that Remus glossed this passage by referring to "collegia Doctorum in Academiis, quae sunt velut oracula provinciarum"—"colleges of doctors in academies, which are as oracles unto the [German] states."[117] Sixty-eight years had seen a startling rise in the prestige of the universities and a wholly new willingness on the part of scholars to be academics.

The shift was well underway in 1540, and it was already associated

[112] For the successful integration of humanists into the universities, see J. Overfield, *Humanism and Scholasticism in Late Medieval Germany* (Princeton, N.J., 1985), 298ff.

[113] See Burmeister, *Studium der Rechte*, 31–58.

[114] Diestelkamp, "Das Reichskammergericht," 453; Stintzing, *Geschichte*, 1:479ff.

[115] Cf., e.g., E. Kern, *Geschichte des Gerichtsverfassungsrechts* (Munich, 1954), 36.

[116] *Peinliche Gerichtsordnung Karls V. von 1532*, Article 219. Cf. Conrad, *Rechtsgeschichte*, 2:286ff.

[117] Remus, *Nemesis Carolina* (orig. Herborn, 1600). Reprinted with Gobler, *Interpretatio Constitutionis Criminalis Carolinae* (orig. Basel, 1543), edited by J.F.H. Abegg (Heidelberg, 1837), 236–37. Gobler's 1543 commentary on this passage simply quoted the text of the *Carolina*.

with Melanchthon's Roman law. In the winter of that year, one of Melanchthon's disciples, Christopher Hegendorffinus, was asked by the leaders of Rostock to come lecture them on the need for a revived university in their own frontier Baltic town. He came. He told them the devil was at work in the world.[118] He reassured them that resources were available to fund new faculties that could counter the devil's influence, resources they need only seize: "There are," he noted, "most ample monasteries."[119] Professors would bring Christian teaching to Rostock, and they would also bring medicine.[120] Finally, Hegendorffinus told his audience that civil law must accompany Christianity, for only civil law could bring peace:

> Now it is certain that societies cannot be preserved, unless they include men who teach Christian piety, unless they include men who compose the disputes that arise among the citizens according to principles of law and justice, who will declare the law unto the people, who will guard the public peace according to the laws, punish the iniquitous and defend the just against violence.[121]

Such men, he said, could only be found in the universities, which must be restored.[122] The Lutheran project to reinstate the old institutions of learning was underway, and with it came a new language of praise for the professoriate, bringers of peace.

Indeed, the campaign to revive the universities owed a great deal to the prestige of Roman law. As the universities rose, the professors were well aware how much the transformation owed to the Roman law of Melanchthon, the principle element of the translatio imperii. For example, the writings of Iacobus Middendorp and Reinerus Reineccius, two publicists of the new university culture, showed a powerful awareness that the triumph of Roman law had helped build the academic order. Middendorp, hailing the university culture that Germans had imported from Italy, praised Roman law, instrumental both in promoting the general revival of classical learning and in bringing scholars closer to power as the advisors of princes. Though a Catholic, he conceived of Rome in thoroughly Melanchthonian terms: the Lotharlegende described the pivotal

---

[118] Christophorus Hegendorffinus, *Oratio de Rationibus Restaurandi Collapsas Academias Publicas* (Rostock, 1540), A iii(r). For the influence of Melanchthonians in Rostock, see Overfield, *Humanism and Scholasticism*, 327, and the literature cited there.

[119] Ibid., B iv(r).

[120] Ibid., A vii(v)–A viii(r).

[121] Ibid., C i(v)–C ii(r): "Nam certum est resp: conservari non posse, nisi sint qui in illis pietatem Christianam doceant, nisı sint, qui legibus & iure dissidia inter cives orta componant, populo Iura dicant, publicam tranquillitatem ex legibus tueantur, improbos punıant, probos adversus vim defendant."

[122] Ibid., C ii(r).

episode in the modern history of Roman law. Eager to promote the claims of the "Academies," Middendorp stressed once again that the emperor had acted with the aid and counsel of Irnerius. In the dark ages, wrote Middendorp, borrowing language directly from Melanchthon, barbarism penetrated Italy, and the laws of Rome "fell silent":

> Until, in the time of the emperor Lothar, when Italy had begun, as it were, to breathe once again, brilliant and learned men, hating the barbarian constitutions, which seemed to taste of tyranny, reestablished the civil law of the Romans, and led it back into the court from which it had been exiled so long. First among them stood Werner, or Irnerius, a certain man of the highest authority and supreme learning. He persuaded the emperor to undertake once again to judge cases by the written laws, and to teach them in the schools of Rome. . . . [Thus] were restored not only jurisprudence, but also scholarship, the purity of the Latin language, and the liberal disciplines.[123]

The success of the universities in which Middendorp was making his career was pinned in his mind to the penetration of Roman law. Reineccius—well-known as an original and influential follower of Melanchthon[124]—was a more sophisticated and learned scholar than Middendorp; he made no mention of Lothar and gave less weight than did Middendorp to Roman law. But his Rome was still the Rome of Melanchthon, and Roman law still served as one of the motors of German academic history in his account of the rise of the universities: as Reineccius recounted it, the muses, routed from Western Europe by the barbarian hordes, had taken refuge in Byzantium. There Justinian had saved them by his codification of the ancient laws, and the study of the ancient laws had done much to bring the muses to Germany after Constantinople fell.[125] Thus German professors perceived themselves to be the benefi-

---

[123] Iacobus Middendorp, *Academiarum Orbis Christiani Libri Duo* (Cologne, 1572), 1:132–33. "Romanae leges oppressae conticuerunt. Donec Lotharij imperatoris temporibus, cùm nonnihil quasi respirare coepisset Italia, homines ingeniosi & eruditi odio barbaricarum constitutionum, quae tyrannidem sapere videbantur, ius civile Romanorum restituerent, & in forum undè iam diu exulârat, reducerent. Inter quos praecipuus ferè extitit VVernerus sive Irnerius quidam vir summae authoritatis & apprimè eruditus. Hic imperatori persuasit, ut praeciperet causas iterùm ex scriptis legibus iudicari, easdemque in scholis Romae doceri. . . . Nec iurisprudentia solum restituta est, verumetiam historia, latinae linguae puritas, & liberales disciplinae." For the borrowing from Melanchthon, cf. "Oratio de Irnerio et Bartolo Iurisconsultis" ("Romanae leges conticuerunt") quoted in Kisch, *Melanchthon*, 216.

[124] See, e.g., Klempt, *Säkularisierung der Universalgeschichte*, 69ff.

[125] Reinerus Reineccius, *Methodus Legendi Cognoscendique Historiam tam Sacram quam Profanam* (Helmstedt, 1583), 26: "Tametsi verò sequentibus temporibus effusae in Italiam, Galliam, Hispaniam & alias provincias peregrinae & barbarae nationes Musas inde fugârunt, tamen cùm alibi tum CONSTANTINOPOLI potissimùm eae domicilium retinuere. Cumque & ibi graviter rei litterariae incommodasset IUSTINIANUS Caes. is inquam,

ciaries of the reception of Roman law: they were mediators of the translatio imperii, modern guardians of "the muses." Status and learning, organized in the reviving universities, were founded on the Roman law of Melanchthon.

With status, learning, and formal institutionalization came an evergrowing influence on the practice of law. Scholars began to declare justice, just as Hegendorffinus had told the knights of Rostock they should. Learned lawyers began to displace the traditional decision makers of the German legal world: the so-called *Schöffen*, regularly sitting lay judges. This "scholarification" often proceeded according to the model of the Reichskammergericht, with scholars joining laymen in equal numbers. But whether or not imperial practice served as the model, learned law extended its dominion. Inevitably the scholars exercised disproportionate influence as they introduced themselves into the practice of justice: able to cite text, to command the difficult terminology of a prestigious system of thought, they drew authority to themselves and away from lay Schöffen who could claim to represent only common sense and experience.[126] The sponsorship of the princes did yet more. A whole new system of learned justice established itself in sixteenth-century Germany on the strength of the new university law.[127]

Indeed, a new kind of academic legal culture grew—one in which professors were called upon to decide cases, one in which the medieval scholastic style of argument began to reassert itself. The law-faculties themselves were directly integrated into the new system. The Empire that Luther and Melanchthon had embraced put adjudicatory power directly into the hands of the professors through the institution of *Aktenversendung*, the submission of cases to law-faculty committees called Spruchkollegien for adjudication. The Spruchkollegien became the institutional embodiments of the idea of Roman-law "impartiality." These learned institutions began growing along with the other new courts of learned justice in the early sixteenth century and attained great importance in mid-

---

qui veterum Iureconsultorum libris abolitis, centones legum nobis reliquit, inserendo ærario suo mercedes, quae in civitatibus bonas artes atque litteras docentibus publicè constitutae essent, rursus hoc sarcijt Michaelis III. Imp. temporibus Bardas Caesar. . . . Ad extremum CONSTANTINOPOLI à Turcis expugnata, Musae inde pulsae in Italiam remigrârunt, & porro Alpes transvolârunt. De quo argumento disserendum hîc non putavimus. Pertractatur enim diversis diversorum scriptis, neque nihil nos alibi conati sumus. Et fecit de IURIS ROM. & legum historia, quae & ipsa huc pertinebat, praeclaro opere operaeprecium VALENTINUS FORSTERUS."

[126] Compare the excellent discussions of G. Dahm, "On the Reception of Roman and Italian Law in Germany," in Strauss, ed., *Pre-Reformation Germany*, 282–315, and Strauss, *Law, Resistance and the State*, esp. 76–83.

[127] See Stölzel, *Entwicklung des gelehrten Richtertums*.

and late century, as the university revival progressed.[128] Indeed, despite their origins early in the century (and in medieval German and Italian models[129]) the formal integration of these institutions into the imperial constitution came only with the late humanist revival of academic life, as imperial ordinances of 1570 and 1600[130] granted litigants the right to demand that law faculties hear their cases as an alternative to regular courts and offices of justice.[131]

The Spruchkollegien whose place in the constitution was thus recognized were like so many smaller, scattered Reichskammergerichte. Like the Reichskammergericht, their ultimate models were the late medieval courts of arbitration.[132] They were associated, like the Reichskammergericht, with a fundamental proposition of appellate justice in early modern Germany: no man who was party to a suit against his sovereign could be tried in the court of that sovereign. Litigants caught up in litigation with their prince had a right to refer their case to a Spruchkollegium as well as a right to appeal to the Reichskammergericht. This idea of an alternative to sovereign justice made the Spruchkollegien welcome resources in mo-

---

[128] Cf. Strauss, *Law, Resistance and the State*, 83.

[129] Like German Roman law itself, the roots of Aktenversendung lay in the German Middle Ages, in the consultation of Schöffen (O. Bülow, *Ende des Aktenversendungsrechts* [Freiburg i.B., 1881], 24, makes this point in unmistakably Savignyan form: "Das Aktenversendungsinstitut ist die getreue Übersetzung der alten Volksrechtssprechung in die Gelehrtenrechtssprechung") and in the medieval use of the *Oberhof*, a metropolitan court that instructed courts in daughter cities on metropolitan law. See E. Klugkist, "Die Aktenversendung an Juristenfakultäten," in *Juristenzeitung* 22 (1967): 155, col. 1; Dawson, *Oracles of the Law*, 161ff. The immediate models for the practice lay, however, in medieval and Renaissance Italy. Dawson, *Oracles of the Law*, 198ff.; Wieacker, *Privatrechtsgeschichte*, 181, and its ultimate inspiration in the ancient ius respondendi. Cf. Klugkist, "Aktenversendung," 155, col. 1; G. Baumgärtel, *Die Gutachter- und Urteilstätigkeit der Erlanger Juristenfakultät in dem ersten Jahrhundert ihres Bestehens*, Erlanger Forschungen. Reihe A: Geisteswissenschaften, vol. 14 (Erlangen, 1962), 14ff.

[130] These were the Imperial Recess of 1570, §85, and the Deputation Recess of 1600, §16.

[131] For the most part, the best introductions to the history of Aktenversendung remain the histories of individual Spruchkollegien. See G. Buchda, "Die Spruchtätigkeit der Hallischen Juristenfakultät," in *ZSS* (G) 62 (1942): 210–94; 63 (1943): 251–318; 64 (1944): 223–75; 68 (1948): 308–47; E. Wohlhaupter, "Die Spruchtätigkeit der Kieler Fakultät," in *ZSS* (G), 58 (1938): 752ff.; E. Seckel, "Geschichte der Berliner Juristenfakultät als Spruchkollegium," in M. Lenz, *Geschichte der Friedrich-Wilhelms-Universität zu Berlin* (Berlin, 1910), 3: 449ff.; Baumgärtel, *Erlanger Juristenfakultät*, 14ff.; N. Hasselwander, *Aus der Gutachter- und Urteilstätigkeit an der alten Mainzer Juristenfakultät* (Wiesbaden, 1956). For a more general treatment, see E. Klugkist, "Die Aktenversendung an Juristenfakultäten." For further literature, see J. Schröder, *Wissenschaftstheorie und Lehre der "praktischen Jurisprudenz" auf deutschen Universitäten an der Wende zum 19. Jahrhundert*, Ius Commune Sonderheft 11 (Frankfurt a.M., 1979), 1 n. 5. B. Schildt, "Die Rechtsprüche deutscher Juristenfakultäten als Quelle rechtshistorischer Forschung" in *Staat und Recht* 32 (1983): 470–77 offers little that is helpful.

[132] Strauss, *Law, Resistance and the State*, 84, citing Krause, *Schiedsgerichtswesen*.

ments of political uncertainty: like the Reichskammergericht, the Spruchkollegien were the resort of Renaissance Germans faced with delicate political questions from the election of Charles V to the writing of the Saxon
constitutions in 1572.[133]

And, indeed, the purpose of the new academic institution was to extend
the constitutional benefits of Roman-law impartiality to all: the title given
Aktenversendung by the imperial law of 1570 was "the benefit of sending
[the record of the case] to impartial outsiders."[134] The centuries-old Italian idea that learned law, as the law of no party, was "impartial"[135] had
been introduced into the German legal-constitutional system. Carefully
formulated procedures attempted to guarantee the impartiality of the
Spruchkollegien. Cases were submitted to faculties at distant universities,
most often in different states, and with the names of litigants omitted.
Accordingly, professors seemed to have no opportunity for exercising favoritism; they were in any case presumed to be interested only in impartially and abstractly elaborating legal doctrine.[136] Thus, when the Empire
adopted Aktenversendung, it adopted yet another "impartial" institution
in its ongoing attempt to govern by mediating between competing powers. The law faculties were to extend a political principle of impartial
umpiring to all of the emperor's subjects.

At the same time, medieval modes of thought reestablished themselves.
When Roman lawyers accepted their integration into the institutional
structure of the Empire, they accepted, of course, their integration into a
tradition older than the Reformation itself. It is perhaps not surprising,
then, that as the sixteenth century wore on, lawyers began to return to
recognizably pre-Reformation styles of thought. Fine distinctions and intricately parsed arguments in the scholastic manner became the stuff of a
new school of Lutheran lawyers, lawyers not afraid to avow the influence
of Bartolus, and who were, like the first Lutherans, capable of taking a
benevolent view of at least some of Canon law.[137] Aristotle's influence

---

[133] Baumgärtel, *Gutachter- und Urteilstätigkeit der Erlanger Juristenfakultät*, 24.

[134] *Reichsabschied*, 1570, §85. Quoted in Welcker, "Aktenversendung" in *Staats-Lexikon*, 2d ed. (Leipzig, 1845), 1:228.

[135] Cf. above, p. 9.

[136] Dawson, *Oracles of the Law*, 203; Schildt, "Rechtsprüche deutscher Juristenfakultäten," 473. As early as 1534, a Mainz territorial ordinance creating a Spruchkollegium testified to the contemporary presumption of professorial impartiality:

> Wo aber der handel wichtig oder irrig / und sie durch der Urtheyl nit entschließen kund-
> ten / sollen sie Rath bey unverdachten und unpartheyschen rechterfahrenen / auff der
> partheyen zimlichen kosten suchen / urtheyl fassen lassen / und folgents eröffnen.

Quoted in Hasselwander, *Aus der Gutachter- und Urteilstätigkeit an der alten Mainzer Juristenfakultät*, 22–23.

[137] See Wolter, *Ius Canonicum*, 62–64. Neo-Bartolism was not just a German phenome-

grew, too: the old language of impartiality, which had always partaken of Canon-law equitable doctrine, took on an association with humanist doctrines of Aristotelean *epieikeia*, equity.[138] A new passion for systems grew at the same time. The law was organized by Lutheran neoscholastics into an ordered body of categories and subcategories, carefully distinguished and ranked.[139] Here, again, Melanchthon was the great founder of the revivalist style, and Melanchthonians were the great expositors. Hegendorffinus, the proselytizer for learned law in Rostock, was one of the most prominent of the new systematizers[140]; and there were many others, too, in whose work an affiliation with the medieval universities went hand in hand with both the medieval style in legal reasoning and a medieval fondness for arguments from natural law.[141]

Thus it was in the midst of a revival of institutions of learned law, colored by neoscholastic associations, that the professors began to sound their claims to impartiality, the claims whose history I wish to trace into the nineteenth century. In their apologetic literature, the scholars worked hard to reinforce the impartial associations of learned justice, established over centuries of arbitration and decades of institutional rebuilding in Germany. By the mid sixteenth century, it became standard language of praise to describe the ius commune as *unparteiisch*, (impartial), and its professorial representatives as "impartial outsiders." Many reasons and many historical and philosophical arguments were given to explain and defend professorial impartiality. Melchior von Osse, for example, writing in 1555, declared the impartiality of learned law to be a necessary consequence of the fact that it was a product of the communis opinio doctorum: "No single individual has an understanding so pure and excellent that his reason should be preferred to written laws and statutes that have been made, following objective [*unparteisch*] consideration, by the har-

---

non. For contemporaneous French neo-Bartolism, see, e.g., R. Tuck, *Natural Rights Theories: Their Origin and Development* (Cambridge, 1979), 41.

[138] See generally Kisch, *Melanchthon*. The Germans were, it should be noted, not alone in adapting the idea of epieikeia to the interpretation of Roman law. For contemporary French parallels, see A. Guzmán, *Ratio Scripta*, Ius Commune Sonderheft 14 (Frankfurt a.M., 1981), 61–68. For the place of Lutheran thinkers in the sixteenth century more generally, see O. W. Krause, *Naturrechtler des Sechzehnten Jahrhunderts*, Rechtshistorische Reihe, vol. 5 (Frankfurt a.M./Bern, 1982).

[139] Burmeister, *Studium der Rechte*, 107, 258. Note Burmeister's discussion of "wie sehr das Reformprogramm in der Scholastik wurzelte," in ibid., 257. Cf. also Troje, "Die Literatur des gemeinen Rechts unter dem Einfluß des Humanismus," in *Coing Handbuch*, vol. 2, pt. 1, 718–30. On this topic, I have profited from reading advance copies of sections of volume two of H. Berman, "The Transformation of Western Legal Scholarship." My thanks to Professor Berman.

[140] Troje, "Literatur des gemeinen Rechts," 734.

[141] For Lutheran natural law, in its connection with Luther's "*Zwei-Reiche-Lehre*," see Cargill Thompson, *Political Thought of Luther*, 80.

monious agreement of many wise and prudent men."[142] The ius commune had for centuries been the law of no party. Now the professors themselves became representatives of equal justice.[143]

To be sure, such professors cannot always have found it easy to portray themselves as impartial. Indeed, they were forced to respond to violent invective that argued just the opposite. The widespread hatred of learned law often expressed itself in accusations that lawyers (and judges) were partisan in the worst sense: willing to take payment to serve the unjust cause of any litigant.[144] Contemporaries found adversary justice immoral; accordingly, a kind of defensive undertone must be heard in the professors' insistent invocation of learned "impartiality." Moreover, it was a complex matter to integrate professorial authority into the delicate equilibrum of the German political system of emperor and princes, of corporate allegiances and rights. Among all these powerful bodies, professors had to stand somehow independent. Thus Hieronymus Treutler, a law professor writing at the beginning of the seventeenth century at the Melanchthonian unversity of Marburg,[145] felt obliged carefully to distinguish the power of the ius respondendi, derived from the emperor, from the status of "doctor," derived from the lesser princes. He cited Middendorp and Reineccius:

> Today lawyers receive their title from the Universities, which, in turn, speak in the name of the emperor, having been specially endowed with this power of creating doctors. Since the creation of doctors of any kind is the province of the monarch, the same imperial authority is present in every one of these kinds of public acts: otherwise these acts are legally null and void; this is not the case with the conferring of bachelor's degrees, which is not a royal matter. On academic honors, see Jac. Middendorp. *tract. de Academiis*, & Reiner Reineccium *in method. histor. tit. de histor. Scholast. in fin. pag. 28.* However, it is not only through the Universities, but also through the princes, that doctors are created, the princes having been granted this imperial power.[146]

---

[142] Quoted in Strauss, *Law, Resistance and the State*, 92.

[143] Cf. also Strauss's discussion of Jacob Lersner in *Law, Resistance and the State*, 93–95.

[144] See generally the treatment in ibid., 4–30.

[145] On Treutler, see Stintzing, *Geschichte*, 1:465–67.

[146] Hieronymus Treutler, *Selectarum disputationum ad jus civile Justinianeum quinquaginta libris Pandectarum comprehensum, volumina duo* (Marburg, 1606), vol. 1, "Disputatio I, VII a" (p. 11). "Hodie Imp. nomine Jurisconsulti renunciantur ab Academiis, quibus hoc specialiter indultum est, & quia Doctorum in quavis arte creatio est de reservatis Principis, ideo in singulis ejusmodi actibus publicis auctoritas Imperatoria interponitur: aliâs enim essent ipso iure nulli: quod secus est in baccalaureis, quorum creatio nihil habet Regalium. vide de honoribus scholasticis Jac. Middendorp. *tract. de Academiis, & Reiner Reineccium in method. histor. tit. de histor. Scholast. in fin. pag. 28.* nec tantum ab Academiis,

Contemporary Italians were by no means so obsessed with defining such elaborate and legalistic relations of power[147]; it was a delicate labor, finding a place for the professors in the interstices of the German power structure, establishing their corporate identity in independent law faculties.

But a place was found. The professors, their claims enunciated by Melanchthon and his followers, could now view themselves as the representatives of learned law and of no party. From Melanchthon's time on, Roman lawyers did not cease to conceive themselves as uniquely impartial, and as the guardians of constitutional peace.

CONCLUSION

By the 1620s war was wrecking most German constitutional hopes of the sixteenth century, founded as they were on the promise of peace. But in 1623, the Roman dream of the century of Melanchthon could still be heard from Martin Opitz, the great poet of the Thirty Years' War. The Greek classics were his spiritual comfort, and his sense of citizenship lay ultimately in Rome:

> Dann wolt' ich auch zu Rom / der Königin der Erden
> Was mein Latein belangt / mit Ehren Bürger werden.
> Trotz einem der herumb mich führte für den Raht
> Als wer' ich wie gebührt / kein Glied nicht von der Statt.
> Der grosse Cicero / Sallustius ingleichen
> Und Maro würden mir die Hände selber reichen.

> Fain would I turn to Rome / the Empress of the Earth,
> Where Latin makes a man as much a citizen as birth.
> And though I have been treated / contumaciously
> By whosoever thinks me less a citizen than he,
> No less a man than Virgil / would offer me his hand,
> Tully and Sallust would take me / into their solemn band.[148]

---

sed etiam à Comitibus Palatinis, hanc potestatem in specie ab Imperatore concessam habentibus, Doctores creantur, quos bullatos vulgo appellant."

[147] Thus Pax Scala, writing in Venice in 1560, could treat the questions of the sources of professorial adjudicative power much more casually than his northern contemporary Treutler was able to do. Scala made no effort to sort out whether scholars were "a Principe insignitus, vel a Comite, vel ab iis approbatus, quibus Princeps suam impertiverit auctoritatem." Scala was much more interested in professional credentials than in power relations: his principle concern was over whether the functions of "iurisperiti" should be reserved to those scholars affiliated with a "collegium." See his *De Consilio Sapientis in Forensibus Causis Adhibendo Libri IIII* (Venice, 1560), bk. I, chap. 5, p. 7, Tit. "An quilibet iurisperitus consulat, vel is tantum, qui publice in aliquo collegio sit constitutus?"

[148] Opitz, *Zlatna* (1623), 477–82. Quoted in W. Kuhlmann, *Gelehrtenrepublik und Fürstenstaat*, Studien und Texte zur Sozialgeschichte der Literatur, vol. 31 (Tübingen, 1982),

Such were the constitutional hopes Rome inspired in Germans: Roman law was the system of justice for parties of all social classes; to have the benefit of Rome was to have the benefit of unimpeachable citizenship. Whatever the success of the Roman program of peace in the sixteenth century—and it is beyond the scope of this chapter to evaluate its success in practice—it established a tradition that could rise again among the men of the generation of Savigny. Because Roman law had signified social peace to Melanchthon, 250 years later it could signify social peace once more.

---

282. See ibid., vv. 461–71, for the consolation of the Greek antiquities. My thanks to Professor Lorna Martens for her aid in interpreting this passage.

Chapter II

DECLINE OF THE ROMAN-LAW CORPORATE TRADITION IN THE EIGHTEENTH CENTURY

WITHIN a generation after the Melanchthonian program had established itself, the Public Peace gave way. The organized violence of the Thirty Years' War, far more systematic and technologically accomplished than any faced by Germans before 1495, ruined vast stretches of the German world. Inevitably, Melanchthonian constitutionalism suffered. The Reichskammergericht was thoroughly politicized during the wars, becoming an instrument of the emperor.[1] Moreover, as the wars drew to a close, one of Europe's greatest polymaths mounted a direct challenge to Melanchthon's legal-historical order. In 1643 Hermann Conring, then professor of medicine at Helmstedt, decisively disproved the legend of Emperor Lothar's formal ratification of Roman law[2] and attempted to put an end to the favored position of Roman law in the German courts.[3]

Still, while the program of Melanchthon was damaged by the Thirty Years' War, it was not destroyed. The Melanchthonian vision was far from dead when the wars ended in 1648. Conring offered no radically new vision of Rome himself: he remained a member of a scholarly community whose understanding of the world was still fundamentally founded on the Four Monarchies of Carion as edited by Melanchthon.[4] And while the Reichskammergericht enjoyed no new flowering after

---

[1] Diestelkamp, "Reichskammergericht," 457. Cf. Smend, Reichskammergericht, 202. Revealing figures on the number of cases received by the Reichskammergericht between 1495 and 1700 are given and discussed by F. Ranieri, "Die Tätigkeit des Reichskammergerichts und seine Inanspruchnahme während des 16. Jahrhunderts," in B. Diestelkamp, ed., Forschungen aus Akten des Reichskammergerichts, Quellen und Forschungen zur höchsten Gerichtsbarkeit im Alten Reich, vol. 14 (Cologne/Vienna, 1984), 43–73.

[2] Conring's revolutionizing work was the De Origine Iuris Germanici, in Conring, Opera, 7 vols., edited by J. W. Gobel, (repr. Aalen, 1970–73), 6:75–188, esp. 132–42. Conring's startlingly vast learning is now explored in its scholarly context by a team of modern scholars in M. Stolleis, ed., Hermann Conring (1606–1681): Beiträge zu Leben und Werk, Historische Forschungen, vol. 23 (Berlin, 1983). His place in legal history is analyzed there in articles by D. Willoweit, H.-J. Becker, and esp. K. Luig (for the disproof of the Lotharlegende) on pp. 321–95.

[3] See below, p. 47.

[4] N. Hammerstein, "Die Historie bei Conring," in Stolleis, Conring, 233. Cf. H. Dreitzel, "Hermann Conring und die politische Wissenschaft," in ibid., 137, and D. Willoweit, "Kaiser, Reich und Reichsstände bei Hermann Conring," in ibid., 326.

1654,[5] peace had finally returned, and some of the losses were modestly recouped.[6] Devastating as the wars had been, they left the Melanchthonian tradition intact. For this reason, I must pass rapidly (for the most part) over the bulk of the seventeenth century.

It was only at the end of the century, when the princes began successfully seizing control of the German states, that the decisive blow to Melanchthonianism came. Absolutism threatened to crush the sixteenth-century institutions of justice, as indeed it threatened all sixteenth-century corporate bodies. In this chapter I wish to trace the decline of the sixteenth-century corporate tradition of the Roman-law professors in the age of absolutism, a decline the memory of which was still strong in Savigny's time. As I hope to show, in good times and in bad Roman-law professors interpreted their place in German society as analogous to that of their distant intellectual ancestors, the jurists of the Roman world.

The decline of the corporate tradition of the sixteenth-century Roman lawyers was by and large the work of two linked forces: Enlightenment and Absolutism. Neither of these would be easy to explain or describe, even if this were a study concerned principally with the eighteenth century. As it is a study principally concerned with Friedrich Carl von Savigny and his contemporaries of the early nineteenth century, I must present the world of the eighteenth century largely through their eyes, leaving the difficult task of explaining the eighteenth century in its own terms to other scholars.

In the eyes of the early nineteenth century, the eighteenth century had been the era of pernicious French influence. And indeed there is no doubt the French influence was in many ways at work in eighteenth-century Germany. This, of course, is particularly true of Absolutism. In Germany as in Locke's England, Absolutism, the great destructive counterforce to the corporate constitution of the sixteenth century, was the "French disease"—the *morbus gallicus*. Indeed, the Reichskammergericht suffered the impact of French absolutism directly in 1689, when the armies of Louis XIV conquered Speyer and confiscated the court's files. The court was reestablished in Wetzlar four years later, but the rival *Reichshofrat*, located at the Court in Vienna and much more closely associated with imperial power, had gained considerable ground in the interim.[7] But, of course, it was not so much the armed forces of the French as the immense prestige of their state innovations that put the sixteenth-century constitution in danger. German princely admirers of Louis XIV worked all

[5] Cf. the figures in Ranieri, "Tätigkeit des Reichskammergerichts."

[6] Smend, *Reichskammergericht*, 212. Cf. the figures in Ranieri, "Tätigkeit des Reichskammergerichts."

[7] On these events, see Smend, *Reichskammergericht*, 215–17.

through the eighteenth century to clear away the institutional clutter of inherited forms. The eighteenth-century Reichskammergericht became, in fact, a symbol of prerational corporate decay, notorious for its backlog and embarrassed by some spectacular instances of corruption. The eighteenth-century court was one of the favorite targets of enlightened princely reformers: immediately upon his accession, Joseph II initiated a "Visitation," a formal several-year-long investigation, of the Reichskammergericht,[8] and F. C. Moser mounted a publicistic attack during his Josephine years.[9] Nor was it the emperor alone whose new power threatened the old court: the territorial princes, in their eagerness to shuffle off the bonds of the Holy Roman Empire, sought and increasingly acquired the so-called "privilegium de non appellando," the "exemption from appeals," which removed their courts from the appellate jurisdiction of the Reichskammergericht.[10] The German princes, determined to end the disaggregation of power in the old constitution, could no longer tolerate this old, central, constitutional institution.

Moreover, French influence was not confined to the world of institutional reform. The influence of new French institutions was paralleled by the influence of new French legal ideas—though not all of them were the sort of legal ideas that Savigny and his contemporaries would find objectionable. Over the course of the seventeenth and eighteenth centuries, two powerful doctrinal movements in particular began to challenge the place of Roman law in the world of German justice: customary-law constitutionalism and natural law. Both doctrinal movements were in some measure imports from the prestigious and powerful French state, where the medieval legal system had collapsed in the political maelstrom of the sixteenth century.

Customary-law constitutionalism offered perhaps the most direct challenge to Roman law's position in the new societies of early modern Europe. In the sixteenth century the venerable Italian ius commune formula, which had always met with some resistance in France, fell into full-scale

---

[8] Ibid., 232.

[9] Ibid., 231, citing F. C. Moser, *Patriotische Briefe* (n.p., 1767), 263ff.

[10] The long history of the princely efforts to escape the appellate jurisdiction of the Reichskammergericht is traced by J. Weitzel, *Der Kampf um die Appellation ans Reichskammergericht*, Quellen und Forschungen zur höchsten Gerichtsbarkeit im alten Reich, vol. 4 (Cologne/Vienna, 1976); cf. also P. Cappellini, *Systema Iuris*, 2:237. For Prussia, see also W. Rüfner, *Verwaltungsrechtsschutz in Preußen, 1749–1842*, Bonner Rechtswissenschaftliche Abhandlungen, vol. 53 (Bonn, 1962). So strong was the belief that subjection to the jurisdiction of the court was indispensable to true membership in the Reich that one Berlin newspaper could declare in 1794 that the *privilegium de non appellando* meant that Prussia had no emperor. See K. O. von Aretin, *Heiliges Römisches Reich*, Veröffentlichungen des Instituts für Europäische Geschichte, Mainz, Abt. Universalgeschichte, vol. 38 (Wiesbaden, 1967), 1:319.

disarray as the growing French state began to displace the old customary order of the French countryside. The resulting grand crisis of custom was the driving force behind the growth of new legal ideologies of constitutionalism mounted in the name of customary law. Since the Middle Ages French lawyers had compiled custumals—written compilations of custom that could serve as evidence in court when witnesses were unavailable.[11] The production of these custumals continued through the sixteenth century, but with a critical change: by the second half of the sixteenth century, their editors had begun to preface them with vigorous defenses of customary law against the encroachments of princes—and Roman lawyers.

The approach taken by these custumal editors—most prominent among them DuMoulin[12] and Coquille[13]—inevitably altered the received conception of customary law. In previous centuries, customary law had been by definition local, and thus provable only by local witnesses or documents. DuMoulin and Coquille, by contrast, spoke of a "common customary law" of the entire realm, hoping in this way to produce written sources of custom applicable in courts all over France, sources that would always be available as an alternative to sources of learned law.[14] These attempts to postulate a "common customary law" were received by some French lawyers with an understandable skepticism.[15] Nevertheless, the

[11] See esp. V. Piano Mortari, *Diritto Romano e Diritto Nazionale in Francia nel Secolo XVI* (Milan, 1962), and V. Guizzi, "Il Diritto Commune in Francia nel XVII secolo," in *Tijdschrift voor Rechtsgeschiedenis* 37 (1969): 1–7. The work of these Italian scholars forms the basis of the discussions in J. Gaudemet, "Tendances à l'Unification de droit en France," in *Formazione Storica del Diritto Moderno in Europa*, Atti del Terzo Congresso Internazionale della Società Italiana di Storia del Diritto, 3 vols. (1977), 1:157–94. See also K. Luig, "The Institutes of National Law in the Seventeenth and Eighteenth Centuries," *Juridical Review* (1972): 203–7 (translation and revision of an article that first appeared in *Ius Commune* 3 [1970]: 64–97); J.G.A. Pocock, *The Ancient Constitution and the Feudal Law*, 2d ed. (Cambridge, 1987), 23–25; J. Franklin, *Jean Bodin and the Sixteenth-Century Revolution in the Methodology of Law and History* (New York, 1963).

[12] On Dumoulin, see Kelley, *Foundations of Modern Historical Scholarship*, 151–82; J.-L. Thireau, *Charles du Moulin*, Travaux d'humanisme et renaissance, no. 176 (Geneva, 1980).

[13] See, e.g., Guizzi, "Diritto Commune," 5. Cf. Gaudemet, "Tendances à l'Unification du Droit," 182ff., on similar tendencies in various lawyers.

[14] See, e.g., Coquille, *La Coutume de Nivernais*, edited by M. Dupin (Paris, 1864), 81: "Les coustumes des provinces de France, qu'on appelle *coustumières*, sont *leur vray droict civil et commun*." Emphasis in original.

[15] As one lawyer put it, the whole idea of a "common customary law" made little sense, since even the two or three local witnesses who ordinarily testified as to a given custom often disagreed among themselves: "[Q]ui me dira ceste raison commune? vue qu'entre deux ou trois personnes, se trouvent bien souvent opinions diverses et contraires." DuPré, *Apologie contre un livre intitulé Catacrise du droit romain* (1601), 15. Quoted in Guizzi, "Diritto Commune in Francia," 7. Customary law, this objection said in effect, often

new notions spread throughout the sixteenth and seventeenth centuries and, indeed, came to be associated with the idea that the "common customary law" of France represented the sum of French constitutional principles.[16] Agitation for unification of a *droit coutumier*, a customary law, grew particularly strong in the 1660s and 1670s.[17] At the same time, university chairs for the teaching of "national" law were established[18]—a development that inevitably boded ill for the old law of the universities, Roman law.[19]

New ideas of natural law were a threat as well. Customary-law constitutionalism was very much a French innovation; natural-law reasoning, by contrast, was an international phenomenon. Nevertheless, the kind of natural-law reasoning that most directly threatened Roman law—the idea of Roman law as *ratio scripta*, "written reason"—while international in scope, attained its fullest development in France. Ever since the Middle Ages, French lawyers had spoken of written bodies of law, including Roman law, as ratio scripta.[20] "Ratio scripta," came, in the mid-sixteenth century, to refer exclusively to Roman law,[21] and French lawyers, like their contemporary, Melanchthon, began insisting that Roman law could claim to serve as the ius commune in any given litigation only to the extent that it represented Aristotelean epieikeia, rational justice or equity.[22] These scholarly innovations set in motion a whole new line of

---

failed to reflect even the shared understanding of a small village; how could there be any "common customary law" of all France? Cf. also Gaudemet, "Tendances à l'Unification de droit," 167, 181–82.

[16] For the connection between the traditions of French customary-law scholarship and incipient constitutionalism, see D. R. Kelley, "Civil Science in the Renaissance: Jurisprudence in the French Manner," in *History of European Ideas* 2 (1981): 270ff.

[17] See A. de Curzon, "L'Enseignement du Droit Français dans les Universités aux XVIIᵉ et XVIIIᵉ siècles," *Nouvelle Revue Historique de Droit Français et Étranger* 43 (1919): 209–69, 305–64. Cf. Gaudemet, "Tendances à l'Unification de droit en France," 187.

[18] See generally, Curzon, "Enseignement du Droit Français."

[19] The new treatments of customary law did not, to be sure, contemplate wholesale displacement of Roman law. Thus, to take only one of many examples, Loyseau set up a hierarchy of laws: C. Loyseau, *Traité du Déguerpissement*: "[I]l faut tenir que devant qu'estendre aux autres Coustumes la décision de celle de Paris il faut premièrement sonder le Droict Romain: et si il contient certaine et résolue décision du poinct controversé, non répugnante à l'usage général de la France; alors posé ores que la Coutumes [sic] de Paris soit contraire, il faut plustot que la suivre, s'arrester à la disposition du Droict commun." Quoted in Guizzi, "Diritto Commune in Francia," 10. Nevertheless, as the phrase "non répugnant à l'usage général de la France" suggests, the revolution in customary-law thinking was very much an anti-Roman revolution.

[20] For the medieval use of the phrase, see Guzmán, *Ratio Scripta*, 38ff.

[21] Ibid. 25 and often.

[22] Ibid., 61ff. For literature on the sources of natural law thought in Antiquity, see Wieacker, *Privatrechtsgeschichte*, 249 n. 1. The new emphasis on reason could also be found among the customary-law theorists. See, for example, A. Loisel, *Institutes Coustu-*

thinking about Roman law, one deeply subversive of received doctrine. In the medieval legal order, Roman law had been applicable as a "ius commune"—a body of fixed doctrinal principles generally applicable because presumptively the personal law of all litigants—and "equity" had been applied to temper its rigors. According to the new line of thinking, Roman law was not a universal body of fixed doctrine, but rather natural reasoning set out in written form, a source of equity itself, and not a rigid body of rules. None of the traditional interpretations of Roman law were safe once lawyers began thinking in such terms. A given Roman rule was not a rule but a starting point for reasoning about the world. This idea— that Roman law was the law of reasoning—spread widely in France, and spread at a critical juncture in the history of natural-law thinking, during the very generations when late scholastic natural-law thinking was reviving in the Spain of Suarez, during the very generations when Descartes and Grotius were both migrating back and forth between the intellectually vigorous and periodically intolerant worlds of France and Holland. By the end of the seventeenth century, a new view of Roman law as ratio scripta, as the law of "reason" at a time when "reason" was in singularly high repute in the intellectual world, had received its definitive statement from Jean Domat.[23]

By the end of the seventeenth century, the militarily powerful and culturally prestigious French state was thus the home of new legal ideas throughly irreconcilable with, and indeed deeply subversive of, the place of Roman law within ius commune tradition. A number of the great French legal thinkers of the sixteenth century, among them DuMoulin himself, had taught in Germany,[24] and by the end of the seventeenth cen-

---

mieres, ou Manuel de Plusieurs et Diverses Regles, Sentences & Proverbes, tant anciens que modernes, du droict Coustumier & plus ordinaire de la France (Paris, 1665), Preface (without page numbers): "[T]out ainsi que les Prouinces, Duchez, Comtez, & Seigneuries de ce Royaume regies & gouuernées sous diuerses Coustumes, se sont auec le temps rangées sous l'obéissáce d'un seul Roy, & quasi de sa seule & unique monnoye ainsi enfin se pourroient-elles reduire à la conformité, raison, & equité d'une seule loy, coustume, poids & mesure sous l'auctorité de sa M." That customary-law treatises should have included references to "reason" is not surprising. Customary practices had always, in Europe, been subject to a test of reasonableness; it was thus natural that jurists should begin to identify custom with reason. More importantly, "customary common law," as I have indicated, hardly existed as such in France. Faced with a nonexistent subject matter, the authors of treatises about the customary common law of their homeland had to resort to Bentham's "formidable nonentity, the Law of Nature." Without "general" or "natural" principles of reason, treatise writers could hardly produce systematic and comprehensive works. Thus the rise of natural-law thinking in the late seventeenth century was arguably in part the result of the same French breakdown of the ius commune system that produced the new theories of customary law.

[23] On Domat see Guzmán, Ratio Scripta, 114ff.

[24] See H. Coing, "L'Influence de la France sur le Droit Allemand," in Gesammelte Aufsätze (Frankfurt a.M., 1982), 1:267–68.

tury, German lawyers (like English ones[25]) began to develop their own traditions of scholarship at least in part on the French pattern. In Germany, the place of Roman law within the ius commune system had survived an initial, unsuccessful attack in the seventeenth century, at the hands of Conring.[26] But by the beginning of the eighteenth century, university teaching of so-called "national" law—teaching, that is, of a "customary common law" essentially invented by scholars—began in Germany as in France. By the early eighteenth century, Conring's successors began to introduce professorships of local customary and statute law— *ius patrium* and *statutarium* (national and statutory law), as it was called in Kiel, where such a professorship was established in 1712, or *vatherländisches Recht* (law of the fatherland), as it was called in Tübingen in 1727.[27] This new form of customary-law scholarship had an effect potentially just as destructive as any new choice-of-law formula. In theory, proof of the existence of custom was still quite difficult in the eighteenth century.[28] But once German professors began to publish accounts of customary law, it became far easier to prove the existence of custom: a court need only examine a scholarly treatise. There was no need to collect testimony, no need to produce special documents, no need to give the opposing side an opportunity to examine witnesses. Customary law had found a new strength.

So, at the same time, had natural law. As early as 1669 Leibniz had declared that fully half of Roman law was nothing other than natural

[25] J.G.A. Pocock has recently posed the question of why English lawyers began, early in the seventeenth century, to refer to the common law as "the common custom of the realm." See Pocock, "Retrospect," in idem, *The Ancient Constitution and the Feudal Law*, 267 n. 16. The answer surely lies in the French influence whose study Pocock himself pioneered.

[26] Conring attempted to alter the old choice-of-law formula that had favored Roman law within the ius commune for centuries. Conring's new choice-of-law formula, had it come into general use, would have inverted the old ius commune formula. As Conring envisioned it, any litigant who wished the court to apply Roman law would be obliged to prove that members of the estate to which the opposing party belonged had submitted to the use of Roman law in the sixteenth century. In effect, this would have shifted the burden of proving the applicability of the legal system from the party alleging personal rights to the party alleging ius commune. Conring's proposal for shifting the burden of proof to the advocate of Roman law did not, however, prevail. See Wieacker, *Privatrechtsgeschichte*, 208.

[27] These examples are from Wieacker, *Privatrechtsgeschichte*, 210.

[28] Parties would be expected to produce official documentation—a *Lehnbuch* (a formal record of the infeudation of property) or *documenta ex archivo publico*. Such documents were naturally not easy to produce in Wetzlar. Failing production of such a document, litigants could, as always in the customary-law regime, produce notarized testimony by witnesses. But these witnesses had to be made available for deposition by the opposing party— once again a requirement that would presumably have been a practical impossibility most of the time. For these details, I have relied on J. S. Pütter, *Nova Epitome Processus Imperii Amborum Tribunalium Supremorum*, 4th ed. (Göttingen, 1786), 92–93.

law.[29] A generation later, natural law had thoroughly established itself in the language of German legal argument; indeed, leading lawyers like Just Henning Boehmer could chastise lawyers of earlier generations for devoting too much attention to Roman law and too little to natural law.[30] To Boehmer, Roman law was no longer a universal law at all but rather a collection of particular rules. The only true universal law was natural law. Meanwhile, the authors of treatises on customary law had, like the French lawyers, begun to introduce ideas of natural law into their own discussions.[31] Clearly, at least some of this represented French influence.

Nevertheless, it would be wrong—despite the traditions of early nineteenth-century nationalism—to imagine that the Germany of the eighteenth century was an intellectual colony of France.[32] If foreign influence provided many of the starting points, Germans soon developed native traditions. In particular, the German tradition of natural-law thought took on a peculiar character. For in the German-speaking world the international natural law movement became bound up with the peculiarly German traditions of systematic academic philosophy. I have already described, if only briefly, the rise of the systematic style that characterized the Melanchthonian jurists who returned to the universities in the sixteenth century, bringing with them the revived Aristoteleanism of the doctrine of epieikeia.[33] When the natural-law revival that was spurred by the work of Suarez and Grotius entered Germany, it took on a distinctly scholastic, systematic coloring—particularly in the person of the greatest of Germany's theorists of natural law, Christian Wolff.[34] The systematic

[29] Guzmán, Ratio Scripta, 147ff.

[30] J. H. Boehmer, Introductio in Ius Publicum Universale ex Genuinis Iuris Naturae Principiis deductum (Frankfurt/Leipzig, 1758) (orig. 1709), A 5: "Cum vero particularia tantum universalibus superaddita sint, inde statim apparet, fundamentum omnium quaestionum, quae huc spectant, ex universali, hoc est, iure naturae petendum esse, & ita in addiscendo iure publico particulari initium ab universali esse faciendum. Quemadmodum vero in iure privato haec inversa methodus ab eruditioribus iam notata est, quod plurimi, derelicto studio iuris naturae, statim scita particularia iuris Romani excolere studeant." For Boehmer on the natural-law origins of Roman law, see W. Neusüss, Gesunde Vernunft und Natur der Sache: Studien zur Juristischen Argumentation im Achtzehnten Jahrhundert, Schriften zur Rechtsgeschichte, Heft 2 (Berlin, 1970), 32.

[31] E.g., G.A. Struve, Syntagma Juris Feudalis, 8th ed. (Frankfurt a.M., 1703), 1–6.

[32] See the discussions of Wieacker, Privatrechtsgeschichte, 168; Coing, "Influence de la France," 268.

[33] See above, pp. 36–37. The connection between sixteenth-century doctrines of epieikeia and natural-law thinking remained present throughout the period of German natural-law thinking—as evidenced, for example, in J. F. Gildemeister's 1783 declaration that the "Grundsatz des Naturrechts ist: Laß einem jeden das Seinige (suum cuique)." Quoted in H.-U. Stühler, Die Diskussion um die Erneuerung der Rechtswissenschaft von 1780–1815, Schriften zur Rechtsgeschichte, Heft 15 (Berlin, 1978), 74. See also the discussion by R. F. Terlinden in ibid., 83.

[34] For recent discussions of Wolff and Wolffianism, see Cappellini, Systema Iuris, 1:62 n.

impulse was, of course, to be found throughout Europe in the seventeenth century,[35] and among German scholars with approaches different from that of Wolff.[36] Nevertheless, it was in the hands of Wolff and his growing following that the German natural-law tradition entered its characteristic paths of systematicity, paths that remained unexplored in the rest of Europe. In large measure, clearly, this Wolffianism represented a revival of the neoscholastic systematic tradition of the sixteenth-century Lutherans. But Roman law as such no longer had pride of place in their systems: it was principles of universal truth, not of Roman tradition, that had captured the allegiance of the new quasi-scholastics of the early eighteenth century.

Whether its competitors were native or foreign in origin, there is no doubt that Roman law was suffering by the mid-eighteenth century. As "national customary law" and intricately reasoned natural-law treatises began to appear, German legal life assumed a thoroughly eclectic character. Indeed, it was eclecticism above all that characterized German legal life in the first half of the eighteenth century, which is known as the era of the "Usus modernus pandectarum," the "up-to-date use of Roman law." The uncertain place of a much-disrespected "updated" Roman law[37] within the diffuse eclecticism of German legal life showed in the midcentury practice of the Reichskammergericht. As the leading journal of the Reichskammergericht—J. U. Cramer's *Wetzlarische Nebenstunden*—shows, even in this old institutional home of imperial Roman justice, the ancient law had pride of place only in principle. The sixteenth-century choice-of-law formula was still in force: the court applied Roman law unless applicable custom or statute could be proven. But in practice this left the advanced Roman-law scholarship of the day diminishing room.[38] Only when custom or statute could not be proven did classical scholarship have its day. Roman law was, to be sure, often still applied. I will recite the details of one 1767 case in which Roman law was applied,

---

19 and vol. 1 often; J. Schröder, *Wissenschaftstheorie*, 83ff.; Neusüss, *Gesunde Vernunft und Natur der Sache*, 35ff.

[35] See, e.g., the discussion in Wieacker, *Privatrechtsgeschichte*, 257.

[36] For the respective systematic ideas of Pütter and of Heineccius, see Schröder, *Wissenschaftstheorie*, 105ff., 140ff.

[37] For the example of Ludewig, see N. Hammerstein, *Jus und Historie* (Göttingen, 1972), pp. 174ff.

[38] Cf. the discussion of the law applied by the Reichskammergericht in H. Wiggenhorn, "Das Reichskammergerichtsprozeß am Ende des alten Reichs" (Diss., Münster, 1966), 260ff. In the middle of the eighteenth century, Roman law was not by any means the source most commonly applied by the Reichskammergericht, as a casual glance at any volume of Cramer's *Wetzlarische Nebenstunden* shows. *Wetzlarische Nebenstunden: Auserlesene beym Hochstprießlichen Cammergericht entschiedene Rechtshändel*. Edited by J. U. Freiherr von Cramer. 128 pts. in 32 vols. (Ulm, 1755–73).

as an example of the pattern of litigation in the mid-eighteenth-century Reichskammergericht. In this case the court rejected a claim of custom and relied on careful and learned reasoning in applying pre-Justinianian law. The case involved a coach, burglarized while garaged overnight in a Swabian inn. The innkeeper, sued by the coachman for damages, mounted two defenses. First he claimed that innkeepers had no liability for the property of guests under the *Observatio Sueviae*, the customary law of Swabia. The court rejected this claim, as the innkeeper had offered neither the testimony of proper witnesses, nor the scholarly opinion of the professors of Tübingen—the professors of "vatherländisches Recht," who could have been presumed to be expert on Swabian custom.[39] Alternatively, the innkeeper claimed the benefit of an exception under Roman law: innkeepers were not liable for property stolen by "vis major," *force majeure,* and such had been the case here—for the theft was performed at night, and "by a band of gypsies with firearms, who were so bold that they fired on a troop of territorial militia thirty strong, one of whom they wounded."[40] But the court noted that the gypsies, even when tortured, admitted that there had been no more than four men and two women in their party. Taking the opportunity for a learned disquisition, the court held that four men and two women in the village in question would not have constituted *force majeure* under the relevant rules of Roman law.[41] Finally, the innkeeper pleaded that the Roman rule had fallen into disuse, for modern Germany was different from ancient Rome: innkeepers were accustomed to better, more civilized conditions, and could not be expected to keep a watch out for thieves as the ancients had had to do.[42] The court cited one of Germany's most important scholars, Augustin Leyser, to show that this rule had indeed never fallen out of use,[43] and it condemned the innkeeper to damages and costs. Sometimes pre-Justinianian law, cultivated by leading scholars, prevailed.

But Roman law most often did not prevail, at least in the cases Cramer reported. Statutes appeared often in the jurisprudence of the Reichskammergericht as Cramer reported it.[44] Natural law too made its claims. In-

---

[39] "Vom heutigen Gebrauch des Edict. Praetoris in Tit. ff. de Nautis, insbesondere bey Landkutschern, die durch Diebstahl Schaden in Wirthshäusern erlitten, und dem wahren Verstand der darinnen erwehnten Vis majoris," in Cramer, ed., *Wetzlarische Nebenstunden*, vol. 73, pt. 2 (1767): 42–44.

[40] Ibid., 33.

[41] Ibid., 35–36.

[42] Ibid., 42.

[43] Ibid., 44–45.

[44] See, for example, a case revolving in part around the *Osnabrückische Eigentums-Ordnung* of 1722: "Ob ein Guts-Herr auf seiner Eigenbehörigen Prædiis in Casu exigentiæ auch fruchtbare Bäume zu fällen und zum Bauen verwenden zu lassen befugt, und solche Befugniß per solum non usum erlöschen oder verlohren gehen möge?" in Cramer, ed., *Wet-*

deed, Cramer was himself a Wolffian and a champion of the new natural-law style, which brought with it grave dangers for Roman law.[45] Cramer and the Reichskammergericht of his time were quite willing to abandon Roman-law rules that failed to meet their test of reason. For example, Cramer and the Reichskammergericht could reject the conditions the ancient law imposed on widows as simply too unenlightened for the eighteenth century.[46] The same sort of corrosive innovation was at work undermining the jurisprudence of the Spruchkollegien, as we can see in an anonymous Dutch handbook, written in 1722 for those unfortunate enough to become entangled in the German legal system. The author warned his readers that German professors relied on "their own bits of reasoning" and sought to explode the "ius commune, and accepted ideas of equity and justice, as though they were useless traditions."[47] Natural-law thinking, in the eclectic first half of the eighteenth century, threatened to displace substantive Roman law even within the learned institutions that historically had sworn to apply it.

Moreover, the very existence of the Spruchkollegien was in doubt. If the princes could not tolerate the Reichskammergericht, still less could they tolerate the far weaker Spruchkollegien. The chronology of the waning of Aktenversendung, the old home of professorial constitutional power, is a year-by-year chronology of the collapse of Melanchthonianism as directly expressed in institutional forms. At the beginning of the eighteenth century, Germans continued to submit their political disputes to law faculties, and scholars continued to speak in the old constitutionalist terms about the value of professorial adjudication. In the early 1700s, scholarly dissertations about the institution learnedly traced its doctrinal history and procedural forms, betraying little sense that its place in the German legal constitution was in any way precarious. Princely power was not yet conceived to be the sole source of law: a 1708 dissertation, for example, declared that judges in Saxony were required to send cases to a law faculty, not only when statutes mandated it, but also when scholarly adjudication was customary or when either litigant desired it.[48]

zlarısche Nebenstunden, vol. 117, pt. 9 (1771): 68–92. For a further discussion of the *Osnabrückische Eigentums-Ordnung*, and in general of the impact of princely statutes on land law, see also below, Chapter V.

[45] On Cramer's Wolffianism, see Cappellini, *Systema Iuris*, 1:421ff.

[46] "Ob conditio viduitatis bey Vermächtnüssen heut zu Tag gültig seye?" in Cramer, *Wetzlarısche Nebenstunden*, vol. 12, pt. 5 (1758): 68–72.

[47] D.S.N.H.P., *Observatio Juris Practica [sic] de Academiis Germaniae in Transmittendis Actis* (Leiden, 1722), 8–9. Note the author's scepticism about the traditional German claim that Aktenversendung provided impartial justice (Ibid., 27ff., esp. 29).

[48] Martin Lange, *De Actorum Transmissione secundum Usum Fori hodierni praecipue saxonici* (Leipzig, 1708), 15: "si id requirant statuta & superioris Magistratus rescripta

Even J. P. Ludewig of Halle,[49] a scholar generally hostile to Roman law, praised professorial adjudication in old constitutionalist terms. Aktenversendung was quintessentially impartial:

> Legal decision making by faculties and *Schöppenstühle* [the old Germanic lay courts] are free of all fear [of partiality and incompetence]. . . . The parties are unknown to the members of these legal bodies, and so [the judges] cannot stand in any relationship [to the litigants] of favoritism or partiality; accordingly, they cannot be led astray by their emotions.[50]

At least in the first decade of the eighteenth century, the old language of praise was still vigorous.

But the trend as the century wore on was against such relics of the old constitution as law-faculty justice. Territorial governments began to forbid the practice in one measure or another in the first decade of the eighteenth century: Prussia circumscribed the practice as early as 1703.[51] Other states followed, especially in the 1720s and after.[52] To enlightened Germans, the old imperial constitution began to seem dark and antiquated. The juristic dissertations of the time reflected the changing climate: even a writer who in 1716 still lauded Aktenversendung in the old style as banishing "all suspicion of bias" from German adjudication felt obliged to denounce its abuses at the same time. The institution, he admitted, was costly and time-consuming.[53] The brilliant Roman lawyer Augustin Leyser, himself writing as a member of a Spruchkollegium, declared that the judge had full authority, as representative of the prince who was the source of legal power, to refuse Aktenversendung.[54] The institution got a boost when Gerlach von Münchhausen, convinced that

---

singularia, aut consuetudines inveteratae . . . si vel uterque vel alteruter litigantium id desideret."

[49] On Ludewig, see N. Hammerstein, *Jus und Historie*, 169–204.

[50] Quoted in F. E. Behmer (praeside J. J. Moser), *De Transmissione Actorum* (Frankfurt a. Oder, 1739), 6–8 n. 2: "Von aller diser Besorgniß . . . sind die Rechtssprüche in Facultäten und Schöppen-Stühlen befreyet. . . . Und wie den Beysizern in Rechts-Collegien die streitenden Partheyen unbekannt, so können sie auch denselben weder in Liebe noch Leid verwandt und folglich keine Ursach vorhanden seyn, durch Leidenschafften des Gemüthes sich von dem richtigen Weg auf Abwege verleiten zu lassen."

[51] Baumgärtel, *Erlanger Juristenfakultät*, 28.

[52] See A. Stölzel, *Die Entwicklung der gelehrten Rechtsprechung*, 2 vols. (Berlin, 1901–10), 1:313ff.; A. Jammers, *Die Heidelberger Juristenfakultät im Neunzehnten Jahrhundert als Spruchkollegium* (Heidelberg, 1964), 15; Baumgärtel, *Erlanger Juristenfakultät*, 27ff.; Dawson, *Oracles of the Law*, 202–3.

[53] D.T.J. Rheinhardt, *Dissertatio Juridica de Transmissionis Actorum Jure, ejusve abusu* (Erfurt, 1716), 25 ("Judex . . . [se] ab omni suspicione partialitatis liberet") and 27 ("partes . . . sumtus perdant, tempusque frustra comsumant").

[54] A. Leyser, "De Responsis Prudentum," in *Meditationes ad Pandectas* (Leipzig, 1741), vol. 1, specimen 6, 54–55 (originally 1713).

law professors should have practical experience, established a Spruchkollegium at the new university of Göttingen in 1736.[55] But Göttingen, left comparatively free by the departure of the Dukes of Hannover for England, was far from typical. In other territories, Aktenversendung and princely rationalization of government could not easily coexist.

By the 1730s Aktenversendung seemed to be dying. The precarious state of the old institution shows vividly in the brief brush of the great constitutional scholar J. J. Moser with the Prussian government. Moser, the famous and forthright champion of old imperial institutions, was a proponent of Aktenversendung in the mid-1730s; indeed, if a committed constitutionalist like Moser had not supported professorial adjudication, no German of the time would have. In 1736 Moser was called by the Prussian government to revive the law faculty of the decaying university of Frankfurt an Oder. Moser (whose thoroughly un-Prussian constitutionalism was soon to make him a spectacular failure at Frankfurt[56]) began his mission with a lecture on university reform entitled "Frank Thoughts." Among other measures, Moser promoted a revival of Aktenversendung.[57] But close inspection of the ancient institutions of Frankfurt undermined Moser's idealism. His attempts at practical reform quickly soured—not least in the Spruchkollegium, where he discovered that he was obliged to fill in for his shirking colleagues, the not very worthy successors of the sixteenth-century professoriate.[58] Indeed, the only place his "Frank Thoughts" had any influence was Göttingen, where they inspired a critical response from Münchhausen.[59] By 1739, as the princely Prussian bureaucratic machine mobilized to remove Moser from his botched deanship, he was willing to preside as a student launched a thoroughly nasty attack on Aktenversendung. Moser's student delivered a public disputation lampooning J. P. Ludewig—not coincidentally a professor at the Prussian university of Halle—for his praise of "impartial" Aktenversend-

[55] Hammerstein, *Jus und Historie*, 326 and n. 77.

[56] The often hilarious events of this episode are described by Moser in his *Lebensgeschichte* ([Offenbach], 1768), 63–83. (I have not seen the later, augmented edition of the work used by most scholars.) Moser's own account should be supplemented by C. Bornhak, "J. J. Moser als Professor in Frankfurt/Oder," *Forschungen zur Brandenburgischen und Preußischen Geschichte* 11 (1898): 329–39. See also, M. Walker, *J. J. Moser and the Holy Roman Empire of the German Nation* (Chapel Hill, 1981), 84–102.

[57] Moser, "Freye, aber wohlgemeinte und auf die Erfahrung gegründete Gedancken, wie Universitäten, Besonders in der Juridischen Facultät, sowohl in einen guten Ruf und Aufnahm zu bringen und darinnen zu erhalten, als auch recht nützlich und brauchbar zu machen seyn möchten?" in *Opuscula Academica* (Jena, 1744), 440.

[58] Moser was obliged to write no fewer than forty-five opinions in his first six months—"ob gleich die Arbeiten meistens nicht nach meinem Geschmack waren." Moser, *Lebensgeschichte*, 67–68; Cf. Bornhak, "Moser," 332–34; R. Rürup, *J. J. Moser: Pietismus und Reform* (Wiesbaden, 1965), 67.

[59] For the influence of this address on von Münchhausen, see Rürup, *Moser*, 68–69.

ung. The student limited himself to ironic Latin comments on Ludewig's German text:

> They are free of all fear [of partiality and incompetence] (*utinam!*) [if only!]
> ... The parties are unknown to the members of these legal bodies, and so
> [the judges] cannot stand in any relationship [to the litigants] of favoritism
> or partiality; accordingly they cannot be led astray by their emotions. (*Sae-*
> *pissime hoc verum esse fatemur; saepius vero & hoc fallere in aprico est.*)
> [Very often true, but more often, in truth, false.][60]

In the age of princely enlightenment, professorial justice could not count on much support in the rising generation, even from students supervised by its most likely supporters.

Still, the old institutions, and the old patterns of scholarship, survived. The first half of the eighteenth century threatened Roman law with diminished status, but not with destruction. It was only in the second half of the century that the great mortal threat to the traditions of learned law appeared, the threat that would be most vividly remembered in the time of Savigny—enlightened codificationism. For by the second half of the century, the new state power and the new legal ideas had liberated an urge to legislate among the German princes. Absolutist positivism, the drive to identify the problems of this world and eliminate them, began slowly to appear in Germany.

In this, German princes outpaced the rationalizers of France.[61] At first, in the second half of the century, German princely codemakers had the modest goal of compiling the laws of their societies to make them easily ascertainable and available. But as the century wore on, the tendency grew among enlightened princes to experiment with rationalizing the laws collected for purposes of political reform.[62] Just as natural-law thinking had penetrated the work of scholars in the first half of the century, it began to penetrate the work of legislators, transforming their work from compilation into codification. The new idea of codification stood sharply at odds with the traditions of legal scholarship. For in a codified legal world, the work of lawyers would presumably involve not the exegesis of legal texts but the consultation of authoritative codes. Indeed, legal thinking in the second half of the century—particularly in

[60] Behmer (praeside Moser), *De Transmissione Actorum*, 6–8 n. 2. Quoted in full, n. 50, above.

[61] See the discussion of A. Watson, *The Making of the Civil Law* (Cambridge, Mass., 1981), 103ff.

[62] See G. Tarello, *Le Ideologie della Codificazione nel secolo XVIII*, Università di Genova. Facoltà die Giurisprudenza. Corso di Filosofia di Diritto, Parte 1 (Genoa, n.d.), 173 and ff.

Prussia, the German heartland of enlightened codificationism—threatened to eliminate the professors themselves from the whole of German legal life. Princely jurists of the absolutist era had begun to see the value in a new ideal: the making of complete codes that would provide positive commands for every possible legal eventuality from the mouth of the prince himself, codes with no "holes," no "interstices"[63]—and this anti-interstitial idea of justice left, quite intentionally, no room whatsoever for scholars to interpret the law.

Indeed, as codification got underway in Prussia, Frederick II, three years after the edict forbidding Aktenversendung, went on in his plans for codification to forbid "private citizens, and in particular professors" from publishing commentaries on the law.[64] Thirty-one years later, as work on Prussia's great ultimate contribution to the work of codification, the *Allgemeines Landrecht*, the General Territorial Law, began, the king gave voice to codificationist hostility towards the other class of professional jurists, the judges: "I will not allow any judge to dream of interpreting, extending, or limiting the laws, still less of making new laws."[65] Similar expressions of hostility towards both segments of the juristic community were heard throughout the period of codification in the later eighteenth century.[66] Both of the two major codes inspired by the late-Enlightenment codificationist movement ultimately adopted in the German lands, the Prussian *Allgemeines Landrecht* of 1794 and the Austrian *Allgemeines Bürgerliches Gesetzbuch* of 1811, embodied these hostilities.[67]

To be sure, the rise of the codes did not mean that the work of scholars would be permanently displaced. Quite the contrary, they were directed at fixing and rationalizing existing law—existing law that was, of course, the creation of scholars. But once their work was fixed, scholars would no longer be able to exercise their old interpretive practices. Moreover, the existing law that the codes proposed to fix was, in Germany, the eclectic law of the *usus modernus*, a style of legal thought in which Roman

[63] On the intended "gaplessness" of the Allgemeines Landrecht, see Wieacker, *Privatrechtsgeschichte*, 331–32.

[64] "Project des Corporis Iuris Fridericiani (1749)" Vorrede §28 IX. Cited in H. Weller, *Die Bedeutung der Präjudizien im Verständnis der deutschen Rechtswissenschaft*, Schriften zur Rechtstheorie, vol. 77 (Berlin, 1979), 72 n. 28. See generally H.-J. Becker, "Kommentier- und Auslegungsverbot," in *Handwörterbuch zur deutschen Rechtsgeschichte* (1978), 2: cols. 963–74.

[65] Quoted in H. Hübner, *Kodifikation und Entscheidungsfreiheit des Richters in der Geschichte des Privatrechts* (Königstein, 1980), 31. For similar sentiments from Joseph II, see Kern, *Geschichte des Gerichtsverfassungsrechts*, 43.

[66] See, generally, Weller, *Bedeutung der Präjudizien*, 60–76.

[67] See generally Becker, "Kommentier- und Auslegungsverbot," cols. 963ff.; H. Mohnhaupt, "Potestas Legislatoria und Gesetzesbegriff im Ancien Régime," *Ius Commune* 4 (1972): 188–239.

law had lost much of its pride of place and constitutionalist associations. Indeed, it was the ultimate measure of the decline in sixteenth-century constitutionalism that this princely movement drew on the ratio scripta of Roman law itself: Princely codificationism had, of course, exemplary support for its program in the very existence of the *Corpus Iuris*, a code compiled (if not in Enlightenment fashion) by order of Emperor Justinian. Moreover princes and their partisans could cite the letter of C. 7, 45, 13, which forbade recourse to precedent in the famous phrase "non exemplis sed legibus iudicandum est"—"judgment should be based on laws, not on cases."[68] Or they could cite Justinian explicitly forbidding juristic interpretation as a derogation of "august" power: "If indeed . . . [any law] seems ambiguous, the case is to be sent by the judges to the highest imperial seat, that it may be made plain through the august authority, which has the sole right to make and interpret laws."[69] Inspired largely by this passage,[70] the German princes set about reducing the power of the professors. By the third quarter of the eighteenth century, the corporate tradition of the Roman-law professoriate had been disastrously weakened.

A ROME FOR THE DECLINING PROFESSORIATE

How did the professors experience this decline? As in the age of Melanchthon, they continued to think of themselves as the representatives of Rome. Accordingly, they interpreted their own estate in absolutist Germany through a new interpretation of Roman history: that of Justus Lipsius, a scholar with a view of Rome very different from Melanchthon's. Lipsius's ideas were already known to Conring,[71] but they only matured in the corporate tradition of the professoriate at the end of the seventeenth century, along with the new absolutist states of which Conring became a champion in his old age.[72]

The connection between princely absolutism and the changed view of Rome was pan-European. Lipsius, the leader of the neo-stoic movment in the Netherlands, was a scholar of international fame. An editor of Tacitus, he brought a Tacitean cynicism, and a Tacitean fascination with the power of princes, to the analysis of politics. Roman history was the his-

---

[68] Quoted in Weller, *Bedeutung der Präjudizien*, 41.

[69] C. 1, 17, 2, 21: "Si quid vero, ut supra dictum est, ambiguum fuerit visum, hoc ad imperiale culmen per iudices referatur et ex auctoritate Augusta manifestetur, cui soli concessum est leges condere et interpretari."

[70] Mohnhaupt, "Potestas Legislatoria," 223.

[71] Hammerstein, "Historie bei Conring," 232.

[72] J. Kunisch, "Hermann Conrings Mächtepolitisches Weltbild," in Stolleis, ed., *Conring*, 250.

tory of Tiberius and Sejanus, the history of perpetually impending power-plays and princely coups. Especially in the minds of Lipsius's German followers, Roman history was the history of Augustus's seizure of power at the end of the Roman civil wars. In his belief that politics was the science of princely government, Lipsius resembled the post-Machiavellian *ragione di stato* thinkers who were his Italian contemporaries.[73] But Lipsius went beyond Mediterranean ragione di stato to formulate a new conception not only of the state but of society as a whole. Lipsius based his social philosophy on the Roman writers on military discipline. He envisioned a world of social "discipline" and a new ethic of public service in which the soldier's loyalty toward his commander would serve as a model for society as a whole.[74] Lipsian "discipline" boded great changes for the German lawyers: lawyers ranked first among the citizens of the new state who came to view themselves, under Lipsius's influence, as *Fürstendiener*, "servants of the prince."[75]

This vision of their role was wholly incompatible with Melanchthonianism. For the heart of the Melanchthonian tradition was the claim of "impartiality," a claim no Fürstendiener could make. As absolutism grew, Lipsianism spread, and lawyers ceased to view Roman law as impartial, and ceased to view themselves as the neutral mediators among the possessors of German power. The Melanchthonian Rome had been a Rome for constitutionalists, a Roman imperial principle in which law mediated impartially among Germany's feuding estates, preserving the Public Peace. Such constitutionalism could find no support among the northern European coevals of Italian ragione di stato theory. In the minds of Lipsian Germans, lawyers had to be the men of one party, the party of their prince.

The law of this Lipsian worldview is to be sought in the ius respondendi, "the right to give legal opinions," which I have already described.[76] The corporate sense of self of the Roman law professoriate continued to find its legal basis in the ius respondendi, the ancient principle of privileged authority for learned lawyers, the legal doctrine that provided the framework for Aktenversendung in particular and for the authority of the jurists in general. But as absolutism and Lipsianism established them-

[73] Cf. F. Meinecke, *Machiavellism*, translated by D. Scott (London, 1957), 117–45, on the spread of ragione di stato thinking in Italy and Germany.

[74] Esp. G. Oestreich, *Neo-Stoicism and the Early Modern State* (Cambridge, 1982); G. Abel, *Stoizismus und Frühe Neuzeit* (Berlin, 1977).

[75] On the development of the mentality of the Fürstendiener, see esp. M. Stolleis, "Grundzüge der Beamtenethik," *Die Verwaltung* 13 (1980): 447–75; H. Hattenhauer, *Geschichte des Beamtentums* (Cologne, 1980), 91–159.

[76] See above, pp. 29–30.

selves, German lawyers began to reinterpret the historical background to the ius respondendi.

One critical text lent itself to this Lipsian reinterpretation, a fragment of the *Handbook of Pomponius* preserved in Justinian's Digest. This fragment laid out the history of the ius respondendi. According to Pomponius, Emperor Augustus had conferred some kind of privilege on certain jurists, a "ius publice respondendi," "the right of giving opinions publicly." This ius respondendi had been somehow modified, a century later, by the emperor Hadrian:

> Before the time of Augustus, the right of giving opinions publicly was not granted by the emperors, but the practice was that opinions were given by people who had confidence in their own studies. . . . It was the deified Augustus who, in order to enhance the authority of the law, first established that opinions might be given under his authority [*ex auctoritate eius*]. And from that time [on] this began to be sought as a favor. As a consequence of this, our most excellent emperor Hadrian issued a rescript on an occasion when some men of praetorian rank were petitioning him for permission to grant opinions; he said that this was customarily not merely begged for but earned [*hoc non peti, sed praestari solere*], and that he [the emperor] would accordingly be delighted if whoever had faith in himself would prepare himself for giving public opinions.[77]

Modern scholars find the meaning of this passage (which is apparently textually corrupt[78]) obscure. What was the "ius respondendi"? Clearly it was some sort of right to give legal opinions. But did these opinions bind the ancient judges? What exactly did "publice" signify?[79] Did Augustus confer an exclusive privilege on jurists whom he favored?[80] Or did he simply acknowledge jurists already considered pre-eminent, attempting to conserve the republican tradition under his own aegis?[81] Perhaps most important, how, precisely, did Hadrian alter whatever it was that Augustus did?[82] How was the ius respondendi of Augustus's political revolution different from that of Hadrian's governmental revolution?

If all of these problems seem insoluble to scholars today, they did not trouble Lipsians in the age of absolutism. For Lipsians in Germany, Ro-

---

[77] D. 1, 2, 2, 49. The translation, which I have slightly revised, appears in T. Mommsen, P. Krueger, and A. Watson, eds., *The Digest of Justinian* (Philadelphia, 1985).

[78] See the discussion of Schulz, *Römische Rechtswissenschaft*, 135ff.

[79] A. Honoré, in particular, has attempted to reinterpret this word. *Emperors and Lawyers* (London, 1981), 5.

[80] W. Kunkel, *Römische Rechtsgeschichte* (Cologne/Vienna, 1972), 101.

[81] Schulz, *Rechtswissenschaft*, 132; Kaser, *Römische Rechtsgeschichte*, 178.

[82] Hadrian's role is also left obscure by our other principle source, Gaius, *Institutes*, I 7. This passage is, in any case, irrelevant to my discussion here, since the *Institutes* were not discovered until 1816.

man history revolved unambiguously around Augustus's seizure of power. It was Augustus who had first identified himself with the Roman state and thereby framed the model of princely power for all ages to come. Accordingly, the meaning of Pomponius's passage, the main source for the ius respondendi and therefore the formal legal basis for the authority of Roman-law scholars,[83] was clear: Augustus, not Hadrian, had been the decisive actor in the legal rise of scholarly power. And it had been Augustus's act to take command of the practice of law and convert the ancient jurists into servants of his own power. Accordingly, a proper understanding of Roman law dictated a wholly subordinate place in society for the professors: they were to serve their prince, not represent old ideals of justice within an obsolete corporate tradition.

The Lipsian Rome appeared on the German scene almost immediately after Conring's refutation of the *Lotharlegende* in the waning years of the Thirty Years' War. Like much of Roman-law scholarship, it came from Holland, which, from the late sixteenth century on, was the great European center of Roman legal studies. As early as 1645, Cyriacus Lentulus, a German expatriate living in the Lipsian stronghold of Holland, published his *Augustus: Sive de Convertenda in Monarchiam Republica*. The book was a typical product of the Tacitean political historiography of princely power that had grown up since Lipsius.[84] The title of Lentulus's book revealed its thesis: Lentulus recast Roman history in quasi-Machiavellian form, locating its focal point in Augustus's seizure of princely power. Augustus's intervention in the practice of law played its part in Lentulus's account of the Augustan revolution. Speaking in characteristically Machiavellian terms, Lentulus presented Augustus's reliance on his council of legal advisers as a piece of public image-making: Augustus, wrote Lentulus, "wished to appear most observant of justice."[85] There was little more than this brief mention of law in Lentulus's account, but other readers of Tacitus and followers of Lipsius soon began to engage in more elaborate post-Machiavellian analyses of the forms of Augustan princely legal plotting. Twenty years after Lentulus, Ulrich Huber, professor of law at the Dutch University of Franeker, offered the first thorough analysis of the arcane considerations of power behind Augustus's grant of authority to the jurists: the new emperor had granted authority to jurists because he preferred lawyers to statesmen, because he wished to efface the dignity of the praetor, and because he wished to plunge the populace into endless legal disputes, disputes that would drain their en-

---

[83] See above, pp. 29–30, 35.

[84] For Lentulus as a typical German Tacitean, see Christ, *Römische Geschichte und Deutsche Geschichtswissenschaft*, 22.

[85] C. Lentulus, *Augustus, sive de convertenda in Monarchiam Republica* (Amsterdam, 1645), 263–64, esp. 264: "Iustitiae se observantissimum videri volebat."

ergy and obscure their memory of the Republic.[86] With Huber's account, often cited by Germans of the following decades, Machiavellian forms of analysis, as well as a new Lipsian notion of what Huber called "harsh princely discipline,"[87] entered the jurists' interpretation of Rome. Inevitably, the "impartiality" of the jurists was put to flight.

As Lipsianism spread from the learned Dutch world into Germany, it transformed German constitutional thought on the subject of Roman law. By the end of the seventeenth century, the German jurists began to view Augustus's princely coup as the source of their own power, and themselves, accordingly, as Fürstendiener. The Lipsian/Tacitean Rome entered the self-definitions of the German jurists from the first moments of the revival of German learning that marked the end of the century. The appearance of the *Usus Modernus Pandectarum* of Samuel Stryk in 1690 marked the watershed year for German jurisprudence. Stryk's work, which gave its name to the whole age of the usus modernus,[88] showed clearly the transition to a new conception of Rome, centered squarely on Augustus's seizure of power.[89] As he wrote, Stryk, a professor at the Prussian university of Frankfurt on the Oder, still relied on sixteenth-century scholarship: when he discussed the ius respondendi, he cited Hieronymus Treutler. But Stryk altered Treutler's sixteenth-century reading of Roman history. Treutler had known Pomponius, of course, and had stated that the authority of the jurists derived from Augustus.[90] But ancient politics had no relevance for Treutler, who was writing in a Melanchthonian world. Treutler simply observed that the German world of his own time—"hodie," "nowadays"—was different. The Rome of Melanchthon's Fourth Monarchy was a living imperium rather than a fixed model; accordingly, events in ancient Rome created no inescapable polit-

---

[86] Huber's influential passage is framed as an apostrophe to Augustus himself. Huber, "Oratio Exhibens Historiam Juris Romani, & ex ejus argumento continuam probationem, literas humaniores cum jurisprudentia esse conjungendas," in idem, *Opera Minora*, edited by A. Wieling (Trier, 1746) (originally 1665 as "Auspicia Domestica, Oratio V"), 109: "Interpretes Juris non modo auctoritate, quam & olim populari consensu obtinebant, sed insuper immensa Legislatorum potestate armasti. An ita dominationi visum expedire? ut nova responsa vetus Edictum, & Prudentium auctoritas judiciale regnum Praetoris everteret? An ut otii dulcedine plebs emollita, nobilioresque animi civilibus studiis ac forensi occupatione, partium & armorum obliti, pristinam ferociam & atrocem Reipublicae memoriam deponerent? Sed interim gloriae atque dissentiendi libido docentium copia & dignitate aucta, non modo judicum religionem multitudine sententiarum distraxit; sed & Graeculorum exemplo scholasticas contentiones & sectarum nomina sanctissimis auditoriis intulit."

[87] Ibid.

[88] Cf. Wieacker, *Privatrechtsgeschichte*, 205ff.

[89] The influence of Dutch jurisprudence on Stryk is noted by Hammerstein, *Jus und Historie*, 156–57.

[90] Treutler, passage cited above p. 38.

ical precedents. For Stryk, by contrast, Rome was a fixed model—a model fixed by Augustus's politics, which made it a Rome that belonged only to princes. As ancient lawyers received their authority from Augustus, so lawyers of Stryk's own time received their authority from their princes:

> The power of the ius respondendi was once granted to any Roman, but afterwards, when Augustus was emperor, it was established that this faculty of publicly giving opinions should be obtained from the Emperor, so that those who were consulted should have greater authority. See D. 1, 2, 2, 49. Nowadays, in my judgment, the law on this matter is no different [*hodie diversum jus obtinere non puto*].[91]

"Hodie diversum jus obtinere non puto": the change in interpretation since Treutler's time may seem innocuous. But Stryk's Rome was fundamentally different from Treutler's. "Publice," in Stryk's mind, had come to signify "conferred by the state." And Stryk's state was no longer the state of Treutler's sixteenth-century constitution, with its elaborate balance of power among corporations, princes, and emperor. The state, in Stryk's time, had been seized by a new class of princes, and, while it continued to offer protection, it had begun to demand a new kind of service.

The Lipsian interpretation of Pomponius was rapidly adopted by the principal enemies of Roman law—a new class of constitutional scholars, the so-called *Reichspublizisten*. The Reichspublizisten, German intellectual descendants of the French customary-law constitutional thinkers of the sixteenth century, were eager to make their mark as the innovators of a new science of government, one that would be largely founded on the Lipsian mode of analysis,[92] and one that would set some constitutional limits to the exercise of princely power; they considered themselves sophisticated guardians of constitutional tradition in the post-Machiavellian German world. As the would-be founders of a new discipline, they felt obliged to put distance between themselves and the old dominant faculty of Roman law.[93] Thus they combined suspicion of princes with hostility toward Roman law, and the Lentulan rereading of Pomponius could

---

[91] S. Stryk, *Specimen Usus Moderni Pandectarum* (Florence, 1841), 14: cols. 33–34: "Praecipue vero ex hoc titulo quoad usum modernum monendum, potestatem de jure respondendi, fuisse olim unicuivis apud Romanos permissam, sed postea imperante Augusto effectum, ut haec facultas publice respondendi beneficii loco ab imper. peteretur, quo eo major auctoritas esset eorum qui consulerentur per *l. 2. §. 47. vers. et ut Obiter ff. h. t. add. §. 8. i. de i. n. g. et c.* Hodie diversum jus obtinere non puto, sed facultatem de jure respondendi adhuc nemini competere assero, nisi cui illa publice collata. Et eapropter juris doctores, qui in locum veterum illorum prudentum successerunt *Carpz. p. 2. c. 10. def. 4. n. 3.* potestatem consulendi et respondendi ex auctoritate imperatoria in promotione solemniter collata sibi rectissime vindicant *Cothmann* [et al.]."

[92] Cf. Hammerstein, *Jus und Historie*, 95.

[93] Hammerstein, "Das Römische am Heiligen Römischen Reich," 121.

not fail to attract them. In 1695 Stryk's pupil (and later opponent) Christian Thomasius, a leading representative of the new Reichspublizistik, published a book with the strange title *Naevorum Jurisprudentiae Romanae Antejustinianeae Libri Duo*—"Two Books of Warts on Pre-Justinianian Jurisprudence." This widely influential work was partly inspired by the Dutch learning to which Thomasius had been exposed in his *peregrinatio academica* (the then customary young scholars' pilgrimage) to Holland, where he had traveled to acquire learning at the centers of Roman-law scholarship.[94] Augustus's grant of the ius respondendi was the twentieth wart Thomasius identified, a disfigurement given jurisprudence in the guise of an ornament. Thomasius cited Huber, and elaborated on his analysis of Augustus's tactic: the emperor wished to embroil the people in litigation, and at the same time to corrupt men of juristic talent by inducing them to seek the favor of his grant of authority. Thomasius, indeed, could detect no end of stratagems in Augustus's supposed boon to the jurists.[95] As Lentulus had written, the emperors wished to *appear* observant of justice. The old "impartial" professoriate, the mediator between emperor and the Estates of the empire, lost its footing in Roman history as the scholarly ground shifted underneath it.

By the early eighteenth century, the Lipsian view of juristic power was universal and by no means limited to the Reichspublizisten. The new princely Rome was on display, for example, in the work of one of the best Roman-law scholars of the early eighteenth century, Augustin Leyser. Firmly fixed in the Lipsian tradition of Lentulus, Leyser, writing from his Spruchkollegium in 1713, located the pivotal moment in Roman his-

[94] On the importance of Thomasius's studies in Holland, see Hammerstein, *Jus und Historie*, 47f. On the *De Naevis*, see ibid., 90.

[95] The passage shows just how intricate Lipsian political analysis of princely plotting could be. Augustus granted the ius respondendi not only for the reasons adduced by Huber, wrote Thomasius ("Naevus XX: 'Maximum damnum Jurisprudentia passa est, quod Augustus facultatem respondendi per modum beneficii concesserit,' " in *Naevorum Jurisprudentiae Romanae Antejustinianeae Libri Duo*, 2d ed. [Halle, 1707]), 70: "quam ideo, ut propter necessarium ex negotii natura dissensum, aut potius ob dissensus infinitam multiplicationem lites inter privatos multiplicarentur, & ita populus infinitis istis dissidiis & jure incertissimo distractus non uniretur ad repetendam antiquam libertatem. Non poterat autoritas JCtorum contemni, quod aliqui, adde etiam multi ante hanc constitutionem Augusti, Juris parum periti vana fiducia virium propriarum aggrederentur, & ipsi de jure respondere. Hoc non poterat detrahere autoritati verorum JCtorum, quin potius ut pulchritudo gratior apparet, inter deformes, ita JCti genuini melius fulgent inter medios Rabulas. Et annon major metuenda erat autoritatis Responsorum Juris labefactio, cum a Principe per modum beneficii peteretur, quod quis viribus propriis praestare debebat. Necesse erat, monopoliis ejusmodi viam intercludi multis egregiis ingeniis dona divina expediendi publice, & allici fratres ignorantiae ad honores ambiendos favore, gratia, argento. Aut forte alia tempora tum erant atque hodie. Et forte ibi non regnabat in aulis fraus, dolus, ambitio, avaritia, insipientia."

tory—and in the history of the ancient jurists—at the instant of Augustus's seizure of power.[96] Jurists were creations of the prince, and had no independent power to make law.[97] By mid-century all learned lawyers were of the same opinion: as one leading Göttingen legal historian put it in 1757, the emperors had invented the ius respondendi because they believed the jurists could be "a great intrument of domination."[98] The semipopular legal literature was as Lipsian as the most learned treatise: the author of *Der Teutsche Justinianus*, a 1718 German translation of the Institutes with commentary, fully accepted Thomasius's Machiavellian reading of the origins of the ius respondendi.[99]

The Lipsian orthodoxy was hardly challenged throughout the century. So unthinking was the concentration on the Augustan revolution that learned jurists thoroughly neglected the republican history of Roman law: to J. Ritter, reviewing the biographies of the ancient jurists in 1752, it was natural to write an account that began "in the time of Augustus"; republican tradition played no part.[100] This fascination with Augustus lasted well down into the 1790s: C. F. Glück, perhaps the last of the great eighteenth-century commentators on Roman law, in 1797 still viewed the power of the ancient jurists as the handiwork of Augustus—handiwork undertaken, Glück said, still speaking in the seventeenth-century language of ragione del stato theory, "out of political considerations of state."[101] Rome no longer gave any sanction to the "impartiality" of the Roman-law jurists.

Rome had found its focus in Augustus's "conversion" of the republic into a monarchy; Roman tradition had become the property of the princes. The new idea of Roman law received, fittingly, its most succinct expression from the leader of the newly ascendant school of natural law-

---

[96] Leyser, "De Responsis Prudentum," 49ff. On Leyser, see K. Luig "Universales Recht und Partikulares Recht in den 'Meditationes ad Pandectas' von Augustin Leyser," in *Diritto Commune e Diritti Locali nella Storia dell'Europa* (Atti del Convegno di Varenna) (Milan, 1980).

[97] Ibid., 59. According to Leyser, the same wise measure had been taken by the ancient Hebrews, who entrusted the "collegium Levitarum" with the ius respondendi (ibid., 53).

[98] J.H.C. von Selchow, *Elementa Antiquitatum Juris Romani Publici et Privati* (Göttingen, 1757), 143.

[99] Anon., *Der Teutsche Justinianus* (Augsburg, 1718), 29: "Als aber die Kayser die Römische Freyheit unterzudrucken begonnen, haben selbige, und zumahlen Tiberius, die Macht, Gesetze zu geben, von dem gantzen Volck genommen, und dem Rath zugelegt, weilen sie solchen ehender, als das gantze Volck, auch hierinn zu ihrem Willen zu haben, gehoffet. *add. Thomas. in Naev. Jurisprud. Antejust. Lib. I, cap. 9.*"

[100] See the "Observatio" of J. Ritter to Heineccius, *Historia Juris Civilis Romani et Germanici*, Lib. I, § 178, edited by Ritter (Strasbourg, 1751), 268. Discussed in C. L. Neuber, *Die Juristischen Classiker: Ein Beitrag zur Civilistischen Biographie* (Berlin, 1806) pt. I (no more appeared), VIIn.

[101] C. F. Glück, *Ausfuhrliche Erläuterung der Pandecten*, 2d ed. (Erlangen, 1797), 433.

yers, Christian Wolff, who declared in the driest language of legal analysis that Roman law had its validity in Germany not by virtue of its being either Roman or German, but rather because it had the endorsement of the prince, "who has the legislative power in his territory."[102] By the end of the century a leading scholar like A. D. Weber could take Wolff's line of thought a threatening step further: the fate of Roman law did indeed depend on the will of the prince, wrote Weber, and "it would be no evil, but rather a boon to the public, if the legislative power eliminated the Roman legal texts entirely from our courts."[103] For legal scholars Roman law had become the instrument of princes just as Rome had become the Rome of Augustus. As the old pride of sixteenth-century corporate society in general faded, their own corporate history had lost its sixteenth-century meaning.

CONCLUSION

As the old corporate society weakened, the social prestige of the professors sank. Roman law fell into a disrepute new in its post-classical history,[104] and lawyers were held in low regard.[105] The status of professors had declined precipitously.[106] Despite the successes of the new universities of Halle and Göttingen, most academic men suffered from poor pay and ugly associations with the prerational past; reformers did not shy from proposing the complete abolition of the German universities.[107] The momentum of modernism was with the princes, and learned law seemed likely to vanish.

Yet, after the late 1780s, the prestige of the princes faltered. In direct response, the professors regained their sense of self. Their pretensions and

[102] Wolff, *Jus Naturae*, Pars VIII, § 967, 745: "*Jus Romanum in Germania* non valet tamquam Jus Romanum, *nec tamquam Jus Germanicum*; sed tamquam Jus superioris, qui in suo territorio potestatem legislatoriam habet" (emphasis in original). Quoted in Cappellini, *Systema Iuris*, 1:509–10.

[103] Weber, *Reflexionen zur Beförderung einer gründlichen Theorie vom heutigen Gebrauch des römischen Rechts* (Schwerin, 1782), 6. Quoted in Cappellini, *Systema Iuris*, 1:114. On Weber, see also Neusüss, *Gesunde Vernunft und Natur der Sache*, 106–7, and the literature cited in Cappellini, *Systema Iuris*, 1:108ff.

[104] Cf. H. Thieme, "Die Zeit des Späten Naturrechts," *ZSS* (G) 56 (1936): 241ff.

[105] See H. Brunschwig, *Enlightenment and Romanticism in Eighteenth-Century Prussia*, translated by F. Jellinek (Chicago, 1974), 135–36.

[106] Cf. R. Kawakami, "Die Begründung des 'neuen' gelehrten Rechts durch Savigny," *ZSS* (R) 98 (1981): 308 nn. 8 and 9. On the status of professors, see generally the discussion of R. S. Turner, "University Reformers and Professorial Scholarship in Germany, 1760–1806," in L. Stone, ed., *The University in Society* (Princeton, N.J., 1974), 2:495–531.

[107] See A. Stölzel, "Die Berliner Mitwochgesellschaft über Aufhebung oder Reform der Universitäten," *Forschungen zur Brandenburgischen und Preußischen Geschichte* 2 (1889): 201–22; R. König, *Vom Wesen der Deutschen Universitäten* (Berlin, 1935), 34.

their sense of their own dignity rose. They began, slowly, to reject the enlightened notion of "natural" reorderings of the world. And their attention shifted, within the text of Pomponius, from Augustus, the prince of power, to Hadrian, the prince of reform. As the first romantic decade began, Rome changed in German minds, and the corporate tradition of the professors was reborn.

Chapter III

IMPERIAL REVIVAL IN THE FIRST ROMANTIC
DECADE AND THE DISCOVERY OF THE ANTONINES

THE ENLIGHTENMENT had enemies among German literary men early on. Their work, beginning with the activity of Möser and Herder in the late 1760s, is familiar to all students of German history. But if the literary Anti-Enlightenment has long been familiar, it is only recently that historians have rediscovered what could be called the great political Anti-Enlightenment: the startling revival of the Holy Roman Empire, linked with growing intellectual antiabsolutism, that began in the late 1780s. So-called *Reichspatriotismus*, love of the Holy Roman Empire, appeared far and wide in the last years of the eighteenth century. Germans began once again to praise the old imperial institutions as checks on princely power and to demand that the emperor resume his historic role as a counterweight to the territorial lords. A number of recent historians have pioneered the historiographical revival of the Holy Roman Empire and demonstrated the new strength of the old empire in German minds.[1] These historians have succeeded in demonstrating how powerful the Holy Roman Empire became in the German public mind of the late 1780s and 1790s, and how strong the German constitutionalist movement had become before the French Revolution burst across the Rhine. The German reform movement began gathering strength two years before the Tennis Court Oath and continued strong until the French overwhelmed the German forces in the second half of the decade. Even after the decisive defeat embodied in the Peace of Campo Formio (1797), the conviction that a revival of sixteenth-century constitutionalism could somehow peacefully form a new foundation for "German freedom" kept its grip on the minds of German thinkers.

This great political movement—inextricably bound together with literary romanticism—brought with it a revival of the sixteenth-century tradition of the Roman-law professoriate. Indeed, the imperial revival of the

[1] K. O. von Aretin, *Heiliges Römisches Reich*; J. G. Gagliardo, *Reich and Nation* (Bloomington, Ind., 1980); E. Bussi, *Il Diritto Publico del Sacro Romano Impero alla fine del XVIII Secolo*, 2 vols. (Padua, 1957); G. Walter, *Der Zusammenbruch des Heiligen Römischen Reichs deutscher Nation und die Problematik seiner Restauration in den Jahren 1814/1815*, Studien und Quellen zur Geschichte des deutschen Verfassungsrechts, Series A, vol. 12 (Heidelberg/Karlsruhe, 1980).

1790s set the terms for the following decades of legal history in Germany. In this chapter I wish to discuss the imperial revival as political twin of literary romanticism and to show how the Roman-law professors shook off their Lipsian toils and reconstituted their own sixteenth-century corporate tradition, as one of many remade corporate traditions in a romantic age of corporate renewal. With the romantic revival of the ancient constitution of the Holy Roman Empire, the professors of Roman law recovered something that had been lost since the age of Melanchthonianism: the sense that they could be bearers of Roman civilization in Germany, independent of princely government.

Roman law mixed high cultural tradition with politics, and, in order to understand the place of Roman law in the romantic era, we must understand how cultural and political life hung together. Yet German political life is rarely placed in the context of German romantic literature in a way that would set the proper background for the impact of romanticism on Roman law. This is entirely understandable, to be sure, since romanticism was, by and large, a thing of the literary rather than of the political world. German romanticism was, for the most part, a movement among literary figures with a wide variety of vaguely conjoined goals: to substitute sensuousness for reason in experiencing the world, to break the hold of French classical and English Augustan forms in verse writing, to elevate the reputation of the Greeks at the expense of that of the Romans. Even though, as we shall see, a kind of opposition to reason played a part in the legal life of the era, most of the features of literary romanticism were devoid of any immediately obvious political implications.

Nevertheless, one central feature of the movement did have supreme significance for the mix of culture and politics that forms the background to romantic Roman law: the fascination with the Middle Ages and the Reformation. It was in this fascination that politics and literature converged. Fascination with medieval and Reformation tradition—and, more specifically, with the constitution of the Holy Roman Empire as it had been reformed in the sixteenth century—was as central to German politics as to German literature. To be sure, there were political currents in German society of the romantic era that owed nothing to the cult of the Middle Ages and the Reformation.[2] Nevertheless, I will refer to the period after 1780 as "the romantic era" in German political history, and I will focus on the medievalizing strain so typical of the time, the desire to revive the ancient constitution of the Holy Roman Empire.[3]

[2] For a general survey of political romanticism, see U. Scheuner, *Der Beitrag der deutschen Romantik zur politischen Theorie*, Rheinisch-Westfälische Akademie der Wissenschaften (Geisteswissenschaften), Vorträge G 248 (Opladen, 1980).

[3] "Romanticism" is a term to be used cautiously in describing politics. Strictly speaking,

The medievalizing character of the romantic era has often been neglected by historians.[4] But contemporaries had no doubt that the revival of pre-absolutist tradition lay at the movement's heart. To Germans, literary romanticism was always a medievalizing movement first and foremost: to Hegel, for example, the romantic aesthetic was an aesthetic of knightly honor and gothic architecture.[5] The identification of romanticism with the Middle Ages lasted down into the last years of the movement. Heinrich Heine, for example, portrayed romanticism as a cult of the Christian Middle Ages:

> What was the romantic school in Germany?
> It was nothing other than the reawakening of the poetics of the Middle Ages, as it had manifested itself in songs, in painting and architecture, in art and life.[6]

To Heine's younger left-wing contemporary, Arnold Ruge, too, romanticism was a "golden age of 'christian-German' magnificence, wholly poetic."[7] Whatever the other political movements in the air during the long romantic period, the medieval revival was always especially powerful.[8]

This medievalizing literary movement grew from the mid-1760s on, and by the 1780s it began to call forth a new kind of traditionalist politics. In politics the medievalizing movement was, in one respect, different

---

there never was any such thing as romantic political thought. In the romantic era the term "romantic" was only applied to literature. (See C. Schmitt, *Politische Romantik*, 3d ed. [Berlin, 1968]; Scheuner, *Beitrag der deutschen Romantik*, 13–16.) Nevertheless, Germans on virtually all points of the political spectrum shared common, recognizably "romantic" politics, politics of medieval revival, at least until 1848.

[4] Most often, the substantive fascination with the Middle Ages and the Reformation has been neglected in favor of an emphasis on romanticism as a "style of thought," to use Karl Mannheim's phrase, as a new mode of thinking that replaced the mode of thinking characteristic of the Enlightenment. To Mannheim himself, the romantic era was characterized not by medievalizing traditionalism but by a conservative "style of thought"; according to Mannheim, encroaching capitalism had broken down the medieval social structure too far for true traditionalism to flourish. See generally, K. Mannheim, "Conservative Thought," in *Essays on Sociology and Social Psychology* (New York, 1953), 74–164. Mannheim was hardly alone: many of the finest intellectual historians have focused, in one manner or another, on "irrationalism" or some other "style of thought" as the key feature of the period: these include G. Lukács, *Die Zerstörung der Vernunft* (Berlin, 1954); Brunschwig, *Enlightenment and Romanticism*; E. Cassirer, *The Philosophy of the Enlightenment*, translated by F. Koelnn and J. Pettegrove (Princeton, N.J., 1951); Schmitt, *Politische Romantik*. Meinecke, of course, treated historicism as the defining style of thought of the period. See F. Meinecke, *Historism*, translated by J. E. Anderson (London, 1972).

[5] Hegel, *Vorlesungen über die Aesthetik* (Frankfurt a.M., 1970), 2:141–42, 330.

[6] Heine, *Die Romantische Schule* (Stuttgart, 1976) (orig. 1833), 10–11.

[7] Ruge, "Die Wahre Romantik," in *Gesammelte Schriften* (Mannheim, 1846), 3:126.

[8] For works that call attention to the medievalizing tendency in German post-Napoleonic political life, see below, p. 93.

from the literary medievalizing movement: for political men, revivalism tended to focus on the early sixteenth century, on the resurrection of the Holy Roman Imperial constitution in the last medieval moment of Ulrich von Hutten and his contemporaries. For romantics in politics, the ideal was less the Middle Ages narrowly conceived than the whole of pre-absolutist corporate society. Möser's famous introduction to his 1768 history of his native town of Osnabrück, the classic statement of early romantic thought, was a first sign of the new flowering of the old particulate constitution of the Holy Roman Empire:

> German history can, in my judgment, hope to take a new turn, if we trace the old territorial bodies ["die gemeinen Landeigentümer"—a term with a special meaning in Möser's vocabulary, referring to the pre-absolutist order], the true component parts of the nation, through all their mutations.[9]

The great political project that began twenty years later, the project to revive the old particulate constitutions, and to reawaken the parts of the old "monstrosity," as Pufendorf called the Holy Roman Empire, was Möser put into political action. It was a remarkable revival. In the 1780s and 1790s faith in the ancient constitution became as much part of a consensus as faith in the ancient constitution was among English oppositional Whigs and American revolutionaries in the eighteenth century—indeed, gothic politics in the German romantic era owed a great deal to gothic oppositional politics in the English Whig era. Everywhere in Germany one found the same pervasive traditionalism and corporatism, the same spirit as gripped the poets: the politics that favored revival of what F. C. Moser in 1796 called, using a favorite romantic topos, "the ruined structure of the Holy Roman Empire,"[10] the politics that favored revival of the old Germanic institutions, especially as they had been reformed at the very end of the Middle Ages, during the imperial recovery of the late fifteenth and sixteenth centuries, the recovery that had centered on the new Reichskammergericht. The cult of the "ruined structure of the Holy Roman Empire" served as the center of romanticism, both political and literary.

What was the significance of this great political ferment? Historians once tended to argue or imply that the political changes of the romantic

---

[9] Möser, *Osnabrückische Geschichte*, in Sämtliche Werke, Historisch-Kritische Ausgabe, vol. 12, pt. 1 (Oldenburg/Hamburg, 1964) (orig. 1768), 34.

[10] F. C. Moser, *Politische Wahrheiten* (Zürich, 1796), 1:121 on "unserer alten baufälligen deutschen Reichsverfassung." For E. Brandes on the idea, typical of the time, of a "gothische Staats-Verfassung," see S. Haikala, *"Britische Freiheit" und das Englandbild in der öffentlichen deutschen Diskussion im ausgehenden achtzehnten Jahrhundert*, Studia Historica Jyväskyläensia 32 (Jyväskylä, 1985), 68. For the favorite romantic topos of the ruined structure, see L. Kunder, "Die Deutsche Ruinenpoesie" (diss., Heidelberg, 1933).

era marked Germany's deviation from the West.[11] That view is no longer tenable—though less because our understanding of Germany has changed, than because our understanding of the West has changed. We should now be able to recognize that the medievalizing Germany of the romantic era was a Germany yielding once again to Western influence—and, in particular, to the continuing influence of the customary-law constitutionalist tradition whose earlier penetration into Germany I have already described.[12] The constitutionalism of the romantic era belonged to the same tradition in legal thought that had produced the French ideas of "national customary law"; "German freedom" and "the Germanic constitution" were old ideas everywhere in Europe when the German intellectuals of the late eighteenth century initiated the cult of their ancient institutions. When Herder described Ulrich von Hutten admiringly as a defender of ancient liberty against the absolutist state,[13] he could draw on more than two centuries of Western tradition that opposed the ancient Germanic constitution to princely despotism. It was in the France of Dumoulin that lawyers and publicists had first begun opposing claims of historic customary rights, claims of the right to conserve "Germanic freedom," to the encroachments of princely power.[14] Opposition founded on the idea of customary right had grown all through the sixteenth century, as I have already recounted, and had culminated in the great historical works of the period of religious wars in the 1560s and 1570s—works of Du Moulin, of Bodin, and of François Hotman and his Huguenot comrades-in-arms.[15] The learned lawyers who pioneered this politics of customary law had, by and large, been forced to flee France. Nevertheless, a French strain of customary-law thought survived, if with declining

[11] See, e.g., Troeltsch, "The Idea of Natural Law," Appendix to O. Gierke, *Natural Law and the Theory of Society*, translated by E. Barker (Cambridge, 1934), esp. 209ff. on the romantic "revolution" against (Western) natural right. American historians since World War II, eager to find the roots of fascism—historians such as Professors Iggers and Krieger—often tended to endorse this interpretation. See G. Iggers, *The German Conception of History*, 2d ed. (Middletown, 1982); L. Krieger, *The German Idea of Freedom* (Chicago, 1957). Indeed, it is still often asserted that a medievalizing Germany deviated from the natural-law West during the romantic era. See, e.g., Scheuner, *Beitrag der deutschen Romantik*, 11–12.

[12] See above, pp. 47, 61.

[13] Cf. the discussion of K. Siblewski, *Ritterlicher Patriotismus und Romantischer Nationalismus in der deutschen Literatur, 1770–1830* (Munich, 1981), 63ff.

[14] See the discussion above, pp. 43–45.

[15] On French customary-law thought see, along with the literature cited above pp. 43–45, E. Hölzle, *Die Idee einer altdeutschen Freiheit vor Montesquieu*, Historische Zeitschrift, Beiheft 5 (Munich/Berlin, 1925); Olivier-Martin, *Histoire du droit français* (Montchréstien, 1948), esp. 424ff. The most important works have been published more recently: see esp. J. Franklin, *Jean Bodin*; Kelley, *Foundations of Modern Historical Scholarship*; idem, "Civil Science in the Renaissance: Jurisprudence in the French Manner"; Q. Skinner, *Foundations of Modern Political Thought* (Cambridge, 1978), vol. 2.

vigor, down into the time of Boulainvilliers and Montesquieu.[16] Indeed, it would be particularly through the work of Montesquieu that the French tradition would influence the German romantics.

To be sure, by the time of the rise of German romanticism England, much more than France, had become the center of the tradition. It was in the eighteenth-century English world that the opposition between customary right and princely power remained a prominent and creative political force. In the seventeenth century, Huguenot ideas had been embraced by Coke and his circle, the advocates of an ancient English constitution against the princely government of the Stuarts. From then on the advocacy of the ancient constitution, as Professor Pocock has called this political platform,[17] became the basis of English anti-princely politics for two centuries. Ideas of the ancient constitution marked the parliamentary revolution of 1688, and ideas of the ancient constitution became the basis of oppositional politics for the following century and a half. Constitutionalist, anti-princely political strains in England and its American colonies had become extraordinarily complex and varied by the eighteenth century, embracing Old Whigs, Radical Whigs, and a variety of country and court ideologists of the eighteenth century in England and colonial America—all English-speakers who shared a faith in England's "gothic constitution" and a conviction that princely corruption of that constitution was a perpetual and imminent threat.[18] And in Britain the celebratory public politics of the ancient constitution remained strong through the 1830s, when the gothic buildings of Parliament were erected, in the era of the Young England movement.

Germany joined this Europe in the romantic era.[19] As the romantic movement gained momentum, Germans in general began to feel the force of a customary-law tradition that had been making converts among German lawyers since 1690. Germans began to feel the power, in particular, of an English world in which the philosophy of "custom" had "helped to

[16] Cf. N. Keohane, *Philosophy and the State in France* (Princeton, N.J., 1980), 346–48. Cf. also H. A. Ellis, "Genealogy, History and Aristocratic Reaction in Eighteenth-Century France: The Case of Henri de Boulainvilliers," *Journal of Modern History* 58 (1986): 414–51, and the literature cited there.

[17] Pocock, *The Ancient Constitution and the Feudal Law*.

[18] Cf., e.g., I. Kramnick, *Bolingbroke and his Circle* (Cambridge, Mass., 1968); D. Forbes, *Hume's Philosophical Politics* (Cambridge, 1975); B. Bailyn, *Ideological Origins of the American Revolution* (Cambridge, Mass., 1967).

[19] For a statement of this important point from a historian who earlier would have argued otherwise, see R. R. Palmer, in his foreword to H. Dippel, *Germany and the American Revolution, 1770–1800: A Sociohistorical Investigation of Late Eighteenth-Century Political Thinking*, Veröffentlichungen des Instituts für Europäische Geschichte Mainz, Band 90 (Abteilung Universalgeschichte) (Wiesbaden, 1978), ix.

generate the philosophy of historicism."[20] In politics Germans (like the French[21]) began a conscious effort to imitate the traditions of "Britische Freiheit" (British freedom), as embodied in the Magna Charta, the writ of habeas corpus, jury trial, and all the rest.[22] Eighteenth-century Germans of Göttingen, Westphalia, and Schleswig regularly looked across the North Sea for their political models (though after 1776 many of them looked to America rather than to England). In England they saw a gothicizing subculture, one in which leading whigs had begun to write gothic novels and build gothic manors, one which had begun to cultivate a taste for the ruins of the Middle Ages even as Englishmen spoke of limiting the powers of their prince through a constitution generally (if not universally) believed to predate the Norman Conquest. Germans saw British constitutionalists who were believers in the ancient liberties of Englishmen more than in liberty as such, believers in rights rather than in reason—though these believers did not believe that those ancient liberties were secure in the England of their own time. The virtues of this gothic England were publicized by the great scholars of Göttingen, themselves subjects of the British Hannoverian king from the middle of the eighteenth century on—like Gottfried Achenwall, who praised the freedom of the English secured by the Revolution of 1688.[23] For C. D. Erhard the example of gothic England seemed to serve as the best rebuke to the raging French revolutionaries—in the preface to his translation of Algernon Sidney in 1793, he described how 1688 had been "the epoch of the political rebirth of the constitution" in Britain and the salvation of "British freedom."[24] The gothic English constitution, revived in America, inspired Duke Ernest of Gotha to believe that the League of Princes, a campaign to revive the Holy Roman Imperial constitution, had been a struggle against despotism comparable to the American Revolution.[25] The well-known anglophilia of the German romantics must be seen in the light of West European politics: we must recognize that the politics that defended

---

[20] J.G.A. Pocock, "Modes of Political and Historical Time," in idem, *Virtue, Commerce and History* (Cambridge, 1985), 95; idem, "Virtues, Rights and Manners," in ibid., 37–38.

[21] Cf. the discussion of the influence of the English "commonwealthman" tradition on the French in K. M. Baker, "A Script for the French Revolution."

[22] Haikala, *"Britische Freiheit,"* 42ff. and passim. For the influence of American political ideals, which during the American Revolution were often viewed with great sympathy in Germany, see generally Dippel, *Germany and the American Revolution.*

[23] G. Achenwall, *Staatsverfassung der Europäischen Reiche*, 3d ed. (Göttingen, 1756), 227. For Göttingen as the center of pro-English sentiment in Germany, see Haikala, *"Britische Freiheit,"* 14, and the literature cited there; cf. also Cappellini, *Systema Iuris,* 1:344–45.

[24] Erhard, "Vorrede," to A. Sidney, *Betrachtungen über die Regierungsformen*, 2 vols., translated by Erhard (Leipzig, 1793), 1:XXIX–XXX.

[25] Cf. Krieger, *German Idea of Freedom,* 19.

the Glorious Revolution and stirred the American Revolution were close to the politics of the romantic era in Germany, politics fought out on all sides over the true nature of the ancient constitution.

The German ancient constitution—that of the Holy Roman Empire as reformed in the sixteenth century—had had its champions all through the eighteenth century, though they had been weak. From 1690 on[26]—that is, from the moment the absolutist state sat astride France—there was indigenous constitutionalist opposition to state power in Germany just as there was in England. Absolutists encountered fear of enlightened practices and enthusiasm for the old corporate order. The Reichspublizisten, whose late seventeenth-century rise I have already described,[27] fought tenaciously against the territorial princes who extricated themselves from the many legal restrictions of the old empire and worked to constitute themselves, like Louis XIV, as supreme rulers. The greatest of the Reichspublizisten, J. J. Moser, for example, attempted to reduce the aspirations of absolutism to pettiness and self-indulgence:

> More and more the urge to be "sovereign" is mastering electoral and princely courts: how many soldiers does one have? *as many as one wants*; how many taxes does one order? *as many as one wants*; how many excises and duties does one impose? *as many as one wants*; in short: one does what one wants, and the territorial estates and subjects can howl. . . .

As this attitude spread, said Moser, the old imperial constitution could in many places be found only on impotent pieces of paper and old documents.[28] Moser was a clever polemicist and a courageous man, but he could not have felt much hope; he was trying to stem a very powerful tide.

But in the late 1780s the situation began to change. Opposition to the princely state became more potent, more widespread, more filled with passionate love for pre-absolutist forms and traditions. Talk of the beauty of the old constitution became common; more important, this talk took on a wholly new elegiac tone. Moser had expressed himself with the indignation of a lawyer who saw long-established rights being violated. His romantic successors expressed more than indignation and viewed the old constitution as more than just established rights. They thought of the old constitution with longing and love, with a yearning for simpler times. And they began to consider how they could reconstruct German public life along pre-absolutist lines.

[26] See generally Hammerstein, *Jus und Historie.*

[27] Above, pp. 61–62.

[28] J. J. Moser, *Von der Landeshoheit derer Teutschen Reichsstände überhaupt* (Frankfurt/Leipzig, 1773), 253, 257.

It was a Habsburg failure, the collapse of the Bavarian schemes of the emperor Joseph II, that gave the romanticism of imperial revival its political opening. Joseph was not a man of the old Reich; his policies often seemed calculated to aggrandize the power of the Habsburgs at the expense of the empire, and, indeed, aimed at converting Joseph himself from emperor into territorial prince. Whether or not he had any intention of abandoning the emperorship, the idea that he might do so was plausible within the politics of absolutism. For absolutism was a thing of the territorial princes; it was distinctly opposed to the old elaborate corporate legal order of the Reich. But in 1787 Joseph's plans to acquire Bavaria for the Habsburg house were checked by the so-called League of Princes, which presented itself as the guardian of the imperial constitution. No doubt the League of Princes was largely engaged in a kind of cynical manipulation of tradition, but its talk of the old constitution caused an intellectual sensation. Lawyers and publicists everywhere began to speak of old institutional traditions, of German freedom.

This literature preached a revival of an ancient German constitution that was, to be sure, very different from the ancient constitution of the English.[29] The German territorial estates general were historically weak[30]; conversely, the German princes were historically strong. The principal counterweight to the German princes had historically been not parliament but the emperor. Accordingly, in the "ancient constitution" of the Holy Roman Empire the emperor, and not any assembly, was viewed as the prime guardian of freedom. In 1787 and 1788 numerous pamphleteers raised the old standard of "imperial justice," of imperial power as guarantor of impartiality and freedom in a system of quasi-independent states. The emperor was, in a proper constitutional order, a judge, not a wielder of power, and the Reichskammergericht was the "shield of German freedom."[31] The Reich meant civil rights for Germans, said C. E. Weisse in 1790; only in the Reich, wrote the leading constitutional theorist of the day, C. F. Häberlin, were German citizens protected from the depredations of their princes.[32]

The abrupt death of Joseph in 1790 brought the renewed enthusiasm

[29] Cf. H. Heffter, *Die Deutsche Selbstverwaltung im Neunzehnten Jahrhundert: Geschichte der Ideen und Institutionen* (Stuttgart, 1950), 102.

[30] Cf. F. L. Carsten, *Princes and Parliaments in Germany* (Oxford, 1959), e.g., 441: "The struggle between princes and Estates had much in common with the conflicts between crown and Parliament, but the outcome was usually the opposite."

[31] Thus [Julius von Soden] *Teutschland muss einen Kaiser haben* (1788), as quoted in Gagliardo, *Reich and Nation*, 101–2.

[32] Weisse, *Von den Vortheilen der teutschen Reichsverbindung* (1790), Häberlin, "Über die Güte der deutschen Staatsverfassung," in *Braunschweigisches Magazin*, October 1792, reprinted in *Deutsche Monatsschrift*, n.s., 1 (1793): 3–33. Both discussed in Gagliardo, *Reich and Nation*, 119–22.

for the sixteenth century constitution to the pitch of fervor. For, with the death of an emperor, a new constitutional settlement—a so-called electoral capitulation—was to be negotiated with his successor. The constitutional revivalism that focused on the new electoral capitulation[33] triggered several years of a political literature of longing for the old patrimonial state and of praise for the old constitution, a literature that came to an end only with the triumph of the French armies. The constitutionalist movement that grew up in these years put its faith in three political measures, all designed to limit the power of the territorial princes. First was the cult of the person of the emperor, who was seen as a counterweight to princely power. Alongside this external check, Germans sought to limit the power of territorial princes within the princes' own governments by guaranteeing that the servants of princes would be independent of their whims—a kind of governmental revolt against Lipsianism. Last, and most important for the professorial revival, Germans sought to revive the old imperial institutions of justice.

As the enthusiastic constitutionalist movement gripped politically minded Germans, a new ethic took hold, one that revolved around establishing the independence of high officials from the person of the prince. Officials were now to regard themselves as *Staatsdiener*, "servants of the state," rather than *Fürstendiener*, "servants of the prince."[34] A great German project to neutralize the state, to take it out of the control of the princes, was underway,[35] and Lipsian discipline was at an end. This reform movement had two distinct strains, a late Enlightenment strain in Prussia, and an early romantic strain in the smaller states.

The Prussian movement has been the better known since Dilthey. The powerful Prussian state of the northeast was little touched by the romantic movement for anti-absolutist reform. Rather, Prussia experienced the attempt to build a "rule of law" in Prussia without sacrificing the absolute power of the Prussian king. Under the leadership of C. G. Svarez, who betrayed the influence of a natural-law tradition that dated back to Wolff[36] and was a firm believer in royal power,[37] the Prussian lawyers and

[33] On the excitement surrounding the electoral capitulation, see Aretin, *Heiliges Römisches Reich*, 1:229ff.; Gagliardo, *Reich and Nation*, 104ff.

[34] See K.G.A. Jeserich, "Die Entstehung des öffentlichen Dienstes," in Jeserich, H. Pohl, G.-C. Unruh, *Deutsche Verwaltungsgeschichte* (Stuttgart, 1983), 2:302ff., and the literature cited there. See also Cappellini, *Systema Iuris*, 1:144.

[35] M. Stolleis, "Verwaltungslehre und Verwaltungswissenschaft," in Jeserich et al., *Deutsche Verwaltungsgeschichte*, 2:58ff. The same new belief in a neutralized state encouraged new notions of judicial independence.

[36] Cf. E. Hellmuth, *Naturrechtsphilosophie und bürokratischer Werthorizont*, Veröffentlichungen des Max-Planck-Instituts für Geschichte, vol. 78 (Göttingen, 1985).

[37] Cf. H. Conrad, *Rechtsstaatliche Bestrebungen im Absolutismus* (Arbeitsgemeinschaft

politicians attempted to establish, as a matter of enlightened reason, that the king should not interfere in his officials' administration of justice. This attempt to pit enlightenment against absolutism, which was uncommonly successful[38] has long been viewed as the movement that laid the foundation for the modern German Rechtsstaat, with its conception of high officials as Staatsdiener rather than Fürstendiener, servants of the state and not of the prince.[39]

But the enlightened Prussian movement was by no means the only one at work. Germans of the smaller states, committed to the new romanticism, were also attempting to limit absolutism on wholly different (often Montesquieuian[40]) grounds; indeed, they explicitly defined their work in opposition to the efforts of the Prussians.[41] In the south, a program of establishing independent corps of Staatsdiener was laid out in the 1790s by Roman lawyers like L. T. Spittler and Hofacker in Württemberg, defenders of *das alte Recht*, the old law.[42] In northern and central Germany a similar program was the work of imperial revivalists like Häberlin or J. A. Remer of Helmstedt, on the one hand, and the great historians of Göttingen, on the other. These men were medievalists, romantic idealizers of the princely states of the past. Remer delivered an address in 1790 that showed how much the constitutionalist movement had ceased to base itself on the legalism of Reichspublizisten like J. J. Moser[43] and how much it had begun to draw its ideological force from an idealization of the Mid-

---

für Forschung des Landes Nordrhein-Westfalen, Abt. Geisteswissenschaft, Hft. 95, 1961), 21.

[38] Cf. most recently C.B.A. Behrens, *Society, Government and the Enlightenment: The Experience of Eighteenth-Century France and Prussia* (New York, 1985).

[39] See esp. W. Dilthey, "Das Allgemeine Landrecht," in *Gesammelte Schriften*, 19 vols. (Leipzig, 1958), 12:131–207; H. Conrad, *Die Geistigen Grundlagen des Allgemeinen Landrechts* (Arbeitsgemeinschaft für Forschung des Landes Nordrhein-Westfalen, Abt. Geisteswissenschaft, Hft. 77, 1957); D. Merten, "Rechtsstaatliche Anfänge im Preußischen Absolutismus," *Deutsches Verwaltungsblatt* 96 (1981): 701–9. Cf. O. Hintze, "Preußens Entwicklung zum Rechtsstaat," in *Gesammelte Abhandlungen*, vol. 3, *Regierung und Verwaltung* (Göttingen, 1967), 151ff.

[40] For Montesquieuianism among several of these men, see R. Vierhaus, "Montesquieu in Deutschland: Zur Geschichte seiner Wirkung als politischer Schriftsteller im achtzehnten Jahrhundert," in *Collegium Philosophicum: Festschrift für J. Ritter* (Basel/Stuttgart, 1965), 403–37.

[41] Cf. J. G. Schlosser's constitutionalist critique of Prussian reform: *Briefe über die Gesezgebung überhaupt und den Entwurf des preussischen Gesezbuchs insbesondere* (Frankfurt a.M., 1789). Discussed in Cappellini, *Systema Iuris*, 2:240–56.

[42] Cf. E. Hölzle, *Das Alte Recht and die Revolution: Eine politische Geschichte Württembergs in der Revolutionszeit, 1789–1805* (Munich/Berlin, 1931), 76ff. Both Spittler and Hofacker, like many of their forbears in the customary-law tradition, confused customary and natural law. On Spittler, see Cappellini, *Systema Iuris*, 1:332ff.; on Hofacker, see idem, 1:591, 596ff.

[43] Cf. above, p. 73.

dle Ages. Remer—who was quoted with approval by Moser's learned successor, Häberlin—declared that princes of the middle-sized German states had the great advantage in forming good governments, for as their realms were small they could be "fathers to their subjects." As for princes of larger realms, their success depended on their having "wise and benevolent servants."[44] In the romantic era, legal argument had given way to medievalizing sentimentality. But sentimentality can make for strong politics. J. J. Moser's son, the penetrating F. C. Moser, certainly believed so. Five years after these statements by Remer, he attempted to build a new ethic of independent "state service" that would replace the old submissiveness of absolutist courtiers. Moser, who had argued for many years that princes had come to view themselves too much as military commanders, now insisted that they must return to their old feudal self-conception—and that their servants, too, must cultivate the old mentality of the feudal state:

What the old princes believed, and what the thoughtful ones still believe, is this: that they are not all-wise, or all-knowing, or all-powerful; that they need, for the government of their house and their people, advice and aid. . . .

What the old princely world believed, and what the thoughtful princely world still believes, is this: that their advisers, helpers and servants, have not only the right but also the duty to form opinions [*Vorstellungen*] about the life and the acts of their prince, whether with or without or against his will, whether they are asked or not; whence the beautiful pledge in the customary oath: *Seinem Herrn treu, hold und gewärtig zu seyn, seinen Schaden zu warnen, seinen Nutzen und Bestes aber zu befördern. [To be faithful, pleasing, and attentive to his Lord, to caution him about matters that may harm him, but to advance that which is useful and good for him.]*[45]

The elder Moser had always spoken of the rigor of the old law; by the mid-1790s the younger Moser was attempting to rest a new ethic of state service on the beauty of the old pledges.[46] Romanticism had begun to make its passionate, strangely diffident political claims.

The new climate brought on a revival of sixteenth-century institutions. As the Empire regained its political strength in the romantic atmosphere,

---

[44] Remer, "Die charakteristischen Züge des Bildes eines vorzüglichen Regenten der mittlern deutschen Staaten." Quoted by Häberlin, "Über die Güte der deutschen Staatsverfassung," 31–32.

[45] Moser, "Das Kabinet der Könige und Fürsten," in *Politische Wahrheiten*, 1:211–12.

[46] This attempt to revive an old feudal ethic of loyalty cum independence is surely best understood within the context of Max Weber's interpretation of the rise of central European bureaucracy as a transformation of the "patrimonial" household of the feudal king into a system in which state servants were loyal to, but independent from, the prince. Cf. Weber, *Economy and Society*, 3:1085–87.

so too did the Reichskammergericht.[47] The Reichskammergericht had remained a favorite of Reichspublizisten throughout the century, and from the middle of the eighteenth century on, under their influence, young lawyers began to spend their student years of wandering at imperial courts rather than in Holland.[48] From the beginning the imperial revival was associated with a revival of the Reichskammergericht. Already in 1787 the Reichskammergericht was acting to curb abuses of princely power. A. L. Schlözer published an account of the court's decision, and it became a favorite of the constitutionalist Häberlin.[49] As the imperial revival proceeded, the publicists who declared the emperor to be the supreme judge and the empire to be a system of justice rather than of power reserved special praise for the imperial courts.[50] The old court figured prominently in the negotiations for the electoral capitulation of 1790. Häberlin, who had himself been sent to the negotiations on official business,[51] declared that no clause of the emerging document was as important as that concerning the imperial high courts. For without "impartial" justice, wrote Häberlin, speaking in terms familiar in the sixteenth century, no country is happy.[52] And, indeed, the Reichskammergericht had active champions at the negotiations.[53] In subsequent years, Häberlin followed Schlözer's lead by publishing, in his new magazine, the Staats-Archiv, accounts of the newly assertive court under the regular heading "German Imperial Justice." The first edition of the Staats-Archiv carried excerpts from court decisions of 1787, 1792, 1793, and 1794 vindicating the rights of German peasants against landlords and princes—"revolutionary trials," as Häberlin called them, that typified the German reform movement's faith that resuscitated imperial institutions could render justice in Germany without French upheavals.[54] These "revolutionary trials" established one

---

[47] See Aretin, Heiliges Römisches Reich, 1:97ff.

[48] Hammerstein, Jus und Historie, 48 n. 31.

[49] A. L. von Schlözer, "Deutsche Reichsjustiz," in Stats-Anzeigen, vol. 11, Heft 43 (1787): 257–71. Cited by Häberlin, "Güte der deutschen Staatsverfassung," 6–7.

[50] [Von Soden], Teutschland muss einen Kaiser haben, cited in Gagliardo, Reich and Nation, 101–2.

[51] C.F. Häberlin, Dedication, in idem, Pragmatische Geschichte der neuesten kaiserlichen Wahlcapitulation und der an kaiserliche Majestät erlassenen kurfürstlichen Collegialschreiben (Leipzig, 1792) (without page numbers).

[52] Ibid., 223–24. It is interesting to note that according to Häberlin, the most hotly debated phase of the negotiations concerned relations with the Vatican (ibid., 198ff.). It was still, in Germany, the age of Febronianism.

[53] Notably, electoral Braunschweig. See ibid., 231 and often.

[54] Häberlin, "Teutsche Reichsjustiz," in Staats-Archiv 1, no. 1 (1796): 83–90. On Häberlin and the Staats-Archiv, see Walter, Zusammenbruch, 37. Häberlin's faith in the Reichskammergericht as the guardian of social justice in Germany was shaken but not broken by the court's 1796 vote to punish a litigant for using the phrase "inalienable human rights" in his complaint. See Häberlin, "Darf der Ausdruck: unveräusserliche Menschenrechte in Satz-

of the many early ties between legal romanticism and agrarian reform that I will explore in detail below.[55] During the same years the Reichskammergericht intervened to protect the independence of state servants, as government officials had begun to view themselves.[56] The old court had reemerged as a political actor.

The Reichskammergericht died with the Empire in 1806, but a renewed faith in the sixteenth century professorial institution of Aktenversendung continued strong throughout the Napoleonic era; indeed, the law faculties gained strength in every respect. Like the Reichskammergericht, Aktenversendung had energetic sponsorship among the princes who met to compose the electoral capitulation: electoral Braunschweig proposed a formal endorsement of Aktenversendung as a protection for subjects involved in litigation with their governments.[57] That a good word should be spoken for Aktenversendung at such a momentous constitutional moment reflects a startling turnaround in the fortunes of the professorial institution. Until recently, most states had worked to abolish the Spruchkollegien; even in Hannover, where there had been no abolition, only a few years before a leading lawyer was still reporting that the institution was falling into disuse.[58] But as "Imperial Patriotism" soared, the imperial professoriate suddenly recovered its institutional sense of self. In 1804 N. T. Gönner, an eminent constitutionalist, could declare Aktenversendung to be the "palladium of German freedom"[59]—the same phrase that imperial revivalists had used ten years earlier for the Reichskammergericht. As I shall discuss below, this revival of Aktenversendung would go on gathering strength for three decades.

THE REVIVAL OF THE LAW PROFESSORS AND THE NEW ROME

The Reichskammergericht and Aktenversendung were historically professorial institutions, and their revival was symptomatic of a more general revival of the law faculties. Heidelberg's law faculty underwent an his-

---

schriften bey dem Reichskammergericht nicht gebraucht werden?" *Staats-Archiv* 3, no. 11 (1797): 365–68.

[55] On the "revolutionary trials" in the Reichskammergericht and in other courts, see below, Chapter V.

[56] E.g., Häberlin, "Justizrath Kober wider den Fürsten von Hohenloh-Schillingsfürst," in *Staats-Archiv* 3, no. 9 (1797): 102–5 (Reichskammergericht directs prince to allow state servant hearing before "impartial" commission).

[57] Häberlin, *Pragmatische Geschichte*, 280–81.

[58] Cf. D. G. Struben [sometimes Strube], "Bedenken 112: Von Verschickung der Acten in Peinlichen Sachen," in *Rechtliche Bedenken*, 2d ed., 3 pts. (Hannover, 1787), 2:329–32.

[59] N. T. Gönner, *Handbuch des deutschen gemeinen Prozeßes*, 2d ed. (Erlangen, 1804), 1:279. Cited in Bülow, *Ende des Aktenversendungsrechts*, 1.

toric renovation beginning in 1803.[60] Starting in 1790, law surpassed theology as the most popular faculty in the Prussian universities.[61] These
were institutional signs of a revival of professorial tradition. Perhaps
most significant, the law faculties began to assume their central place in
the system of the *Staatsdienerschaft*: to protect their status as state servants, the new bureaucrats began receiving legal protections against arbitrary discharge by princes.[62]

A new spirit of enthusiasm infused the German universities at the same
time. And with this university revival came a new turn in the systematic
tradition in German law. For the romantic movement in law was by no
means an anti-systematic one. To be sure, the rebellion against the Enlightenment in German law was often a rebellion against the ideas of
Christian Wolff and his followers (whose method the leading romantic
lawyer Gustav Hugo called a "plague" on German scholarship[63]). Nevertheless, it never became a rebellion against the systematic ideal that
Wolff had made his own early in the century. Quite the contrary. As the
enthusiastic spirit of the period grew, German lawyers attempted not to
abolish the systematic method, but rather to reform and revivify it.[64] The
hope of lawyers in this "era of late natural law"[65] was to introduce into
their systematic treatments a knowledge both of the particular details of
the historical world and of the practical wisdom of everyday legal problems.[66] Like the philosopher to whom many of them declared allegiance—
Immanuel Kant—they hoped to find some means of being empiricists and
deductivists at the same time, thinkers capable of beginning with the contingent things of this world but also of rising to some systematic understanding that would permit them to draw true conclusions without relying exclusively on empirical investigation.[67] Indeed, Kant's work loosed
in the universities a new excitement about the possibilities of legal scholarship, and a large volume of innovative work appeared.

[60] See generally J. Rückert, "Heidelberg um 1804, oder: die erfolgreiche Modernisierung
der Jurisprudenz durch Thibaut, Savigny, Heise, Martin, Zachariä, u.a.," in F. Strack, ed.,
Heidelberg im säkularen Umbruch: Traditionsbewußtsein und Kulturpolitik um 1800
(Stuttgart, 1987), 83–116.

[61] Brunschwig, *Enlightenment and Romanticism*, 169–70.

[62] Cf. W. Bleek, *Von der Kameralausbildung zum Juristenprivileg* (Berlin, 1972).

[63] Quoted in Stühler, *Erneuerung der Rechtswissenschaft*, 135.

[64] The remaking of the German systematic tradition in this period is the subject of Cappellini, *Systema Iuris*, and Schröder, *Wissenschaftstheorie*. Both should be consulted for
wide-ranging and learned treatments.

[65] Cf. H. Thieme, "Die Zeit des Späten Naturrechts," 202–63.

[66] See generally Schröder, *Wissenschaftstheorie*, with detailed discussions of a large number of important lawyers of the period.

[67] For Kant's simultaneously deductivist and empiricist views of law and his influence
among professional lawyers, see Schröder, *Wissenschaftstheorie*, 147ff.; Cappellini, *Systema Iuris*, 1:146ff.

In this atmosphere of renewal, romantic lawyers perceived their world, with its many moribund early modern institutions, as a place alive with possibilities of renovation. For example, K. S. Zachariä, one of the most prominent of German legal Kantians,[68] received his first professorship in this period at Wittenberg, which had been Germany's leading university as the home of Luther and Melanchthon, but which now, in the 1790s, was a backwater. There Zachariä became a member both of a busy Spruchkollegium[69] and of a territorial court that still had the form of a sixteenth-century institution. This latter court had, in the old manner, a *Gelehrtenbank* and a *Herrenbank*—a "scholars' bench" and a "lords' bench." Zachariä, sitting as one of six scholars on the court, had the opportunity to experience the whole range of legal life in Saxony. A man of his time—one of reform and revival both—he saw in Saxon institutions both ugly feudal remnants and the tradition of true imperial justice: "It is true, the knights and the cities enjoyed privileges whose disadvantageous consequences were all too noticeable. But the justice was impartial [unpartheyisch] and administered gently in criminal matters."[70] These institutions needed only a few simple reforms to allow the true classical spirit to enter into them. Zachariä was convinced that once oral procedure (mündliches Verfahren) was introduced to replace the written procedure then used, Greek and Roman rhetoric would revive in Germany.[71] When the young lawyers of the 1790s looked upon sixteenth-century institutions, they saw the possibility of a revived Antiquity in a reformed Empire.[72]

The Discovery of the Antonines

It was a new Antiquity they saw: the Rome of the Antonines, of the great age of imperial revival in the second century A.D. The Rome of the Antonines was the characteristic object of the enthusiasm of early romantic lawyers; the study of the Rome of the Antonines linked imperial revival and the revival of the professorial corporate tradition with a characteristic neohumanist romanticism that began with Gustav Hugo and culmi-

---

[68] See, e.g., the discussion of Cappellini, *Systema Iuris*, 1:144–73.

[69] K. S. Zachariä, *Biographischer und Juristischer Nachlaß* (Tübingen, 1843), 38.

[70] Ibid., 41.

[71] Ibid., 38. Zachariä's commitment to "mündliches Verfahren" reflected his larger commitment to a return to Germanic forms of justice, and his belief that Roman institutions had ultimately Germanic origins. Cf. below, p. 142.

[72] Baumgärtel, *Erlanger Juristenfakultät*, 105, notes that the Erlangen Spruchkollegium, departing from Enlightenment patterns of adjudication, relied on "the pure theory of Roman law" for the first time in 1790. This is difficult to evaluate, but it may be another early example of the revival of classical scholarship in tandem with the renewal of early modern institutions.

nated in the work of Savigny. The Roman civilization of the romantics was, for the first time, an Antonine civilization.

Finding the new Rome was not easy, for Rome played in general only a small part in the German romantic movement. It is familiar history that though they felt passion for Antiquity, the romantics felt passion emphatically for Greece and not for Rome. For Europeans in general, by contrast, Antiquity had always been first and foremost Roman Antiquity. Indeed, non-German Europe experienced a renaissance of Roman studies in the eighteenth century. The immediate forerunner of the cult of Greece associated with Winckelmann and Lessing was the new European (and especially English) cult of Roman architecture that marked the middle of this century: the discoveries of Pompeii and Herculaneum gave a powerful impulse to the neoclassical revival in architecture, a revival that brought Berlin its simple, grand, Romanizing Opera House.[73] Roman history, meanwhile, enjoyed a spectacular Europe-wide revival. Montesquieu and Gibbon set entirely new standards of research with their writings on Rome; Mably and others kept it alive as a political icon, maintaining Roman history as a kind of injunction to political action.[74]

But Germany was slow to join in in this European Roman revival. The absence of Germany from the scholarly and political rebirth of Rome before the 1790s was due in part to the influence of Conring. German lawyers and historians spread their energies thin throughout the eighteenth century—inevitably so, in a legal order that required them to be intimate with the historic rights of so many persons and corporations in Germany as well as with the difficult texts of the *Corpus Iuris*. Germany was the land of an immense scholarly eclecticism in all things, not only in law.[75] Accordingly, the great innovative currents in Roman-law scholarship ran outside Germany, for scholars could not afford to concentrate solely on Roman law.[76] In part the German neglect of Rome was the reverse of the medal of Greek neohumanism: even if Winckelmann had learned his idea of "edle Einfalt und stille Größe"—"noble simplicity and quiet grandeur"—from the Romanizing neoclassical movement, he made it famous as a Greek idea. And, under the sponsorship of Lessing, Klopstock, and

[73] Cf. F. Schnabel, *Deutsche Geschichte im Neunzehnten Jahrhundert*, 3d ed., 4 vols. (Freiburg i.B., 1947), 1:161–62.

[74] Cf. Baker, "Script for the French Revolution," 242–43.

[75] On the eclecticism of the polyhistors, see R.J.W. Evans, "Culture and Anarchy in the Empire," *Central European History* 18 (March 1985), 14–29; A. Grafton, "The World of the Polyhistors," ibid., 31–47.

[76] This was Hugo's diagnosis of the weakness of Roman-law scholarship in eighteenth-century Germany. Hugo, *Lehrbuch der Rechtsgeschichte bis auf unsere Zeiten* (Berlin, 1790), 231.

the other intellectual leaders of literary neohumanism, Greece became, in most minds, Germany's Antiquity.

Nevertheless, neohumanist lawyers needed a Rome. It was not until the imperial revival of the late 1780s that the lawyers of Göttingen broke the hold of Lipsianism, and discovered a new Rome in the Rome of the Antonines. Enlightenment authors had never been able to grapple satisfactorily with the Antonines.[77] For the German lawyers, the Antonines became intelligible in the 1790's, as imperial reform became their most pressing political cause. It was Gibbon who brought sudden color to the ancient epoch of imperial reform. His *Decline and Fall of the Roman Empire* opened with a description of the glory of the Rome of the Antonines:

> In the second century of the Christian Era, the Empire of Rome comprehended the fairest part of the earth, and the most civilised portion of mankind. . . . During a happy period (A.D. 98–180) of more than fourscore years, the public administration was conducted by the virtue and abilities of Nerva, Trajan, Hadrian, and the two Antonines.[78]

Germans of the decade of imperial revival were enthralled by Gibbon's picture. D. H. Hegewisch of Kiel, writing in 1800 of the age of the Antonines as *The Epoch of Roman History Most Fortunate for Humanity*, began his book by adverting to the intellectual sensation Gibbon had created: "You ask, dear friend, if one can prove that the period of Roman history that begins with the emperor Nerva and ends with the death of Marcus Aurelius was really such a happy period for humanity as Gibbon claims in his famous work."[79] Hegewisch affirmed that the age of the Antonines had been happy—and not only, as his readers might suspect, for the imperial party in the city of Rome, but for all classes of the Empire.[80] The Roman constitution had been a model of "Harmonie"[81]—the influence of Leibniz's analysis of the Holy Roman Imperial constitution on Hegewisch can be clearly detected—and while the self-aggrandizing ambitions of princes had diminished the happiness of the Empire's peoples, nevertheless wise and self-restrained emperors like the Antonines

[77] Cf. A. D. Momigliano, "La Formazione della moderna storiografia sull'impero Romano," reprinted in *Contributo alla Storia degli Studi Classici* (Rome, 1955), 125: "descrizioni illuministiche dell'età degli Antonini . . . insoddisfatti."

[78] Gibbon, *Decline and Fall of the Roman Empire*, The Modern Library (New York, n.d.), 1:1. Cf. esp. Chapter 2 of Gibbon's book, "Of the Union and Internal Prosperity of the Roman Empire, in the Age of the Antonines."

[79] Hegewisch, *Über die für die Menschheit glücklichste Epoche in der Römischen Geschichte* (Hamburg, 1800), 1.

[80] Ibid.

[81] Ibid., 11–12.

had been able to bring into being a blessed state of affairs.[82] This was a Roman history for the new party in German politics, the party that hoped for constitutionalism through a revival of the old role of the emperor as a force for restraint. The example of Rome would now serve to inspire and strengthen German constitutionalism.

The new Roman history was perfectly tailored for a revival of the Roman-law professoriate. The revival of the sixteenth-century constitution promised also to be a revival of the sixteenth-century glory of professors. For the new emphasis on the Rome of the Antonines brought with it as an inevitable corollary a rereading of Pomponius on the ius respondendi.[83]

Pomponius's vague description of Hadrian's actions on behalf of the ancient lawyers—that he had restored an old order in which authority was "customarily not merely begged for but earned"—had not attracted much attention in Germany in the years before 1788. One great Roman lawyer, in the dark Lipsian years of the eighteenth century, had spoken a brief word in praise of Pomponius's Hadrian: J. G. Heineccius, the student of Thomasius who spent much of his career at Franeker. Heineccius is often mentioned as an important eighteenth-century precursor of Savigny. He was a learned and painstaking scholar of the Roman legal sources.[84] But even he had comparatively little to say. Like other scholars of his time, he cited Thomasius's "Warts" in devoting many words to Augustus's purposes in inventing the ius respondendi.[85] But Heineccius, writing in 1719, added an afterthought on Hadrian: "On Tiberius, see *L. 2 §47 D. de Orig.* [i.e., Pomponius's *Handbook*], from which passage it is also evident that Hadrian revived the old custom of granting the power of giving legal opinions to everybody who had confidence in his abilities."[86] Gibbon, a vocal admirer of Heineccius, repeated this reading of Pomponius without further elaboration in his famous Chapter 44, his history of Roman law.[87] Gibbon's Chapter 44, in turn, inspired the great revival of Roman-law scholarship in Germany that began with Gustav Hugo of Göttingen (who translated Gibbon's chapter) and culminated with Savigny.[88] Filtered through Gibbon, Heineccius's passing observa-

[82] Ibid., 12–13.

[83] Quoted above, p. 58.

[84] Cf. Stintzing-Landsberg, *Geschichte*, vol. 3, pt. 1, 197.

[85] J. G. Heineccius, *Antiquitatum Romanarum Jurisprudentiam Illustrantium Syntagma* (Strasbourg, 1741) (orig. 1719), 67ff. Cf. Heineccius, *Elementa Juris Civilis* (Utrecht, 1772), 1:15.

[86] Heineccius, *Antiquitatum*, 69.

[87] Gibbon, *Decline and Fall*, 2:338: "Hadrian restored the freedom of the profession to every citizen conscious of his abilities and knowledge," citing Heineccius.

[88] Cf. G. Marini, *L'Opera di Gustav Hugo nella Crisi del Giusnaturalismo Tedesco* (Milan, 1969), 14–15; Cappellini, *Systema Iuris*, 1:175ff.

tion on Hadrian triggered an explosion of interest in Hadrian and the Roman lawyers. Hadrian, the prince of reform, had given the scholars back their dignity, their place of ethical leadership in the legal world.

The Roman historiography of the lawyers began its shift of course under the changing winds of imperial politics in 1788, with the "De Consistorio Principum" of C. G. Haubold, professor at Leipzig, and a leading representative of the "elegant" tradition in German Roman-law scholarship.[89] Haubold's modest sixty-eight-page essay looked like any learned Latin dissertation of the usus modernus. But it embodied a new view of Rome and a new lesson for German jurisprudence. Haubold reviewed in detail the activities of the ancient Roman emperors as judges sitting in courts called "consistories" or "auditoriums." In itself, any essay on the adjudicative function of the Roman emperors would have been politically charged in 1788, when so much reforming commentary demanded that the emperor resume his sixteenth-century role as judge, not general. But Haubold did more: he radically departed from the Lipsian tradition that had dominated German historiography of Rome since the time of Thomasius. The most important constitutional developments had taken place, in Haubold's account, not under Augustus, but under Hadrian.[90] This seemingly innocuous shift of scholarly focus had weighty political implications. For in abandoning Augustus for Hadrian, Haubold was abandoning the era of the semi-mystical origins of imperial power in favor of the era of imperial reform. Moreover, the era of imperial reform, this second-century analogue of German politics was marked, in Haubold's account, by a new and increasingly heavy reliance on legal scholars in the process of adjudication.[91] Imperial reform and scholarly lawmaking—such was Haubold's lesson—went hand in hand.

Haubold was heeded at Göttingen, Germany's leading university, where C. G. Heyne and Gustav Hugo drew great conclusions from his new Hadrianic focus in Roman historiography. Jurists were no longer to be the agents of princely domination. Rather, the substitution of Hadrian for Augustus meant that jurists were the authors of their own power. It was no accident that Hugo and Heyne worked at Göttingen. This great new German university was located in Hannover, the German soil most favorable to imperial revival. Since the departure of its dukes for England in 1714, Hannover had been peculiarly free of princely absolutism; after 1760, when George III, the first of the Hannoverians to concentrate his

---

[89] C. G. Haubold, *De Consistorio Principum, Specimina II* (Leipzig, 1788–89). The second "specimen," published in 1789, is essentially an appendix to the main body of the work. For Haubold's place among the "elegant" jurists, see Stühler, *Erneuerung der Rechtswissenschaft*, 65.

[90] Haubold, *De Consistorio Principum*, 29ff.

[91] Ibid., esp. 52ff.

energies on Britain, acceded to the British crown, citizens of Hannover, left on their own, felt a particularly strong attachment to imperial tradition.[92] Göttingen, flourishing in the absence of princely interference, had an active and important Spruchkollegium, and C. G. Heyne was attracting brilliant pupils, notably F. A. Wolf. Thus F. C. Moser could praise Göttingen as an honorable guardian of constitutional tradition.[93] Hannover and Göttingen were both prime representatives of institutional constitutionalism and the natural homes of Roman law revival.[94]

In 1790, even as the representative of nearby Braunschweig spoke for Aktenversendung at the negotiations for the new electoral capitulation, Heyne addressed the anniversary convocation of Göttingen, taking as his topic the high honors of the Roman jurists, their status in ancient society, their power, and their true glory as the authors of Roman law.[95] Heyne—who was active as one of the publicistic praisers of the old constitution,[96] and who was himself one of the true authors of the stunning revival of classical culture in romantic Germany[97]—drew on the essay of Haubold as well as on new writings by Hugo to show the ancient lawyers in a new light as men of the greatest influence. The address was a vigorous and stylish reformulation of Haubold's Hadrianic revolution, his reorientation of Roman legal history to the second century. Heyne distinguished between the republican period, in which men had been accorded legal authority because of their social status, and the imperial period, in which

[92] Gagliardo, *Reich and Nation*, 10.

[93] Moser, *Patriotische Wahrheiten*, 1:125–26.

[94] Another noteworthy piece of anti-Lipsian Roman historiography to come out of Göttingen in this period took a different approach from that of Heyne and Hugo. This was the Montesquieuian essay of C. Meiners, entitled "Geschichte der Sitten der Römer in den beyden ersten Jahrhunderten nach Christi geburt," which appeared in the *Göttingisches Historisches Magazin* 5 (1789), esp. 372: "Der Untergang der Freyheit unter den Römern, und die auf den Ruinen der Republik errichtete unumschränkte Allein-Herrschaft der Kaiser war nicht so wohl die Wirkung des unersättlichen Ehrgeitzes einiger nach unrechtmässiger Gewalt strebender Mit-Bürger, als vielmehr der bisherigen Schicksale und gegenwärtigen Lage der Republik, besonders der Feilheit, und Nichtswürdigkeit des Römischen Pöbels, der Ohnmacht des Senats, und der Raubsucht, und anderer verderblicher Laster der Grossen und Mächtigen des Volks. Wenn also auch kein Cäsar, kein August, und Tiber geboren worden wären, so würde dennoch Allein-Herrschaft in Rom entstanden, und allgemein gewünscht worden seyn." For Montesquieu's influence in Göttingen, see Cappellini, *Systema Iuris*, 1:212ff; A. Buschmann, "Ursprung und Grundlagen der geschichtlichen Rechtswissenschaft: Untersuchungen und Interpretationen zur Rechtslehre Gustav Hugos" (diss., Münster, 1963), 116ff.

[95] Heyne, "Honores Iurisconsultis habiti ab Impp. Romanis" in *Opuscula Academica* (Göttingen, 1796), 4:211–30 (orig. 1790).

[96] Cf. Heyne, "Über Freyheits-Revolutionen," in *Deutsche Monatsschrift* (August, 1790), esp. 325.

[97] See A. Grafton, "Prolegomena to F. A. Wolf," *Journal of the Warburg and Courtauld Institutes* 44 (1981): 101–29.

men had been accorded social status because of their legal learning. Throughout the imperial period, said Heyne, respect for and influence of the scholars grew.[98] Finally, the evolution of legal scholarly authority created the need for constitutional change. This need was met by Hadrian's transferral of power from the senate to his own council, which was predominantly made up of scholars.[99] From then on, knowlege of the law by itself led to the highest honors.[100] Thus Heyne, greatly elaborating on Heineccius's reading of Pomponius, located the source of legal authority not in the "august" power of the emperors,[101] but in the learning of the scholars themselves; the Hadrianic reforms were, as it were, merely a reflection of the growth of acumen among the jurists, the constitution was a superstructure on the base of legal learning. Heyne went on to connect this high imperial constitutional-legal tradition directly to the scholarly revival of his own day. The years after Alexander Severus were bad ones for the scholars and for law, which had passed the years of its great efflorescence. But the rise of the late imperial law schools in the age of Constantine maintained the scholarly tradition of ancient Rome, whose heirs now congregated in the hall of Göttingen where Heyne spoke.[102] Rome and Roman-law scholarship were still alive in the German university.[103]

While Heyne worked to enliven Roman-law scholarship, his colleague Gustav Hugo worked to sacralize it. Hugo was the single most important Romanist lawyer of the decade, and one of the most important lawyers in Germany for decades after. In his youth he was a leading disseminator of the work of Montesquieu and Gibbon in Germany; in his old age, he would still be prominent enough to attract an attack by the young Karl Marx. Newly appointed at Göttingen in the late 1780s, Hugo was deeply caught up, as Heyne was not, in the new romantic philosophy of the time—indeed, he cultivated a kind of romantic poet's timidity about power[104] that set him apart from most of the imperial reformers with whose cause he allied himself. When in 1790 he published his *Textbook of Legal History up to the Present*, a conspectus of the entire history of Roman-law doctrine, past and present, Hugo declared the book to be

[98] Heyne, "Honores," 215ff.

[99] Ibid., 218–20.

[100] Ibid., 220.

[101] On the "august" legal power of the emperors, cf. above p. 56.

[102] Heyne, "Honores," 227–29.

[103] Hugo later published a German-language version of Heyne's convocation address on the ancient jurists. "Herr Hofrath Heyne über die Ehrenbezeugungen welche den Römischen Rechtsgelehrten unter den Kaisern wiederfuhren," in *Hugos Civilistisches Magazin* 1, no. 4 (1791): 477–89.

[104] On Hugo's attitude, see Cappellini, *Systema Iuris*, 1:180–81, and esp. Schröder, *Wissenschaftstheorie*, 155ff. For this attitude as typical of Romantics, see generally Schmitt, *Politische Romantik*.

modeled on the doctrinal histories of the church historians. It was his
intention to write a history, though an unabashedly critical one, of the
Church Fathers of jurisprudence.[105] This "Church History" was written
with a shrewd eye to the politics of the Holy Roman Empire. Hugo belonged with his whole heart to the imperial revival.[106] He also espoused
anti-Enlightenment views that would, a decade and a half later, become
internationally associated with his great follower Friedrich Carl von Savigny. Indeed, the imperial revival belonged, in Hugo's mind, entirely to
the great rebellion against the Enlightenment: Wolff, as Hugo put it con-
temptuously in 1797, would have tried to demonstrate both the new
French constitution (*constitution*) and the constitution of the Holy Roman Empire (*Verfassung*) a priori.[107] In his summary of the modern history of Roman law, the plotting of the German emperors and the plotting
of the German princes both received sharp words. On the whole, the state
of the Empire looked bleak to Hugo. The Reichspublizisten had bravely
defended German freedom against the emperors since the Peace of Westphalia, but the despotism of the territorial lords had nevertheless grown
at the expense of the freedoms of their subjects;[108] now the old Reich was
growing weaker before the territorial princes.[109] Moreover, the princely
codification movement, which was so strong as Hugo wrote, seemed, in
the romantic parlance of the day, to signify that the spirit of the age had
turned away from Roman law and from scholarship in general: "The new
codes offer, perhaps, further evidence that learned knowledge of law has
fallen off as sterile reasoning [*Raisonniren*—a catchphrase for Enlightenment approaches] about legal propositions has become more common,
otherwise one would not have felt a need for the codes." One might even
be led to suppose, wrote Hugo, that the Germans were abandoning Roman law at the same moment that they were embracing classical literature
in the triumphs of the past fifty years. However, "it is almost impossible
that Roman law not benefit, now that ancient literature is cultivated
among us with infinitely more taste than ever."[110] This was Hugo's answer to the trials of the Empire: the literary revival of Antiquity gave him
faith that scholars of Roman law could successfully step in where the
Reichspublizisten had failed, as the defenders of German freedoms. The

[105] Hugo, "Vorrede" (without page numbers), to *Lehrbuch*, [1], [3]–[4], main text, 2. For
the importance of Hugo's work in establishing the periodization of Roman law, see Buschmann, "Ursprung und Grundlagen," 26.

[106] Hugo's philosophy of the "harmonious" constitution, full of the language of the sixteenth century that became so widely popular in the 1790s, is summarized in Marini, *Gustav Hugo*, 27–28.

[107] Quoted in Stühler, *Erneuerung der Rechtswissenschaft*, 135.

[108] Hugo, *Lehrbuch*, 240.

[109] Ibid., 249.

[110] Ibid., 249.

power of the enthusiasm abroad in Germany seemed to silence all political doubts.

Like Heyne, Hugo borrowed from Haubold[111] the image of Rome that best suited his political hopes, that of a Rome whose focal point lay in the reign of Hadrian. The classical years of Roman jurisprudence, in his anti-Lipsian rendition, began before Augustus, in the late Republican age, and reached their intellectual peak in the age of the Antonines, when Romans shook off Augustus's influence.[112] Hugo denied outright the Lipsian account of Augustus's reign. Augustus had never destroyed republican jurisprudence. Hadrian, too, had his central place.[113] Indeed, Hadrian had had no choice but to recognize the growing merit of the lawyers: like Heyne, Hugo emphasized that the scholars had risen high by their own strength, until Hadrian, who "exercised his activity [primarily] in personal supervision of the governors and professors" of the empire,[114] felt forced to acknowledge their de facto power. Moreover, wrote Hugo (again like Heyne, tracing the high imperial tradition into his own times) the success of Roman law in Germany had been, similarly, no more than the product of the age: Maximilian and the estates, when they established the Reichskammergericht in 1495, had simply acknowledged the fact that the people had already embraced learned law. Hugo returned to his favorite analogy, theology, in summarizing the grand lesson of his history—that scholarship is wholly independent of power: "Scholarship is never improved by an imperial law, or by a cabinet decree, any more than theology is improved by a council. The spirit of the age renders all commands either ineffective or irrelevant."[115] This was Hugo's Holy Roman Empire: a church whose living magistrates were the professors, heirs to and guardians of the old imperial spirit against its new imperial and territorial enemies, a church that would inevitably reform itself to fit its priesthood.[116]

Thus, in the era of crisis and renewal for the Holy Roman Empire, the Göttingen school formed, under the banner of Hadrianic Rome, to provide a classicizing vanguard for constitutional renewal. The influence of this school could be found in virtually any German Roman historian writing by the beginning of the 1800s. For example, Hegewisch, in his historical allegory of princely constitutionalism, did not neglect the jurists. He,

[111] Hugo's admiration for Haubold is noted in Marini, *Hugo*, 75.

[112] Cf. Hugo's chart of the ages of Roman law in the *Lehrbuch*, 5.

[113] Ibid., 95, 106ff.

[114] Ibid., 116.

[115] Ibid., 228.

[116] For a parallel attempt to theologize Roman law, cf. the distinguished J. G. Schlosser's contribution to the first number of Hugo's *Civilistisches Magazin*. Schlosser suggested that jurists should study pure Roman law just as theologians should study the Old Testament. Schlosser, "Über das Studium des Reinen Römischen Rechts," *Hugos Civilistisches Magazin*, 4th ed. (Berlin, 1823), 20–21, 32, 47 (orig. 1791).

too, still accepted the Lipsian account of the events of the reign of Augustus. But where the Lipsian jurists had admired Augustus, Hegewisch condemned him. And where Enlightenment historians in general had neglected Hadrian, Hegewisch made him the hero of a juristic renovation in Rome.[117] Other historians and lawyers also accepted the Göttingen Rome. C. L. Neuber, thanking Haubold and citing Hugo, composed a biographical history of "the classic figures of jurisprudence" that followed Hugo's chronology, beginning in the republican period and reaching its high point in the age of the Antonines.[118] Neuber cited Hume for the proposition that only jurisprudence had survived into the imperial era as the embodiment of a living republican tradition.[119] The new interpretation, so much the common coin of German historiography, appeared in the universal history of J. A. Remer of Helmstedt as well,[120] and in the legal polemics of N. T. Gönner.[121] A new anti-Lipsian orthodoxy was in place.

CONCLUSION

In the end, the Göttingen Roman-law movement could not have carried great political weight. Men who believed that constitutional change

[117] Hegewisch, *Glücklichste Epoche*, 99–100: "Von den ältesten Zeiten der Republik her wurden die Rechtsgelehrten häufig consulirt, und sie ertheilten ihre Gutachten über vorkommende Fälle. . . . August, welcher wußte, wie viel auf die Erklärung der Gesetze ankam, die noch in republicanischen Zeiten gegeben waren, um alles Andenken an jene Zeiten zu vertilgen und den Wunsch nach ihrer Wiederherstellung zu unterdrücken, schränkte die vorher allgemeine Befugniß eines jeden Juristen dergleichen Gutachten zu ertheilen, auf eine gewisse Zahl derer ein, auf die er Vertrauen setzte. . . . Hadrian gab jene Befugniß wieder frey; 'es müsse,' sagte er, 'kein Privilegium seyn, was eigentlich die Pflicht erfahrner Juristen wäre.' " Hadrian himself, declared Hegewisch, knew his law quite well, and sat in judgment in his court, where he always chose the most experienced legal scholars as his colleagues. Ibid., 97.

[118] Neuber, *Die Juristischen Classiker*, XLV (acknowledgment of Haubold), e.g., 120 (citation to Hugo). Neuber's book is discussed by Schulz, *Geschichte der römischen Rechtswissenschaft*, 117 n. 2.

[119] Neuber, *Die Juristischen Classiker*, 119, quoting Hume's *History of England* (London, 1763), 3:314. Hume's influence on Hugo is noted by Marini, *Hugo*, 14–15, and Cappellini, *Systema Iuris*, 1:192.

[120] J. A. Remer, *Darstellung der historischen Welt durch alle Jahrhunderte* (Berlin/Stettin, 1801), 91: "Die Rechtsgelehrten fingen seit dem punischen Kriege an, sie [the twelve tables] zu commentiren, und Responsa darüber zu ertheilen. Servius Sulpitius gab die Rechtsgelehrsamkeit zu Ciceros Zeiten eine scientifische Gestalt." The contribution of the classical jurists had been in producing reliable compilations of the laws of the Empire, whose "Menge" was " eine der härtesten Geißeln des Reichs." Ibid., 92.

[121] Cf. Gönner's declaration that historical and philosophical jurisprudence could, together, resurrect "das schöne Zeitalter der Antonine." Quoted in Rückert, *Idealismus, Jurisprudenz und Politik* 84. For Zachariä's contemporary insistence on the importance of the post-Republican jurists, see Cappellini, *Systema Iuris*, 1:160 n. 53.

would somehow take place simply because great respect was due the accomplishment of highly cultured Romanist lawyers would never be powerful men. And, indeed, Hugo's movement was marked by a deep-seated lack of political will. Hugo's preface to the new journal he founded in 1791 as an organ of the movement, the *Civilistisches Magazin*, showed a kind of romantic diffidence, a willingness to cultivate Roman law for its own sake without responding to the practical demands of this world. In his journal would be found, wrote Hugo, "only those aspects of modern Roman law that ordinarily interest nobody: doctrinal elaboration of concepts, overviews of the whole, matters that nobody learns by heart, and that even if one learned them by heart, would be useless."[122] This passage, which conjures up so vividly the image of the professor as alienated poet, is charming evidence of the ultimate political unfitness of a romantic of the early 1790s. Romantic diffidence, too, goes far to explain one belief that set Hugo apart from the imperial revivalists of his day: Hugo, true to his conviction that Roman-law professors should be theorists, caring little for this world, favored an abolition of Aktenversendung. Expressing his admiration for the scholarship of the Dutch Universities, in which there were no Spruchkollegien, Hugo declared his belief that scholarship in Germany required that professors be relieved of their adjudicative duties.[123] Here the limitations of the Göttingen school, as long as Hugo was its leading spirit, was clearly displayed. As much as Hugo might talk of German freedoms in a revived Reich, he was too deeply immersed in the romantic conviction that legislators must be poets. If Hugo's Göttingen school had been the only hope of imperial reformers in the first romantic decade, their hope would have been slim.

But, of course, Hugo's was not the only movement, and it was the French Revolution, not romantic diffidence, that put an end to German constitutional reform. And, whatever his political otherworldliness, Hugo had made a resonant new claim for the old "Angels of the Empire." When Hugo's disciple Savigny appeared at the end of the 1790s, the apostolic sensibility of the Roman-law church was strong. And Savigny was much more a man of this world than Hugo had been, and much more eager to leave his mark on German society. He was prepared to unite the practical institutionalism of Häberlin with the romantic theorizing of Hugo under the common banner of the Holy Roman Empire, in a new constitution in which the German law professors would lead a society-wide revival of Rome.

[122] G. Hugo, "Über den Plan dieses Journals," *Hugos Civilistisches Magazin*, 4th ed. (Berlin, 1823) (orig. 1791), 9.

[123] G. Hugo, "Juristische Nachrichten von der Leydenschen Universität, 1790," in ibid., 2:228–29. Similar sentiments were expressed in Elsässer, "Uber den Geschäftsgang der Acten an Rechtscollegien," appendix to W.A.F. Danz, *Grundsaze des gemeinen, ordentlichen, burgerlichen Prozesses*, 3d ed. (Stuttgart, 1800).

Chapter IV

IMPERIAL TRADITION AND THE NEW
PROFESSORIATE AFTER 1814

SEVENTEEN MONTHS after Napoleon's final defeat, Count von Buol Schauenstein opened the first session of the Bundesversammlung, the new federal assembly of the German states at Frankfurt. His speech is jarring to read. Though Count von Buol, the Austrian ambassador, was addressing the delegates of the victorious German states, he did not speak about victory. He spoke about the German universities and professors. Germany, said Count von Buol, was a land of poets, thinkers, artists, and adventurous merchants.[1] False modesty would not prevent him from expressing his conviction that Germany stood in the first rank of literary, artistic, and practically minded nations. And the universities should be marked out for special praise: "To whom are our universities not a proud monument of German development? Even foreigners who are not just to us in weighing our merits grant the superiority of the form of our scholarly institutions, which unite all of knowledge, the individual main disciplines and the subordinate disciplines, in a single whole."[2] This odd speech offended German nationalists at the time and continued to offend them all through the nineteenth century.[3] It was, transparently, Metternich's attempt to commandeer the proud new ideology of German scholars and put it in the service of suppression of the new nationalism of the day: as Buol phrased it, the Germans should not pursue unity, for political strength could only come at the expense of cultural genius—Would the German spirit be so inventive and diverse if the Germans had only one capital and one prince?[4] Thus did the romantic cult of scholarship—for Buol's speech was a pastiche of romantic *topoi* borrowed from Savigny and Schleiermacher and Schelling[5]—make its debut as an intellectual in-

---

[1] "Eröffnung der Bundesversammlung," in J. L. Klüber, ed., *Staatsarchiv des teutschen Bundes* 5 (1817): 30.

[2] Ibid., 31.

[3] Cf. Treitschke's bitter account in the *History of Germany*, 7 vols., translated by E. and C. Paul (New York, 1968), 2:401–2.

[4] "Eröffnung der Bundesversammlung," in Klüber, *Staatsarchiv*, 32.

[5] For the romantic philosophy that lay behind Count von Buol's speech, see esp. the discussions of Fichte and Schelling in König, *Wesen der Deutschen Universität*, 65ff., 125ff. For Savigny's contribution, see below, pp. 106–7. The importance of the romantic philos-

strument of reaction. In the future, romanticism would be at least as much an instrument of revolution as reaction. But whether it was invoked by the left or the right, the new ideology of the German scholars had gathered such force in the twenty years since the mid-1790s that it would remain central to German political life for a generation. In the chapters that follow I wish to show how the Roman-law professoriate became a political force in post-Napoleonic Germany, bringing with it visions and hopes for a revival of Roman civilization.

As the French revolutionary wave receded, the political forces of post-Napoleonic Germany drew their strength, by and large, from the traditions of the Holy Roman Empire. The still-surviving old corporate traditions and institutions of the Middle Ages and the Reformation were revered in the romantic German society that emerged after the French occupation. Germans saw their society as a tangle of long-lived institutions, corporations with imposing traditions, and professions that commanded intense loyalty from their members; the impulse toward the creation of a new society that German liberals felt was very much one toward the creation of new forms on the old corporative model.[6] The old villages and the free cities, the guilds, the armies—Germans took their sense of belonging from these many surviving bodies and organizations. In the chapters that follow, I wish to discuss German politics as politics of reverence for Holy Roman Imperial tradition, as a resumption of the ancient constitutionalist politics borrowed from the West in the 1790s. I will portray the professors of Roman law as possessing one of the greatest of the old corporate traditions—a corporate tradition that, as we have seen, dated back to the sixteenth-century reforms of the Holy Roman Empire and one that had matured under the leadership of no less a figure than Melanchthon. Within the German society of particulate traditions, members of the Roman-law professoriate had a sense of corporate loyalty and of corporate history just as townsmen or guildsmen did. They were German. But they also had a special tradition of their own, a tradition that remained certain and powerful whatever the vicissitudes of German

ophers for Savigny, and Savigny's place in the history of romantic philosophy, are emphasized by Rückert, *Savigny*, 95–96 and often.

[6] For this theme generally in recent interpretation of post-Napoleonic German history, see W. Schieder, "Probleme einer Sozialgeschichte des frühen Liberalismus in Deutschland," in idem, ed., *Liberalismus in der Gesellschaft des deutschen Vormärz*, Geschichte und Gesellschaft, Sonderheft 9 (Göttingen, 1983), 9–21, esp. 13–14 and the literature cited there. Among older German and American historians who have emphasized the backward-looking character of the period, see, e.g., Gerhard Ritter, *Stein: Eine politische Biographie*, 2 vols. (Stuttgart, 1931); Heinrich Heffter, *Deutsche Selbstverwaltung*; Leonard Krieger, *German Idea of Freedom*; and Mack Walker, *German Home Towns*.

politics, of revolutions from above and below, of westernizations and re-actions.

But first I must pause for a cautionary word about the general character of German politics in this period. Savigny and his followers, whose polit-ical beliefs will occupy much of my attention in this and the following chapter, have, over the years, too often been considered to be exception-ally backward-looking men, too often thought of as extreme opponents of a new forward-looking liberalism of the nineteenth century. They were indeed backward-looking men. But—as thoughtful recent historians have recognized—they were neither exceptional nor extreme. For the forward-looking liberalism that general readers (and even sophisticated historians) occasionally imagine Savigny to be opposing hardly existed, as such, in immediately post-Napoleonic Germany.

This is a point that students of German history have from time to time forgotten. Particularly in the aftermath of Nazism, historians eager to trace the roots of the failure of German liberalism in the early nineteenth century tended to forget how unknown forward-looking liberalism was in the twenty or so years after 1815. Even the most learned historians have occasionally portrayed the Germany of Count von Buol as a society struggling to introduce or thwart a late-nineteenth-century Western-style liberalism that was hardly yet in evidence. Professor Krieger, for example, describes "the liberal spirit," the prime legacy of nineteenth-century Eu-rope, as never establishing itself in Germany. This liberal spirit embraced the following freedoms: "freedom of the spirit, which included the right to hold and communicate beliefs and opinions; material liberties, which included rights of free economic initiative and exchange, of social mobil-ity and juridical security; and finally the broad distribution of political powers, which conferred control over public institutions upon represen-tative sections of the governed."[7] In romantic Germany, "conservatism" triumphed over this "liberalism,"[8] and the liberal spirit—so recognizably a thing of a later age—was able to produce only a "half-finished struc-ture."[9] Other historians describe the romantic era as a time of latent crisis over ministerial independence, a crisis that emerged from this latency only in the era of Bismarck.[10] The truth of the 1820s and 1830s, in these

---

[7] Krieger, *German Idea of Freedom*, 3.

[8] Krieger, *German Idea of Freedom*, ix.

[9] Ibid., 3.

[10] See J. Sheehan, *German Liberalism in the Nineteenth-Century* (Chicago, 1977), 45–46, discussing O. Pflanze, "Juridical and Political Responsibility in Nineteenth-Century Germany," in *The Responsibility of Power*, edited by L. Krieger and F. Stern (Garden City, N.Y., 1967), 162–82; F. Schnabel, "Geschichte der Ministerialverantwortlichkeit in Ba-den," *Zeitschrift für die Geschichte des Oberrheins* 75, nos. 1–3 (1921): 87–110, 171–91, 303–31. This tendency to project the life of the second half of the century back into the first receives a striking formulation in Böckenförde's article, "Der deutsche Typ der konstitu-

accounts, is to be found not in the perceptions of contemporaries, but in the politics of the unification era—or, indeed, in the brutal world of post-1933 Germany.

To be sure, historians of recent years have written more sensitively of the period, discerning in Germany "a broad camp of moderates stretching from reforming conservatives to . . . 'organic liberals.' "[11] Nevertheless, the occasional tendency to dramatize post-Napoleonic German political life as a great conflict between the forward drive of history and the reactionary tug of society is, for my purposes, quite dangerous. For it is a tendency that remains particularly strong in discussions of the philosophy of the Rechtsstaat, the peculiarly German[12] idea of "rule of law," which dominated political discourse of the day and which will form the focus of my discussion. The philosophy of the Rechtsstaat was a kind of third-way-ism. German advocates of a Rechtsstaat offered their "rule of law" as a third way between *Volkssouveränität* and *Absolutismus*, between the absolutism of the popular revolutionaries and that of the princes. This third-way-ism was nearly universal among leading German thinkers, whatever their political tendencies—and their political tendencies diverged widely: R. V. Mohl, the popularizer of the term "Rechtsstaat," later became strongly parliamentarian in his convictions[13]; K. S. Zachariä, for many Germans of the time the leading Rechtsstaatler, was an obstinate moderate, difficult to classify[14]; and F. J. Stahl was a prominent monarchist. Stahl's Rechtsstaat, for example, was characterized by its unconditional refusal to justify the use of arbitrary power, even used for ethical ends, with a claim to sovereignty—monarchical or popular. By

---

tionellen Monarchie." Taking as his starting point Carl Schmitt's analysis of century-long unresolved tension between military and bourgeois principles of government, Böckenförde characterizes nineteenth-century constitutional monarchy as a "transitional form" produced by the impossibility of deciding the conflict between monarchical and popular sovereignty. E.-W. Böckenförde, "Der deutsche Typ der Konstitutionellen Monarchie im neunzehnten Jahrhundert," in idem, *Staat, Gesellschaft und Freiheit*, 130. Among the legal historians, note also that Wieacker, *Privatrechtsgeschichte*, 447, has written that the "political locus" of nineteenth-century jurisprudence was "the system of civil standoff." For a study dating struggles over ministerial responsibility in Schleswig-Holstein to the 1850s, see F. Greve, *Die Ministerialverantwortlichkeit im Konstitutionellen Staat* (Berlin, 1977).

[11] John, *Politics and the Law*, 21.

[12] The "peculiarly German" character of the Rechtsstaat has been the boast of German theorists since Lorenz von Stein. Stein, *Verwaltungslehre*, 8 vols. in 4 (Stuttgart, 1866–84), 1:295–96. For the Rechtsstaat as peculiarly German, see, U. Scheuner, "Die neuere Entwicklung des Rechtsstaats in Deutschland," in idem, *Staatstheorie und Staatsrecht* (Berlin, 1978), 165; E.-W. Böckenförde, "Entstehung und Wandel des Rechtsstaatsbegriffs" in idem, *Staat, Gesellschaft und Freiheit* (Frankfurt a.M., 1976), 66 (originally in *Festschrift für A. Arndt* [1969]).

[13] Cf. M. Stolleis, "Verwaltungslehre und Verwaltungswissenschaft," 2:69f.

[14] Cf. Stolleis, "Verwaltungslehre und Verwaltungswissenschaft," 67–68.

this means, Stahl hoped to place his Rechtsstaat entirely outside the realm of the political disputes that had riven the eighteenth century:

> The Rechtsstaat stands in opposition, above all, to the patriarchal, to the patrimonial, to the mere police state, in which the authorities are bent on realizing ethical ideas and utilitarian goals according to a moral, and therefore arbitrary valuation of every given case; no less, however, does it stand in opposition to the Volksstaat (Rousseau, Robespierre), as I would call it, in which the Volk, acting by means of the state, attributes perfect positive political virtue to each citizen and recognizes no legal limits on its own ethical valuations at any given moment.[15]

Interpretations of this Rechtsstaat philosophy have been very much marked by the tendency to see Germany as a realm of conflict between progressivism and reaction. Indeed, most historians have treated Rechtsstaat philosophy as the product of a "sovereignty crisis," of the complete delegitimation of traditional German society caused by the flood of new liberal ideas from across the Rhine. The old society had been exposed as irrelevant. The legitimacy of the princes had been "inwardly wounded" by the events of the French Revolution.[16] But the new society was not yet ready for power. The new liberals, while convinced that the forward movement of history was with them, were too weak or timid to assert their own sovereignty, were unwilling "to define the final location of sovereignty . . . an unwillingness that came from the liberals' reluctance to confront the full practical and theoretical implications of their desire to represent the Volk against the state."[17] Liberals and monarchists alike in the German lands thus favored a "rule of law" because neither party was able to effect its own rule; the general sovereignty crisis forced Germans into a delicate "balancing act,"[18] the nineteenth-century Rechtsstaat.[19]

---

[15] F. J. Stahl, *Philosophie des Rechts*, 3 vols. in 2, 2d ed. (Heidelberg, 1846), vol. 2, pt. 2, 106.

[16] M. Stolleis, "Verwaltungslehre und Verwaltungswissenschaft," 58. Cf. the careful statement of the political situation in 1814 of F. Valjavec, *Die Entstehung der politischen Strömungen in Deutschland, 1770–1815* (Vienna, 1951), 412–15.

[17] Sheehan, *German Liberalism*, 45.

[18] Böckenförde, "Der deutsche Typ," 130: "Balancierung."

[19] Virtually all historians see a sovereignty crisis at work. See H. Gangl, "Der deutsche Weg zum Verfassungsstaat im neunzehnten Jahrhundert," in Böckenförde et al., eds., *Probleme des Konstitutionalismus im Neunzehnten Jahrhundert* (Berlin, 1975), 46ff. To be sure, there are variations. Eckhart Kehr, for example, tends to view the Rechtsstaat not as a compromise acceptable both to princes and to constitutional liberals, but as the defensive weapon of the liberals alone. See E. Kehr, "Zur Genesis der preußischen Bürokratie" in *Primat der Innenpolitik*, Veröffentlichungen der historischen Commission zu Berlin, vol. 19 (Berlin, 1965), 41.

It is this perduring tendency to think of Germany as a battleground between change and the dark forces of reaction, between the dynamic New and the static Old, that one must shake off if one is to understand Savigny and his contemporaries. It makes undeniable dramatic sense to think about the German world in these terms. One reads about the French invasion and the French expulsion and feels that Germany was caught up in the sweep of history for the first time. It makes undeniable dramatic sense, too, to suppose that German history was, in the early nineteenth century, already grinding toward Hitler—that the post-Napoleonic years were years when liberalism, introduced by the French armies into a dreary and static German world, met a pivotal defeat, when great abstract political principles collided: "liberalism" against "conservatism," forward-looking Western political progressivism against reaction—conflicts in which, of course, liberalism was crushed.

But a sense of drama can be a grave handicap in understanding history. To some degree, it is surely true that German "liberals" of the period thought of themselves as representing the forward march of history. It is undeniably true that German liberals of the romantic era tried and failed to introduce some Western innovations; in some sense, liberalism did fail in the romantic era. Moreover, it is true that the fear of political power, still strong after the experience of the French Revolution, did indeed often echo in the work of Rechtsstaat thinkers. The world had revealed a new danger since 1789. The Rechtsstaat thinkers of early nineteenth-century Germany bore the visible scars of the experience of revolution: the forth-right, self-confident tone of German political writings of the early 1790s had largely dissipated; the successors of Häberlin and of Kant felt obliged always to expend a portion of their effort in declaring what they were not: they were not radicals; they were not popular revolutionaries; they stood only for a "rule of law."

Yet if it is true that German political life was deeply shaken by the dynamic new forces revealed in the course of the French Revolution, it is not true that the Germans' only alternative was a static older German world. As I have already suggested, German political life had been marked by a rising tide of change in the years before the French Revolution. In large measure, the French Revolution had broken in, not upon a petrified ancien régime in Germany, but rather upon the constitutionalist reformism of Reichspatriotismus. It was this constitutionalist reformism that the German "liberals" of the period resumed after 1815, opposing to the dynamic New a dynamic Old. German liberalism was "fundamental law" liberalism, comparable to the "fundamental law" politics of the previous century elsewhere in Europe.[20] It was backward- not forward-

---

[20] See L. Gall, *Der Liberalismus als regierende Partei* (Wiesbaden, 1968), 41ff.

looking, and was characterized not by a struggle for principled freedom, but by a struggle for Germanic freedom that was the German analogue of the gothic freedom that formed the (perceived) basis of English and American political life. To be sure, there were backward-looking Germans who were reactionaries, who did indeed favor a kind of new stasis, a return to an imagined unchanging medieval world. But "backward-looking" was by no means necessarily an equivalent of "reactionary" in the Germany that emerged after 1815.

All of this is not to deny that early nineteenth-century Germany was, in some sense, a conservative society as compared with the West. Quite the contrary. My object is to show that the politics of German lawyers were politics of a kind that had already become common in the previous centuries in England and France; Germany, seen from this point of view, very much "lagged" behind the West (as even sensitive recent historians have perhaps failed to note). But German lawyers uniformly "lagged"; it is quite wrong to differentiate radically between the "conservatives" and the "liberals" among them. If something tragic began during this period, it did not begin because German anti-Western conservatives triumphed over German pro-Western liberals—though perhaps something tragic began because German "conservatives" and German "liberals" together tried to westernize too eagerly, too late.

In this chapter, I will present the politics of Roman law as politics of ancient constitutionalism in the old Western style, of a kind of Romanist lawyers' Germanic freedom. I will present Savigny's "Historical School" as only one of many backward-looking reformist movements of the time—though as one committed to reviving its own, quite distinctive, eighteenth-century tradition of change. I will present the resurgent professoriate of Savigny's time as deeply conscious of its Holy Roman Imperial ancestry. I will attempt to show that the German lawyers of the Romantic era, like ancient constitutionalists of previous centuries, thought of themselves as representing not only the constitution of their native country, but also the political and social traditions of Antiquity. Indeed, it is only part of the tale to call them either reform conservatives or organic liberals; they were political antiquarians of an older type. There were two schools of professorial revival, which drew different lessons from different aspects of early modern tradition. The universities of the constitutionalist south—Tübingen, Erlangen, above all Heidelberg—drew on the old traditions of corporate liberty and especially on the institution of Aktenversendung as they developed the philosophy of the Rechtsstaat. Savigny's own school of followers, centered at Prussian Berlin but drawing its ideas from Hannover and Hesse, the heartlands of philosophical romanticism, where seventeenth- and eighteenth-century legal practices still survived on a large scale, looked to very different elements of early modern tradition. But both schools harbored the same hope, that the Roman-law professorial tradition could, on the one hand, infuse political life with the strength and free sensibility of old corporate society, and, on the other, lend a sense of moral mission to the Germans, a sense drawn from the grandeur of the classical tradition. I will consider these two varieties of romantic thought in succession, turning first to Savigny, then to a discussion of the early modern professorial tradition among the Rechtsstaat thinkers of the south.

THE HISTORICAL SCHOOL

Napoleon was driven out of a Germany rich with the signs of university revival. The renewed sense of self so noticeable among Heyne, Gustav Hugo, and their contemporaries at Göttingen in the early 1790s had spread all through the German-speaking states in the years of the Napoleonic occupation; the romantic dream of rebuilding ancient institutions survived even as Germans lost full control of their own governments.[21] Prince Karl Friedrich of Baden, with his reforms of 1803, succeeded in transforming Heidelberg, a moribund small-state university, into a national legal center.[22] The founding of the University of Berlin followed seven years later. Both universities became focuses of a new academic élan, and both could benefit from the unprecedented national pride in the German universities that Count von Buol had attempted to make his own. Meanwhile the vigorous flowering of legal philosophy that had begun in the 1780s and 1790s, during the period of Reichspatriotismus and spreading Kantianism, had continued through the war years.[23] The changed state of the universities made itself felt in law as elsewhere: law professors shared in the newly soaring prestige of scholars, the national prominence first of figures like Kant and F. A. Wolf, still recognizably professors in an eighteenth-century mold, later of figures like Hegel and Schelling, near-cult objects in the early decades of romanticism. Alongside this growth in prestige, clearly present but difficult to describe or explain, came concrete additions to the direct professorial exercise of power: the recrudescent professorial law set its stamp on the emerging professional bureaucratic state. The use of trained lawyers as bureaucrats

---

[21] Cf. esp. the fine discussions of the Prussian reform movement in Ritter, Stein, 1:271ff., esp. 287, commenting upon Stein's hope of "eine Erneuerung altdeutscher Gemeinfreiheit, genossenschaftlicher Organisation an Stelle der obrigkeitlichen Zwangsanstalt," and, generally, Heffter, Deutsche Selbstverwaltung.

[22] See Rückert, "Heidelberg um 1804."

[23] For surveys of jurisprudence during the Napoleonic period, see generally Stühler, Erneuerung der Rechtswissenschaft; Cappellini, Systema Iuris. Also informative is Rückert, "Heidelberg um 1804."

had begun in the eighteenth century. But only beginning in 1817 did the study of law become the requirement for entry into state bureaucracies.[24] From then on law professors would continue to leave their mark on the powerful state apparatuses of central Europe.[25]

Perhaps the most salient sign that the old status of the law professors was reviving after its long decline since the sixteenth century was the sudden success of Aktenversendung. As professors attained a quite unprecedented cultural status in the first years of the nineteenth century, the old institution continued the climb into renewed prominence that had begun with the electoral capitulation of 1790.[26] In 1804 N. T. Gönner, a leading specialist in Public Law, made the declaration I have already quoted: Aktenversendung was the "palladium of German freedom."[27] The university of Tübingen received its highest number of Aktenversendungen in 1805, the re-founded university of Heidelberg in 1810.[28] This reversal in the ideological fortunes of the institution culminated in two quite unexpected triumphs: faculty agitation at the new Prussian university of Berlin resulted in the creation of an unplanned Spruchkollegium there[29]; and the *Bundesacte* of 1815—the basic document of the *Bund*, the federation of German states established at the Vienna Congress—included, despite considerable adverse agitation,[30] a partial guarantee of the right to Aktenversendung.[31] The *Bundesacte* would continue to generate interest in the old institution. As we shall see, the renewed Spruchkollegien soon became focuses for the development of professorial politics in an altered Germany.

[24] See generally Bleek, *Von der Kameralausbildung zum Juristenprivilege.* The effective date for Prussian territories was 1817. Ibid., 104. The practice established itself more gradually in the rest of the German lands, especially in the south. See ibid., 262–85, for a survey.

[25] Cf. C. J. Friedrich, "The Continental Tradition of Training Administrators in Law and Jurisprudence," *Journal of Modern History* 11 (1939): 129–48.

[26] See above, p. 79.

[27] Gönner, *Handbuch des deutschen gemeinen Prozeßes,* cited in Bülow, *Ende des Aktenversendungsrechts,* 1. Cf. G. A. Löning, "Spätes Lob der Aktenversendung" *ZSS (G)* 63 (1943): 333.

[28] Klugkist, "Die Aktenversendung," 157. Klugkist does not see the signficance in these dates, but rather views the decline of the institution as uninterrupted after the mid-eighteenth century. Cf. ibid., 156, col. 1. Similar views are to be found in all the literature on this subject. Decade-by-decade figures for the various faculties can be found in Jammers, *Heidelberger Juristenfakultät,* 179, and Klugkist, *Göttinger Juristenfakultät als Spruchkollegium,* 106.

[29] E. Seckel, "Berliner juristische Fakultät als Spruchkollegium," 3:449ff. The erroneous idea that Savigny himself was responsible for establishing the Berlin Spruchkollegium is dismissed by Rückert, *Savigny,* 41–42.

[30] Cf. Löning, "Spätes Lob der Aktenversendung."

[31] Deutsche Bundes-Acte, June 8, 1815, Art. 12, Abs. 4. Cf., e.g., Kern, *Geschichte des Gerichtsverfassungsrechts,* 38. Cf. below, pp. 135–36.

Amid all these new signs of professorial power, the law professors were claiming for themselves a new role as national leaders of what was increasingly to be denominated the "Rechtsstaat"—the society of rule of law. "Rule of law" suggests "rule of lawyers." And indeed, in the years 1814–15 a new generation of "political professors"[32] came on the scene, making the political philosophy of the Rechtsstaat almost the exclusive province of law professors. The word "Rechtsstaat" was coined by K. T. Welcker, then professor of law at Giessen, as liberation neared in 1813.[33] Of its best-known representatives, K. S. Zachariä[34] was a professor at the renewed university at Heidelberg, and the Hegelian F. J. Stahl, often declared by later generations to have given the Rechtsstaat its canonical definition,[35] was a professor at the new university at Berlin. These were only the most important representatives of the new philosophy. Many other comparatively forgotten professors prominent in the years of the liberation contributed, from N. T. Gönner, the champion of Aktenversendung[36] and insufferable tyrant of the Bavarian university at Landshut,[37] to J. L. Klüber of Heidelberg, publicist, in eighteenth-century style, of the new German Federation.[38] In the life of German polemics, as in the life of German institutions, a professorial age had begun. Most important, of course, were Friedrich Carl von Savigny and his followers and emulators; it was these Romanist lawyers who mounted the most unabashed and influential campaign for professorial leadership in a Romanist Rechtsstaat. Their campaign, too, began in the immediate aftermath of the liberation, with Savigny's internationally famous pamphlet,[39] "On the Vocation of our Time for Codification and for Legal Scholarship."

[32] Cf. Schnabel, *Deutsche Geschichte im Neunzehnten Jahrhundert*, 2:204ff.

[33] E.-W. Böckenforde, "Entstehung und Wandel des Rechtsstaatsbegriffs."

[34] Especially in his *Vierzig Bücher vom Staate*, 7 vols. in 5 (Stuttgart/Tübingen, 1820–32). Cf. Stolleis, "Verwaltungslehre und Verwaltungswissenschaft," 67–68. On Zachariä, see C. Brocher, *K. S. Zachariä, sa vie et ses oeuvres* (Paris, 1869); Mohl, *Staatswissenschaften*, 2:512–28; Rückert, "Heidelberg um 1804," 91, 95–96; and below pp. 141–42.

[35] The importance of Stahl's definition was declared by Otto Bähr in his *Rechtsstaat* (Cassel/Göttingen, 1864), 1, and is generally recognized in the literature. See Scheuner, "Neuere Entwicklung des Rechtsstaats," 202 (originally in *Hundert Jahre Deutsches Rechtsleben* [Karlsruhe, 1960], 229–62). H. Boldt, however (*Die Deutsche Staatsrechtslehre im Vormärz*, Beiträge zur Geschichte des Parlamentarismus und der politischen Parteien, 56 [Düsseldorf, 1975]: 213–15) calls the influence of Stahl into question.

[36] See above p. 79.

[37] See G. Radbruch, *Paul Anselm Johann Feuerbach: Ein Juristenleben* (repr. Gottingen, 1969), 69–70. For bad relations of Savigny and others with Gönner, see Rückert, *Savigny*, 78ff. Cf. Stuhler, *Erneuerung der Rechtswissenschaft*, 86–91.

[38] See Mohl, *Staatswissenschaften*, 2:473–87.

[39] Cf. D. R. Kelley, *Historians and the Law in France* (Princeton, N.J., 1984), 72ff.; P. Stein, *Legal Evolution* (Cambridge, 1980), 72ff.

Savigny and Thibaut

Friedrich Carl von Savigny became famous as the subtlest advocate of legal reform when legal reform came to seem urgent in 1814 and 1815. To be sure, it had seemed urgent to the enlightened princes. But this sense of urgency had now spread more widely. The French occupation had deeply disrupted the German sense of proper order. Forms of life that had been able to withstand the most determined princely despotism would not withstand the disorientation of Germans in lands where the old political order would vanish unless reformed and revivified.

The German-speaking lands were an extraordinary legal patchwork. The old ius commune remained law in many parts of Germany; indeed, judges still swore the 1495 oath of the Reichskammergericht. As the important Hessian jurist Burchard Wilhelm Pfeiffer described it in 1815, this rule of ius commune had come to be a practicing lawyer's nightmare:

> Roman law is the main source of civil law [in Hesse]; various territorial laws have changed a great deal of it; but the greatest multiplication of laws is based on customs, which can be viewed in part as common German customs (in a historical sense), in part as customs of all Hesse, in part as customs of single provinces, and in part merely as customs of the kind of which J. v. Müller says that often nothing more than a large village has preserved them "in an old tale and in a grimy community chest." Through an ordinance of Landgrave Wilhelm II [promulgated in 1524] it is made the duty of every judge and law-finder "nach gemeynen kayserlichen beschriebenn Rechten, auch nach reddelichen und erbarn Statuten, Ordenungen und Gewonheyten unsers Fürstenthumbs und Landschaft, wo die für sie bracht werden, nach jrem bestenn Verstentniß glich zu richten und zu urteiln" ["to judge all equally, according to their best understanding, and according to the common imperial laws as well as honest and proper statutes, ordinances, and customs of our principate and country, where the latter are made available to them"—a version of the oath of the Reichskammergericht]. This great heterogeneity of legal sources has had, as its inevitable consequence, the most remarkable lack of uniformity in the civil law of the individual parts of this state.[40]

[40] B. W. Pfeiffer, *Ideen zu einer neuen Civil-Gesetzgebung für Teutsche Staaten* (Göttingen, 1815), 102. It is noteworthy that Pfeiffer did not recognize the local Hessian judge's oath as having been modeled on the oath of the Reichskammergericht. This Hessian oath is noted as a close relative of the oath of the Reichskammergericht in H. Kiefner, "Rezeption (privatrechtlich)," in *Handwörterbuch zur deutschen Rechtsgeschichte*, 4: 979. On the important Pfeiffer, Chief Justice of the High Appellate Court for Hesse in Cassel, see below, pp. 131–32.

It was this centuries-old order that enlightened codificationists had sought, in the second half of the eighteenth century, to abolish, and that their successors of the Napoleonic era continued to attack. Indeed, the *Code Napoléon*, which drew both on the work of scholars of "national customary law" and on the work of Romanist lawyers,[41] had been introduced in many parts of Europe in part in order to end the "heterogeneity of legal sources" in places like Hesse. Where codes (whether French, Austrian, or Prussian) had come in, the old world of legal scholarship, with its learned interrogation of witnesses and ancient texts, was at an end. Yet codification had by no means settled all matters. If one no longer needed, in code states, to consult ancient texts or local witnesses, one still needed answers to unanswered questions. The enlightened codes had proved far from definitive: lawyers in the code states (notably Prussia) found themselves faced with a monumental task of interstitial lawmaking, of doctrinal stuggles to fill the many gaps in their codes.[42] Legal uncertainty was compounded by political opposition to an order based on territorial codes: the existence of territorial codes offended the widespread sentiment for national unification. Perhaps the most deeply felt disaffection was created by the situation in formerly French territories where the *Code Napoléon* (soon renamed the *Code Civil*) was in force, loved by many but viewed by others with suspicion.[43] Sentiment for reform was strong, and jurists published a variety of programmatic proposals. Some favored general adoption of the *Code Civil*, some the general adoption of the Austrian Code, newly promulgated in 1811, others the drafting of a wholly new native German code.[44] Among the welter of proposals were a number that strongly favored both affirmation of the status of Roman law as the common law of Germany and an explicit entrusting of lawmaking

[41] See, generally, A.-J. Arnaud, *Les origines doctrinales du Code Civil Français*, Bibliothèque de philosophie du droit, vol. 9 (Paris, 1969).

[42] For a sense of the immense labor that was required to make the Allgemeines Landrecht fit the needs of Prussian life, see, e.g., the *Jahrbücher für die Preußische Rechtswissenschaft und Rechtsverwaltung*, edited by K. A. v. Kamptz (1813ff.), and the *Allgemeine Juristische Monatsschrift für die Preußischen Staaten*, edited by Mathis (1805ff.). Prussian lawyers faced, in general, exactly the same doctrinal problems that lawyers in states with no code faced. For the similarity in problems with agrarian law, see below, p. 189, n. 160.

[43] See the discussion of K.-G. Faber, *Die Rheinlande zwischen Restauration und Revolution* (Wiesbaden, 1966), 118ff.; W. Schubert, "Das französische Recht in Deutschland zu Beginn der Restaurationszeit," *ZSS* (G) 94 (1977): 129ff.; idem, *Das Französische Recht in Deutschland* (Cologne/Vienna, 1977). For the widespread popularity of the French Code in the Rheinland, see E. Fehrenbach, "Zur sozialen Problematik des rheinischen Rechts im Vormärz," in H. Berding et al., eds., *Vom Staat des Ancien Regime zum Modernen Parteienstaat: Festschrift für Theodor Schieder* (Munich/Vienna, 1978), 200.

[44] For the post-Napoleonic legal controversies in Germany, see H. Hattenhauer, "Einleitung," to idem, ed., *Thibaut und Savigny: Ihre Programmatischen Schriften* (München, 1973), 9–51; Rückert, *Savigny*, 166.

power to the professors. Karl Ernst Schmid, proposing a comprehensive program of reform and renewal in his *Deutschlands Wiedergeburt* (Germany's Rebirth) of 1814, declared that a new system of appellate courts should be established, with each court located near a university.[45] A Tübingen professor, the indefatigable student of the *Corpus Iuris* Eduard Schrader,[46] suggested that all the German states adopt the system of the praetorian Edict as it had existed in ancient Rome; rule of ancient law, he said, would maximize the capacity of law professors to create a uniform, flexible legal order for all Germany.[47] It was as one of many such pamphleteers that Savigny became an internationally famous advocate of the continued rule of legal scholarship.

Savigny wrote his famous pamphlet in response to perhaps the most important forgotten jurist of the period, and certainly the most prominent opponent of professorial lawmaking: Anton Friedrich Justus Thibaut, the leading figure at the renewed university of Heidelberg.[48] Thibaut, in many ways as influential and original a Romanist lawyer as Savigny,[49] published in 1814 a pamphlet advocating the drafting of a general German code. In embracing codification, the great Enlightenment ideal, Thibaut was not, however, rejecting the new romantic currents. Quite the contrary: he was uniting the enlightened ambition to remake the world with a romantic conviction that the best things of the world pre-dated the Enlightenment. Thibaut embraced one of the commanding new romantic causes: he wished to see the rule of lawyers learned in the Roman-Canon tradition at an end; he wished a revival, somehow, of the native German legal forms that had prevailed before the governmental revolution of the sixteenth century.

Indeed, Thibaut went to great pains to attack the learned professoriate to which he himself belonged. From the beginning of his pamphlet, Thibaut denounced Roman law precisely because its rule entrusted the

---

[45] K. E. Schmid, *Deutschlands Wiedergeburt* (Jena, 1814), 278: "Noch besser würde es freilich für die so nothwendige Verbindung zwischen dem Leben und der Schule seyn, wenn die Kreisgerichte ihren Sitz an Orten bekämen, wo zugleich Universitäten sind."

[46] Cf. R. v. Mohl, *Lebenserinnerungen* (Stuttgart/Leipzig, 1902), 1:146.

[47] E. Schrader, *Die Prätorischen Edicte der Römer auf unsere Verhältnisse übertragen, ein Hauptmittel unser Recht allmälich gut and volksmäßig zu bilden* (Weimar, 1815) (also repr. in idem, *Civilistische Abhandlungen* [Weimar, 1816]), esp. 17ff., 49–50. Similarly Pfeiffer, though he was no supporter of Savigny (cf. *Ideen zu einer neuen Civil-Gesetzgebung für Teutsche Staaten*, 6–7 [hostility toward Savigny's political elevation of professoriate], argued in favor of Roman law as the basis for a new code and conceded the need for a special place for the universities. (Ibid., 67 [judges need scholarly training]).

[48] On Thibaut, see R. Polley, *Anton Friedrich Justus Thibaut (A.D. 1772–1840) in seinen Selbstzeugnissen und Briefen*, Rechtshistorische Reihe, no. 13, 3 vols. (Frankfurt a.M./Bern, 1982).

[49] See below pp. 141, 180–81; Rückert, "Heidelberg um 1804," 92–93.

well-being of the German people to scholars. Roman law required philo-
logically correct texts, which could be established only by consulting
manuscripts scattered throughout the libraries of Europe. "Accordingly,"
wrote Thibaut, "the happiness of our citizens depends on whether our
scholars are treated liberally in Rome and in Paris, and on whether they
collect [their readings] industriously, or not!" ("Not."—he added drily in
a footnote.)[50] Accordingly, the code he proposed was to be exhaustive,
leaving no room for interpretation.[51] He mixed his attack on the scholars
with jibes at the greed of lawyers familiar since Roman law first appeared
in Germany: "All your learnedness, all your variants and conjectures—
all of this has disturbed the peaceful security of the citizen a thousand
times over, and filled the pockets of the lawyers alone."[52] He drew on the
new romantic vocabulary of "national character"—a vocabulary Herder
had pioneered and Thibaut had adopted years before[53]—to deny that
German scholars could construct adequate law out of the Roman inheritance. The Corpus Iuris, Thibaut said, was "the work of an alien nation,
very much unlike ourselves, from the period of that nation's decline [i.e.,
the sixth century, when Justinian ordered its compilation], and bearing
the traces of this decline on all sides." "We lack," he continued, "the national ideas [Volks-ideen] of the Romans, which must have made infinitely much [of their law] easy to understand."[54] Not only had scholars
failed to resurrect the national legal mind of the Romans, they had done
much to destroy the German legal mind by introducing into it their un-
healthy philological spirit. "For ages, your best scholarliness, instead of
enlivening the true, pure juristic sensibility of the civil community [das
bürgerliche Wesen], has killed [the juristic sensibility]."[55] We have, he
concluded, more and more philology and less and less sense for law.[56] His
solution would have taken the interpretation of law decisively out of the
hands of the scholars by eliminating the authority of the Roman texts. He
proposed the making of a new, comprehensive, wholly German code for
use in all the German lands.[57]

Savigny responded to Thibaut as a champion of Roman civilization

---

[50] Thibaut, "Über die Notwendigkeit," in Hattenhauer, ed., Thibaut und Savigny, 71–72
and 195 n. 5.

[51] Ibid., 67. Cf. Hubner, Kodifikation und Entscheidungsfreiheit, 47.

[52] Thibaut, "Über die Notwendigkeit," 72.

[53] As early as 1797, Thibaut denied that the "deutscher Geist" would have produced
Roman law (Bender, Rezeption des Romischen Rechts, 59).

[54] Thibaut, "Über die Notwendigkeit," 69.

[55] Ibid., 73.

[56] Ibid., 74. Thibaut's attacks were directed largely against Hugo. See Ruckert, Savigny,
181.

[57] For the differences between Savigny and Thibaut, see generally the discussion of Rückert, Savigny, 178, 190–91.

and of the professorial class, and as a skeptic of the Enlightenment tradition of codification. He was a charismatic man. One of the very few members of the highest nobility to make an academic career—his most prominent colleagues, Thibaut and P.J.A. Feuerbach,[58] were, by contrast, a
poor man and a bastard, respectively—Savigny brought a lasting prestige
to the profession and acquired a kind of "sacrosanct" name in the academic literature of succeeding generations.[59] He had visionary hopes for
the professoriate that had fallen into such decline in the eighteenth century. In a short essay written for an English magazine, he had enunciated
the doctrine of national pride in the universities that would reappear thir-
teen years later as Count von Buol spoke before the federal assembly.
Germany had great shortcomings compared to England or France:

> But that which in Germany supplies the want of almost all these advantages,
> and in which it is unparalleled in any other country, is its *Universities*. To
> them, more than to any thing else, Germany is indebted for its vast progress
> in the arts and sciences. By means of them, Germany is that which it in all
> other respects is in so slight degree—a nation. It may even be asserted that
> Germany is contained in its Universities.[60]

Nationalist hopes were the highest hopes a German could express in
1803; Savigny justified them by a wholly new, wholly elevated conception
of the activity of the professor and of the meaning of Universities. Universities were the focus of freedom: what Germany's *gebildete Stände*—
educated estates—experienced in their university years was "the freedom
of an academic life"[61]; indeed, the first universities had been founded, he
wrote five years later, on the free initiative of learned men.[62] And the professor had the opportunity to convey knowledge and wisdom with a force
only personal communication could muster: lecturing to his students, the
teacher would "not narrate what he knows, but allow his knowledge to
emerge before his listeners, so that they can 'witness, and witnessing, im-

[58] On Feuerbach's life, see esp. Radbruch, *Feuerbach*.

[59] Cf. H. Kantorowicz, "Savigny and the Historical School of Law," *Law Quarterly Review* 53 (1937): 326 and passim. Three generations later, Savigny was followed by Ulrich von Wilamowitz-Moellendorff, another great renovator of the prestige of classical scholarship in Germany, in entering academics from the nobility.

[60] Savigny, "On the Present State of the German Universities" (1803), published in R. Wellek, "Ein unbekannter Artikel Savignys über die deutschen Universitäten," *ZSS* (G) 51 (1931): 534. For the German version, of this essay, see H. Marquardt, "Ein unbekannter Aufsatz F. C. von Savignys," in *Die Sammlung: Zeitschrift für Kultur und Erziehung* 6 (1951): 321–36.

[61] Savigny, "On the Present State," 535.

[62] Savigny, review of Schleiermacher, *Gelegentliche Gedanken über Universitäten in deutschem Sinn* in *Vermischte Schriften* (repr. Darmstadt, 1968) (orig. 1808), 4:264.

itate, the activity of reason as it gives birth to understanding.' "[63] This belief in the special power of the professor to inspire was common to the age: not only figures like Schelling and Schleiermacher but also law professors spoke in such terms. When Schrader pleaded for the use of pure Roman law, he defended his position by asserting that only an "unmediated and many-sided penetration of scholarship into life itself" could produce the "necessary inspiration [*Begeisterung*]" to revive the legal spirit of Germany, a legal life led by scholars who were "Schöpfer und Bildner," "creators and plastic artists."[64] Savigny would continue in succeeding years to promulgate this romantic vision of 1814. "The more elevated effect of personal communication," he wrote in 1832, "this is what lends the universities their high, their irreplaceable value."[65] And students would continue to respond to this visionary mode of education through the intimate contact of personalities. As one student wrote, "The beautiful and imposing man stepped to his lectern like a priest of scholarship"; another spoke of him as an evangelist.[66] Savigny gave new life to Hugo's twenty-year-old idea that the Roman lawyers formed an apostolic succession.[67] It was not only noble birth, it was fire of conviction and power of personality that Savigny brought to the renovation of the early modern professoriate and its *mission civilisatrice*.[68]

Where the teaching of Roman law had brought honor to Thibaut, the aristocrat Savigny had brought honor to the teaching of Roman law and

[63] Savigny, quoting Schleiermacher in ibid., 262. Compare Savigny's description in his English article: "And what can be more animating to the student, than the knowledge that he hears the best that can be said on the topic; that ideas are made known to him first, which he is convinced will be accepted hereafter, even by scholars themselves, with gratitude and admiration. Thus teacher and learner have a reciprocal effect on each other; the one feels himself compelled to foresight and correctness, the other learns to esteem himself, and thus each gives to the other what he receives from him." Savigny, "On the Present State," 535.

[64] Schrader, *Die Prätorischen Edicte*, 50.

[65] Savigny, "Wesen und Wert der deutschen Universitäten," in *Vermischte Schriften*, 4:274 (orig. 1832). Cf. his description of the lecture-room scene, still very much that he had described in 1808: "Indem nun so der Lehrer die Genesis des wissenschaftlichen Denkens unmittelbar zur Anschauung bringt, wird in dem Schuler die verwandte geistige Kraft geweckt und zur Reproduction gereizt; er wird nicht blos lernen und aufnehmen, sondern lebendig nachbilden, was ihm in lebendigem Werden zur Anschauung gebracht ward" (ibid.). It is worthy of note that as early as 1800 Savigny criticized Feuerbach for neglecting the power of personally communicated conviction: "Feuerbach lehrt sehr gründlich und gut, nur hat sein Äußeres zu wenig; man vernachlässigt das überhaupt zu sehr, ohne zu bedenken, daß das der einzige Punkt ist, der mündliche Vorträge nützlich und in gewissen Fällen unentbehrlich macht." Quoted in Radbruch, *Feuerbach*, 51.

[66] These were, respectively, no less than Bluntschli and Jhering. See H. Vonessen, "Friedrich Karl von Savigny und Jakob Grimm" (diss., Munich, 1958), 53–54.

[67] Cf. above, pp. 87–88.

[68] Cf. the interesting discussion of R. Kawakami, "Die Begründung des 'neuen' gelehrten Rechts," on Savigny's conception of "Schule."

sought to bring more, and against Thibaut he mounted a vigorous defense
of the traditions of legal scholarship against the code ideal. Like Hugo
twenty-five years earlier, he saw the new codes as the product of a "sterile
reasoning" about legal propositions that formed a poor substitute for
"learned knowledge of law."[69] The code ideal was the product of an age
of false Enlightenment, when men had lost their understanding of human
history and their sense of proportion about their own powers:

> Men lost their sensitivity to the majesty and particularity of other eras, as
> well as for the natural development of nations and constitutions—to every-
> thing that makes history invigorating and fruitful. What replaced that sensi-
> tivity was a unbounded expectation that the present age was called to no less
> a task than to make absolute perfection a reality.[70]

The product of this great human overreaching was enlightened codification, and in particular the three leading codes, the Prussian, French, and
Austrian, whose claims so many of Savigny's contemporaries trumpeted.
These codes were inevitably flawed, overblown in their ambitions, and
poorly suited to the societies in which they had been introduced.[71] As for
the idea of producing a new German code: it overestimated, Savigny said,
the mastery among German lawyers of the traditions of the German people. The German tradition of legal scholarship was simply not sufficiently
learned to allow lawyers to fit code to nation:

> Unfortunately, the German eighteenth century was very poor in great jurists.
> To be sure, the number of diligent men was large, and they produced very
> valuable preliminary work. But only rarely was it more than preliminary
> work. A jurist must have a double sensibility: he must think both historically,
> in order to form a clear understanding of the peculiarities of each age and
> each legal form, and systematically, in order to allocate to every concept and
> proposition its proper place in a living interactive union with the whole—
> that is to say, its only true and natural place. One finds uncommonly little of
> this double scholarly sensibility in the jurists of the eighteenth century, par-
> ticularly with the baleful influence of a kind of diffuse and superficial philos-
> ophizing.[72]

Things had improved in his own time,[73] but not by enough to make attempts at codification desirable. That must wait while scholars deepened
their grasp of the world around them.

This of course meant that precisely what Thibaut had opposed must

[69] See above, p. 88.
[70] Savigny, *Vom Beruf*, 100.
[71] Ibid., 128ff.
[72] Ibid., 125.
[73] Ibid.

come to pass: the legal order must continue to depend on the skill of German scholars. The proper place for the cultivation of law was the universities; indeed, university reform and standardization of the legal curriculum was the first prerequisite for the renovation of Germany's juristic order.[74] Savigny insisted that the strength of centuries of Roman-law tradition in Germany offered an answer to all Thibaut's charges. Roman law was indeed the product of an alien people, but German jurists had expended their scholarly energies upon it for centuries; accordingly, it had become effectively German.[75] These generations of scholars had made themselves fit to make law for a society in which the people had lost its intuitive feel for the proper forms of law. Savigny conceded Thibaut's accusation that professorial adjudication had been abused by lawyers: Aktenversendung was in need of reform. Nevertheless, once reformed it could render "the most excellent services."[76] Even if the Holy Roman Empire could not be revived,[77] Germany should abide by the usus modernus, for the German Volk was not ready for the task of lawmaking.[78] The jurists must step in, and make law as the "impartial" vicars of the Volk: "We have uncovered, in the estate of the jurists, a subject for living customary law, and so for true progress."[79] The people would rule in theory, and the people's cause would be advanced in fact. Authority would remain with the learned jurists.[80]

---

[74] Ibid., 187.

[75] It is also noteworthy that Savigny insisted that the Germans had never been in a position to enjoy independent development, for the German nation had never been centered on any fixed locality—a point Count von Buol was later to echo. Savigny was not the only classicist to emphasize fixed locality: consider Karl Otfried Müller's similar emphasis in his later theorizing about mythology. What is the history of this early nineteenth-century scholarly association of national culture and *unverrückte Localität*? For *unverrückte Localität* in Savigny, see also D. Strauch, *Recht, Gesetz und Staat bei Friedrich Carl von Savigny*, Schriften zur Rechtslehre und Politik, vol. 23 (Bonn, 1960), 41.

[76] Quoted in H. Mohnhaupt, "Richter und Rechtsprechung im Werk Savignys," in W. Wilhelm, ed., *Studien zur Europäischen Rechtsgeschichte* (Frankfurt a.M., 1972), 253.

[77] For Savigny's wistful concession that the Holy Roman Empire could not be revived, see Strauch, *Recht, Gesetz und Staat*, 57.

[78] For the usefulness of the usus modernus to Savigny, see Stühler, *Erneuerung der Rechtswissenschaft*, 27. Later, Savigny would take pains to insist that the death of the Holy Roman Empire had not ended the validity of the ius commune. See Cappellini, *Systema Iuris*, 2:121 n. 49. For the survival of the usus modernus into the late eighteenth century, see idem, 1:103. For even Thibaut's invocation of the old ius commune choice-of-law formula, see ibid., 2:110–11.

[79] Savigny, "Vom Beruf," 175. Cf. the discussion of W. Wilhelm, *Zur Juristischen Methodenlehre im Neunzehnten Jahrhundert*, Frankfurter wissenschaftliche Beiträge, Rechts- und Wirtschaftswissenschaftliche Reihe, vol. 14 (Frankfurt a.M., 1958), 74–75. For the centrality of "impartiality" to Savigny's public image, see Rückert, *Idealismus*, 194 and ff.

[80] For fine discussions of Savigny's "programma di riforma del diritto vigente," see

Many of Savigny's readers were appalled. As one anonymous reviewer of "Vom Beruf" declared: "It is not to be expected that the German princes will simply surrender their peoples to the famous lawmaking of the *representative jurists*, or juristic Brahmins, who eternalize their Sanskrit, rule everywhere all silent and still, suck the people's marrow dry, and would like to mark themselves out as the teachers of laws and morals, like the Rabbis of the Jews."[81] Savigny had a mild answer: "If one could get at the marrow of the people through learned jurisprudence," he responded, "it would probably have acquired more disciples!"[82] But Savigny damned himself with these words, for learned jurisprudence did indeed acquire more and more disciples. Thibaut, too, was not done with angry words: "The Volk has waited long enough for the results of the work of professors and lawyers, and nobody is going to convince it that its historical friends [i.e., the historical school of Savigny] will produce a wise and simple legal constitution for the fatherland at any time."[83] Thibaut's Volk notwithstanding, historians have agreed ever since that professorial law revived and flourished under Savigny's banner. From Savigny's time onward, the great German nineteenth-century Roman-law tradition gained in social and intellectual standing for decades. Under the name "Pandektistik"—the study of the "Pandects," or Digest of Justinian—Savigny's Romanist followers succeeded in reestablishing scholarly Roman law in German legal life. A hundred years later, Hermann Kantorowicz, the sharpest critic Savigny has had since Thibaut, had only one kind thing to say of him: Savigny, said Kantorowicz, had greatly improved the lot of the professors.[84]

What were the sources of the great professorial clamor, led by Savigny, in the years 1814 and 1815? In part, perhaps, the new prominence of law professors on the political stage simply reflected changes in the composition of the German faculties: as cameralistics and Reichspublizistik vanished from the curricula, only law professors were left to take up the burden of reasoning about the state. But the law professors of the Rechtsstaat era had larger purposes and a sense of a more important mission than simply filling the shoes of the vanished public philosophers of the eighteenth century. Like Count von Buol, they believed that the professorial

---

P. Caroni, "La Cifra Codificatoria nell'opera di Savigny," *Q. Fior.* 9 (1980): 69–111; and esp. idem, "Savigny und die Kodifikation," *ZSS* (G) 86 (1969): 97–176.

[81] Quoted by Savigny in the "Nachträge" to "Vom Beruf," 245.

[82] Ibid.

[83] Thibaut, "Besprechung des Einleitungssatzes der *Zeitschrift für Geschichtliche Rechtswissenschaft*" in Hattenhauer, ed., *Thibaut und Savigny*, 273.

[84] Kantorowicz, "Savigny and the Historical School," 331–32. As Hugo put it, Savigny wanted to "save scholarship from codification." Quoted in Rückert, *Savigny*, 74.

tradition could satisfy the new nationalistic urge in Germany, that the old "impartial" professoriate could step into the tense political void of the Rechtsstaat left behind by the expelled armies of the French. They were traditionalists, both of the great and of the little tradition[85]: they represented old ways of lawmaking in the German countryside, and they represented the magnificent legal civilization of the Romans. It is impossible to comprehend the full significance of the title commonly given Savigny's movement—"Historical School"—without a full sense of the wide range of historical traditions that German Romanist lawyers of the early nineteenth century felt they represented. To trace the traditionalist politics of the Roman-law professors, I will begin with Savigny's hopes for post-Revolutionary Germany before moving on to the rather different hopes of the Rechtsstaat thinkers of the south.

In some measure, the Savigny who mounted his influential defense of professorial lawmaking could be called, not a traditionalist, but a kind scholarly anti-statist. It was Savigny's hope that the charismatic Roman-law professors, sheltered within the free universities, could form the basis for a true spontaneous order, an order that, in an odd way, represented a kind of intellectual laissez-faire.[86] Thus his *Vom Beruf unserer Zeit* attacked codificationism on liberal grounds: those who demanded a code, Savigny said, proceeded from the false belief that all law must grow out of "statutes—that is, express prescriptions of the highest state power."[87] His proposal for a rule of jurists was intended, accordingly, as an alternative to state power: "Properly considered," he wrote, "it can well be supposed that the labor [of producing authoritative legal literature] can be consummated by individual legal scholars uncommanded and unratified by the state."[88] As Savigny conceived it, an order based on legal scholarship would thus be truly, radically liberal: judges would, in making their decisions, choose from among scholarly treatises as a source for their holding. No single treatise would be authoritative; rather legal decisions would be made by the free competition among published works for the confidence of the judge. Thus scholarly lawmaking embodied precisely a kind of freedom that was impossible in a legal system bound, as absolutist rulers had envisioned, by a code: as Savigny put it, the free "scholarly person" provided the ideal alternative to the rigid provisions

[85] On the great and little tradition, cf. R. Redfield, *Peasant Society and Culture* (Chicago, 1956), 70ff.

[86] For somewhat differing accounts of the political beliefs of the young Savigny on the propriety of state action, contrast G. Marini, *Friedrich Carl von Savigny* (Napoli, 1978), 55–57, with Rückert, *Savigny*, 322ff.

[87] Savigny, "Vom Beruf," 101.

[88] Ibid., 108.

of a code.[89] Moreover, the leadership of the jurists would make possible a national legal system adopted by the spontaneous will of the jurists themselves, and without state action.[90] In all of this, Savigny's thought belonged to the new tradition of laissez-faire.

Nevertheless, the heart of Savigny's defense of the professoriate lay in his faith in old traditions and institutions, in the long, German history of the use of Roman law. Savigny and his followers wished to revive the old constitution, insofar as it had survived the Enlightenment—an old order that, they were convinced, had all the resources necessary to carry Germany safely into the post-French Revolutionary world without losing hold of German tradition. This was the fundamental tenet of Savigny's reform conservatism: he wished, not to prevent change—for he was, like other prominent law professors, an avowed sponsor of legal change—but rather to stand by the old mechanisms of change that had sufficed in the legal world of the pre-absolutist order, a legal world governed in part by long-standing custom and in part by the texts of the learned high culture. As he stated his program in 1815:

> The Historical School starts from the assumption that the substance of law is to be drawn from the entire past of a nation . . . from the innermost essence of the nation itself, and its history. The prudent activity of every age should be directed at comprehending, rejuvenating, and sustaining this raw material, the necessary product of the nation's inner development.[91]

To understand the social implications of this, Savigny's version of Herderite *Volksgeist* (national-soul) theory, we must know more than historians have yet attempted to learn about the existing (but slowly changing) order that Savigny wished to "comprehend, rejuvenate, and sustain." We must look where historians, convinced that Savigny represented some kind of abstract conservatism, have failed to look: in the particularities of the legal world of the German countryside.

[89] Cf. H. Coing, "Das Verhältniß der positiven Rechtswissenschaft zur Ethik im Neunzehnten Jahrhundert," in J. Blühdorn and J. Ritter, eds., *Recht und Ethik*, Studien zur Philosophie und Literatur des neunzehnten Jahrhunderts, vol. 9 (Frankfurt a.M., 1970), 23–24 (not distinguishing with sufficient care, however, between judges and learned jurists as classes in Savigny's thought). Cited in Mohnhaupt, "Richter und Rechtssprechung," 250.

[90] Cf. Savigny, "Vom Beruf," 186. This claim to represent effective national unification continued in the statements of Pandektisten in the ensuing decades. The realization of the promise of national legal unification was, however, hampered throughout the century by the absence of a national high civil court (cf. Wieacker, *Privatrechtsgechichte*, 446; H. Müller-Kinet, *Die höchste Gerichtsbarkeit im deutschen Staatenbund* [Bern/Frankfurt a.M., 1975]). Thibaut, it should be noted, had made a similar claim.

[91] Savigny, "Ueber den Zweck der Zeitschrift für geschichtliche Rechtswissenschaft," in *Vermischte Schriften*, 1:113.

The Existing Order in Hannover

For the pre-absolutist order had survived: the old order as Savigny conceived it was the existing order of the states in which he had spent his youth, Hannover and Hesse, the central German states that had never been changed by the imposition of enlightened codes. In the legal worlds of Hannover and Hesse, there were two different principal legal systems in place during Savigny's lifetime: Roman law and customary law. Let me quote once again B. W. Pfeiffer's description of the legal situation in Hesse:

> Roman law is the main source of civil law [in Hesse]; various territorial laws have changed a great deal of it; but the greatest multiplication of laws is based on customs, which can be viewed in part as common German customs (in a historical sense), in part as customs of all Hesse, in part as customs of single provinces, and in part merely as customs of the kind of which J. v. Müller says that often nothing more than a large village has preserved them "in an old tale and in a grimy community chest."[92]

Savigny built his idea of the role of the professoriate on this pre-absolutist world, the world in which he had formed his philosophy while a young scholar at Marburg. To understand Savigny's conception of law, one must understand how he saw the role of professors in the formation of the two dominant legal traditions of the pre-absolutist order: Roman law and customary law. I will consider each in turn.

Most historians distinguish between two Germanies in the early nineteenth century: the Prussian North and the constitutionalist South.[93] But there was a neglected third Germany as well: the world of Hannover and Hesse in central and northern Germany, where neither Prussian state reformism nor Western constitutionalism had succeeded in displacing the old legal order. Savigny's intellectual formation took place in this third Germany, in the universities of Göttingen and Marburg, where scholarly romanticism grew up in the middle of a countryside in which the pre-absolutist world still survived. It was this world that he failed to bring with him to Berlin, when he failed to establish a revived usus modernus as the basis of the curriculum in place of the *Allgemeines Landrecht*.[94] To

---

[92] Pfeiffer, *Ideen zu einer neuen Civil-Gesetzgebung für Teutsche Staaten*, 102.

[93] E.g., R. Rürup, *Deutschland im Neunzehnten Jahrhundert, 1815–1871* (Göttingen, 1984), 130. Contrast W. H. Riehl, *Land und Leute*, 6th ed. (Stuttgart, 1867), 125–39, on the tripartite character of Germany.

[94] Cf. E. Wolf, *Grosse Rechtsdenker der Deutschen Geistesgeschichte*, 4th ed. (Tübingen, 1963), 521–22. Savigny continued to lecture on the *Allgemeines Landrecht*. Notes on Savigny's lectures on the *Allgemeines Landrecht* are available and have been discussed by D. Strauch, "F. C. von Savignys Landrechtsvorlesungen," 245–64. Cf. also Savigny, "Vom

understand Savigny, we must look at this pre-absolutist legal world—
which to a large extent still existed, comparatively undisturbed, in his
own time in the German states that had never experienced enlightened
codification.[95]

Hannover, for example, the home of romanticism and of Hugo's Göttingen school, was a kingdom without an enlightened code. That does not
mean that Hannover lacked princely legislation: such legislation (but of
a distinctly nonabsolutist type) played a crucial role in Hannoverian justice of the late 1820s and early 1830s. But in practice, as we shall see, the
exercise of princely power was little felt.

The newly constituted Kingdom of Hannover had emerged little-
changed from the French occupation. French legislation had been introduced into Hannover's constituent principates and duchies late, and with
little effect. In all parts of the kingdom, French legislation and the results
of occupation-period litigation were declared null and void in 1813–14.[96]
As a result, Pfeiffer's description of Hesse[97] could have fit Hannover as
well: there was only the most minimal legal uniformity over the kingdom.
Hannover was a legal patchwork of unintegrated localities. The records
of its legal life give a rich sense of the motley, the profusion of laws and
varying customs of which Thibaut and Pfeiffer complained. I will take
most of my examples from the *Juristische Zeitung für das Königreich
Hannover*, a privately published journal that served the needs of the legal
community in this codeless state. Only in a codeless state could a journal
like the *Juristische Zeitung* exist: precisely because the sources of law
were so various, Hannoverian lawyers needed some kind of general organ
that could publish information on the customs, statutes, and interpretations of Roman law that were the matter of court decisions. Accordingly
the journal offered an assortment of short scholarly essays, reportage on
court decisions and on local customs, as well as the texts of laws and
decrees new and old. It thus functioned simultaneously as law review,
court reporter, and official journal for the kingdom.[98]

Beruf," 118–20 (asserting that the Landrechte could in practice only be understood by reference to the doctrines of Roman law).

[95] Scheuermann, *Einflüße der historischen Rechtsschule*, 40, correctly observes that the
states without codes offered the most favorable ground for the Savignyan program.

[96] See generally W. Schubert, "Das Französische Recht in Deutschland zu Beginn der Restaurationszeit," *ZSS* (G) 94 (1977): 134–41. See also R. Oberschelp, *Niedersachsen 1760–
1820: Wirtschaft, Gesellschaft, Kultur im Land Hannover und Nachbargebieten*, 2 vols.,
Veröffentlichungen der Historischen Kommission für Niedersachsen und Bremen, 35; Quellen und Untersuchungen zur allgemeinen Geschichte Niedersachsens in der Neuzeit, vol. 4,
pts. 1 and 2 (Hildesheim, 1982), 1:124–25.

[97] For abolition of French law in Hesse, see Schubert, "Französisches Recht," 142–44.

[98] For a general survey of the legal institutions of Hannover, which included a complex
variety of courts that I do not review in detail here, see Oberschelp, *Niedersachsen*, 2:100–
111.

An example from the *Juristische Zeitung* for 1826 gives some idea of the baroque character of Hannoverian law, centered on the smallest jurisdictions and determined by a mix of princely ordinances and popular customs both centuries old. Like most contributions to the *Juristische Zeitung*, this short piece was sent in by a local lawyer:

ON THE CUSTOMARY MEASURES OF HILDESHEIM

Doubt frequently arises in Hildesheim about which measures should be used in boundary and other disputes.

In his *Meyerrecht* (Pt. 2, p. 36) Gesenius teaches that:

> in the principate of Hildesheim, the *Morgen* equals 120 sq. *Ruthen* of Calenberg feet; land has also been measured in the same way.

But this view is false, and its testimony deserves no credence, as no particular cases are offered.

I, on the other hand, can testify from personal experience [*aus eigener Erfahrung*], for in the matter of Amelunke et al. v. Spengler, both parties from Dahlum, the royal ministry in Bilderlahe took cognizance of the customary measures.

The entire controversy is rendered irrelevant by a now *very rare* [emphasis in original] ordinance on taxation by His Highness the Duke and Bishop Ferdinand promulgated and published in 1646, in which it is stated, for example, in tit. I, art. I, that:

> Henceforth in our Bishopric, and all the cloisters, offices, courts, cities, towns, and villages belonging to it, in all selling, buying, and other contracts, in measuring and weighing, whether in ells, weights, grain, wine, beers, and *all other measures* [emphasis in original], the ells, the measures, and weights of the city of Braunschweig shall be taken as the norm.

Subsequent ordinances in Hildesheim (of the 20th of January, 1777, and the 21st of September, 1786) also agree perfectly, in that they determine, for example, that the windlass should be measured according to Braunschweig measures. . . .

In the aforementioned case brought before the ministry at Bilderlahe, Amelunke et al. conceded that in their area Braunschweig measures had earlier been customary, and several field witnesses and old people [*Feldgeschworene und alte Leute*] from Bockenem were willing to testify to the same effect.

One may therefore assume, according to earlier determinations, that Braunschweig measures are the norm in Hildesheim until it can be demonstrated that other measures are desired and chosen.

Lammspringe.   Kleinschmidt, Dr.[99]

---

[99] *Juristische Zeitung für das Königreich Hannover* 1, no. 1 (1826): 61–63.

The horror of enlightened reformers at the uncertainty of legal life at its most basic levels in Hildesheim, as reflected in this passage, can well be imagined. Custom, legal scholarship, and casual legislation mix in unpredictable proportions. Judicial officials base their decisions in part on a treatise by Gesenius—a local practitioner and scholar[100]—and in part on the testimony of "old people from Bockenem." The officials rely on these sources only because they are ignorant of ordinances 180 years old, copies of which are *"very rare."* Those ordinances themselves, rather than carefully specifying law, declare to be law in Hildesheim that which is customary in Braunschweig—thus forcing officials to determine, not only what is customary, but what is customary in a different jurisdiction. All this to establish measures and weights different from those used perhaps thirty miles away.

But if enlightened reformers would have been horrified, romantic political theorists of the Rechtsstaat could take great comfort from the law of Hildesheim. For on the everyday level of law-finding, as Dr. Kleinschmidt, the collector of rare legal documents, knew it, "popular sovereignty" and the "monarchical principle" were difficult to distinguish. Volk and Fürst (prince), from the point of view of a romantic, were exercising authority concurrently in Hildesheim and without distinct spheres. What "His Highness the Duke and Bishop Ferdinand" declared to be law was law for all time; on the other hand, legal officals relied on the "old people of Bockenem" for the state of Hildesheimer law, or else on learned treatises that purported to embody only what was customary. Knowledge of everyday life continued to be the main source of law: Dr. Kleinschmidt drew his knowledge of the law "aus eigener Erfahrung." "Feldgeschworene und alte Leute" also knew the law from experience.

The life of this customary-law order was attested in item after item of the *Juristische Zeitung.* There was, lawyers could easily believe, no necessary conflict between prince and people. Even when princes asserted their power in the "cloisters, offices and courts, cities, towns, and villages" of Hannover, they were also often careful to defer in large measure to popular custom, as this 1822 ministerial rescript for the Duchies of Bremen and Verden (a single region in northern Hannover) testifies:

MINISTERIAL RESCRIPT OF THE 29TH OF MAY, 1822,
REGARDING THE PUNISHMENT OF ADULTERY

A ministerial rescript, dated the 29th of May, 1822, was given to the Chancellery of Justice in Stade, which first of all left undisturbed the previous custom, according to which both single and double adultery is punished only by imprisonment in the Duchies of Bremen and Verden, adding however, that

---

[100] Karl Gesenius was Canzley- und Hofgerichtsprocurator in Wolfenbüttel. Cf. the title page of his *Das Meyerrecht,* 2 vols. (Wolfenbüttel, 1801–03).

the (up until now express) authority to commute this imprisonment to a money fine could no longer be allowed, but that whatever applications to commute an imposed or a pending sentence of imprisonment on account of adultery into a money fine must be retracted as not belonging to the authority of the Justice Chancellery. If necessary, the condemned parties should be directed to the Royal Cabinet Ministry. Similarly, with respect to patrimonial and other courts . . .[101]

To be sure, the prince, in this case, was attempting to assume a prerogative. But it was only a very limited prerogative, the right to collect fines as substitutes for imprisonment. And the royal ministry was careful explicitly to ratify custom (*Observanz*) with respect to the original penalty itself. To romantics this could only mean that law-finding power remained in the first instance with the people.[102] If royal decrees could themselves defer to custom, the courts and local justice ministries generally based their decisions on nothing else. Thus, in most cases, customary law governed; in some sense, it could be truly said that princes and courts deferred to a "rule of law."

But it was centrally important for the Savignyan program that the customary law that ruled was not precisely speaking the direct creation of the Volk. For customary law was by and large based on learned treatises, some of them produced by local lawyers, some by the professoriate. This reliance on learned treatises was inevitable: determining custom was most often a more complex business than simply calling in "the old people" as the officials described by Dr. Kleinschmidt did. There were great and recurring uncertainties about the details of customary law, and the people

---

[101] *Juristische Zeitung*, 1, no. 2 (1826): 49–50.

[102] Another case concerning the morals of Bremen and Verden shows that the state could also give its recognition to the *usus fori*, the custom of local courts. Here the Royal Ministry had, on request, confirmed an appellate finding:

> Rescript des königlichen Cabinetts-Ministern an das Stadtgericht
> zu Stade, vom 9. July 1829, daß das stuprum tertia vel quarta vice
> reiteratum in den Herzogtümern Bremen und Verden als
> Criminaldelict nicht betrachtet werden könne.

Da die Vorschriften der Reichsgesetze über Bestrafung gemeiner Unzucht keine Norm geben, nach welcher über die policeiliche oder peinliche Bestrafung dieses Vergehens sich etwas bestimmen ließe, in den Herzogtümern Bremen und Verden auch ein die peinliche Bestrafung des mehrmals wiederholten stupri vorschreibendes Gesetz nicht besteht, nach dem früheren dortigen Gerichtsgebrauche aber, wie sich jetzt ergeben hat, auch die zum dritten Male und öfter wiederholte außereheliche Schwangerung stets nur policeilich geahndet ist.

The ministry went on to ratify court practice (*Juristische Zeitung* 5, no. 1 [1830]: 81–83). The case sheds interesting light on status of "judicial" custom as opposed to "popular" custom.

were often quite unable to settle mooted questions.[103] If customary agrarian law was lacking in Lauenberg, could officials there apply the customary law of neighboring regions, when those regions had historically been enserfed while Lauenberg had not?[104] Here historical scholarship had pressing daily purposes in Hannover. So did the great characteristic activity of romantic scholarship: the collection of customs. The *Juristische Zeitung* published long compilations of Hannoverian customs, precisely because officials of justice could not decide cases without such information.[105] It also published jurisprudential essays on how the existence of a custom could be proven in court.[106] Thus local lawyers were part of a learned culture that sustained the customary-law regime.

The leaders of the learned community that served the needs of the customary-law order were the professors. The prominence of professorial treatises among the sources courts cited dated back to the eighteenth century. Under the influence of Conring, professors at the German universities had been expected to acquire expertise in "German law"—i.e., the "common customary law" I have already discussed at length. The treatises they produced had long served as evidence of customary law, and they continued to do so.[107] In the immediate aftermath of the French occupation, some Hannoverian local governments had made some attempts to forbid courts to cite scholars,[108] and procedural ordinances declared emphatically that courts were not to rely upon the "mere opinions" of professors.[109] But whatever might constitute "mere opinions," both adjudicative branches—the courts and the chancelleries of justice—regularly cited the professoriate not only for propositions of Roman law, but also on the specifics of the customary law on every type of legal ques-

---

[103] Cf. Watson, *Evolution of Law*, 43–65.

[104] *Juristische Zeitung* 2, no. 2 (1827): 136–43, 154–56; cf. T. Hagemann, in F. von Bülow (continued first by T. Hagemann, then by E. P. J. Spangenberg) *Practische Erörterungen aus allen Theilen der Rechtsgelehrsamkeit*, 10 vols. (Hannover, 1818), 6:112ff.

[105] E.g., "Nachrichten über die in den Herzogtümern Bremen und Verden bestehenden Local–Statuten und Gewohnheiten, so wie über die in dieser Provinz vorhandenen Deich- und Holzgerichte (aus officiellen Quellen vom Jahre 1806)" in *Juristische Zeitung* 20, no. 1 and 2 passim (1845); "Alphabetische Zusammenstellung der gebräuchlichen Grundzinse und Dienste von Lehn-, Meier- und Zinsgütern im Fürstentum Lüneburg," in ibid. 3, no. 1 (1828): 53–63.

[106] "Über das Wesen und den Beweis einer Gewohnheit," in *Juristische Zeitung*, 7, no. 1 (1832): 120–25.

[107] See above, pp. 47, 50.

[108] For legislation against Aktenversendung in this period, see Schubert, "Französisches Recht," 140–41. Cf. *Juristische Zeitung*, 14, no. 1 (1839): 97 (reporting an 1814 ordinance from Osnabrück against Aktenversendung to Privatdoctoren). For struggles over Aktenversendung, see ibid., 19, no. 3 (1844): 99; 5, no. 1 (1830): 113–14; 12, no. 2 (1837): 93–95.

[109] Hagemann, *Practische Erörterungen*, 7: 119.

tion.[110] Savigny himself was not least among the scholars considered authoritative by both the highest court and the highest chancery in Hannover.[111] Professorial authority was exercised not only through judicial citations, but also through Aktenversendung. The Göttingen faculty, for example, could adjudicate a typical case in which an old statute had to be tested against a countervailing custom. In this case, the legal validity of the 1580 ordinance in question, which outlawed a six-percent interest rate, was doubtful. The professors found that the ordinance had never established itself in Germany, and that custom justified the high interest rate:

> The imperial-legal prohibition of six-percent interest never generally penetrated in Germany, either in older or in more recent periods; the imperial courts would have recognized six-percent interest as soon as it became customary in the territory [sobald dieser landüblich gewesen]
>
> cf. Meiern, Gedanken über der Rechtmäßigkeit des 6ten. Zinsthalers, S. 13f.
> Mevii, Decision. P. IV. D. 205.
> Mittermaier, Grundsätze des gem. dt. Privatr. §90.[112]

This mixed scholarship of the usus modernus the very latest work of the universities (Mittermaier was the chair of the Heidelberg Spruchkollegium), in service of the old principle that custom bound the Hannoverian courts of Bremen and Verden.

Savigny and his followers acquired a sense of their own place in German society from the use of scholarship in these countryside courts. Roman law existed alongside custom. The main sources of prevailing custom were two: testimony of local witnesses, and writings of university professors. As the romantics of the Historical School interpreted this state of affairs, Professoren and Volk together made law in the central German courts. This tendency to identify the Professoren with the Volk showed in the demand of one scholar that Aktenversendung be guaranteed to the poor of Hannover. Writing in 1844, when the courts were beginning to deny the right of Aktenversendung outright,[113] this anonymous contributor to the Juristische Zeitung protested on behalf of the poor. "I may be permitted," he wrote, "to present a few cases that have come before courts in provinces where pure Roman law applies and that have involved sums under 30 Thaler." In these cases the poor had been allowed neither

---

[110] E.g., Juristische Zeitung 2, no. 2 (1827): 145–46, in which a chancellery cited scholars on the permissibility of putting women on the wheel.

[111] E.g., Juristische Zeitung 7, no. 1 (1832): 78–79 (authoritative status of Savigny's Recht des Besitzes).

[112] "Über die Rechtmäßigkeit des 6. Zinsthalers," Juristische Zeitung 3, no. 1 (1829): 38.

[113] See below, p. 203.

an appeal outside ordinary channels such as had been available since the
founding of the Reichskammergericht ("Nichtigkeitsbeschwerde") nor
Aktenversendung:

> Many matters involving 300 and 600 Thaler are not as important to the
> parties involved as a dispute over 10–20 Thaler for these people. Thirty Tha-
> ler is rather more for a man who earns, by hard labor, 90 Thaler a year, than
> 300 Thaler for a man who every year collects more than a 1000 Thaler in
> dues, rents, and crop percentages. What has become, here, of "equality be-
> fore the law"?[114]

The professors at Göttingen who took such an interest in *Volksgewohn-
heiten* (the customs of the people) thus served, in the eyes of scholars such
as this, as the potential administrative hope of the poorer Volk.[115]

The Jurisprudence of the Existing Order:
Professorial Lawmaking in the Thought of Savigny and Puchta

The legal order of this Hannoverian Rechtsstaat provided Savigny and
his followers with the village tradition, the little tradition, on which they
could base their traditionalist program. Of the members of the Historical
School, it was Savigny who made the first effort to formulate a coherent
account of the pre-abolutist legal order: in his *Vom Beruf unserer Zeit*,
he accounted for the predominance of learned treatises in court customary law-finding by postulating that the Volk, the original source of custom, had ceased to be the principal maker of law as culture evolved; jurists had accordingly stepped in and carried on the task of developing
customary law. The same jurists had brought Roman law with them.[116]
But the classic statement of the Historical School's little tradition did not
appear until some years later. This was G. F. Puchta's *Das Gewohnheitsrecht*, which was published in two volumes, the first in 1828, the second
in 1837. *Das Gewohnheitsrecht* was the most influential and fully argued
statement of the Historical School's attempts to base a legal order on the
work of professors of law.[117] It was instantly controversial—indeed, the
publication of the first volume was a signal for the great jurisprudential

---

[114] "Über die Nothwendigkeit der Zulassung der Nichtigkeits-Beschwerde und Aktenversendung bei den Untergerichten in nicht appellablen Sachen," in *Juristische Zeitung* 19, no.
3 (1844): 99, 140.

[115] *Volk*, in the German of the time, it should be remembered, was often used to mean
"poor people" or "subject classes." See esp. the range of meanings given in J. and
W. Grimm, s.v. "Volk," *Deutsches Wörterbuch* (Leipzig, 1852), vol. 12, no. 2, cols. 463–69.

[116] E.g., Savigny, "Vom Beruf," 104.

[117] Puchta's version was "in der historischen Rechtsschule fast absolut herrschend."
Scheuermann, *Einflüße der historischen Rechtsschule*, 83.

wars that split the German legal world throughout the 1830s and 1840s. Puchta ignited this controversy by his forthright defense of the idea that professors should, ultimately, be the source of law in a modern state; that Germany should be ruled by what he called a "Juristenrecht," a "jurists' law."

Puchta was conservative by temperament like so many who became prominent in the years of political romanticism in Germany. He was profoundly religious. He maintained "a decidedly monarchical and conservative" standpoint[118]—which, to be sure, did not alienate him from the Rechtsstaat consensus of his day. He spent many years in Heidelberg and continued to correspond with the leading Rechtsstaat thinker Robert von Mohl,[119] and, like his contemporaries of all political tendencies, he believed it to be the task of his age to steer clear of both Volk and Fürst: the state, said Puchta, has as its only purpose the preservation of a lawful order of freedom that stood above all party interest.[120] He was an immensely influential jurist. His textbooks of Roman law, the *Institutes* and the *Pandects*, were standard for law students for years. His contribution to the grand German tradition of systematization—the attempt to organize legal doctrine according to what he called the "pyramid of principles"—became, over the course of the nineteenth century, the standard methodology not only of systematic German private law but also of systematic German public law. Puchta was, as historians have increasingly recognized, very much the father of the nineteenth-century Rechtsstaat.[121]

This father of the Rechtsstaat always had one eye on the world of Han-

---

[118] See the obituaries reproduced by Puchta's editor as an introduction to his *Kleine civilistische Schriften*, ed. Rudorff (Leipzig, 1851), e.g., X and XLIV. Cf. Puchta, *Das Gewohnheitsrecht* (repr. Darmstadt, 1965) (originally 1828), 1:136–37, on "die Lehre von der Volkssouveränität und . . . ähnliche Verkehrtheiten."

[119] Cf. J. Bohnert, "Beiträge zu einer Biographie Georg Friedrich Puchtas," ZSS (G) 96 (1979): 239 n. 85. On Puchta's legal thought more generally, see J. Bohnert, *Über die Rechtslehre Georg Friedrich Puchtas*, Freiburger rechts- und staatswissenschaftliche Abhandlungen, vol. 41 (Karlsruhe, 1975).

[120] Puchta, *Cursus der Institutionen*, 2d ed. (Leipzig, 1845), 67–68: "Dieß ist der gemeinschaftliche Irrthum zweier großer politischer Parteien, die einander gegenüber stehen. Die eine Partei giebt dem Recht des Fürsten einen privatrechtlichen Charakter, indem sie es entweder wie ein Analogon der väterlichen Gewalt, oder der Vormundschaft, oder nicht gar als ein Eigenthum betrachtet; die andere behandelt das Recht der Unterthanen als ein Privatrecht, indem sie es jedem Einzelnen als solchem zuschreibt, und so die Einzelnen als solche, vereinzelt oder in beliebig von ihnen eingegangenen Associationen, zum Widerstand gegen die Regierung, und zur Theilnahme an derselben berechtigt."

[121] Puchta's influence is traced by W. Wilhelm, *Zur Juristischen Methodenlehre im neunzehnten Jahrhundert*, 70 and passim. The critical importance of Puchta's theories for later Rechtsstaat thought is also declared by, e.g., M. Stolleis, "Verwaltungslehre und Verwaltungswissenschaft," in Jeserich et al., eds., *Deutsche Verwaltungsgeschichte*, 2:81.

nover, the world I have described, where customary law formed a kind of neutral ground between prince and people, and professorial treatises were the principle source of customary law. The eminence of professors in this customary Rechtsstaat gave Puchta's justification for professorial law-making its force and plausibility. Starting from the living world of Hannover, Puchta developed Savigny's postulate of the role of jurists as the organs of the Volksgeist into an account of the existing order and a philosophy for the future.

Puchta built his argument on one jurisprudential proposition, one shift of interpretation in procedural law, which today might seem trivial but which was informed by the most sophisticated philosophy of the universities, and which had startlingly far-reaching political implications. Puchta's fundamental assertion was that customary law, if it existed at all, must be the product of the *gemeinsame Überzeugung*, the "common conviction," of the Volk. This assertion, simple as it seems, had highly significant legal and political implications. Pursued to its logical conclusion, the idea of "common conviction" called into question the vitality of the Volk as a lawmaking force and left room for the professors to step in as leaders of the legal order.

The requirement of "common conviction" lent support to the claims of the professors by altering the jurisprudential status of what were called *Übungen* or *Handlungen*, of actions that could be the basis of a court finding that a particular customary right or duty existed. Suppose that a feudal lord alleged that a peasant owed him a certain service (or money payment in lieu of some traditional service) as a matter of customary law. In order to prove that the peasant owed him the obligation in question, the lord might adduce evidence in court that this peasant or other peasants had performed the service in the past. These past performances were called *Übungen* or *Handlungen*, and they had some (though varying) status as proof of the existence of customary law. Puchta addressed himself to the exact legal status of these *Übungen*. The question was whether *Übungen created* custom or were *evidence* of custom. Puchta maintained that *Übungen* were *evidence* of the existence of a customary duty or right that both peasant and lord believed to exist. Customary law existed in the Volksgeist, and both peasant and lord were aware of it through their gemeinsame Überzeugung, their "common conviction" that the act in question was mandated by customary law. [122]

By taking this position, Puchta set himself against a new breed of so-called "Germanist" lawyers. The Germanists maintained, against Puchta, that Übungen actually did *create* law. In so arguing, they believed them-

---

[122] For Puchta's views, see, e.g., *Das Gewohnheitsrecht*, 1:109, 2:85, and often. On Puchta and Savigny on this point, see Rückert, *Savigny*, 305ff.

selves to be defending the supremacy of the German Volk. For if the
Übungen of country people created customary law, then the peasants
themselves were somehow the legislators of their own lives; the Volk was,
in some sense, sovereign in Germany.[123] This conviction was informed,
moreover, by a kind of mystical scholarly medievalism typical of the romantic era. The "Germanist" lawyers, who favored expulsion of Roman
law and a return to German law, were pioneers in the study of medieval
legal systems. They had discovered a critical fact about primitive legal
systems: that in primitive legal systems, obligations are created by the
performance of ritual acts, not by the intent of the parties. Thus, in the
medieval German world lord and vassal were bound to each other as soon
as they performed the ritual of infeudation. No court would consider it
relevant to ask whether lord and vassal had ever *intended* to be bound.
The only legal question was whether they had performed the critical ritual
act. Romantic Germanists were entranced by this medieval world, in
which act was all that mattered and shared intent counted, legally speaking, for naught. They wished to revive the old Germanic world of binding
legal rituals—of what they called "publicity and solemnity"—as the basis
of the legal system. Because they believed in "publicity and solemnity," it
was critically important to the Germanists to insist that Übungen created
customary obligations—for if Übungen created customary obligations,
not only did the Volk in some sense rule, but Germany still had a "public
and solemn" "Germanic" act-based legal system. These Germanist lawyers made many converts, among them Hegel, who maintained in his own
writings on contract law that contracts could be formed only by ritual
acts, not by the shared intent of the parties.[124]

Puchta had political reasons of his own for taking his own view. For by
insisting that Übungen were only evidence of obligations, Puchta could
insist that the Volksgeist had ceased to produce law; he could also plausibly plead for a continued predominance of learned lawyers. That the
Volksgeist should yield to the jurists, while not a necessary implication of
Puchta's theory, was compatible with it: if Übungen were only evidence
of customary law, and not themselves customary law, then it was quite
possible that the Volksgeist was, as Savigny said, in need of scholarly rep-

[123] Cf., e.g., G. Beseler, *Volksrecht und Juristenrecht* (Leipzig, 1843), 63ff., 111–12. See
also, B.-R. Kern, *Georg Beseler*, Schriften zur Rechtsgeschichte, Heft 26 (Berlin, 1982),
378f.; J. Rückert, *A. L. Reyschers Leben und Rechtstheorie*, Abhandlungen zur Rechtswissenschaftlichen Grundlagenforschung, vol. 13 (Berlin, 1974), 328f.; S. Buchholz, *Abstraktionsprinzip und Immobiliarrecht: Zur Geschichte der Auflassung und der Grundschuld*,
Ius Commune Sonderheft 8 (Frankfurt a.M., 1978), 110–11.

[124] For a discussion of Hegel against Savigny on contract law, see P. Landau, "Hegels
Begründung des Vertragsrechts," in M. Riedel, ed., *Materialien zu Hegels Rechtsphilosophie*, 2 vols. (Frankfurt a.M., 1975), 2:180–86.

resentatives. Even if new Übungen could be found in daily German life, this did not mean that the Volksgeist was still producing new law. Moreover, if Übungen were only evidence of customary law, then scholars were not bound by the Übungen of the Volk in elaborating a new *Juristenrecht*. Juristenrecht, systematic scholarly lawmaking, declared Puchta, was just as much the product of a gemeinsame Überzeugung as customary law.[125] The scholars "must act as the representatives of the people,"[126] for they had a special responsibility to elaborate their gemeinsame Überzeugung into a national law. Indeed, they could serve the nation's lawmaking needs better than any other force, for, through scholarly systematization and elaboration, they were able to transcend the merely "receptive" and become "productive."[127]

The continued dominance of Roman law followed, in turn, from the postulate that scholars were the representatives of the nation. If scholars had faith in Roman law, that faith must be a product of their gemeinsame Überzeugung. Nor was the faith of the scholars in Roman law misguided: as a general proposition, customary law was no longer truly possible, for the old Germanic legal constitution had faded, the simpler times had vanished well before the Reception of Roman law.[128] The existing Roman-law order was no affront to the Volksgeist, which had long since lost its capacity to deal with a complex modern world. To be sure, many of the local customs were sensible and durable; state action to eliminate them would be inappropriate.[129] But if state action would be inappropriate, Roman-law reform was not: "Our entire mode of legal thinking," Puchta wrote, "is based on Roman jurisprudence."[130] Indeed, without Roman law, no scholarship—and therefore no productive lawmaking—would be possible.[131] Hostility to Roman law was a forgivable "human weakness"[132], but Roman law was truly a *Weltrecht*, a law of world civilization, and had firmly established itself in Germany.[133] The age of Juristenrecht had come. The Romanist lawyers were the only representatives of "common conviction," and village life justified the common embrace of a higher Roman tradition.

[125] Puchta, *Gewohnheitsrecht*, 1:161.
[126] Ibid., 1:166.
[127] Ibid., 1:146.
[128] Ibid., 1:205, 214, 233.
[129] Ibid., 1:224–25.
[130] Ibid., 1:56–57 n.1.
[131] Ibid., 1:202.
[132] Ibid., 1:203.
[133] Ibid., 1:202–3. For the development of Roman law as a *Weltrecht* through the elaboration of the *ius gentium*, the body of Roman rules presumptively applicable to all peoples, see ibid., 1:34ff.

Savigny's Grand Tradition: The Historical School's Roman Civilization

Thus Savigny and Puchta founded their hopes in part on the homeliest kind of tradition, on what could be called the village legal life of Germany. But they also believed that the homely tradition empowered them to represent the great tradition. As Romanist lawyers in Germany had done for centuries, they thought of themselves as men of Rome. Savigny and Puchta were men of an age of *Begeisterung*, of inspiration, and they wanted the grander, more momentous, grounding that only reinterpreting history could give them. Thus Puchta insisted that the rule of jurists in Germany was the manifestation of an evolutionary tendency that marked world history as a whole:

> With every Volk, and in every period of the existence of every Volk, even in the earliest period, in which knowledge of the law is a common possession of all members, we find men who, through their intellectual preferences, their inclinations, or vocation, acquire a superior familiarity with law, a familiarity that is distinguished from the familiarity possessed by others only quantitatively, not qualitatively, through its extent and not its character. It is a consequence of the heterogeneity of the mass of propositions into which law evolves that the familiarity of these others grows increasingly more imperfect, that their consciousness becomes ever less truly filled by their law. In equal measure do those who are knowledgeable about law become the natural representatives of the national legal consciousness. . . . This relationship establishes itself most decisively when knowledge of the law becomes the possession of those who are set aside from the rest of the people because scholarship has become a vocation, and the jurists have become a special class.[134]

Determined to see Germany within the unfolding of world history, Savigny and Puchta turned to the reinterpretation of Antiquity.

Antiquity, like the Hannoverian countryside, seemed to Savigny and his contemporaries to exist untouched by politics. As the great historian of Rome, B. G. Niebuhr, put it, "sound philology" offered "the best antidote to fanaticism."[135] This belief in the neutrality of Antiquity appeared and reappeared in all corners of German society. Antiquity offered a minimally charged curriculum for the German schools: as Paulsen has written of the secondary schools in this period, caught, during curriculum fights, between the rival educational schemes of princes and of republicans, Antiquity offered "neutral ground," an educational alternative ac-

---

[134] Ibid., 2:18–19.
[135] Quoted in M. Hoffmann, *August Boeckh* (Leipzig, 1901), 219.

ceptable, on the strength of its prestige, to all.[136] By the same token, conferring bureaucratic appointments on the basis of classical education seemed to eliminate politics and favoritism from the process: it was a great virtue of Roman-law training for bureaucrats that making Bildung, the peculiarly German ideal of a cultivated education, the prerequisite for power created equality of opportunity.[137]

As Savigny and Puchta worked to construct their own version of a neutral Antiquity, they were able to build on the work of the 1790s. Haubold, Heyne, and especially Hugo had reclaimed the ius respondendi during the imperial revival of the 1790s and had made Roman law once again a source of justification for professorial preeminence. Savigny and Puchta extended and refined this two-decades-old interpretation of Roman history into an elaborate historical theory of the role of the Volksgeist, in which scholars became the dominant productive source of Roman law. As I have shown, the scholars of the 1790s seized upon Pomponius's account of the reign of Hadrian in reinterpreting Roman legal history. Hadrian had been forced to acknowledge the special authority of the jurists because the brilliance of the jurists themselves could not be ignored. As Hugo concluded: "Scholarship is never improved by an imperial law, or by a cabinet decree, any more than theology is improved by a council. The spirit of the age renders all commands either ineffective or irrelevant."[138] The legal order had established itself spontaneously, unbeckoned by the emperor. This was a vision of history perfectly suited to the hopes of the Savigny's generation; this was rule of law that utterly excluded rule of men, legal order without the sovereignty of either Volk or Fürst. Savigny and Puchta set about elaborating the Roman history of the decade of imperial revival into the basis for their own Rechtsstaat.

Savigny wanted his truth to emerge from Roman history. In his *Vom Beruf*, he found his interpretation. He postulated three stages in the ancient history of Roman law: first, an age in which the Volksgeist itself made law; second, an age in which jurists stood in for the Volksgeist, making law as its representatives; and finally, a disastrous age of codification, in which late-antique bunglers had edited and rehashed the writings of the golden eras before, creating the *Corpus Iuris*.[139] The *Corpus Iuris* was the typical product of premature codification. Codification was

[136] F. Paulsen, *Geschichte des Gelehrten Unterrichts in Deutschland*, 2:322.

[137] Bleek, *Von der Kameralausbildung zum Juristenprivileg*, 39–40. "Chancengleichheit" must of course be viewed in light of the obligation of servants of the state to serve some time without pay. Cf. K.G.A. Jeserich, "Die Ausbildung der höheren Verwaltungsbeamten," in Jeserich et al., eds., *Deutsche Verwaltungsgeschichte*, 2:324.

[138] Hugo, *Lehrbuch der Rechtsgeschichte*, 228.

[139] Savigny, "Vom Beruf unsrer Zeit," 114–17.

most often the work of a people in cultural decline.[140] A lesson for Germany lay in this Roman history: Germany was as yet in an evolutionary stage analogous to the second stage of Rome, the age in which jurists made law as the vicars of the Volk[141]; accordingly, the German jurists must hold off the claims of codificationists, the usurpers of the legislative power of a Volksgeist sovereign but quiescent. Only through an unyielding defense of their own power to elaborate legal doctrine—a power they did in fact enjoy in the pre-absolutist Hannoverian and Hessian heart of the German world—could jurists faithfully advance the causes of the Volksgeist.

Savigny's outline of Roman history became canonical for the historical school, but it was no more than an outline. As with the theory of customary law, it was Puchta who elaborated Savigny's postulates into volumes of legal history and jurisprudence, and into the standard texts of German legal education. He explained that the promulgation of the Twelve Tables had not yet signaled the exhaustion of the Roman Volksgeist. Law lived in the consciousness of the people—but at the same time was cultivated by legal specialists:

> Alongside what was written, a great part of the law existed unwritten, living and evolving in the consciousness of the people as customary law. Both written and unwritten law were perfectly equivalent, both were the property of the people. The twelve tables were intended to present the fundamental principles of the entire legal system, the rest of Roman law appeared as an extension of it, as the twigs that shot forth from its trunk and branches. The newly developing and growing law that existed undelineated in the conviction of the people was put in the context of the twelve tables. This was the business of the legal specialist [Rechtskundigen] of the age. Accordingly the customary law that existed alongside the written law was called *interpretatio duodecim tabularum* [the interpretation of the twelve tables].[142]

But the later development of Roman law was primarily the development of Roman legal scholarship as the guardian of popular private law. With the end of the republic and the vast extension of the empire, the Roman Volk inevitably began to lose touch with its sense of law, but the jurists were able to step in:

> The jurists cannot fail to feel themselves the natural representatives of their nation in law; law lives in their consciousness, as it had, until that time, lived in the unmediated consciousness of the entire people—from which it had, to

---

[140] Ibid., 113, 117.

[141] Cf. the discussion of Polay, *Ursprung, Entwicklung, und Untergang*, 55.

[142] Puchta, *Cursus der Institutionen*, 281. Cf. Puchta, *Gewohnheitsrecht*, 1:15–16. For similar views in the work of Johannes Christiansen, see Cappellini, *Systema Iuris*, 2:301.

be sure, not disappeared, by which it was, however, no longer completely comprehended. This feeling gives legal scholarship for the first time the inner dignity that cannot be lacking if it is to flourish; without this inner dignity, the jurist is either an obscure pedant, or a laborer half-compelled to serve.[143]

Thus legal scholarship took its whole meaning from its representative character. It continued to embody the legal sensibility of all: the *edictum perpetuum* (the collection of procedural and substantive principles established by the praetors and the basis of most Roman law in later centuries) was, like the twelve tables, a product of gemeinsame Überzeugung,[144] of the "common conviction" that was the mark of true customary law with its seat in the Volksgeist. The authority of the jurists was confirmed by the establishment of the ius respondendi (which Puchta, interestingly, credited to Augustus, not Hadrian[145]); it gave force of law not only to the opinions in specific cases, but also to the published writings of the jurists.[146] Rome was the model society of scholarly lawmaking.

It was a feature of this model society that neither Volk nor Fürst exercised real power. If the theoretical authority of assemblies and princes was great, in practice they too refrained from lawmaking. Even in the republican period, special enactments were made to apply to private law only where weighty political questions required them.[147] In the principate, the many rescripts, decrees, and *constitutiones* of the emperors in general only confirmed the law made by the learned:

> [For the most part] they did not depart from their natural purpose of expressing established law, while, however, influencing the law by giving a clear determination to principles that were controversial or the extent of whose applicability was uncertain. Finally, instances did not lack in which the Emperor used the opportunity presented to them by the decision of cases to introduce new legal principles. But this was not the original purpose of decrees and rescripts; when he spoke as a judge, the prince was bound, like any other, to pronounce according to existing law and create nothing new.[148]

The regime of learning thus maintained itself in Roman law through the principate. Despite the fall of the Republic, the princes never usurped the proper power of the scholars, who continued to be the living guardians of private law. Puchta's analysis of the legal status of imperial decrees and rescripts in the Roman principate can be fully understood only against the background of legal life in a place like Hannover. His emperors, who

---

[143] Puchta, *Cursus der Institutionen*, 1:425.
[144] Ibid., 1:340.
[145] Ibid., 1:559–60.
[146] Ibid., 1:564.
[147] Ibid., 1:284ff.
[148] Ibid., 1:543.

"did not depart from the natural purpose of expressing established law," had their counterparts Hannover's duchies and princedoms.

As he closed his account, Puchta was careful to declare for the law students that read his text the differences between the legal scholars of their own time and the jurists of ancient Rome. The ancients had had a livelier sense of their law than any modern:

> As in all objects of knowledge, we have a wider horizon in law than the ancients did, our law had its origin, to a large extent, in ages long past, in another world, among other peoples. Knowledge of it demands a considerable scholarly apparatus, we need the context provided by historical research in order to be masters of our law from all sides and in order that the otherwise dead residue that we are left with in the present may be born within us as a living organism.[149]

There was no perfect analogy between Rome and Germany, but what set Germany apart only made the work of law professors that much more important. The young lawyers who heard Puchta lecture were instructed to consider themselves the only guardians of the national spirit, the only revivers of an "otherwise dead residue." With their work, history would come alive in German society.

At this point I must pause to introduce one more element in the Savignyan theory of law and legal history. In promoting the lawmaking claims of learned jurists, Savigny and his followers were obliged to oppose more than just the claims of the Germanist-sponsored Volk. They were also obliged to oppose the claims of another class of lawyers: judges who might be inclined to claim legal authority for precedent. It was very important for Savigny and Puchta that the principal source of law not be prior court decisions but rather learned essays and treatises. Thus they were fundamentally hostile to the judicial exercise of power through the making of binding precedent. Their hostility to precedent very much set Savigny and Puchta apart from the law professors of the south, to whom I will turn in a moment.[150]

Indeed, the Historical School's Juristenrecht was emphatically intended

---

[149] Ibid., 1:471.

[150] It bears emphasizing that in insisting that propositions of law received their authority through the support of scholarship, not through prior citation by the courts, Savigny and his followers were setting themselves against what had been the traditional basis for use of Roman law in Germany. For, in theory, Roman law had its legitimacy in Germany because courts had customarily cited it. See H. H. Jakobs, *Wissenschaft und Gesetzgebung im bürgerlichen Recht nach der Rechtsquellenlehre des neunzehnten Jahrhunderts*, Rechts- und Staatswissenschaftliche Veröffentlichungen der Görres-Gesselschaft, N.F., Heft 38 (Paderborn, 1983), 82–93.

as a rule of scholars, not judges. Accordingly, at least until the late 1830s—a time of sea change in German legal thought—Savigny remained firmly opposed to judicial lawmaking.[151] In this, as in all things, the Historical School gave its beliefs ideological force through the interpretation of Roman history: Puchta built a kind of anti-judicial bias directly into his interpretation of Roman legal history by focusing on the Roman practice of dividing the decision making in legal cases between magistrate (*praetor*) and judge (*iudex*). In Roman private law, a magistrate made a decision on the legal issues in the abstract before delegating the authority to determine factual liability to a judge. Puchta saw in this procedural division of labor a wise diminishment of the judicial role in favor of the scholarly, for the praetor generally yielded, in his finding of law, to the opinions of the learned. "The jurists," he wrote of the key element in the excellent Roman legal constitution, "were not judges, and the judges were not jurists."[152] Of these two classes it was the jurists who ruled. Although to a certain extent the authority of precedent was recognized, it was the general rule from an early date that judges were simply and directly bound by the opinions of legal scholars,[153] and so were the high magistrates who gave legal doctrine formal sanction.[154]

Puchta used denunciation of judicial power to explain away difficult points both in Roman legal history and in the jurisprudence of customary law. Why, for example, had the twelve tables been necessary? Surely the Roman people had already known the law, which after all was a creation of their own, common Volksgeist? Puchta's answer: the twelve tables had expressed no new substantive law, but rather only procedural law. Such a publication of procedure was necessary, for the plebeians were oppressed by judges: the simple citizen "was thrown upon the good will of the deciding judge, who perhaps encountered him as a political opponent."[155] Was it not true that Germans had historically been hostile to juristic authority? They had indeed, but the blame lay with the judges: it had been the misidentification of scholarship with the ugly doctrine of judicial precedent that had brought Roman law into ill repute.[156]

As we shall see in a moment, hostility to judges set the Historical School profoundly apart from the much more politically minded constitutionalists of the south. Indeed, it was not only the political activists of

---

[151] Cf. Mohnhaupt, "Richter und Rechtssprechung im Werke Savignys," 258ff.

[152] Puchta, *Cursus der Institutionen*, 1:424–25. Cf. Puchta, *Gewohnheitsrecht*, 2:125–26.

[153] Puchta, *Cursus der Institutionen*, e.g., 1:325.

[154] Ibid., 1:325: "Die prudentes waren es, die das Recht durch Interpretation fortbildeten, für den Magistrat war kein Raum zu einer positiven Wirkung auf dasselbe."

[155] Ibid., 1:184.

[156] Puchta, *Gewohnheitsrecht*, 1:164. Cf. above n. 150.

the south who were more willing than Savigny to put their energy behind the campaign for judicial independence. Hostility to precedent even set the Savignyans apart from the old-world scholars of Hannover. Theodor Hagemann can serve as an example. Hagemann was a leading Hannoverian scholar, active since the 1790s, and an enthusiastic convert to the pure Roman law movement. Like Schrader of Tübingen, Hagemann argued, in 1824, for the establishment of a *ius honorarium*, of a juristic order that would replicate the law by which the Romans had lived. But for Hagemann such a ius honorarium clearly had to be a rule of judges: "The crowd of controversies in the common law [i.e., applicable Roman law], multiplied further by the great number of disputed matters in statutory and local law, . . . can only be avoided through a ius honorarium created by following the decisions of the highest state court."[157]

Hostility to precedent was a telling feature of Savigny's program, a measure of his unwillingness to embrace practical politics. For there was a profound impracticality in his anti-judicial bent. It was hostility to precedent more than any other aspect of their program that made the Historical School radical advocates of a Professorenrecht, a "professors' law." And Savigny's dream of exclusively professorial lawmaking was too radical to command much support in the end: when he conceived his civilization, he neglected too much the practical problems of the exercise of power. Judges were in a much better position to exercise power than professors; the hopes of the legal profession could ultimately only repose in the judiciary. And, indeed, as Savigny's program crumbled in the 1840s, even he began to accept the claims of the judges. As I shall show below, the immediate consequence of the collapse of the Savignyan program in the 1840s was a comparative rise in the prestige of judges over the prestige of professors.[158] In the end, Savigny's program could not be carried out.

THE REVIVAL OF *AKTENVERSENDUNG* IN SOUTH GERMANY

Memories of professorial tradition never quite dominated the political talk of the constitutionalist south, as they did the talk of Savigny's Berlin. There were brilliant jurists who looked askance at the aspiring national leaders in the universities. Even in Hesse, B. W. Pfeiffer, for example, turned decisively away from the professoriate after an early flirtation with university life. A *Duzfreund* of Savigny (and a man who exercised direct influence on Savigny's thinking[159]), he became disenchanted with aca-

---

[157] T. Hagemann, "Meinungen der Rechtsgelehrten: Präjudicien," in *Practische Erorterungen*, 7:124–25.

[158] See below, Chapter VI.

[159] See below, p. 185. A *Duzfreund* is a friend close enough to address one with the informal and more intimate *du*.

demic life during the first years of liberation and turned down offers of professorships in order to pursue what he considered to be more practical work as justice of the highest court of Hesse.[160] Moreover, even the leading law professors themselves could be slow to embrace professorial tradition. For professorial tradition was predominantly a Roman-law tradition, and Roman law was always difficult to reconcile with romanticism, powerfully colored as romanticism was by the love of all things German. Adam Müller's attack on the use of Roman law as a "Roman French Revolution" was only one expression of a widespread antipathy that at first stood in the way of the southern revival of the old tradition of "impartiality." Thibaut's sponsorship of the "national ideas" of the Germans in his conflict with Savigny, and his corresponding contempt for the professoriate, is only one example: in the first years after the liberation many southern professors were eager to discard Roman law, and the Roman-law professoriate, in favor of some native alternative.

But after the reaction set in in 1819, professorial tradition revived in the south just as it had in Berlin. Even Thibaut returned to the old faith. In this section I wish to trace the meaning of the old faith in the constitutionalist south. The southern Romanists were not committed to the existing order in the way Savigny and Puchta were. They sought not to strengthen the old traditions, but to build on the old institutions of the sixteenth-century constitution in erecting a new popular constitution in Germany. In this sense, they were "liberals" where the members of the Historical School were "conservatives." But the lawyers of the south were nevertheless sixteenth-century revivalists, advocates of traditionalist politics.

In tracing the traditionalist politics of the southern professoriate, I will discuss only one aspect of professorial tradition: Aktenversendung. As I hope to show, this was a critically important aspect. Aktenversendung took on startling new significance after 1819. Through the revived Spruchkollegien of the southern universities, Holy Roman Imperial tradition was transformed into classical nineteenth-century constitutionalist thought, as professors attempted to build a new ethic of judicial independence on the strength of their own corporate tradition.

The southern German states were, historians agree, the center of Rechtsstaat thought, of the new constitutionalism of the nineteenth century.[161] The elements of the southern Rechtsstaat program, as developed pre-eminently in Baden, were all variations on the characteristic political proposition of the 1790s: that powerful officials should consider them-

---

[160] See J. Nolte, *Burchard Wilhelm Pfeiffer*, Göttinger Studien zur Rechtsgeschichte (Göttingen, 1969), esp. 13 and n. 2, 20–22.

[161] E.g., Krieger, *German Idea of Freedom*, 229ff.

selves Staatsdiener, not Fürstendiener, servants of the state, not personal servants of the prince. The state was to be built on an independent officialdom with independent corporate ethics, ethics founded on legal training and loyalty to law: an independent judiciary would work alongside an independent, legally trained bureaucracy.[162] This Rechtsstaat movement of the post-1814 era was a resumption of the interrupted reform movement that had preceded the French Revolution. Judged by its own goals, the movement was entirely successful: Germany became "the classical land of the bureaucracy in the European world, as China in Asia or as Egypt in Antiquity."[163] And it is important to keep in mind what the goals of the reform movement were. Bureaucratic and judical independence was not just a *pis-aller* for Germans who could not establish either popular or princely sovereignty—though in part it was undoubtedly that.[164] When the romantic political thinkers erected Staatsdienerschaften, they were attempting to revive and transmute institutions of ancient freedom and ancient corporate spirit; they were consciously attempting to engineer the transformation that Max Weber declared to be the characteristic transformation of continental European constitutional development: from patrimonal state to bureaucratic state.[165]

For the basis of the southern Rechtsstaat was to be the old feudal corporate sensibility. The new corps of bureaucrats and judges were to be aware of their own special status, legally protected, and independent of the prince while loyal to him. The law that was to rule was not a general law, but the several law-based ethics and legal protections of the individual state-servant bodies.[166] Hegel, with his highly corporatized society and his insistence on the importance of bureaucratic spirit, was the characteristic philosopher of this romantic movement. But he was hardly alone. The corporatist Rechtsstaat could be found in the thought of "political professors" all throughout the south, in Baden as well as in Hegel's native Württemberg.

All this did not, at first, bode well for Roman law.[167] For most of these Rechtsstaat thinkers in the years immediately after the Napoleonic wars,

---

[162] See above, pp. 76–77.

[163] O. Hintze, "Der Beamtenstand," in *Gesammelte Abhandlungen*, vol. 2, *Soziologie und Geschichte* (Göttingen, 1964), 95.

[164] Cf. Bleek, *Von der Kameralausbildung zum Juristenprivileg*, 31.

[165] Weber, *Economy and Society*, 3:1085–87.

[166] Ibid., 3:1099: "The feudal association and also the related patrimonial forms that have a stereotyped status structure constitute a synthesis of purely concrete rights and duties. They amount, as we have pointed out, to a 'constitutional state' (Rechtsstaat) on the basis of 'subjective' rights, not 'objective' law."

[167] The best accounts of the Germanist movement are to be found in biographies of its leading figures. See esp. Kern, *Beseler*, and Rückert, *Reyscher*. See further below, pp. 204–8.

a commitment to medieval tradition at first implied a rejection, and indeed, a vigorous rejection, of Roman law. The southwest was one of the centers of the new Germanist movement of the post-1814 years, the movement that boasted among its leaders figures as prominent as Jakob Grimm,[168] among its interested readers figures as discerning as Hegel,[169] and among its disciples figures as important as the young Karl Marx.[170] The Germanists mustered great political power from the denunciation of Roman law. Their attacks were, to be sure, directed largely at Roman-Canon criminal procedure, and the heart of their campaign lay in the demand for jury trial to replace bench trials, with judgment rendered according to the elaborate *gesetzliche Beweisregeln*, the complex evidentiary rules developed by postclassical Romanists and Canonists.[171] Nevertheless, Germanists did not by any means confine themselves to criminal procedure: the emotional power of the Germanist campaign against what was widely perceived as an unjust criminal system[172] became the emotional power of a legal campaign on all fronts, criminal and civil.[173] Distrust of Roman law was a force of first political importance in the south.

And yet southern Rechtsstaat thought had profoundly important debts to the Roman-law professorial tradition. As I hope to show, the pressure of political events after 1818–19 forced the southern Rechtsstaat thinkers to shift their political hopes, by and large, from jury trial to the corporate

[168] On Grimm's central role in the Germanist movement, see Wieacker, *Privatrechtsgeschichte*, 405–6.

[169] Hegel's interest in the Germanists is most evident in his commitment to jury trial. For his importance in the campaign for jury trial, see P. Landau, "Schwurgerichte und Schöffengerichte in Deutschland im 19. Jahrhundert bis 1870," in A. Padoa Schioppa, ed., *The Trial Jury in England, France, and Germany, 1700–1900*, Comparative Studies in Continental and Anglo-American Legal History (Berlin, 1987), 251–54.

[170] See below, pp. 207–8.

[171] For the campaign against the "gesetzliche Beweisregeln" and in favor of some form of jury trial or Schöffengericht, see Landau, "Schwurgerichte und Schöffengerichte in Deutschland im 19. Jahrhundert bis 1870," 244 and passim; J. Langbein, "The Constitutio Criminalis Carolina in Comparative Perspective," in P. Landau and F.-C. Schroeder, eds., *Strafrecht, Strafprozess und Rezeption* (Frankfurt a.M., 1984), 222–23; idem, *Torture and the Law of Proof* (Chicago, 1977) chaps. 1, 3–4. For the centrality of jury trial to the Germanist movement, see generally E. Sjöholm, *Rechtsgeschichte als Wissenschaft und Politik: Studien zur germanistischen Theorie des neunzehnten Jahrhunderts*, Abhandlungen zur rechtswissenschaftlichen Grundlagenforschung, vol. 10 (Berlin, 1972).

[172] For a vivid account of passionate German debate over criminal law during the post-Napoleonic period, see E. Schwinge, *Der Kampf um die Schwurgerichte bis zur Frankfurter Nationalversammlung*, Strafrechtliche Abhandlungen, Heft 213 (Breslau, 1926).

[173] I have attempted elsewhere to show that the terms of debate over criminal jury trial deeply influenced nineteenth-century German commercial law. See J. Whitman, "Commercial Law and the American *Volk*: A Note on Llewellyn's German Sources for the Uniform Commercial Code," *Yale Law Journal* 97, no. 1 (1987): 160–66.

tradition of the professoriate. In particular, the professorial tradition served as the historical basis for the one feature that set the southern Rechtsstaat decisively apart from that of Savigny's Berlin: judicial independence. For unlike Savigny and his followers, the lawyers of the south hoped to revive their own corporate tradition only in order to pass the crozier of independence and authority on to the judges; they believed that the professoriate had to yield, in coming ages, its role of leadership to an independent bench presiding over courts staffed by lay jurors. The ancient constitution had to be metamorphosed into a new Rechtsstaat. In this metamorphosis the old Spruchkollegien would provide the foundation for an independent judiciary.

THE *BUNDESACTE* AND THE REVIVAL OF *AKTENVERSENDUNG*

As the long Napoleonic occupation ended, German lawyers of the south saw heady possibilities of reform. Their lodestar was the famous Article 13 of the fundamental law of the new German Federation, the Bundesacte of 1815. Article 13 promised a revival, in every German state, of the old representative institutions of the pre-absolutist world, the territorial Estates General. Lawyers all throughout Germany hoped these revived institutions would form the basis of representative government.[174] They were, of course, disappointed. Article 13 was flouted everywhere but the south, and even there the reaction that began with the Carlsbad Decrees of 1819 made a mockery of Western forms. Parliamentarism was never successfully established until after 1945. But the guarantee of territorial Estates was not the only one on which Germans could rest their hopes for a revival of the ancient constitution. The Bundesacte, despite considerable adverse agitation,[175] also included a partial guarantee of the right to Aktenversendung.[176] This guarantee was placed, significantly, at the very beginning of the section on the free institutions of the new Bund. The Bundesacte permitted the four Free Cities (Frankfurt, Hamburg, Lübeck, and Bremen), which were much loved among romantic lawyers,[177] to establish, along with other small territories, their own appellate courts in order to insure their own independence; litigants in these courts were to be guaranteed Aktenversendung:

[174] See generally H. Brandt, *Landständische Repräsentation im deutschen Vormärz: Politisches Denken im Einflußfeld des monarchischen Prinzips* (Neuwied/Berlin, 1968).

[175] Cf. Loning, "Spätes Lob der Aktenversendung."

[176] Cf., e.g., Kern, *Geschichte des Gerichtsverfassungsrechts*, 38.

[177] For the importance of the idea of the four Free Cities in forming Savigny's thought, see W. Schubert, "Savigny und die Rheinisch-Französische Gerichtsverfassung," *ZSS* (G) 95 (1978): 158. The importance of these cities for the development of German law in general is argued in Buchholz, *Abstraktionsprinzip und Immobiliarrecht*, 14–15. The ideological significance and the vibrant commercial and cultural life of the four Free Cities made them central to German intellectual history in this period. They deserve a study of their own.

ARTICLE 12

In these common appellate courts . . . each party shall be entitled to Aktenversendung to a German faculty or to a Schöppenstuhl [old German lay
court], where a final decision will be made.

ARTICLE 13

In every federal state there will be a constitution based on a territorial estates
general.[178]

The guarantee of Aktenversendung written into the Bundesacte stimulated a flowering of praise for the institution.[179] The guarantee was dou-
bly significant: great political meaning attached to Aktenversendung because its use had been guaranteed in the Four Free cities, the only
governments in Germany free from princely rule.[180] And the very place-
ment of this guarantee next to that of representative assemblies showed
how much significance the old free institution had acquired in the minds
of Germans of the time. As reaction gathered momentum after 1819 and
the realization of Article 13 became more and more remote, lawyers fell
back increasingly upon Article 12. For twenty years after 1819, Aktenversendung became a kind of constitutionalist refuge for the professors of
the south. With their renewed embrace of Aktenversendung came a renewed faith in the power of Roman tradition to preserve order and freedom in Germany.

For the most part the revival of Aktenversendung, and of the Roman-
law professoriate, did not begin in the south until 1819. To be sure, the
general revival of Aktenversendung that was part of the imperial revival
everywhere in Germany was felt in the south, too. Early in the nineteenth
century the Heidelberg Spruchkollegium was working to defend the independence of civil servants[181] and thus to make itself a guardian of the
principles of Staatsdiener constitutionalism inherited from the Holy Roman Imperial revival of the 1790s. Few of the law professors who would
soon become Germany's leading political thinkers condemned Aktenversendung outright. But few had more than tepid praise. Thibaut, for example, had specifically requested not to be relieved of his duties on the

---

[178] Bundesacte, in J. L. Klüber, ed., *Staatsarchiv des teutschen Bundes* 1 (1816): 28.

[179] Löning, "Spätes Lob der Aktenversendung."

[180] This would be particularly true after the *Wiener Schlußakte* of 1820.

[181] Cf. "Ueber die Notwendigkeit einer genauen Prüfung eines Verbrechens und über den Werth der sorgfältigen Beobachtung aller Förmlichkeit des Beweisverfahrens," in C. Martin, ed., *Rechtsgutachten und Entscheidungen des Spruchcollegii der Universität Heidelberg* (Heidelberg, 1808) vol. 1 (no more appeared), 1–164. According to Martin, this volume of decisions was published only because the civil servant involved in the case wished to see his record before the public. Ibid., vi–vii.

Spruchkollegium during the negotiations over his move to Heidelberg.[182] But over the succeeding few years, he praised the Heidelberg institution only for being not too burdensome on his time[183]—and, of course, he made himself famous in 1814 as an opponent of the Roman-law tradition.[184] Thibaut's colleague K. T. Welcker, the constitutionalist leader, was a firmer opponent of the Spruchkollegien than Thibaut, though he was far from being a bitter one. In 1818 Welcker belonged to a radical Germanist strain of codificationists committed, like Thibaut, to the drafting of a wholly native German code[185] and vehemently opposed to Roman and Canon law.[186] He willingly admitted to having been a member of two Spruchkollegien (Giessen and Heidelberg) staffed "by the most first-rate and estimable colleagues."[187] Nevertheless he was hostile. Denouncing the "exclusive caste-like domination of the administration of justice by jurists,"[188] he declared himself convinced of the "inadequacy and perversity" of a system founded on Aktenversendung rather than on jury trial.[189] For men like Thibaut and Welcker, caught up in enthusiasm for the Volks-Ideen of the Germans, the Spruchkollegium, a relic of a Romanizing age in German history, at first held little attraction.

But politics changed all that. In the years after 1819—Meinecke's "year of misfortune in the nineteenth century"[190]—it became clear that constitutional government would not be established soon. The Carlsbad Decrees were followed by the 1820 Final Act of the Congress of Vienna, which declared that "the German Federation, with the exception of the free cities, is composed of sovereign princes."[191] The old, pre-1787 absolutism had powerful and committed champions, whom talk of Volks-Ideen was not likely to defeat. As the constitutionalist movement faltered and threatened to buckle under the ever-heavier arm of reaction, Thibaut and Welcker (who soon came under serious attack himself) began to speak in wholly new tones about Aktenversendung and the Ro-

---

[182] Thibaut, letter to Heise, February 22, 1805: "[v]on practischen Arbeiten im Spruch-Collegio wünsche ich keineswegs Dispensation." Reproduced in Polley, Thibaut, 2:131.

[183] Thibaut, letter to Zachariä, November 14, 1806. In ibid., 2:200.

[184] For Thibaut's support, à la Dahlmann, for Landstände in 1815, see Rückert, Savigny, 171; cf. also idem, 191.

[185] Cf. Welcker, Review of "Gutachten der (Königl. Preußischen) Immediat-Justiz-Commission (zu Köln) über das Geschworenengericht," Heidelberger Jahrbucher der Litteratur 11 (1818): 786, on the need to expel "das verderbliche und Unvatherländische" from German law.

[186] Ibid., 789ff.

[187] Ibid., 817.

[188] Ibid., 806.

[189] Ibid., 817.

[190] F. Meinecke, Erlebtes, 1862–1901, in Werke, 9 vols. (Stuttgart, 1969), 8:125.

[191] Cf. Böckenförde, "Der deutsche Typ," 114–115.

man-law tradition. The Roman-law tradition revived despite its discordance with romantic thought in the south, because it was an old, strong tradition associated with old, strong institutions.

The Dynamic of Roman-Law Revival in the South: Retreat into the Ancient Constitution

The Roman-law tradition showed its strength during the *Demagogenverfolgung*, the persecution of liberals (literally: of demagogues) managed by standing princely inquisitional courts.[192] As increasing numbers of leading liberals came under attack, the tradition of appealing to law faculties for decisions in politically charged cases resurfaced. The university Spruchkollegien were called on again and again to decide questions involving the lawfulness of princely actions during the years of the Demagogenverfolgung.[193] Thibaut's university, Heidelberg, was particularly sought after in the 1820s and early 1830s to serve as a judge in political matters.[194] But the University of Erlangen, too, was asked in the mid-1820s to decide questions involving delicate political content.[195] In a time of persecution, the constitutional tradition proved to be stronger than liberal slogans. The liberals needed well-established institutions: political innovation was becoming impossible, so constitutionalists sought refuge in political tradition.

The experience of the strength of Roman-law tradition in the face of persecution converted Welcker and Thibaut into advocates of Aktenversendung. Like other Spruchkollegien, that of Welcker's university, Freiburg, was asked to intervene in the constitutional conflicts of the 1820s. In 1823 Friedrich List, condemned to hard labor for his political activities in the Württemberg Assembly, appealed to the Freiburg Spruchkollegium for vindication. There is some evidence that Welcker, perhaps still wary of the institution, tried to avoid the task of writing an opinion in the affair.[196] But the Spruchkollegium did make itself heard, and ten years later Welcker was still proud of the fact: when he and Rotteck published their

---

[192] See, generally, L. F. Ilse, *Geschichte der politischen Untersuchungen, welche durch die neben der Bundesversammlung errichteten Commissionen, der Central Untersuchungs-Commission zu Mainz und der Bundes-Central-Behörde zu Frankfurt in den Jahren 1819 bis 1827 und 1833 bis 1842 geführt sind* (Frankfurt a.M., 1860).

[193] See, e.g., Baumgärtel, *Erlanger Juristenfakultät*, 122–23, and below, pp. 143–44.

[194] Jammers, *Heidelberger Juristenfakultät*, 51.

[195] Baumgärtel, *Erlanger Juristenfakultät*, 122–23.

[196] According to H. Müller-Dietz, Welcker, while offering his services in drafting the opinion, attached conditions to the offer that made it "practically a refusal." Müller-Dietz, *Das Leben des Rechtslehrers und Politikers Karl Theodor Welcker*, Beiträge zur Freiburger Wissenschafts- und Universitätsgeschichte, Heft 34 (Freiburg i. B., 1968), 86 n. 328. I have not been able to see C.-D. Schott, "Friedrich List und die Freiburger Juristenfakultät," *Freiburger Universitätsblätter*, Heft 4 (1963): 40ff.

Staats-Lexikon in 1834, Welcker devoted a whole paragraph of his article on List (who in the end served only a short time before being permitted to flee to Pennsylvania) to the Freiburg Spruchkollegium's defense of List as a triumph of constitutional law.[197] Welcker, like so many constitutionalists of the period, had learned that the old institutions were much safer and more effective as bastions of constitutionalism than any modern constitutionalism could invent. By 1833—two years after he had pointedly quoted Count von Buol's praise of the German universities of fifteen years earlier[198]—Welcker, himself feeling reactionary pressures, was collecting and publishing opinions of Spruchkollegien defending his own actions on behalf of freedom of the press.[199] Thibaut's development followed the same course. In 1821, as Aktenversendung took on its new importance in the fierce political struggles of the time, Thibaut declared the Spruchkollegium to be a uniquely valuable guardian of Christian justice, an institution entrusted with "the most important legal questions."[200] Four years later, fighting for enlarged membership for the Spruchkollegium, he adopted the traditional language of praise: the Spruchkollegium had been founded for "impartial [*unpartheyische*] justice and the development of legal doctrine [*Rechtsbildung*]," and the Heidelberg faculty was in its period of "greatest flowering" in its pursuit of these purposes.[201] Thibaut had become a kind of convert to tradition.[202]

The Formation of Rechtsstaat Theory in the Spruchkollegien

The liberals of the south had been driven back behind the bulwark of the sixteenth-century constitution. As a result, Rechtsstaat theory, as it grew

---

[197] Welcker, "List," in Welcker and Rotteck, eds., *Staats-Lexikon*, 2d ed. (Altona, 1847), 8:555.

[198] "Ein stolzes Denkmal deutscher Entwicklung." Quoted in K. T. Welcker, *Die Vervollkommnung der organischen Entwicklung des deutschen Bundes* (Karlsruhe, 1831), 33.

[199] K. T. Welcker, ed., *Neuer Beitrag zur Lehre von den Injurien und der Preßfreiheit durch die Rechtsgutachten der Spruchcollegien von Heidelberg, Kiel und Tubingen über den Preßprozeß des Hofrath [sic] Welcker und durch die Prüfung der hofgerichtlichen Entscheidungsgründe in den Appellationsschriften des Geheimraths Duttlinger und des Hofraths Welcker* (Freiburg, 1833).

[200] Quoted and discussed in Polley, *Thibaut*, 1:150–51. Thibaut made these statements in the unsavory context of a campaign to keep a Jew, S. W. Zimmern, out of the Spruchkollegium. Liberalism of the period was a liberalism more of constitutionalism than of tolerance.

[201] Thibaut, letter to A. H. Fröhlich, December 6, 1825. In Polley, *Thibaut*, 2:464.

[202] Polley, *Thibaut*, 1:87–88, 271, finds Thibaut's "conversion" (the term was used to describe Thibaut's later years by B. G. Niebuhr) difficult to explain. Surely the answer lies in the familiar chronology of the German reaction. J. Rückert is surely correct in rejecting Polley's assertion that Thibaut's "conversion" was a conversion from some kind of "Demokratismus." Rückert, review of Polley, *Thibaut*, in ZSS (R) 101 (1984): 444. Thibaut's "Demokratismus" had not survived the early years of the nineteenth century. However, Rückert is surely also correct in observing that Thibaut's "optimistisch-idealen Zug zur Aktivität" lasted only until 1819. Rückert, *Savigny*, 170.

in the decades of the 1820s and 1830s, developed largely in the work of the Spruchkollegien. The younger generation of constitutionalist thinkers that arrived on the scene in the 1820s was made up of Spruchkollegium members: Mohl—the man who popularized the word "Rechtsstaat" in 1829[203]—was a member of the Tübingen Spruchkollegium from the beginning of his career[204]; H. Zöpfl, a leading constitutionalist down into the Bismarck era, was a long-time member at Heidelberg[205]; F. J. Stahl was a member at Berlin.[206] There these new thinkers drafted judgments on the most urgent political cases of the day, in the company of old theorists like Thibaut, Zachariä, and Klüber, whose experience of the pre-absolutist tradition dated to the years of Holy Roman Imperial revival in the 1790s. Inevitably, the coloring of old corporatist liberty, founded on ancient Roman-law privilege, came to tinge nineteenth-century German constitutionalism.

One Heidelberg decision, often cited as one of the fundamental expositions of Rechtsstaat thought,[207] will serve to show how deeply the conviction had entered southern minds, by the early 1830s, that their modern cause had its roots in the sixteenth-century constitution. The case involved one of the most interesting provinces of German legal history in the period—social insurance, which was already in evidence on the German scene decades before Bismarck. Insurance schemes were as yet at an early stage, and social planners were accordingly unprepared for the problem of moral hazard—a technical term in insurance for the possibility that the insured will destroy the property, or fail to take precautions to ensure its safety, in order to collect. In this case, the grand duke, the responsible ministers, and the territorial assembly of the Grand Duchy of Sachsen-Weimar-Eisenach had cooperated to pass, in 1821, a bill establishing a fire-insurance association and requiring all homeowners to purchase insurance. The bill had, unfortunately, a flaw: it allowed at least some of the homeowners to value their homes themselves. In succeeding years, as economists might predict, homes burned by the score; presumably their owners were unable to resist the temptation of collecting the inflated sums at which they had valued their property. By 1826 the grand duke's government had responded. The government initiated the process of revising the law so that homeowners whose homes were destroyed by fire should be reimbursed according to the true value of their loss. But a

[203] Böckenförde, "Entstehung und Wandel des Rechtsstaatsbegriffs," 66.

[204] Mohl, *Lebenserinnerungen*, 1:145.

[205] On Zöpfl and other members, see Jammers, *Heidelberger Juristenfakultät*, 58ff.

[206] Seckel, "Geschichte der Berliner Juristischen Fakultät," 463.

[207] See Jammers, *Heidelberger Juristenfakultät*, 95, for its importance in Zachariä's oeuvre. Cf. Mohl, *Staatswissenschaften*, 2:517n; Stintzing-Landsberg, *Geschichte*, vol. 3, pt. 2, 110.

number of fires took place before the assembly could pass on this ordinance—among them, fires in a town called Ellersleben. When several Ellersleben homes were destroyed by fire, and the state insurance association paid the homeowners only what it deemed "true value," they sued. When the homeowners lost their claims, they requested, and received, Aktenversendung. The case was sent to Heidelberg.[208]

Heidelberg held for the homeowners,[209] in an opinion written by Thibaut.[210] Thibaut took the opportunity accorded by membership in a Spruchkollegium to promote the judicial corps as an independent guardian of the Rechtsstaat. His decision enunciated a powerful constitutional doctrine, one intended to affirm the special status of judges as the guardians of rule of law. Thibaut gave the judge the constitutional right to decide whether a law had been properly enacted, and the duty to refuse to enforce an improper law.[211] Thibaut's decision did not survive the next round of appeals. The High Appellate Court in Jena sent the matter to the Leipzig Schöppenstuhl, which declared that judges were bound by the command of the sovereign and had no authority to refuse to enforce a ducal ordinance.[212] Nevertheless, Thibaut's reasoning heralded a new movement among south German Rechtsstaat thinkers in favor of a strong judiciary[213] entrusting justice to legal professionals rather than to executive organs.[214]

Thibaut's decision was important, but it was not the most important treatment of the case. The most important treatment came from Thibaut's colleague Zachariä, who wrote a definitive exposition that gave great weight to the fact that the case had been decided by a Spruchkollegium. To Zachariä, the intervention of the Heidelberg faculty in the affairs of Sachsen-Weimar-Eisenach served as an affirmation of the possibility of building a new constitution on centuries-old German tradition; he made his essay into a defense of the proposition that rule of law in Germany took its significance in large part from its origins in a decision by a Spruchkollegium, an historic repository of German freedom and impartiality.

Many anecdotes have survived about Zachariä—that he was unkempt,

---

[208] This account is taken from C. W. Schweitzer, "Ein Rechtsfall, hauptsächlich als Beitrag zur Bestimmung des Verhältnisses zwischen der richterlichen und der gesetzgebenden Gewalt," *Jahrbücher der Gesetzgebung und Rechtspflege in Sachsen* 1 (1829): 299–304. Cf. Jammers, *Heidelberger Juristenfakultät*, 114ff.

[209] Schweitzer, "Rechtsfall," 305–8.

[210] Jammers, *Heidelberger Juristenfakultät*, 95–96.

[211] Schweitzer, "Rechtsfall," 311.

[212] Ibid., 318–21.

[213] Jammers, *Heidelberger Juristenfakultät*, 113ff.

[214] Cf. G. Plathner, *Der Kampf um die Richterliche Unabhängigkeit bis zum Jahre 1848*, Abhandlungen aus dem Staats- und Verwaltungsrecht, Heft 51 (Breslau, 1935).

shabbily dressed, miserly—but there has been too little scholarship on his career.[215] He is one of the great neglected jurists of the nineteenth century, the author of commentaries on the *Code Napoléon* that were standard not only in Germany, but also in Italy and in France itself. He began as a bit of a radical before, like many romantics, shifting gears.[216] He made his permanent fame as coeditor, with Mittermaier, of the *Kritische Zeitschrift für Rechtswissenschaft und Gesetzgebung des Auslandes*,[217] and so as one of the principal importers of Western ideas into Germany. But it would be a misrepresentation of Zachariä's mode of thought to say that he intended to be only an importer of Western ways. Rather, he searched everywhere in Western history for prefigurements, precedents, and institutional relatives of constitutional structures he was convinced were ultimately distinctively German. Thus he declared that Spruchkollegien were a German institution comparable to jury trial,[218] and that Roman iudices,[219] too, being comparable to jury trial, were ultimately of German origin.[220] For Zachariä, the task was to uncover a German framework for Western constitutionalism, a German meaning for English and French freedoms. This comparatism, so much that of the age of Cuvier, made him one of the most insistent sponsors of the idea that Aktenversendung provided a necessary German base for constitutionalist reforms.

It was on this point that he insisted as he built political philosophy on Thibaut's decision. Zachariä, who was caught up in a feud with the president of the Spruchkollegium,[221] had not taken part in the decision.[222] But he saw great significance in the work of his colleagues nevertheless. He elaborated Thibaut's decision on fire insurance into a grand distinction between *Gesetz*—a law enacted according to constitutional forms with the consent of a popular assembly—and *Verordnung*—an administrative police measure.[223] This fundamental constitutionalist distinction was, in

---

[215] There are discussions of Zachariä in all of the best recent literature. See Stühler, *Erneuerung der Rechtswissenschaft*, 151–60; Schröder, *Wissenschaftstheorie*, 149ff.; Rückert, "Heidelberg um 1804," 95–96; Cappellini, *Systema Iuris*, 1:144ff. But he deserves a larger-scale treatment.

[216] Cf. Stühler, *Erneuerung der Rechtswissenschaft*, 158–59.

[217] 1829ff.

[218] Zachariä, *Biographischer und Juristischer Nachlaß*, 41.

[219] See above, p. 130.

[220] Zachariä, *De Originibus Juris Romani ex Jure Germanico Repetendis* (n.p. [Heidelberg], 1817), 22. This remarkable pamphlet, written as a prize for Heidelberg students, was surely one of the first attempts to build a comparative Indo-European constitutional history on the discoveries of Sir William Jones and Friedrich Schlegel.

[221] Jammers, *Heidelberger Juristenfakultät*, 43ff.

[222] Zachariä, "Erstreckt sich das richterliche Entscheidungsrecht auf die Frage, ob die Regierung eine Verordnung, auf welche sich in einer Streitsache die Partheyen beziehen, zu erlassen berechtigt gewesen sey?" *Archiv für die civilistische Praxis*, 16 (1832): 150 n. 5.

[223] Zachariä, "Richterliches Entscheidungsrecht," 145ff.

turn, adopted by Mohl and C. G. Wächter to become one of the classic premises of Rechtsstaat theory.[224] It was, said Zachariä, a distinction that independent courts had a duty to uphold. And independent courts had their necessary models in Spruchkollegien, which were German analogues of the justice of the free states of Italy:

> The Italian free states of the Middle Ages went so far as to call in foreigners, upon whom they conferred the office of judge. A similar acknowledgment of the fundamental proposition [that courts must be independent] lies in Aktenversendung, which is customary in Germany and had its begingins in the German cities.[225]

The fifteen years in which Rechtsstaat thought had been harbored in the Spruchkollegien had focused the attention of men like Zachariä squarely on the ancient constitution.

Still, if the Spruchkollegien seemed strong, politics could make fools of those who hoped for too much from old institutions. The 1830s were years of decisive crisis for the institution, marked by frequent invocations of its old-world associations. The constitutional conflicts of the period deeply weakened the tradition of Aktenversendung, but not before its status as a last bastion of freedom in the Holy Roman Imperial tradition had been widely proclaimed. One of the immediate consequences of the disorders of 1830 was a rash of "political" Aktenversendungen by German dissidents seeking vindication from university faculties. The faculties issued favorable, if ineffective, declarations. The German Federation responded with two decrees that between them sent Aktenversendungen into its final decline. These decrees of 1834 and 1835 denied Spruchkollegien the right to issue judgments in criminal matters—a blanket denial of jurisdiction whose real intent, ministers of Baden conceded, was to end the frequent appeal to the universities in political matters.[226] In the ensuing controversy, all participants recognized that the decisive issue was whether or not the Spruchkollegien deserved their centuries-old reputation for "impartiality." The ministers of the Federation were well aware that public regard for the Spruchkollegien depended on this reputation, and they were careful to justify curtailment of the old institution by denying its historic claims:

> The true reason for the recommended measure lies in a lack of confidence that the judgment of the academic Spruchkollegien in administrative and criminal matters with a political coloring is impartial [unbefangenen], a lack

[224] Jammers, Heidelberger Juristenfakultät, 95–96.
[225] Zachariä, "Richterliches Entscheidungsrecht," 174–75.
[226] Jammers, Heidelberger Juristenfakultät, 52–53.

of confidence that their judgments are free of the influence of political partisanship and of misguided striving for popularity.[227]

In mounting these attacks on the ancient claims of the institution, the
ministers could rely on support from some political intellectuals as well.
As the controversy grew heated in the summer of 1834, August Rehberg,
a grand old figure prominent since the 1790s, wrote an attack on the
predominance of the professoriate in German legal life and declared that
the universities should cease attempting to maintain their independence
from princely power: "The contemporary universities cannot lay claim to
the same independence and self-sufficiency that was theirs as part of their
status as corporations in earlier centuries." To Rehberg, as to Zachariä,
the Spruchkollegien were the German forms of independent justice. But
such independent justice had been rendered impossible by the establishment of princely power in the Reformation:

> The officials of the Schöppenstühle and those of the Spruchkollegien are sim-
> ilar; the advantages and powers associated with academic honors, the high
> dignity of a *rector magnificus* (an honor conferred on leading academics), are
> honors that great princes, the patrons of scholars and friends of scholarship,
> did not disdain to assume for themselves, allowing their actual duties to be
> performed by a prorector. All of this testifies to their connection to the Ger-
> man Empire. In the Empire, one could have compared the great fraternity of
> the universities with the French *parlements*, which, under their high-sound-
> ing title, "cours souveraines," had the hubris to form themselves into an in-
> dependent state body—but which thereby only prepared their own decline.
> The claims of the university were already irreconcilable with the police
> power of the princes, once the latter developed as part of territorial sover-
> eignty.[228]

Such attacks on the old institution called forth indignant responses. Publicists reacted swiftly and with firm declarations that the Spruchkollegien
protected old world freedoms. The *Augsburger Allgemeine Zeitung*
wrote: "Among the unhappy signs of the time is a dislike, often driven to
the point of hatred, against all institutions that owe their existence to the
earlier constitution of Germany or to older German customs." A faculty,
said the newspaper, could render much more impartial judgments than a
court, for it did not know the "political or religious coloring" of the de-

---

[227] Quoted in ibid., 53.
[228] A. W. Rehberg, *Die Erwartungen der Deutschen von dem Bund ihrer Fürsten* (Jena,
1835), 67, 68–69. For Rehberg's hostility to legal scholarship in German political life, see
also 43–47. The date of original composition of the pamphlet is given as July 1834 at the
end of the page-proofs, which are in the possession of the Handschriftenabteilung of the
Niedersächsische Staats- und Universitätsbibliothek Göttingen.

fendant.[229] Thus on all sides the fate of Aktenversendung was fought out by Germans who assumed its worth, if any, lay in its continuing early modern "impartiality."

Perhaps the most thorough attempt to give a simultaneously constitutionalist and old-world coloring to the Spruchkollegien in the conflicts of the 1830s was the response of Welcker. When, in 1834, Rotteck and Welcker published the first volume of their Staats-Lexikon, the bible of liberals of the years before 1848, they included an article by Welcker that passionately argued the value of Aktenversendung and demonstrated clearly the sense among southerners of a direct continuity between old forms of professorial justice and the new judicial law-finding they hoped to introduce. The Staats-Lexikon appeared in 1834, as the agitation for a suppression of Aktenversendung mounted, agitation that would eventually result in decrees clamping down on the institution. By this time, two decades of constitutional politics had converted Welcker to views not very different from Zachariä's, and he expressed them freely in his article "Aktenversendung." He showed a rich sense of the institution's traditions, beginning the article with an account of its unbiased judgments in cases involving the power of the state in the sixteenth century.[230] He proceeded to its revival and constitutional reaffirmation in the Napoleonic and post-Napoleonic years, insisting that the Bundesacte had not only recognized but also extended the right of Aktenversendung as a measure for the protection of German freedom. He quoted Gönner: the institution was the "palladium of German freedom and the security of the citizen."[231] He made Aktenversendung, as an expression of freedom, subject to the characteristic guarantees of the Rechtsstaat: the right to Aktenversendung could not be abolished without the consent of the people.[232] As almost every defender of Aktenversendung felt compelled to do, Welcker conceded that the institution was subject to unfortunate delays; moreover, it would no longer be necessary or practical once the fundamental forms of modern liberal justice—oral procedure and the jury trial—had been introduced into Germany. But the introduction of those forms was far from accomplished, and in the meantime Aktenversendung was indispensable.[233] What Cicero had said of the traditional Roman forms of justice—that they were the "palladium of Roman liberty"—was equally true of Aktenversendung: unbiased justice in matters opposing

[229] Augsburger Allgemeine Zeitung, suppl. to vol. 13, December 13, 1836, 51–52. Quoted in Baumgärtel, Erlanger Fakultät, 125.

[230] Welcker, "Aktenversendung," in Staats-Lexikon, 1:228. In the first edition (Altona, 1834), this article appears at 1:237–47.

[231] Ibid. 1:229.

[232] Ibid.

[233] Ibid., 1:229–30.

citizen to the state was "hardly thinkable" without faculty adjudication.[234] Above all, Aktenversendung afforded protection against the impositions of petty princes, for it was the last remnant of *Reichsjustiz*, imperial justice. The old imperial courts, whose work had been founded on cooperation with the various estates of the German people, were gone; the independence of judges was now everywhere threatened by the German states.[235] Aktenversendung held the answer to this as well as to the threat of petty and arbitrary behavior by local professors, in its tradition of "consensus of German scholars (communis opinio doctorum)."[236] As long as the day of modern, public justice remained far off, only this last "reichgesetzliches Surrogat," "surrogate for imperial law," remained to assure the "security, honor, freedom, and wealth of the citizen."[237] To this leading liberal intellectual as to so many others, these surviving early modern institutions preserved German traditions of freedom and rule of law and could provide the bridge to modern justice. In his last words he warned that if the independence of judges could no longer be safeguarded, the independence of professors was all that assured justice in Germany.[238]

The Göttingen Seven and After

These publicistic conflicts were fought out three centuries after Christophor Hegendorffinus had stood before the leaders of Rostock in the Baltic winter to declare that law professors could bring them justice.[239] It was now Welcker and Zachariä who stood before the German public, to renew the old promise. It was surely the last moment when such a promise could plausibly be made. The most notorious and decisive blow against the political dignity of the German professors was struck in 1837: the dismissal of the famous Göttingen Seven—Dahlmann, the brothers Grimm, and four others who protested the suspension of the Hannoverian constitution by King Ernst August in 1837.[240] Like other constitutional conflicts over the previous fifteen years, the affair of the Göttingen Seven was the occasion for intervention by the law faculties. J.C.B. Stüve, the liberal mayor of Osnabrück and the author of Hannover's agrarian reform legislation, requested opinions from the German Spruchkollegien

[234] Ibid., 1:230.
[235] Ibid., 231.
[236] Ibid., 232.
[237] Ibid., 231.
[238] Ibid., 234.
[239] Cf. above, p. 32.
[240] For the affair of the Göttingen Seven, see, most recently, H.-G. Husung, *Protest und Repression im Vormärz*, Kritische Studien zur Geschichtswissenschaft, 54 (Göttingen, 1983), 95–96.

on the lawfulness of Ernst August's coup d'état. The Prussian faculties—Breslau, Halle, and Berlin—were expressly forbidden to respond to Stüve's application.[241] But four other faculties did respond—Zachariä was the respondent for Heidelberg, the eminent Germanist A. F. Reyscher for Tübingen—and three of their judgments condemning Ernst August were published together by Dahlmann.[242] It was an impressive mustering of academic support, but the course of Hannoverian politics did not change.

Indeed, by 1837, some of the spirit had drained from the Spruchkollegien. Zachariä published in that year a last plea on behalf of the old institution; it was full of proud rhetoric, but it betrayed his awareness that the decrees of 1834 and 1835 had decisively undercut Aktenversendung. His essay, "The National Unity of the Germans and the German Universities," was an attempt to marshal the well-established nationalist defense of the universities in support of Aktenversendung. He deplored the decrees.[243] Other nations had extraordinary courts to deal with cases of great constitutional moment; Germany had none. Aktenversendung must fill the lacuna. If the jurisdiction of the professors had to be limited, it should be limited to cases in which there were charges of crimes against the state.[244] This was an issue not only of justice but of nationalism: "Aktenversendung to professors in a different state has always been, and is to this day, a support, to a certain degree, of German unity."[245] All this was brave language, but there were indications, too, that events had left Zachariä cowed. One parenthetical statement read: "(It goes without saying that I have considered academic life from only *one* side, as was appropriate to the subject of this essay. Anyone who, like myself, has lived in universities for over *fifty* years, hardly needs to be reminded of the dark side of the picture.)"[246] It was true, he admitted, that governments had found that not all university teachers could be trusted.[247] Zachariä hedged this admission with a declaration that most professors belonged to the "Tory party," the "Partei der Tories"[248]; but it was a revealing admission nevertheless. Aktenversendung could make no claims at all if it could not

---

[241] Cf. Buchda, "Die Spruchtätigkeit der Hallischen Juristenfakultät"; Seckel, "Geschichte der Berliner Juristenfakultät," 468f.; Jammers, *Die Heidelberger Juristenfakultät*, 129.

[242] *Gutachten der Juristen-Fakultäten in Heidelberg, Jena und Tübingen, die Hannoversche Verfassungsfrage betreffend*, 2d ed. (Jena, 1839).

[243] Zachariä, "Die Nationaleinheit der Teutschen und die teutschen Universitäten," *Jahrbücher der Geschichte und Politik*, 10, no. 1 (1837): 416–17.

[244] Ibid., 417.

[245] Ibid.

[246] Ibid., 391.

[247] Ibid., 401.

[248] Ibid.

make its traditional claim of impartiality. Political polarization had progressed too far: professors could no longer claim the center.

To my knowledge, the tradition of praise for Aktenversendung had died away by the 1840s, after the crackdown of the previous decade. It is significant that Robert von Mohl declined to join the Heidelberg Spruchkollegium when he became Zachariä's successor in 1846. He explained his refusal to join by saying that he was too ignorant of Roman law to participate. But that was a peculiarly unpersuasive reason. Mohl had been a member of the Tübingen Spruchkollegium for years, and he said himself that his Heidelberg colleagues were eager to have him:

> I could not ... join the Spruchkollegium in Heidelberg although it would have pleased me to do so—and pleased my colleagues even more, perhaps, for questions of public law [staatsrechtliche Fragen] came up frequently. As a rule, I would have had to speak only commonsensically [naturalistisch reden] or vote along with one of my colleagues better versed in Roman law—which I was naturally neither willing nor permitted to do.[249]

I suggest that Mohl declined to join because the old institutional élan was gone by 1846. The Spruchkollegien had, in the end, proved a feeble instrument of constitutionalism when faced with strong repressive measures, in an era when political rhetoric had escalated to a degree of violence too great for tradition to provide much of a shield. Mohl, though he had only kind words for the institution, no longer saw much value in associating himself with it.[250]

CONCLUSION

Aktenversendung fell in the hopes of southern constitutionalists for the same reason it had risen: intensifying political pressure first forced men like Thibaut and Welcker to take refuge in Roman-law tradition, and further intensifying political pressure made the Roman-law tradition untenable in the struggles of the 1830s. A turn of the screw, and they became champions of the sixteenth-century constitution; another turn of the screw, and the sixteenth-century constitution could help no longer. Nevertheless, the old constitution had provided two decades of refuge, and the campaign for judicial independence was surely strengthened by the infusion of the surviving energy of the Spruchkollegien.

Perhaps the real strength of the Spruchkollegien can be measured in the

---

[249] Mohl, Lebenserinnerungen, 1:107. Quoted in Jammers, Die Heidelberger Juristenfakultät, 59.

[250] Mohl's increasingly parliamentarian convictions (cf. Stolleis, "Verwaltungslehre und Verwaltungswissenschaft," in Jeserich et al., eds., Deutsche Verwaltungsgeschichte, 2:69f.) were another sign of his dissatisfaction with the constitutionalism of the previous decade.

fact that politically diffident men like Savigny and his followers were unwilling to make use of them. In the harsher political climate of Prussia professorial tradition never became associated with the kind of vigorous political action typical of the south. The men of Berlin were not political activists. Quite the contrary: they wanted tradition to loft them above politics. Savigny and Puchta therefore rarely became involved in the grand constitutional conflicts that occupied the time of Mohl and Zacharia (although of course there are exceptions[251]); during all the years of constitutional conflict, the north remained unassertive. Thus, the Berlin professors resisted entangling their Spruchkollegium in politics; despite the foundation of a Spruchkollegium at Berlin and Savigny's own activity in it—he himself drafted some 138 opinions[252]—the Berlin professors rarely made their voices heard on major political questions. Indeed, in 1835 they made the antiquity of the Spruchkollegium their grounds for yielding to the decrees that circumscribed professorial authority: Spruchkollegien were, the Berlin professors declared, ancient, *uralt*, and not suited to involvement in "the political confusions of our time."[253] No statement more at odds with the southern conception of the political use of tradition can be imagined: to the southerners, the antiquity of the Spruchkollegien was a basis for constitutionalist action; to the Historical School, the same antiquity was a justification for inaction. Savigny and Puchta hoped only that the old institutions, and the great Roman tradition, could serve to make political conflict unnecessary. The Rechtsstaat thinkers of the south had no such hope. They were determined to draw strength for their political innovations from the old traditions that had eventually to give way to a new world; Savigny and Puchta simply wished to see the great and the little tradition survive.

Nevertheless, in both north and south the professors were constitutionalists of a distinctly eighteenth-century type. Savigny and Puchta appear in most accounts of this period as "conservatives"; Welcker appears as a "liberal." The terms are not meaningless: the professors of Berlin and those of the south belonged to very different schools of thought regarding the propriety of political action. But all of them were revivalists of the ancient constitution. Savigny and Puchta, on the one side, and Welcker

---

[251] For Puchta's concern for, inter alia, press freedom, see *Kleine civilistische Schriften*, XXV–XXVIII. For Savigny on academic freedom during the Demagogenverfolgung, see Stühler, *Erneuerung der Rechtswissenschaft*, 59. Savigny was, on the other hand, capable of referring to the Carlsbad Decrees as a "Verdruß." Rückert, *Savigny*, 215.

[252] Dawson, *Oracles of the Law*, 456 n.16. For Puchta's role as a Spruchkollegium member, see *Kleine civilistische Schriften*, IX. Savigny asked to be excused from duty on the Spruchkollegium at Marburg, but in 1811 could express his "joy" over the institution. Rückert, *Savigny*, 34, 151–53.

[253] Quoted in Seckel, "Geschichte der Berliner Juristenfakultät," 471.

and Zachariä, on the other, were equally rooted in pre-absolutist tradition; both schools of Rechtsstaat thought developed among law professors on the strength of the same old-world associations.[254] The lawyers of the 1820s and 1830s were not struggling to become Western liberals. They did not believe that they lived in the ruins of an old order that could never be repaired. They *did* wish to interpose themselves between prince and people and to save the political peace in Germany; but in so doing they were not responding to the terror of a "sovereignty crisis." They were full of a hope that seemed real: the hope that an ancient constitution could be revived—for the southerners, a constitution of balanced corporations whose legal frictions were smoothed by "impartial" professors of law; for the Berliners, an old imperial constitution of tiny princely Rechtsstaaten in which the political strife that followed Napoleon's expulsion would have no meaning and contain no threat, and in which the traditions of ancient Rome still somehow lived. These lawyers failed. But their plans and aspirations for change were well considered and not wholly foolish. In the next chapter I will discuss in more detail the kind of change they hoped to effect. Whatever their differences about the use of politics, they shared a conviction that German society could be remade on the model of Rome.

[254] Cf. the discussion of the Göttingen Seven affair in M. Fioravanti, *Giuristi e Costituzione Politica nell'Ottocento Tedesco*, Per la Storia del Pensiero Moderno Giuridico, vol. 8 (Milan, 1979), 53–54 (outcry based not on ideas of individual rights but on "diritti della 'storia' ").

Chapter V

HIGH CULTURAL TRADITION AS AN INSTRUMENT OF REFORM: THE PROFESSORIATE AND THE AGRARFRAGE

THE PROMISE of Roman legal civilization as the Roman-law professors conceived it was change without destruction, peaceful reform through the revival of Roman tradition. This was not a completely empty promise. This professorial talk of the saving power of classical tradition may now seem to have been hopeless or fantastic. But the romantic Romanist lawyers had practical plans for change that historians have never understood. In the end these plans did not—and probably could not—succeed. Nevertheless, at least until the decline of rule-of-law romanticism that began in the late 1830s, it seemed possible, without the agency of the state, to achieve civilized reform through the gradual elaboration of legal principles whose beginnings could be traced back to the sixteenth century and beyond into the ancient world. In this chapter I will trace this gradualist program of legal reform and the recasting of Roman tradition that it necessarily demanded.

The so-called *Agrarfrage*, agrarian reform (literally: agrarian question), was the dominant political issue of the romantic period; my subject in this chapter will accordingly be Romanist answers to it. The Agrarfrage was the great test. If the professors had not been able to put the tradition they felt they represented to use in agrarian reform, they would not have seemed a very potent force. The cultural tradition of Rome and of the Holy Roman Empire could seem imposing in the decades of the 1820s and 1830s only because it seemed to offer answers to the Agrarfrage. In this chapter I wish to show how this issue set into motion a great revolution in property law that began in the 1790s and ended only with the greater political revolution of 1848. All the law professors whom I have described above were involved in a complex doctrinal battle against feudalism in the German countryside, a battle that produced far-reaching reinterpretations of Roman history, and deep reconceptualizations of property law that were intended as models of change without political strife.

From the late eighteenth century onward, the Agrarfrage, the debate over putting an end to the feudal landholding order in the German countryside, was the most pressing political question in every part of Germany. The feudal order[1] was not effectively ended in the German countryside until after 1848; indeed, *Bauernbefreiung*—the liberation of the peasants—was in some ways not complete until late in the nineteenth century. Enlightened princes had freed their serfs here and there in the German world as early as 1688.[2] Nevertheless, enlightenment efforts to ease the lot of the peasants had come to little or had affected only royal domains.[3] Until the mid-eighteenth century, most peasants were still in some sense enserfed, in a state of feudal subordination to the lords of the land they tended, with their obligations defined by customary law. To be sure, the medieval feudal order had been significantly altered in many respects: in particular, many peasant obligations to perform services had been commuted into obligations to make regular money payments. Nevertheless, peasants remained subject to taxes, dues, and demands for personal service that were numerous and ill-defined; lords found it possible to impose, on their peasants, duties that regularly received the sanction of the courts. Peasant rights to land, to forage, and to the protection theoretically owed them by their lords was everywhere precarious; they suffered in some places by being tied to the land and in others by being forced off it. Feudalism lived and even flourished in the eighteenth- and nineteenth-century German world.[4] When Savigny wrote his *Vom Beruf unserer Zeit*, aboli-

---

[1] In speaking of "feudalism" throughout this chapter, I should note that I refer only to feudal land tenure, and not to any other aspect of what could be defined as a feudal order. In particular, I do not refer to feudal jurisdiction—the special jurisdiction of manorial courts—whose abolition was an important goal of nineteenth-century reformers.

[2] See K. Kroeschell, "Bauernbefreiung," *Handwörterbuch des Agrarrechts* (Berlin, 1981), 302, for a brief chronology.

[3] Cf., e.g., W. Conze, *Die liberalen Agrarreformen Hannovers* (Hannover, n.d.), 7; R. Gross, *Die bürgerliche Agrarreform in Sachsen in der ersten Hälfte des neunzehnten Jahrhunderts* (Weimar, 1968), 58ff.

[4] The large literature on the subject of agrarian relations and agrarian reform in the late eighteenth and nineteenth centuries begins with G. F. Knapp, *Die Bauern-Befreiung und der Ursprung der Landarbeiter in den älteren Teilen Preußens*, 2 vols. (Leipzig, 1887). For agrarian relations in Hannover, the most important for my purposes here, see esp. a work by a student of Knapp, W. Wittich, *Die Grundherrschaft in Nordwestdeutschland* (Leipzig, 1896); see also Oberschelp, *Niedersachsen*, 1:103ff. Agrarian relations varied widely from area to area, and much literature must be consulted to form a full understanding of them. See, e.g., F. Lütge, *Geschichte der deutschen Agrarverfassung vom frühen Mittelalter bis zum 19. Jahrhundert* (Stuttgart, 1963); idem, *Mitteldeutsche Grundherrschaft*, Quellen und Forschungen zur Agrargeschichte, vol. 4 (Stuttgart, 1957); W. Engels, *Ablösungen und Gemeinheitsteilungen in der Rheinprovinz*, Rheinisches Archiv. Veröffentlichungen des Instituts für geschichtliche Landeskunde der Rheinlands, vol. 51 (Bonn, 1957); F. W. Henning, *Dienste und Abgaben der Bauern im Achtzehnten Jahrhundert*, Quellen und Forschungen zur Agrargeschichte, vol. 21 (Stuttgart, 1969); Conze, *Die liberalen Agrarreformen Hannovers*; Gross, *Bürgerliche Agrarreform in Sachsen*; J. Mooser, "Property and Woodtheft: Agrarian Capitalism and Social Conflict in Rural Society, 1800–1850—A Westphalian Case

tion was still far off. In the parts of Germany that had fallen under direct French rule, feudalism had been legally abolished, and the famous October Edict of 1807 had promised an abolition for the Prussian territories. But the status of former French subjects varied after 1814, and the Prussian promise was implemented at best in a piecemeal and incomplete fashion.[5] In general, Bauernbefreiung was the same slow process in all the German lands during the eighteenth century as well as in the decades after 1814: one by one, the various feudal taxes and obligations were not abolished directly, but either commuted into a fixed rent, or, later, made redeemable for a single capital payment. Reform efforts focused, by and large, on allowing peasants to mortgage their land in order to make it possible for them eventually to acquire clear title.[6] Peasants had various reasons, legal and financial, for refusing the opportunity to redeem their obligations outright. The result was that even in lands where formal abolitionist legislation was enacted, feudalism of a kind continued to exist on a large scale—and, indeed, was the cause of critical unrest in the early 1830s and after.

Nevertheless, since the eighteenth century, various campaigns for agrarian reform, for lightening the load of the German peasants, had deeply shaken the old doctrinal order of German law. By the early 1790s, when the agrarian reform movements, stirred and quickened by the French Revolution, began to reach their peak, German lawyers were faced with the need for a whole new system of property law. This great social reordering, which has been too much neglected by legal historians,[7]

Study," in R. G. Moeller, ed., *Peasants and Lords in Modern Germany* (Boston, 1986), 52–80; R. Koselleck, *Preußen zwischen Reform und Revolution* (Stuttgart, 1967), 487–559; U. Ruhberg, "Die Rechte des Grundeigentümers: Entwicklung des Eigentumsbegriffes in Preußen zwischen ALR und BGB im agrarischen Bodenrecht" (diss., Kiel, 1972); P. Dany, "Grundeigentum und Freiheit: Liberalisierung der preußischen Agrarverfassung in der Zeit von 1794 bis 1850" (diss., Kiel, 1970) is a convenient summary of Prussian agrarian legislation. For a detailed study of two differing regions, see J. Mooser, *Ländliche Klassengesellschaft, 1770–1848*, Kritische Studien zur Geschichtswissenschaft 64 (Göttingen, 1984). Good brief introductions are Kroeschell, "Bauernbefreiung"; S. Buchholz, "Einzelgesetzgebung," in *Coing Handbuch*, vol. 3, pt. 2, 1721–57. For surveys, see T. Hamerow, *Restoration, Revolution, Reaction* (Princeton, 1958), 38–55; C. Dipper, *Die Bauernbefreiung in Deutschland* (Stuttgart, 1980).

[5] For agrarian history during the French occupation of the Rhineland, see E. Fehrenbach, *Traditionale Gesellschaft und Revolutionares Recht: Die Einführung des Code Napoléon in den Rheinbundstaaten*, Kritische Studien zur Geschichtswissenschaft, 13 (Göttingen, 1974).

[6] For a survey of reform legislation, see S. Buchholz, "Die Quellen des deutschen Immobiliarrechts im 19. Jahrhundert," *Ius Commune* 7 (1978): 250–325. For the example of Hannover, see generally Wittich, *Grundherrschaft*; for another example, see E. Sakai, *Der Kurhessische Bauer im Neunzehnten Jahrhundert und die Grundlastenablösung*, Hessische Forschungen zur Geschichtlichen Landes- und Volkskunde, Heft 7 (Melsungen, 1967).

[7] Compare this call for new scholarship by H. Hattenhauer: "In der Tat müssen wir diese

called forth great productive powers from the Romanist lawyers and Roman historians alike. New possibilities and pressing new necessities in property law released tremendous new energies within the community of jurists as well as in the community of Roman historians. I will begin with the new Roman history that emerged as a result, before turning to the new property law.

REMAKING ROMAN HISTORY

Under the social pressure of the Agrarfrage a new Roman history developed, one that mixed desire for agrarian reform with early romantic sentimental philosophizing about German country life. From its earliest years the romantic movement drew much of its strength and sentimental force from a love of the peasantry caught up in a centuries-long process of change. In particular, Möser's many sketches and brief essays on the Osnabrück peasantry, which contained learned and often ironic discussions of the possibilities and consequences of freedom for the peasantry, initiated an elective affinity between romanticism and the peasants that lasted for seventy or eighty years.[8] Möser's sketches were deeply skeptical, and they cultivated a Westphalian slowness to change; accordingly, they had little reformist punch to them. But when Möser was moved to express political ideals, he did so in ways that would lend themselves to the uses of reform in later generations.

Möser's famous fable of the Frisian peasantry, "Kurze Geschichte der Bauerhöfe," established the model for romantic thinking, among classicists as among others. Möser's fable was an account of the inadvertent loss of ancient freedom among the Germans. The Frisian peasants, hypothesized Möser, might once have been free. But in order to stave off common dangers they took on obligations to perform community service, just as they might build a dike to stave off the sea. In time and through historical accidents and human venality, however, originally freely given community service might have been transformed into an obligatory feudal subjection to a class of dynastic nobility. Möser himself hedged ironically on the question of whether such a fable might correspond to the

---

erste Phase der Bauernbefreiung, die Phase der Bauernprozeße um die richterliche Begrenzung ihrer Dienstpflichten gegenüber der Gutsherrschaft, in zukünftiger rechtshistorischer Forschung wohl ernster nehmen, als dies bisher geschehen ist." Hattenhauer, "Burchard Wilhelm Pfeiffer und die Bauernbefreiung in Kurhessen," in *Festschrift für Hermann Krause* (Cologne/Vienna, 1975), 199.

[8] The influence of Möser on Savigny is noted by, e.g., Sjöholm, *Rechtsgeschichte*, 30; Stühler, *Erneuerung der Rechtswissenschaft*, 234–35. Unfortunately, I have not been able to obtain a copy of J. Schröder, *Justus Möser als Jurist*, Osnabrücker Rechtswissenschaftliche Abhandlungen 5 (Cologne, 1987).

truth.[9] But he had established a mode of thought about peasants and peasant freedom that would develop into a new Roman history and a lawyerly romantic program of reform. Romantic Romanist lawyers would continue laboring to demonstrate that peasants had historically been free, and that the proper work of scholarship was to show how that freedom had been lost and could be regained.

But in the effort to free the peasants as in so many things, Roman law and romanticism sat uneasily together. The peasants were German; it was difficult to claim any Roman heritage for them. Worse, angry denouncers of Roman law insisted that it had *destroyed* historic peasant Germanic freedom. From the mid-eighteenth century on, critics of Roman law maintained that its introduction operated to depress the estate of the peasantry, the *Bauernstand*. For Roman law had no provisions easily applicable to German peasant relations[10]—except its law of slavery. The charge that the Roman law of slavery had been employed against German peasants could be heard from opponents of Roman law from C. H. von Senckenberg in 1756 down to G. F. Knapp and Gustav Radbruch in the nineteenth and twentieth centuries.[11] The Göttingen school set to work refuting this charge. In the first volume of his *Civilistisches Magazin*, Gustav Hugo reprinted a brief essay on the inapplicability of the Roman law of slavery to the modern world: the Germans had only a very few African slaves; moreover, the African slave trade was carried on only by nations unfamiliar with Roman law.[12] Furthermore, if Roman law were applied to African slaves, they would almost all be free men.[13] But this sort of ugly accusation was not easily defused.

Because the charge that Roman law had been used to enslave the peasants was so ugly, it was particularly urgent for romantic Romanist lawyers to find some interpretation of Roman history that could alter the coloring of Roman law in the public mind. In the 1790s, eager to join in in the imperial revival, they had rediscovered the Antonines. At the same time they began to rediscover the early Roman republic and to make it the focus of their hopes in a Rome for agrarian reformers.

The new Roman agrarian history began where the new Roman political history did, and at the same time: in Göttingen, during the 1790s. It grew up in reaction to a radical abolitionist reading of Roman history

---

[9] Möser, "Kurze Geschichte der Bauerhöfe," in *Patriotische Phantasien*, in idem, Werke: Historisch-kritische Ausgabe, 14 vols. in 16 (Oldenburg/Berlin, 1944–81), 4:269–76.

[10] Cf. Koschaker, *Europa und das Römische Recht*, 154.

[11] Bender, *Rezeption des Römischen Rechts*, 47, 92.

[12] Hugo, "Über die Institutionen des heutigen römischen Rechts," in *Civilistisches Magazin* 4th ed. (1823), 1:129ff. For Hugo's critique of slavery, see Stühler, *Erneuerung der Rechtswissenschaft*, 140.

[13] Hugo, "Über die Institutionen des heutigen römischen Recht," 134.

that made its appearance during the French Revolution.[14] Babouvistes, radicals of the revolution, had made agrarian laws—*loix agraires*—their rallying cry. These were the leges agrariae of early Rome, laws on the ownership of public land whose exact meaning remains obscure. The most striking provision of these leges agrariae limited ownership of such lands to a certain acreage. European scholars from Machiavelli and Ulrich Obrecht through Harrington, Montesquieu, and Mably had interpreted the leges agrariae as evidence of early Roman limitation on private property, of a willingness to transfer land from the rich to the poor in order to strengthen the state. Babeuf and his circle employed this scholarly-publicistic tradition to justify their socialistic program.[15] German romantics set out to counter the ungradualistic political implications of Babouvism by attacking the scholarly foundations of this Roman history.

In 1793 C. G. Heyne of Göttingen, appalled by the Babouvist use of Roman history, gave a lecture entitled "Leges agrariae pestiferae et execrabiles," in which he demonstrated that the agrarian laws applied only to public land; there was no interference with private property rights in Roman law.[16] Like Heyne's recentering of Roman legal history on the reign of Hadrian,[17] this new and politically urgent interpretation made its way to Kiel a decade later, where Heyne's campaign to de-radicalize Babouvisme was taken up first by D. H. Hegewisch,[18] and then by a man who was to revolutionize Roman historiography, B. G. Niebuhr.

Niebuhr, a Dane and, by profession, a banker, moved in reformist circles in Kiel and later in Berlin, where as a Prussian state servant he contributed a preparatory memorandum to the drafting of the October Edict that promised Bauernbefreiung in Prussia. When he took up the question of the leges agrariae in 1804, he did so not as a reactionary but as a reformer eager to benefit the peasants of Denmark and Germany. Niebuhr was the model of a fervid romantic neohumanist. He believed with the

[14] The history of this episode in Roman historiography has been investigated by a number of classicists in recent years. See A. Heuss, "Niebuhr und Mommsen" in *Antike und Abendland* 14, no. 1 (1968), 1–18; idem, *Niebuhrs Wissenschaftliche Anfänge* (Göttingen, 1981); A. D. Momigliano, "Alle origini dell'interesse su Roma arcaica: Niebuhr e l'India," in *Rivista Storica Italiana* 92 (1980), 561–71; idem, "Niebuhr and the Agrarian Problems of Rome" in idem, *New Paths of Classicism in the Nineteenth Century*, History and Theory, Beiheft 21 (Middletown, 1982), 3–15; K. Christ, *Von Gibbon zu Rostovtzeff* (Darmstadt, 1972); idem, *Römische Geschichte und Deutsche Geschichtswissenschaft*, idem, *Römische Geschichte und Wissenschaftsgeschichte* 3 vols., vol. 3 (Darmstadt, 1983); Z. Yavetz, "Why Rome?" *American Journal of Philology* 97 (1976): 276–96.

[15] On the Ideengeschichte of the "loix agraires" see Heuss, *Niebuhrs Wissenschaftliche Anfänge*, 153–334.

[16] Cf. ibid., 322–28.

[17] See above, pp. 86–87.

[18] Cf. D. H. Hegewisch, *Geschichte der Gracchischen Unruhen in der Römischen Republik* (Hamburg, 1801); cf. Heuss, *Niebuhrs Wissenschaftliche Anfänge*, 328–30.

conviction of a renaissance scholar[19] that Roman history could change German lives. "I went back to a great nation," he wrote, "to strengthen my mind and the mind of my hearers."[20] He would submit the social conflicts of Germany to humanist solutions; his method would be the imitation of the exemplary ways of the Romans: as Niebuhr put it, he made "the heroes and patriots of Rome . . . rise up before our view, not like Milton's angels, but as beings of flesh and blood."[21] They were to be heroes and patriots for Germany, representing a model society based on a strong and free peasantry. For Niebuhr was wholly persuaded, by the writings of Möser along with those of the English champions of the "ancient constitution," that a free, sturdy peasantry was the foundation of a sound state. This "patriotic" (in Möser's sense of the word) conviction was the source of his hostility to the feudalism that hobbled what had once been, and should be again, a free yeoman class, a peasantry that would make Germany as strong as Rome. But Niebuhr had to explain how the Roman peasantry had fallen from its free state, and how it could be liberated again without revolution. He set out to explain the enigmatic leges agrariae as the legal instrument of reform.

His explanation came into existence only with the help of two men: James Grant, a servant of the English East India Company, and Savigny. Conversations with Grant suggested to Niebuhr the model of Indian land under the Zamindar. As a tax official Grant was involved in the reform of Indian landholding, and he had come to the conclusion that the Zamindar had usurped ownership of public lands, which they had originally only superintended as agents of the crown. The Roman nobles, Niebuhr postulated, had perpetrated a similar usurpation; in this they were like Möser's one-time leaders of a free peasantry who had converted themselves into a hereditary nobility. The limit on landholding mentioned in the leges agrariae was a limit on the right of nobles to hold land that remained the property of the public. Ancient Roman efforts to enforce the leges agrariae were thus not assaults on private property, but appropriate reform measures much like those employed by the English in India. The Indian analogy thus afforded Niebuhr the model not only of Roman, but also of English freedom.[22]

---

[19] That Niebuhr remained deeply fixed in Renaissance attitudes shows in his declaration that his researches were intended only as a supplement to Livy (Niebuhr, *Römische Geschichte*, 3 vols. [Berlin, 1853] 1:ix). Cf. Heuss, "Niebuhr und Mommsen," 5–6; B. Bravo, *Philologie, histoire, philosophie de l'histoire: Étude sur Droysen* (Wroclaw, 1968), 168.

[20] Quoted in G. P. Gooch, *History and Historians in the Nineteenth Century* (London, 1952), 18.

[21] Niebuhr, *Römische Geschichte* 1:3.

[22] Cf. Momigliano, "Alle origini dell'interesse su Roma arcaica"; "Niebuhr and the Agrarian Problems of Rome." For the Prussian reformers' English inspiration, see, e.g., Mooser, *Ländliche Klassengesellschaft*, 94.

However, Niebuhr's problem was not yet solved. The Roman nobles did not simply manage public lands; like Möser's nobility, they had become entitled to permanent hereditary occupation. How could they claim such a right against the Roman state? It was Savigny who gave Niebuhr his solution. In 1803 Savigny had made his fame with a book on the new property law, the *Recht des Besitzes*. Savigny's book was a brilliant analysis of the Roman law of possession, whose fundamental thesis (the complexities of which I will explain below[23]) was that possession had been protected in Roman law because it formed a part of the law of prescription: possession, in Savigny's analysis, was a kind of provisional legal state. Savigny's thesis—that *possession is always in the process of maturing into ownership*—illuminated Niebuhr's problem. Together the two scholars formulated an explanation of events in the very ancient Roman countryside. The nobility had begun by possessing public lands; in time (and in conflict with the original understanding of "possession" in Rome) that possession had matured into ownership.[24]

Their conclusions had profoundly significant implications for land and class in Germany. Any declaration that the peasants had historically been free would have done much to delegitimate feudalism. But rooting peasant freedom in Roman history had particularly valuable consequences for the program of reform. For republican Rome, so Niebuhr and Savigny believed, was a polity in which reform had been achieved without the curse of revolution. The plebeians had successfully forced social change through peaceable "secessions"—mass exoduses that the plebeians ended only upon guarantee of their rights. The *plebs*, by its tactic of successive secessions, had established its own rights without a revolution and made Rome Rome as a result.[25] For this reason, Rome offered the model of reform without the sacrifice of "harmonious cooperation of the classes."[26] Not only was the Roman tradition safe from the charge of having enslaved the German peasants, it offered them freedom.

Niebuhr among the Law Professors

Feudalism, Niebuhr seemed thus to proclaim in his lectures on Roman history (1810–11) could be peacefully dismantled in Germany; Roman history, properly understood, demonstrated that the peaceful reinstitution of historic freedoms was the route to strength. Niebuhr's humanist politics of reform proved profoundly appealing among law professors everywhere. But in this as in other matters, the thinkers of the south took

---

[23] See below, pp. 183–84.
[24] Cf. Heuss, *Niebuhrs Wissenschaftliche Anfänge*, 121–22.
[25] Yavetz, "Why Rome?"
[26] Christ, *Römische Geschichte und Deutsche Geschichtswissenschaft*, 41.

Niebuhr's Roman history as an injunction to a much more vigorous and direct attack on feudalism than did the Savignyans.

Thibaut knew Niebuhr in Kiel, but as a young man Thibaut was far too radical for Niebuhr, and he never became one of the advocates of Niebuhrian history.[27] It was rather Zacharia, always closer in spirit to the Savignyans, who sponsored Niebuhrianism most vigorously among the southerners. Zacharia applied Niebuhr's lessons directly, even naively, to the world of Baden. Deeply caught up in fights to free the Baden peasantry,[28] Zacharia published an investigation of Roman history, his two-volume *Lucius Cornelius Sulla, genannt der Glückliche, als Ordner des Römischen Freystaates*.[29] It was wholly in the Niebuhrian mold, a glorification of Sulla as the maker of a constitution that could serve as a model for Germans. "His age," exclaimed Zacharia of his hero, "had so many similarities with our own!" Rome had been riven by conflict between the class that wished to rule by money and the class that wished to rule by numbers.[30] Zacharia, who wished to preserve a nobility in Baden while still ending feudalism, believed that the future lay neither with money nor with numbers, but with landed wealth. Sulla had had the same convictions, and his tool had been fidelity to the *leges agrariae*. Zacharia rehearsed the history of the usurpation of the public land by the nobles, with its dire consequences for Roman freedom.[31] Sulla had sought to end the evil: "One can describe the plan that underlay Sulla's constitutional laws thus: Sulla wanted to recall the good old age of the Roman free state, for this state had had a moderate aristocracy—the legal order from which had developed the before-mentioned *lex Licinia* (the Roman "Reform-bill" [English in the original])."[32] The Sullan aristocracy was to be "landed" not "monied" (the words are again English[33]). Sulla fought his battle for this aristocracy in the same way Zacharia fought his own battles in Baden: by use of scholarship. The constitutional reforms that were to revive Sulla's aristocracy were only possible because Sulla had the aid of *Rechtsgelehrten*—legal scholars. It was these scholars who had drafted Sulla's legislation[34]—and scholars in general who, in conjunction with princes, could remake a free self-governing society.

---

[27] On the relations between Thibaut and Niebuhr, see Polley, *Thibaut*, 1:81ff.

[28] Cf. Zacharia's *Der Kampf des Grundeigenthumes gegen die Grundherrlichkeit* (Heidelberg, 1832).

[29] Zacharia, *Lucius Cornelius Sulla, genannt der Glückliche, als Ordner des Römischen Freystaates*, 2 vols. (Heidelberg, 1834).

[30] Ibid., 1:iii–iv.

[31] Ibid., 1:36–41.

[32] Zacharia, *Sulla*, 2:11–12. *Lex Licinia* was a principle *lex agraria*, agrarian law.

[33] Ibid., 10.

[34] Ibid., 2:6. Zacharia has in mind Q. Mucius Scaevola, whose counsel to Sulla he declares probable.

Zachariä's Niebuhrianism certainly marked him as the southerner closest to the Savignyans. But his was not a Savignyan Niebuhrianism. For Zachariä's book was intended to give support to an abolitionist statute, a piece of legislation. Savigny had devoted a lifetime to denying the vocation of his time for legislation, and he could hardly have accepted Niebuhr's teaching if it had necessarily implied a need for statutes. Rather, he and Puchta attempted to use Niebuhrianism to achieve a very different kind of reform, reform not by legislation but by scholarship. Indeed, the subject of Savignyan Niebuhrianism offers a fine study in how Savigny thought social reform could be achieved through the action of legal scholars alone, without legislative intervention.[35]

It has been said that Savigny simply neglected the German peasants.[36] That is false. It has also been noted that Savigny, as a lord, was distressed by the effect in his own lands of the uprisings of 1830. That is true, but misleading.[37] Whatever his distress in 1830 and after, he was very much committed to reform, particularly in his earlier years. Savigny made his contributions to agrarian reform as a legal historian and as a doctrinal lawyer, and in both capacities he tried to put into practice a program of scholarly reform that claimed to represent a glorious Roman tradition. His principle contribution as a Niebuhrian historian came with his essay on the Roman colonate,[38] written in 1822 as the fiercest struggles over the liberation of peasants were fought in Prussia—struggles in which Savigny participated directly as a member of the Prussian State Council. The essay on the colonate was history with an unmistakeable political purpose. For Savigny denied that any juridical or historical connection existed between the so-called Roman *coloni* and the German *Bauer*. This was near-revolutionary in its reformist implications, for "colonus" was the ordinary legal term for peasants in the German courts.[39] Savigny declared, in effect, that feudalism in Germany rested on a correctable error in legal scholarship, for Roman law contemplated only free *Bauern*.

In Savigny's time (as indeed to this day) the colonate was usually de-

---

[35] Savigny's account of Niebuhr's politics should be consulted: "Niebuhr's Wesen und Wirken," in *Vermischte Schriften*, 4:220–24.

[36] Wolf, *Grosse Rechtsdenker*, 531–32. For varying views, see M. Brutti, "L'intuizione della proprietà nel sistema di Savigny," *Q. Fior.* 5–6 (1976–77): 99ff. Brutti himself wisely states: "Savigny ha sempre davanti agli occhi il regime feudale dei rapporti di appartenenza," ibid., 102.

[37] For a thoughtful discussion of Savigny's reactions to 1830 on his own lands, see Rückert, *Savigny*, 217–18. Rückert, after giving the evidence a close reading, concludes that Savigny was "nicht eigentlich restaurativ oder reaktionär, sondern *quietistisch*." (Emphasis in original.)

[38] Savigny, "Ueber den Römischen Colonat" and "Nachtrag 1849," in *Vermischte Schriften*, 2:1–66.

[39] For examples from cases in Hannover, see e.g., below p. 194.

scribed as the late-Roman precursor of European serfdom. Ending the association of German peasants with the colonate was thus an indispensable first step for putting a revived Roman law in the service of agrarian reform. It was Savigny's tactic to deny the institution any status in the true Roman doctrine of the classical jurists. The colonate, Savigny maintained, postdated the classical law. Thus Savigny could point to the closest Roman analogy to German serfdom and declare it a product of Rome's decline, a manifestation of the same age of decadence that had produced Justinian's code. He began his essay in Niebuhrian fashion, by promising to shed scholarly light on the problems presented to Germans by the French Revolution:

> In the most divergent periods, and among completely different peoples, the cultivation of the soil has brought forth peculiar class relations. These have been restructured in a great part of Europe in our own days, sometimes violently and sometimes peacefully, and this restructuring has drawn general attention to them. Such relations were also widespread in the Roman Empire under the Christian emperors, existing alongside slavery, which they gradually limited and then replaced. A discussion of these late-Roman peasant relations [Bauernverhältnisse] will not be useless, for they have gone almost completely unnoticed in our time.[40]

A learned treatment followed. Savigny gave a general description of the institution and then proceeded to its dating and origins. The colonate was hardly in evidence before Constantine.[41] Its origins were obscure. Something like it had existed in the very earliest age of Roman history (i.e., before the establishment of the Republic): "The clients of the oldest Roman constitution were also propertyless peasants [Bauern], and they too lived by birth in a state of dependency." But they were hardly to be identified with coloni. Neither were the slaves of the intervening centuries.[42] Savigny could only speculate about the introduction of this strange institution into the Roman world.[43] But he was able to deny, at the end of his essay, that the colonate was in any way Rome's contribution to German serfdom. German serfdom had not influenced the Roman colonate:

> And even less ground exists for explaining the origin of German serfdom from the Roman colonate, even if, in Latin versions of German national laws, Roman terms of art were used here as in other matters for the description of German legal concepts. But there is a more important difference in the origins

[40] Savigny, "Ueber den Römischen Colonat," 2.
[41] Ibid., 41.
[42] Ibid., 44–45.
[43] Ibid., 46ff. But see "Nachtrag 1849" for Savigny's later word on the origins of the colonate in the light of subsequent scholarship.

of these two institutions which must above all be mentioned. The development of the Roman colonate falls in the age of the nation's dissolution. . . .
German serfdom coincides with the original development of class relations.
. . . In this regard, [German serfdom] is without doubt more to be compared
with the most ancient Roman clientship than with the colonate, even though
it stands in an immediate temporal connection with the latter.[44]

The implication for the practice of law was clear: if German peasants
were treated as coloni by German courts, this only reflected lack of scholarly sophistication. The colonate had no place in German justice. The
implication for near-revolutionary reform by nonrevolutionary means
was clear as well to readers familiar with Niebuhr's account of the history
of early Rome: Germany's peasants were certainly suffering; so had the
peasants of pre-republican Rome. But the latter had fought their way—
peacefully, not violently—to free status, and German peasants could do
the same. There were indeed no provisions for peasant relations—
Bauernverhältnisse—to be found in classical Roman law. It was a law that
despite the collapse of the Republic, continued to embody the principles
of freedom.[45] But that lack proved only the value of Roman law for a
Germany about to establish freedom in a strong state, just as the Romans
had done, millenia before.

Savigny's essay ignited a scholarly controversy that lasted down into
the time of Max Weber.[46] But it certainly did not achieve its intended
effect on German legal practice. Fifty learned pages were hardly enough
to change centuries of legal practice, and the peasants continued to be
referred to as "coloni" until they were finally freed after 1848. But the
essay had given expression to the conviction that scholarship could help
to end feudalism by giving German law the shape of classical Roman law.
Reform by Romanization was possible, and in their doctrine and practice
Savigny and his followers would be guided by their faith in Niebuhr's
Rome.

It was Puchta who systematized the Niebuhrianism of the Historical
School and integrated it into a coherent interpretation of Roman legal
history.[47] In 1822, as Savigny worked to scour Roman law clean of late

[44] Savigny, "Ueber den Römischen Colonat," 52–53.
[45] Cf. Savigny, "Vom Beruf," 116. Cf. Savigny's rebuttal in his "Nachtrag 1849" of
Huschke's suggestion that the colonate could somehow have grown out of the doctrines of
Roman law itself. "Der Römische Colonat," 56.
[46] Cf. Weber, Die Römische Agrargeschichte in ihrer Bedeutung für das Staats- und Privatrecht (Stuttgart, 1891), 3, on "die seit Savigny nicht wieder entschlafene Streitfrage über
die Entwickelung des Kolonats."
[47] Puchta himself said that the great influences on his work had been Niebuhr and Savigny, not Savigny alone. Puchta, "Autobiographische Notiz," in Kleine civilistische Schriften, XXI n., cited in Brie, Der Volksgeist bei Hegel und in der Historischen Schule (Berlin/

imperial agrarian practice, Puchta—who declared that to expel Roman law from the German legal order would resemble expelling Greek models from German art[48]—was attempting to integrate Niebuhr's researches with constitutional history. In a learned essay, he linked *auctoritas*, used typically as the word for the type of power exercised by the Senate and the magistrates of Rome, with the history of property law as laid out by Niebuhr. Citing Niebuhr and Savigny, Puchta maintained that in very early Roman history the different Roman classes had had different forms of property rights with different Latin names: like *possessio*, *auctoritas* was a term used only in the law of the patricians, not of the plebeians; it meant "having title or a legal claim" to a piece of property. Later, this term of patrician property law had been extended to patrician political power as exercised by magistrates and the Senate. Thus the history of property law, wrote Puchta, and the fate of the Roman constitution were "completely interdependent."[49]

Demonstrating this interdependence remained Puchta's governing ambition as he composed his mature works, the *Gewohnheitsrecht* and the *Cursus der Institutionen*. The Roman history that he wrote, especially in the latter much-reprinted and widely used text, was both grander and closer to Niebuhr's Roman history than what he had written in 1822. Its overarching purpose was to demonstrate how true legal freedom had developed in Niebuhr's early Rome, and how legal scholars had become the sole guardians of that freedom. Again, in Puchta's account, the early "tribal" differences between patricians and plebeians had generated the history of private law for later centuries of Roman history and, indeed, for the world history of Roman law. The patricians, warrior citizens of the original Rome, had had no private property in the many lands they had conquered. In the public land, there had been only possessio: "according to the most ancient legal view, the individual existed in the most intimate connection with the whole, his public still absorbed his private person."[50] Private property had established itself to a certain extent as early Romans had taken possession of movable booty.[51] But only among the plebeians had true private property, and indeed private law, devel-

---

Leipzig, 1909) 11–12. According to one obituary, his accomplishment was his success in combining Savigny and Niebuhr. Puchta, *Kleine civilistische Schriften*, XXXVIII.

[48] Bender, *Rezeption des Römischen Rechts*, 68.

[49] Puchta, "Adversus hostem aeterna auctoritas," in *Kleine civilistische Schriften*, 62–63, 64.

[50] Puchta, *Cursus der Institutionen*, 129–30. Puchta's attempt to show how social role was bound up with property bears the clear traces, here, of Möser's influence: cf. Möser, "Von dem echten Eigentum," in *Patriotische Phantasien*, in *Werke*, 4:138–41.

[51] Puchta, *Cursus der Institutionen*, 131–33. This movable booty naturally included all those things later subject to ownership *ex iure quiritium*, under the special law of Roman citizens.

oped. The plebeians had originally been members of neighboring, conquered tribes. For them there could be no possessio, a term that referred
only to ownership by right of conquest. Thus it had been among the plebeians that ager privatus—private land—and private property as regu-
lated by the complex early Roman law of the *ius quiritium*—the special
private law of Roman citizens—could first arise:

> The ius quiritium received its complete development among the plebs; the
> plebeians gave their acceptance to the concept of the private person, a con-
> cept that the ius quiritium presupposed. The creation of an independent pri-
> vate law alongside the ius publicum dates from this point: in this act of cre-
> ation, the Romans were destined to give birth to something that would long
> outlast the name of the Roman people, and extend itself over a far larger
> space.[52]

This property-owning plebs was however not yet a part of the Roman
state; membership in the state came only with the militarization of the
Roman constitution by Servius.[53] With the integration of the plebs into
the state came full constitutional recognition of private law[54] but also
growing oppression by the patricians, who imposed new *Lasten* (the common German term for feudal burdens) on the plebeians, enriched themselves by harsh debtor-creditor laws, and protected their interest in their
own "patrician courts" (Germans could not fail to be reminded of the
feudal manorial courts, the *Patrimonialgerichte*, of their own time).[55]
Eventually, the ruling classes succeeded in excluding the people entirely
from the land, which inevitably led to the ultimate downfall of the republican constitution[56] (though Rome remained, according to Puchta, fundamentally and irrevocably republican in its institutions[57]). But the struggles of the plebs left their mark on Roman law: private law now existed,
and through the plebeian secessions it was embodied in the twelve tables.

The lesson of Puchta's constitutional history was clear: true private
property was a creation of the peasants, whose primitive legal consciousness remained embodied in Roman law. As we have seen, what was embodied in Roman law had, according to Puchta, become the preserve of

---

[52] Ibid., 150.

[53] Ibid., 152, 157, 161ff.

[54] Especially with the substitution of the Decemvirs for the Pontifices as chief law-finding
body. Ibid., 171.

[55] Ibid., 176. Puchta was, however, careful to insist that there was no direct analogy between the patricians and the nobility of his own time. The institution of slavery, in particular, had prevented Rome from undergoing a development parallel to that of modern Germany. Ibid., 275.

[56] Ibid.

[57] Ibid., 371.

jurists.[58] Any scholarly efforts to elaborate Roman property law to the benefit of the German peasants were accordingly only renderings unto the peasants of a private property order that was their own creation. And, indeed, Puchta did engage in exactly such scholarly efforts, as did all the law professors I have discussed. To explain the nature of scholarly reform as practiced by Puchta, Savigny, and his contemporaries, I must now go more deeply into the doctrines of property law.

REMAKING PROPERTY LAW

Most historians deny that the doctrines of the Romantic Romanist lawyers offered any benefits to Germany's peasants at all. Indeed, the Romanist lawyers have most often been condemned as *bauernfeindlich*, hostile to the peasantry—though, paradoxically, they have been condemned both for destroying and for sponsoring peasant freedom. Both lines of attack are misguided; both miss the strength of romantic Romanist love for the peasantry.

The angriest denouncers of Roman law have always been those who insisted it had enslaved the peasants.[59] But since the late nineteenth century, Roman law has been confronted with an entirely different charge: Savigny and his contemporaries have been declared bauernfeindlich for their undoubted emphasis on freedom of property for peasants as well as for lords. The regime of free property, according to this still common indictment, could only act to the disastrous disadvantage of the peasant. A free market in property would inevitably drive peasants off the land. The Romanist "freeing up" of property was part of a liberal effort with wrenchingly dislocating consequences, an effort to make German society *bürgerlich*—"bourgeois"—the German legal equivalent of "possessive individualist."[60] The only possible result of this legally induced *embourgeoisement* was the proletarianization of the German peasantry.[61]

The charge of embourgeoisement has a sounder basis than the charge of enslavement. It is certainly true that the Romanists did put great emphasis on a "pure" concept of property. Savigny's own definition of prop-

---

[58] See above, pp. 120–24.

[59] See above, p. 155.

[60] See, e.g., Polay, *Ursprung, Entwicklung und Untergang der Pandektistik*, passim; Kawakami, "Die Begründung der 'neuen' gelehrten Rechtswissenschaft durch Savigny." Cf. also W. van Hall, "Savigny als Praktiker: Die Staatsratsgutachten (1817–1842)" (diss., Kiel, 1981), 94ff. This dissertation is summarized in article form under the same title in ZSS (G) 99 (1982): 287–97. Van Hall's assertions that Savigny was a radical advocate of free property are particularly odd in light of the events that van Hall recounts: he describes Savigny arguing for the retention of feudal duties. Cf. the dissertation version of van Hall's work, esp. 100–104.

[61] A charge that goes back to G. F. Knapp, *Die Bauern-Befreiung*.

erty is characteristic of the age: property was "the unlimited and exclusive domination [Herrschaft] of a person over a thing."[62] And his *Recht des Besitzes* certainly was founded, in some sense, on a classical liberal view of the world: he declared in the book that possession was protected by the state as a measure for the protection of the inviolable individual.[63] If Savigny himself believed he was aiding the peasants,[64] that is of course no proof that his program had any beneficial consequences at all.

Nevertheless, there is a fundamental error in the widespread belief that the romantic Romanists were in favor of a kind of ruthlessly free property. In fact, they were not advocates of free property as such at all. Rather, they were advocates of *Roman* property law, with which they hoped to replace the feudal property law that prevailed in the countryside until the late eighteenth century; indeed, their early modern predecessors had, to a lesser extent, also hoped to substitute a Roman-law property regime for a feudal regime that worked against peasant interests. And while Roman property law surely contemplated a freer property regime than did feudal property law, it by no means lacked encumberments on property.[65] Quite the contrary. The main arena of doctrinal struggle among the Romanist lawyers of Savigny's time was the law of property encumberments. Only historiographical neglect of the great legal battles of the romantic era could leave intact the reputation of the Romanists as free property absolutists; only careless neglect of their writings could make them out to have been "bourgeois" enemies of peasant interests. They were not. Their effort to introduce Roman-law rules into the countryside was the soul of their conservative reform movement, of their attempt to use the high cultural legacy to alter Germany.

Two Ways of Conceptualizing Feudalism

To understand that reform movement, it is necessary to understand some technical history of property law—for great social consequences hung in the balance, in Germany as in France,[66] on seemingly minute points of

[62] Savigny, *System des heutigen Römischen Rechts*, 8 vols. (Berlin, 1840–49), 1:367.

[63] E.g., Savigny, *Das Recht des Besitzes*, 7th ed., edited by A. F. Rudorff (Vienna, 1865), 55–56.

[64] Cf. M. A. Bethmann-Hollweg, "Erinnerung an Friedrich Karl von Savigny als Rechtslehrer," *Zeitschrift für Rechtsgeschichte* 6 (1867): 73.

[65] Cf. K. Kroeschell, "Zur Lehre vom 'germanischen Eigentumsbegriff,' " 44: "Der Vorwurf, die romanistische Privatrechtswissenschaft habe in ihrer Realitätsferne die vielen Bindungen namentlich des Grundeigentums übersehen, trifft also daneben." (Citation omitted.)

[66] For developments in French property law, closely akin to (and in part inspired by) German developments, see D. Kelley and B. Smith, "What was Property? Legal Dimensions of the Social Question in France (1789–1848)," in *Proceedings of the American Philosophical Society* 128 (1984): 200–230.

doctrine in the jurisprudential conflicts over Bauernbefreiung. These seemingly minute points concerned the Roman law of prescription and the medieval doctrine of "split property," and their real importance can only be understood against an elaborate background of medieval and early modern history of property law.

It was in his opposition to the doctrine of split property that Savigny seemed most committed to "free" property law. This doctrine was nothing that could be found in classical Roman law. Classical Roman law did not contemplate the typically split ownership characteristic of feudal property, in which both lord and tenant were understood as having ownership rights in the same piece of property. Classical Roman law was marked by the strong insistence that there could be only one owner of real property in law, and that the rights of any others to interfere in his disposition of his property were not themselves rights of ownership but *iura in re aliena*, "rights in something belonging to someone else." The rigor of this classical conceptualization began, however, to falter by late Antiquity;[67] and most medieval European jurists simply abandoned the necessity of single ownership of property. The alternative they most commonly offered was the doctrine of *dominium minus plenum*, "less full property," developed first and foremost by Bartolus in the attempt to give a Roman accounting of European feudal property relations. Bartolus distinguished between *dominium directum*—direct property—and *dominium utile*—equitable property: in German, *Obereigentum*, "over-property," and *Untereigentum*, "under property." The former characterized the property rights, typically, of a feudal lord, the latter those of a peasant.[68] This was the dominant mode of analysis of land ownership in the ius commune of Europe. This Bartolist conception of split property was received with the rest of Italian-Roman law in the German Renaissance, and it continued to be regularly accepted down into the era of the enlightened codes: it was acknowledged as valid by, for example, the *Allgemeines Landrecht* (I, 18, §1) and the Bavarian *Organisches Edikt* of

---

[67] Cf. E. Levy, *West Roman Vulgar Law: The Law of Property* (Philadelphia, 1951).

[68] Cf. Kroeschell, "Zur Lehre vom 'germanischen Eigentumsbegriff,'" 36–37; W. Wiegand, "Zur theoretischen Begründung der Bodenmobilisierung in der Rechtswissenschaft: Der abstrakte Eigentumsbegriff," in Coing and Wilhelm, eds., *Wissenschaft und Kodifikation des Privatrechts im Neunzehnten Jahrhundert*, Studien zur Rechtswissenschaft des neunzehnten Jahrhunderts, 6 vols. (Frankfurt a.M., 1974ff.), 3:119ff.; J. W. Hedemann, *Die Fortschritte des Zivilrechts im Neunzehnten Jahrhundert*, vol. 2, pt. 1, *Das Materielle Bodenrecht* (Berlin, 1930), 3ff. Also of interest is D. Willoweit, "Dominium und Proprietas: Zur Entwicklung des Eigentumsbegriffs in der mittelalterlichen und neuzeitlichen Rechtswissenschaft," *Historisches Jahrbuch* 94 (1974): 132–56. For the medieval background, see generally the discussion of P. Grossi, *Le Situazioni Reali nell'Esperienza Giuridica Medievale* (Padua, 1968), 144–208. Accursius, it should be noted, anticipated Bartolus in making this distinction.

1808; indeed, dual ownership was so generally accepted in Germany that even the *Badisches Landrecht* of 1809, otherwise modeled on the French *Code Civil*, included provisions for the treatment of Obereigentum and Untereigentum.[69]

Nevertheless, Obereigentum and Untereigentum were wholly feudal, purely Bartolist artefacts. Only ignorance or doctrinal perversity could make them Roman, and they were energetically attacked from the Renaissance on—by representatives of French legal humanism including Cujas and Doneau[70] and in Germany, by a number of opponents through the eighteenth century.[71] By the time of Savigny, learned lawyers (among them Savigny himself) had uniformly abandoned the doctrine of split property in favor of exclusive ownership. It is undoubtedly the case that to the extent that learned lawyers of the early modern period and the early nineteenth century were concerned to put an end to the doctrine of split property, it is entirely accurate to describe them as advocates of unfettered "free" property.[72]

But learned lawyers (again among them Savigny himself) were concerned with a great many doctrines, developed since the eleventh century, other than the doctrine of split property. From the late Middle Ages on, learned lawyers developed, alongside the doctrine of split property, a wide range of methods for analyzing the feudal world, methods that did not by any means presuppose "free" unencumbered property. In particular, they developed way of analyzing the various services and payments that members of a feudal society owed others. It was, of course, characteristic of the feudal order that most members of society were obliged to perform specified regular services for, or make specified regular payments to, other members of society, in return for the right to hold certain pieces of land. It was very difficult to analyze such a society in Roman-law terms. The Roman world was, to be sure, a world of status like the feudal world; and most Roman individuals were in some measure subject to the authority of others. Nevertheless, classical Roman law did not contemplate anything like the feudal world of regular, specified, quasi-ritual services as the basis of land tenure. The conceptual difficulties this world

[69] Wiegand, "Zur theoretischen Begründung," 133–34. The doctrine underwent, however, one crucial modification in the course of its development in Germany: where Bartolus had viewed the lord as the principle owner and the peasant as the subsidiary owner, Germans of the eighteenth century attempted to give some measure of ownership to the peasant. (Kroeschell, "Zur Lehre des 'Germanischen Eigentumsbegriffs,' " 37–38.)

[70] Wiegand, "Zur theoretischen Begründung," 126.

[71] Ibid., 131.

[72] Room for disagreement would remain. For differing views on the significance of the abolition of split property for the intepretation of the Historical School, see H. Wagner, *Das geteilte Eigentum im Naturrecht und Postivismus* (Breslau, 1938), 54–70; B. Buss, "Die historische Schule und die Beseitigung des geteilten Eigentums in Deutschland" (diss., Munich, 1966).

presented were, moreover, exacerbated by the fact that Canon law frowned on the payment of regular land rents, which were viewed as disguised interest payments.[73] To the extent that learned Christian lawyers wished to analyze feudal obligations that took the form of regular rents or in-kind payments by the holder of infeudated land, they could find it quite vexatious to distinguish perfectly licit feudalism from illicit money-lending.[74] From the late Middle Ages onward, learned lawyers who were determined to avoid running afoul of the Canon law of usury were obliged to exercise great ingenuity in devising analyses of the feudal order of regular obligations tied to landholding. It is within this tradition of the analysis of feudal obligations, rather than within the history of the rejection of the doctrine of split property, that Savigny developed his characteristic property-law doctrine.

He developed that doctrine within a distinctively German tradition of the analysis of feudal obligations.[75] According to the characteristic German conception, which embodied a vision of the feudal world very different from the vision underlying the doctrine of split property, the feudal rights of the lord were to be viewed as servitudes—legal interests attached to the land that the tenant tilled. The basic meaning of *servitus* in Roman

[73] For the use of a "census" as a money-lending device, see J. T. Noonan, *The Scholastic Analysis of Usury* (Cambridge, Mass., 1957), 154ff.

[74] It is for this reason that the bulk of the early learned treatments of feudal obligations appear in treatises on usury. See, e.g., DuMoulin, *De usuris* (1547); H. Leotardus, *Liber Singularis de Usuris* (Venice, 1761), 193–94.

[75] Indeed, what is perhaps most interesting about the German approach to the problem is that the Germans did *not* conceptualize feudal obligations as the French did. The French, led in this as in other matters by DuMoulin, conceptualized the feudal world as a world of mortgages. The holder of infeudated land was a mortgagor: he had pledged his land as a guarantee that he would perform the obligations he owed his lord and mortgagee. See L. Duncker, *Die Lehre von den Reallasten* (Marburg, 1837), 5ff.; F. Friedlieb, *Die Rechtstheorie der Reallasten* (Jena, 1860), 120ff.; O. Gierke, *Deutsches Privatrecht*, 3 vols. Systematisches Handbuch der deutschen Rechtswissenschaft, Abteilung 2, Teil 3 (Leipzig, 1905), 2:704–5. For the rise of the mortgage analogy in the late Middle Ages and its culmination in the theory of DuMoulin, see B. Schnapper, "Les rentes chez les théologiens et les canonistes du XIIIᵉ au XVIᵉ siècle," in *Études d'histoire du droit canonique dédiées à Gabriel Le Bras*, 2 vols. (Paris, 1965), 2:988ff, and the literature cited there. See also J.-L. Thireau, *Charles Du Moulin*, 384ff. The mortgage theory attracted some limited support in sixteenth- and seventeenth-century Germany, see Friedlieb, *Reallasten*, 121ff.; P. C. Klemm, *Eigentum und Eigentumsbeschränkungen in der Doktrin des usus modernus pandectarum*, Basler Studien zur Rechtswissenschaft, Reihe A: Privatrecht, vol. 10 (Basel/Frankfurt a.M., 1984), 139 and n. 131, and had the voice of Unterholzner in the early nineteenth century. See Duncker, *Reallasten*, 8; Friedlieb, *Reallasten*, 123. Yet for the most part Germans rejected the mortgage theory—oddly enough, as the mortgage theory would have been well suited to the German agrarian order of the early nineteenth century. Reform efforts of the early nineteenth century did, after all, leave peasants by and large the mortgagors of their land. See Buchholz, *Abstraktionsprinzip und Immobiliarrecht*; idem, "Quellen des Immobiliarrechts." Yet here, as so often in legal history, legal theory and economic reality remained disjoint.

law is "right of way" or "easement," a legally recognized entitlement to use someone else's property in a strictly limited manner. Thus, a Roman urban property owner might have the right to prevent his neighbor from building so high as to block off his light. These *servitutes* of Roman law were very few and very limited. In particular, no classical servitude could ever have conferred upon its holder the right to claim services. Servitudes, in the classical law, were conceived as rights to the limited use or control of another's property; they were not rights to demand that another do anything—as the postclassical maxim put it, "servitus in faciendo consistere nequit," "a servitude cannot consist in a performance."[76]

Nevertheless, learned lawyers of the early modern period used the Roman concept of servitus to analyze the world of feudal obligations. No less an authority than the Holy Rota, the great Papal court, for example, declared in 1606 that burdening a piece of land with a regular rent was more or less like burdening it with a servitude.[77] Servitude analysis made headway in the German world of the the sixteenth[78] and seventeenth centuries,[79] and by the early eighteenth century it had captured the German mind.[80] By the end of the century servitude analysis had been extended beyond regular rents to cover all feudal obligations and had risen to the level of "an undoubted dogma."[81] This dogma was employed to characterize both a tenant's obligations to his lord and those of the lord to his tenant: peasant rights to the use of public and noble lands were sometimes described as "Servituten"; so were the rights of the lord on the land of the peasant, including the rights to demand services and payments. The lord's rights, in this analysis, were "rights of way," "easements" attached to the peasant's property. Conversely, the peasant's rights of pasturage and the collection of necessaries in forests and commons were equally "easements."[82]

---

[76] Cf. F. Schulz, *Classical Roman Law* (Oxford, 1951), 384.

[77] The decision of the Holy Rota is reproduced in L. Cenci, *Tractatus de censibus, totam materiam constituendi, conservandi, & extinguendi annuos census juxta formam, & stylum etiam in Romana curia adhiberi solitum, theoricè, & practicè explicatam continens: Cui accesserunt non modo additiones, & Sacrae Rotae romanae decisiones jam separatim impressae, sed & aliae pleraeque ab ipso authore manuscriptae suis locis repositae sunt; necnon Joannis Baptistae Leonelij, & Ludovici Molinae commentaria ad bullam Pij v. De censibus* (Lyons, 1676), 353, of the separately paged "Decisiones": "quia cum census sint impositi super rebus corporalibus, illisque inhaereant quasi quaedam servitus." Cited and discussed in Leotardus, *De Usuris*, 193.

[78] Puchta, *Cursus der Institutionen*, 315. For the sixteenth-century controversy over this point, see Klemm, *Eigentum und Eigentumsbeschränkungen*, 126.

[79] For the example of Franzke, see Friedlieb, *Reallasten*, 124.

[80] See below, pp. 173–75.

[81] Duncker, *Reallasten*, 20 and generally 17ff.

[82] For helpful descriptions of the analysis of German property concepts in these Roman terms, see Buchholz, *Abstraktionsprinzip und Immobiliarrecht*, 24ff., 105–7; Klemm, *Eigentum und Eigentumsbeschränkungen*, 126–39, 142–48.

This servitude analysis would, under any circumstances, have been potentially quite disruptive of the social certainties of a feudal order. For servitude analysis implied that the tenant was the true "owner" of his land and his lord merely, as it were, an intrusive burdener. But servitude analysis became, in practice, even more disruptive than it otherwise might have been when, in the course of German legal history, it came to be coupled with another, even more potentially disruptive body of doctrine: the Roman law of prescription, a complex corpus of rules on the acquisition and extinction of rights that held within it revolutionary implications for Germany society.

The law of prescription provided an answer to the critical social question that remained once it was determined that feudal obligations were servitudes: how were these servitudes created, and how were they destroyed? Through what procedures could a lord obtain servitudes on his tenants' property that would oblige those tenants to serve him, and through what procedures could his tenants put an end to those obligations? In answer, Romanist lawyers pointed to the law of prescription— *Verjährung*, in German. This was the law of the acquisition or loss of title to a thing through possession over a certain period of time. Under the law of prescription, if I hold a piece of property for a certain period and do so "nec vi, nec clam, nec precario" ("not by force, nor by stealth, nor by permission"), I acquire a right to that property; conversely, if I fail to use my property, I may lose it.[83] The standard period of time required for prescription varied widely in the ius commune. Roman legal texts differed in setting this time period, some of them granting prescriptive rights after a short period of time, "immemorial time," or "a long time." The exact purport of these texts was not clear. But they were generally interpreted as requiring ten, twenty, or thirty-odd years, depending on a variety of circumstances.[84] In addition, Canon law, which developed its own very elaborate law of prescription, specified a forty-year period. This period was used in various contexts by German Roman lawyers of the usus modernus.[85] The exact details of the law of prescription were quite uncertain in the early modern period. Lawyers differed over which prescriptive period should be used in which circumstances, and differed over such issues as whether an individual who claimed prescriptive ownership of a piece of property should be required to believe in good faith that the

[83] The possessory interdicts that protected possession "nec vi nec clam nec precario" dated to an early period in Roman law. For a recent discussion, see B. Frier, *The Rise of the Roman Jurists* (Princeton, N.J., 1985), 53ff.

[84] For the "sächsiche Frist" of thirty-one years, six weeks, and three days, see Buchholz, *Abstraktionsprinzip und Immobiliarrecht*, 25.

[85] For the "longi temporis praecriptio" of ten years "inter praesentes" and twenty years "inter absentes," and the "longissimi temporis praescriptio" of thirty or forty years, see Buchholz, *Abstraktionsprinzip und Immobiliarrecht*, 105–6.

property was his.[86] Indeed, the law of prescription was thoroughly uncertain—and therefore full of opportunity for innovative lawyers.

Once lawyers conceptualized feudal rights and duties as Servituten, the question arose as to whether these Servituten could be gained (or lost) through prescription. On the answer to that question hung the meaning of Roman law for the peasantry. In classical Roman law, the law of prescription would not have applied to feudal rights, for prescription applied only to "corporeal," and not to "incorporeal" interests.[87] Here, however, Canon law had wrought an important change on the ius commune. For complex historical reasons, Canon lawyers had long accepted the idea that possessory interests in incorporeal rights could be acquired through prescription.[88] Under the influence of Canon Law, Roman lawyers had long tentatively suggested the same[89] and would suggest it with increasing frequency as the early modern period wore on.

Yet to subject feudalism to the law of prescription was to do more than engage in an abstract doctrinal exercise. By subjecting the world of feudal obligations, conceived of as a world of servitudes, to the ius commune of prescription, lawyers were entering a realm of profound legal indeterminacy. The exact parameters of the law of prescription were wholly undefined; no lawyer could know what the ultimate effect the great reconceptualization would have. The stage was thus set for grand legal battles over prescriptive rights to feudal services, battles that reached their peak intensity only in the time of Savigny.

Doctrinal Battles

Skirmishes over feudalism and the Roman law of prescription were already being fought in the late sixteenth and early seventeenth centuries. Early attempts to invoke the Roman law of prescription on behalf of the peasants were, to be sure, comparatively unambitious and ultimately unsuccessful. In Brandenburg, Romanist lawyers who were *bauernfreundlich*, i.e., "friendly to the peasants," resorted to the law of prescription in an effort to guarantee peasants the right to make cash payments in lieu of feudal services. Presumably the inflation of the sixteenth century had diminished the value of payments the lords had previously accepted. The lords accordingly attempted to reassert their right to demand services rather than cash. The Brandenburg lawyers argued that the peasants had

---

[86] For a survey of views on the questions of *bona fides* and *titulus*, with due attention to legal practice, see, e.g., C. Matthiae, *Controversen-Lexikon des römischen Rechts*, 3 vols. (Leipzig, 1856), vol. 1, pt. 2, 319ff.

[87] For this problem, which involved a wide variety of aspects of property law in early modern law, see Klemm, *Eigentum und Eigentumsbeschränkungen*, 54–56.

[88] Wolter, *Ius Canonicum in Iure Civili*, 12.

[89] Savigny, *Recht des Besitzes*, 504–6; Wolter, *Ius Canonicum in Iure Civili*, 184ff.

acquired a prescriptive right to commutation of their services. This Roman-law argument received some sanction from the Brandenburg *Kammergericht*[90]—as elsewhere the institutional representative of the ius commune. But the nobility protested violently against the ius commune innovation, and no degree of support for a Roman-Canon law of prescription among the jurists could prevent passage of legislation confirming noble customary rights to demand performance of actual services.[91] After 1648 pressure from the nobility in Brandenburg succeeded in forcing a reenserfment of the peasantry that put an end to innovative Romanizing.[92] Brandenburg was not alone in curbing efforts to use the ius commune to benefit the peasantry: by the early eighteenth century, similar moves to restrict the use of the law of prescription on behalf of peasants were underway in other states. In Braunschweig, for example, legislation was enacted in 1709 to prevent peasants from claiming a prescriptive right to deviate from the traditional form of their secular tithes.[93] By the eighteenth century the principle was well established that legislation by the diet of a given German state destroyed the legal effect of any attempts to evade feudal duties through the law of prescription.[94]

Yet despite these legislative efforts, doctrinal innovation continued in the early eighteenth-century era of the usus modernus, even though it brought with it dissension and litigation. Samuel Stryk, for example, acknowledged that there was an unequaled controversy in the courts over the law of servitudes.[95] Nevertheless, he gave his sanction to servitude analysis.[96] So did other leading figures, among them Boehmer,[97] Leyser,[98]

[90] F. Grossmann, *Über die gutsherrlich-bäuerlichen Rechtsverhältnisse in der Mark Brandenburg vom 16. bis 18. Jahrhundert*, Staats- und socialwissenschaftliche Forschungen, vol. 9, Heft 4 (Leipzig, 1890), 20. Cf. also ibid., 26–27, 43, 48, 82, for the *bauernfreundlich* character of Roman law in Brandenburg.

[91] Ibid., 38, 40. For another example of an early Brandenburg polemic against the use of prescription to favor the peasantry, cf. L. Distelmeier, *Statuta und Gewohnheiten der Chur und Marcke Brandenburg* (Jena, 1607), 470–71.

[92] Grossmann, *Über die gutsherrlich-bäuerlichen Rechtsverhältnisse*, 60.

[93] *Chur-Braunschweigische Zehendordnung von 1709*, §25, in *Chur-Braunschweigische Landesordnungen* Cap. IV. , 1105, 1006. Cited in D. G. Struben, "Bedenken CXXXV, 'Ob die Praescriptio immemorialis durch ein Gestz interrumpiret wird?' " in *Rechtliche Bedenken*, 1:319. Cf. below, n. 106.

[94] See the citations in ibid.

[95] Stryk, *Usus Modernus*, Liber VIII, Titulus I, § 1: "Si ulla in foro frequens controversia est, certe de servitutibus est, quae inter vicinos in civitate, et confines in agris toto die nascitur."

[96] For Stryk's acceptance of servitude analysis, see generally ibid., §§ 3ff., and Friedlieb, *Reallasten*, 125.

[97] Boehmer, *Ius ecclesiasticum Protestantium, usum modernum iuris canonici iuxta seriem decretalium ostendens et ipsis rerum argumentis illustrans adiecto triplice indice. 5 vols. in 4* (Halle, 1730–36), 5:384 (Title 19, "De Usuris," §61): "Praesupponi autem ante omnia debet, *censum realem esse instar servitutis praedialis*."

[98] Leyser, *Meditationes*, 2:455 (Spec. 109, no. VI).

Heineccius,[99] and two influential dissertation-writers of 1710.[100] The first
half of the eighteenth century—as natural law thought was spreading, but
before the rise of the enlightened codes—was thus marked by efforts in
the community of learned lawyers to rethink the German world.

Indeed, as servitude analysis established itself over the course of the
eighteenth century, the feudal world began to suffer a conceptual transformation. Lawyers began to think of feudal obligations as arising wholly
from property relations rather than from personal status. According to
the new thinking (already widespread in seventeen-century France), feudal rights and duties ceased to be personal and became attached to
land.[101] Where, earlier on, clergymen or noblemen had enjoyed their feudal freedoms because of their personal status, these freedoms now began
to apply to the land they occupied, so that the land could be sold to a
member of a different feudal status without thereby becoming less valuable. This transformation from "personal freedom" to "real freedom"—
from *Personalfreiheit* to *Realfreiheit*, as it was called—picked up momentum from the early eighteenth century on, and it made the application of
the law of prescription to feudal rights much easier and more doctrinally
logical. Once again, we can look to Möser for a lively account of the
changes of the age. Möser described how profoundly the shift in the legal
conceptualization of freedom could alter the lot of the peasant who came
into possession of formerly free land. He described an early eighteenth-
century deed:

> This 1709 document formally declares that a peasant who came into posses-
> sion of a noble property became as free as a nobleman in respect of hunting
> rights, of subjection to patrimonial courts, and of all the other freedoms at-
> taching to the property; nowadays we have become so accustomed to this
> concept that we are surprised that any such document was needed in this
> case, and that the concept was not taken for granted.[102]

Möser then elaborated on the extent of peasant Realfreiheit as it had established itself in his time.[103] A profound change had taken place. Freedom had formerly been an attribute of unchanging status. Now it was

[99] See, e.g., Friedlieb, *Reallasten*, 125.

[100] Duncker, *Reallasten*, 12–13.

[101] For the shift in Germany, see Wittich, *Grundherrschaft*, 4–5. For the shift in the seventeenth century in south, west, and central Germany, see Klemm, *Eigentum und Eigentumsbeschränkungen*, 131.

[102] Möser, "Von der Real- und Personalfreiheit," in *Patriotische Phantasien*, in *Werke*,
vol. 5, pt. 2, 176–77.

[103] Ibid., 177. On this page Möser also charged *Rechtsgelehrten* with being opposed to
peasant freedom and attempting to maintain status-based feudalism. All scholars, especially
in the early eighteenth century, were not "bauernfreundlich." Nevertheless the "bauernfreundlich" Roman law of the late eighteenth century did have its beginnings in this period.

subject to the rules of property law and could be acquired by prescription. As Möser described matters, the vanishing of the old world opened a whole new realm for prescription law. In the old order, he stated, "if one knows a man's status, one knows whether he is free; and where the former is lost sight of, the latter cannot exist through prescription."[104] "Service," he said, "argues against prescription"[105]—that is to say, the feudal order of subordination and the ius commune of prescription could not be reconciled: as the feudal order disappeared, Roman law acquired a new importance.

This new importance brought with it a social problem potentially far more explosive than any prescriptive guarantee of the commutation of feudal services. In theory prescription law was not only acquisitive but also extinctive—i.e., feudal rights could in theory be lost as well as gained through application of the law of prescription. Indeed, if Roman prescription law were applied in all earnest, lords could lose their rights simply by failing to demand them, perhaps by failing to demand them for as short a period as ten years. In the late seventeenth and early eighteenth centuries, lawyers were wholly uncertain whether such extinguishing prescription were possible,[106] whether in part or in whole. A tradition reaching back to the glossators held that lords could lose only a given year's services through prescription; the ongoing obligation itself could not be lost.[107] But some eighteenth-century lawyers were willing to contemplate the more radical possibility that prescription might destroy obligations for good.[108] By midcentury, learned lawyers were searching for some way, as Möser wrote, to reconcile service and prescription. In particular, the influential Friedrich Esaias Pufendorf, the grandnephew of the great legal theorist Samuel and himself a major figure in jurisprudence, attempted in his often-cited *Observationes Juris Universi* (1744ff.) to fix a compromise position on the Roman law of prescription. Pufendorf, who endeared himself to generations of constitutionalists by his forthright defense of the independence of the Hannoverian High Court in Celle, where he was chief justice (when asked by King George II, "Why do I always

---

[104] Ibid., 179.

[105] Ibid., 180.

[106] Cf. W. A. Schoepff, ed., *Selectae Decisiones et Resolutiones Tubingenses, ex Jure Publico, Feudali, Canonico, Criminali, Civili & Statutario, Nomine Inclutae Facultatis Juridicae Conscriptae*, 2 pts. (Tübingen, 1726–30), 2:13, describing the common wisdom that "die Zehenden-Freyheit unter diejenige Sachen gerechnet wird, welche gar nicht verjährt werden können." There were, however, differences of opinion, some of which are canvassed in this decision.

[107] See Duncker, *Reallasten*, 152–53. Cf. Klemm, *Eigentum und Eigentumsbeschränkungen*, 136, on Lauterbach's willingness to allow only Verjährung of a given year's obligation, not of the whole obligation.

[108] See the discussion of Leyser in Duncker, *Reallasten*, 152.

lose in your court?" Pufendorf is said to have replied, "Because Your Majesty is always wrong"), addressed, in 1756, the revolutionary possibility of extinctive prescription. He attempted a kind of doctrinal compromise. Feudal rights could be lost, he said—but not through the neglect of the lord, only through a direct act of refusal by the peasant, fully understood as such.[109] If a lord merely neglected to demand services, his right to the services was *not* thereby extinguished; nevertheless, a peasant could become free through prescription. If a peasant steadfastly refused to perform a service for ten years in the presence of his lord, or for twenty in his lord's absence,[110] and the lord acquiesced, the peasant would be free. Pufendorf acknowledged that this was a doctrinal novelty: "I am aware," he wrote, "that I depart from the universal view of scholars."[111] Nevertheless, he held to his argument.[112] Pufendorf's compromise was influential. By 1765 the High Court in neighboring Hesse was citing Pufendorf repeatedly as it addressed extinguishing prescription. Feudal rights could be extinguished—but only if the peasants somehow actively did not perform the service. A lord who merely neglected to demand a

---

[109] Pufendorf, "Observatio CLXXXVIII, 'Quemadmodum servitutes praediorum & cetera jura non utendo amittantur,' " in *Observationes Iuris Universi* (Hannover, 1744ff.), 3: esp. 508–9.

[110] This distinction between prescription of ten years "inter praesentes" and twenty years "inter absentes" was common to all usus modernus theorizing. See Buchholz, *Abstraktionsprinzip und Immobiliarrecht*, 105–6.

[111] Ibid., 509: "Sentio a recepta omnium Doctorum sententia me recedere."

[112] A concise account of Pufendorf's theory can be found in an unpublished 1772 document, now posthumously published as *Friedrich Esaias Pufendorfs Entwurf eines hannoverschen Landrechts (vom Jahre 1772)*, edited by W. Ebel, Quellen und Darstellungen zur Geschichte Niedersachsens, vol. 78 (Hildesheim, 1970), 89–90:

> Wir haben vernehmen müssen, daß aus den neueren Kaiserlichen Rechten darunter Zweifel obwalte, ob auch die Dienstbarkeit der Land-Güter durch einen bloßen Nicht-Gebrauch von zehen Jahren verloren gehe, wenn schon deren Gebrauch nicht verwehret, noch an Seiten des dienstbaren Guts die Freyheit verjähret worden. Wir nehmen aber zumal nach der Verfassung unsrer deutschen Länder die Meinung an, welche auch dem natürlichen Recht am gemäßesten zu seyn scheinet, und selbst bey städtischen Gütern von aller Zeit her in den Rechten gegolten hat, daß durch den bloßen Nicht-Gebrauch die Dienstbarkeiten auch der Land-Güter nicht verloren gehen, wenn nicht deren Ausübung verwehret worden, und darauf die den Rechten bestimmte zehen oder zwanzigjährige Zeit verflossen, mithin dadurch oder sonst das dienstbare Gut die Freyheit verjähret hat.
>
> Die Verjährung der Freyheit als eines Rechts bedarf zwar keines besonderen Grundes zu ihrem Anfange, es muß gleichwohl der Besitzer des deinstbaren Guts von Anfang nicht anders geglaubet haben, als daß er befuget sey, den Gebrauch der Dienstbarkeit zu verwehren, oder sonst einer Freyheit sich anzumaßen.

Here again I pass over the complications attendant upon the different periods and types of Verjährung. For followers of Pufendorf in his doctrine of *usucapio libertatis*, see Matthiae, *Controversen-Lexikon*, vol. 1, pt. 2, 328–29.

service could not lose it, since prescription had to be positive, and not negative.[113] This sounds like a legal technicality, and of course it was. Like other will-based legal doctrines, the Pufendorfian compromise could no doubt lead to well-nigh metaphysical disputes in actual litigation: What constituted "active intentional nonperformance" of a feudal duty? But no doubt the doctrine's tendency to resolve itself into such unanswerables formed part of its attraction. Pufendorf's theory allowed the Hessian court to introduce the Roman law of prescription while attempting to evade its most revolutionary implications. The Hessian court was typical of the time. Later lawyers would not be so hesitant to threaten lords with loss of services through prescription. But in 1765 this revolutionary moment in the history of German law was yet to come.

The revolutionary shift came in earnest with the great imperial revival of the late 1780s. By this decade, many peasants west of the Elbe had been freed, in a fashion—some by private act of a lord, some by statute. These peasants were granted legal ownership of their own bodies. This did not, however, make them in the fullest sense free, since extensive duties of personal semifeudal service were still attached to the land they tilled. A second reform measure had, however, also gone into effect: many of the peasants' obligations had been put in writing[114]—as, for example, by a Prussian ordinance of 1784, which required the issuance of "urbaria," documents detailing the mutual obligations of peasants and lords.[115]

These changes were, in a sense, only formal: the peasants remained obligated to perform most services, or, as the case might be in their region, to pay a cash rent in lieu of those services. Yet the fact that their duties had been formalized opened up vast new possibilities for the peasants to contest their circumstances in court. Enough litigation over peas-

[113] "Servitutes iuris germanici, et quae iis aequiparantur singularia iura, per solum non usum amitti non possunt, sed requiritur simul ex altera parte libertatis usucapio," in B. W. Pfeiffer, ed., *Neue Sammlung Bemerkenswerther Entscheidungen des Oberappellationsgerichts zu Cassel* (Hannover, 1819ff.) (originally decided March 27, 1765), 3: esp. 34 (citing Pufendorf, T. I, obs. 151, §22): "da man unmöglich etwas verlieren kann, so lange man dasselbe in Besitz behält, nothwendig erst dieser Besitz durch eine gegentheilige Handlung gestört werden muß, ehe man sagen kann, daß es durch Nichtgebrauch verloren sey, welche gegentheileige Handlung, wenn eine zehnjährige Acquiescenz dazu kommt, die usucapionem libertatis für den Gegentheil ausmacht."

[114] The crucial importance of the introduction of these written records into the countryside at the end of the eighteenth century is a concern of Buchholz, *Abstraktionsprinzip und Immobiliarrecht*, 9 and passim. See also J. W. Hedemann, *Die Fortschritte des Zivilrechts*, vol. 2, pt. 1, 1ff. Buchholz sees the origin of the practice of recordation in the spread of urban practices into the countryside.

[115] The Prussian record of compliance with the requirement of "urbaria" was, however, poor. See Brunschwig, *Enlightenment and Romanticism in Prussia*, 58. The Prussian Allgemeines Landrecht of 1794 incorporated most of these recent reforms at II, 7, §§ 136ff. For contemporary Hannoverian reform agitation, see Oberschelp, *Niedersachsen*, 1:123f.

ant obligations reached the courts to create a sense of crisis. Typical fears were expressed in a violent pamphlet war over agrarian reform in Saxony after 1793[116]—a fight over public opinion which brought K. S. Zachariä, among others, to prominence.[117] The tension and disruptive force of the reform movement were incalculably deepened by the French Revolution, which after 1792 began to encroach directly onto German soil. As Bauernbefreiung proceeded, a whole new and intensely important field of law opened up to the professors of Roman law: property relations, once governed by customary law, were suddenly plunged into highly uncertain litigation. A flood of Roman-law writings followed.

Thus, a revolution in property law began as the new order of written obligations attached to land and not to persons established itself. This revolution was linked with the great revival of the Holy Roman Imperial ancient constitution in the 1790s: the reinvigoration of the Reichskammergericht[118] brought with it a new activism on behalf of the peasants. As Häberlin described it, the old court of the ius commune began to favor the peasants in "revolutionary trials" that constituted "the best praise" for the "teutsche Constitution," the German constitution. Writing in 1796, Häberlin saw the new imperial justice as Germany's legal revolution without political revolution:

> Findings of the supreme imperial courts, such as are communicated here, contain the best praise for the German Constitution. They deserve to be all the more generally known, so that all may see that the peasant in Germany can, the Lord be praised, obtain justice when he is in the right, not only against his lord, but also against his prince, when the latter is his landlord. . . . It is true that many people are not at all well disposed toward these *revolutionary trials* [emphasis in original], as they call them, through which beloved custom (which, however, has no force of law if it does not correspond to reason) is called into question. But let us give thanks to God that we Germans can still lead such revolutionary trials. . . . As long as we can do so, we are safe from the *French* [emphasis in original] kind of revolutionary trial.[119]

[116] See Gross, *Die Bürgerliche Agrarreform in Sachsen*, 63, 72, and the literature cited there.

[117] Zachariä's role is described by W. Behrendts, *Reformbestrebungen in Kursachsen im Zeitalter der französischen Revolution*, Leipziger Historische Abhandlungen, Heft 38 (Leipzig, 1914), 76ff.

[118] See above, pp. 78–79.

[119] Häberlin, ed., "Teutsche Reichsjustiz," in *Staats-Archiv* 1, no. 1 (1796): 83–84n. Häberlin's list of "revolutionary trials" in this section includes trials from 1787 to 1794. Ibid., 83–90. On the new activity of the court in this period, see also F. Hertz, "Die Rechtsprechung der höchsten Reichsgerichte im römisch-deutschen Reich und ihre politische Bedeutung," in *Mitteilungen des Instituts für Österreichische Geschichtsforschung* 69 (1961): 331–58.

This attempt to create not rule of law, but revolution by law, was accompanied by a radicalization of the doctrines of prescription. As E. F. Klein described the situation in Prussia, lawyers had ceased to stop short of the argument that feudal obligations could become unenforceable if a lord failed to demand them. The result was chaos. The new learned law had destroyed the old paternal sense of community among lords and peasants through the pernicious introduction of the *ius commune* of prescription. Learned lawyers had introduced themselves into the countryside in the hope of aiding the "oppressed country-dweller." But they had succeeded only in worsening life for all:

> The more lords and subjects became involved in legal wrangles, the more the idea of a paternal relationship between master and subject was lost.
>
> It did not help matters when legal scholars either applied Roman doctrine to the peasants, or else established legal presuppositions that worked to the benefit of the landlords. Quite the contrary, it was this that ruined everything. The landlords themselves began to view as legal obligations services that they had previously demanded only as praiseworthy dutifulness, and the peasants, who had previously taken into consideration only their lord's needs and their own, began to feel the evil effects of the doctrine of prescription, and preferred to refuse all service, however willingly they would previously have performed it, rather than running the danger of burdening themselves with new legal obligations. The natural consequence was that the landlords, who had also made themselves familiar with the theory of prescription, ceased to deal with their subjects mildly and indulgently, so that this mildness and indulgence should not be held to create a binding duty.[120]

As the passage shows, the new learned law could cut two ways. On the one hand, peasants who performed services could, in the new legal order, discover that those services had become legally binding duties—once the period of prescription had run, and if the lord had not forced or tricked

---

[120] E. F. Klein, "Uber die gesetzliche und richterliche Begünstigung des Bauernstandes," in idem, ed., *Annalen der Gesetzgebung und Rechtsgelehrsamkeit in den Preussischen Staaten [Kleins Annalen]* 24 (1806): 170–71. *National Union Catalog* lists a separate printing of this essay that I have not seen. Klein opposed the reforms of learned law, but not as a reactionary. His article was intended to demonstrate that only wholesale abolition of serfdom would help the peasants in the end. See ibid., 173. As this quote suggests, the promulgation of the *Allgemeines Landrecht* did not spare Prussia any of the common German difficulties over the new law of prescription. Cf. below, footnote, for the work of Prussian lawyers attempting to develop a Prussian law of prescription in the feudal context. On Klein's political beliefs, see G. Birtsch, "Freiheit und Eigentum: Zur Erörterung von Verfassungsfragen in der deutschen Publizistik im Zeichen der Französischen Revolution," in R. Vierhaus, ed., *Eigentum und Verfassung: Zur Eigentumsdiskussion im ausgehenden achtzehnten Jahrhundert*, Veröffentlichungen des Max-Planck-Instituts fur Geschichte, 37 (Göttingen, 1972), 179–92.

the peasant into performing the service, nor requested the service (i.e., as long as the service was performed "nec vi, nec clam, nec precario"). But the lord too could lose out; if he failed to demand the service, or if he asked for it rather than ordering it, he could find that the feudal obligations he expected to enjoy were not enforceable in court. This change boded havoc—but it also seemed to hold the promise of reform. For if Romanist lawyers could manage the application of learned law correctly, they could greatly ease the burdens of the peasants without revolutionary change. And, indeed, as the 1790s progressed, there was a great flowering of Roman-law theorizing, as property law became the realm in which romanticism could go into action.

Advocates of the new property law took two different tacks. First, they discarded the old Bartolist analysis of split property, the distinction between dominium utile and dominium directum. Second, they embarked upon a far-reaching extension of the law of prescription.

As the large-scale reform of agrarian law picked up momentum in the 1790s, the Bartolist analysis of feudal property as split vanished. The abandonment of split property was in some measure the work of the Enlightenment. Natural-right theory introduced a widespread emphasis on absolute property rights: both the French Code Rurale of 1791 and the Geschäftsinstruktion of Freiherr vom Stein in 1808 made declarations directed against feudal dual ownership about the sanctity of property.[121] But within legal practice, it was the versatile and brilliant Thibaut who successfully banished "split property." In 1801 Thibaut published the essay most important for the romanization of agrarian reform. "Über dominium directum und utile," his scholarly demonstration that split property had no place in classical Roman law, was the critical link between the "pure" Romanism of the coming generation of Savigny on the one hand, and the great reform movement on the other.[122]

As Thibaut's view became the dominant one during the first half of the nineteenth century,[123] the rejection of split property created a sink of legal

[121] Hedemann, Fortschritte des Zivilrechts, 1:11–12.

[122] For the importance of this essay in the rise of "pure" Roman law, see Stintzing-Landsberg, Geschichte, vol. 3, pt. 2, 84; Wiegand, "Zur theoretischen Begründung." As H. Wagner puts it, with the abolition of "split" property, "[d]ie Historische Rechtsschule . . . übernahm insoweit die Rolle der französischen Revolution." H. Wagner, Die Politische Pandektistik (Berlin, 1985), 155.

[123] Wiegand, "Zur theoretischen Begründung"; Kroeschell, "Zur Lehre vom 'germanischen Eigentumsbegriff,'" 48ff. For Savigny's reliance on Thibaut on this point, see Brutti, "Proprietà nella sistema di Savigny," 82. Kroeschell demonstrates that the Germanists espoused as "pure" a concept of property as the Romanists at first. The development of a "German" conception of property followed the development of the rift between Germanists and Romanists, beginning in the decisive year of 1828 with W.E.A. Albrecht's Die

confusion. Over the tense decade of the 1790s, fights over the feudal tradition began to resolve themselves into fights over the conceptual changes in property law, over what amounted to a shift from the conception of noble property as dominium directum with established rights and prerogatives to a conception of noble property as servitudes subject to the rules of prescription.[124] The great uncertainty and the seeming promise of the new property law called forth innumerable Romanist treatises in the 1790s. *Besitz, Servitut, Verjährung*—possession, servitude, prescription—were the great topics of the day. In these three terms lay the basic shape of agrarian litigation after the midcentury reforms. If peasant or lord claimed an unwritten property right, courts asked for the proof or disproof of Verjährung. Through Verjährung a Servitut could be gained through several decades of undisturbed possession (Besitz) "nec vi, nec clam, nec precario"; or lost through nonuse. Thus the midcentury reforms, by removing agrarian relations from the realm of customary law, had forced the creation of whole new legal doctrine on the nature of Besitz and Verjährung.

Besitz und Verjährung was, indeed, the title of an 1802 book by Thibaut.[125] Nor was Thibaut the only Roman-law scholar to turn his energies on these topics. From forgotten authors like C. H. Gros, who published a purist account of the pre-Justinianian law of Verjährung in 1795,[126] through barely remembered leaders of jurisprudence like B. W. Pfeiffer[127] or the influential C. F. Glück,[128] and on to include famous names of German law, Savigny[129] and the Kantian K. S. Zach-

Gewere als Grundlage des älteren deutschen Sachenrechts. Ibid. See also Wagner, *Geteiltes Eigentum*, 71.

[124] Thus some were at pains to minimize the significance of the shift: in Saxony, one noble pamphleteer, recognizing that change was underway, declared simply that the change changed nothing: he conceded that only nobility who held their land by *dominium directum* had a right to tax-free status as a matter of ancient feudal contract; however, he added, other nobility had their tax-free status through "Herkommen, Verjährung." ([F. L. Wurmb], *Das Grabmal des Leonidas* [n.p., 1798], 119–20). This attempt to deny that the new property order meant real reform aroused "particularly vehement" objections from an anonymous opponent. Behrendts, *Reformbestrebungen in Kursachsen*, 84.

[125] Thibaut, *Über Besitz und Verjährung* (Jena, 1802).

[126] C. H. Gros, *Geschichte der Verjährung nach römischem Rechte* (Göttingen, 1795).

[127] Pfeiffer, "Über den wesentlichen Unterschied der adquisitiven und extinctiven Verjährung," in *Vermischte Aufsätze über Gegenstände des deutschen und des römischen Rechts* (Marburg, 1803) 272–341. On Pfeiffer's activities in the agrarian reform movement, see Hattenhauer, "Burchard Wilhelm Pfeiffer und die Bauernbefreiung in Kurhessen," and below, p. 185.

[128] See Glück, *Ausführliche Erlauterungen der Pandekten*, 8:105–55, 367–80; 10:264–68.

[129] Savigny's famous first work was, of course, his *Recht des Besitzes*, first published in 1803. Citations are to the 7th ed. edited by A. F. Rudorff (Vienna, 1865). For the prominence of prescription and Verjährung in Savigny's Marburg *Methodenlehre* of 1802, see

ariä[130] among them, Besitz and Verjährung were the stuff of numerous new careers in Roman law beginning in the 1790s.[131]

Thibaut, in his brief 1802 handbook, took a bold approach to the use of the Roman law of prescription. He denied outright that feudal rights could be *acquired* through the law of prescription—but insisted that the same feudal rights, through the same law of prescription, could be *lost*. It was, he conceded, very controversial whether Roman rules on acquisitive prescription applied to "German legal institutions unknown to the Romans, for example corvée or banns."[132] Most legal scholars believed that the Roman law of prescription could be extended to German feudal institutions.[133] But Thibaut denied it: acquisitive prescription applied only to specific rights familiar to the Romans.[134] Extinguishing prescription was, however, a different matter: "Thus all rights whose acquisition is not sanctioned by the letter of the law cannot be acquired according to the [common-law] principles of acquisitive prescription, under which they cannot be subsumed. However, these rights can be subsumed under the principles of extinguishing prescription."[135] Thibaut then went on to discuss the extinction of feudal rights in some detail, noting that the prescriptive period for extinction was uncertain.[136] There were limits to what extinguishing prescription could achieve. Standing by the traditions of medieval analysis, Thibaut wrote that lords who neglected to collect certain kinds of dues lost only the right to those payments they had failed to collect, and not the right to future dues;[137] he was unwilling to push the

---

Cappellini, *Systema Iuris*, 1:620–22, 626. Other major jurists who published on these topics during the period include E. C. Westphal, *System des Römischen Rechts über die Arten der Sachen, Besitz, Eigentum und Verjährung* (Leipzig, 1788), and K.F.W. von Spangenberg, *Versuch einer systematischen Darstellung der Lehre vom Besitz* (Leipzig, 1794). For further bibliography, see the references in Savigny, *Recht des Besitzes*, and in *Lehre von der Verjährung durch forgesetzten Besitz* of Savigny's follower K.A.D. Unterholzner (Breslau, 1815). For the relationship between Unterholzner and Savigny (who was not satisfied by Unterholzner's treatment of Verjährung) see A. Vahlen, ed., *Savigny und Unterholzner: Vierundzwanzig Briefe F. K. v. Savignys aus dem Nachlaß von K. A. D. Unterholzner, mit einem Lebensabriß Unterholzners*. Verhandlungen der Akademie der Wissenschaften zu Berlin (1941), no. 3. On Unterholzner, see the literature cited in Rückert, *Savigny*, 73 n. 324.

[130] Zacharia, "Wissenschaftliche Entwicklung der Lehre des römischen Rechts von den dinglichen Servituten," in *Hugos Civilistisches Magazin* 2 (1795): 320–48. Cf. Cappellini, *Systema Iuris*, 1:171, 171–72 n. 90.

[131] Cappellini, *Systema Iuris*, 1:139–40, notes the prominence of debate over the application of the Roman law of servitudes to feudal rights in the late eighteenth century, but does not recognize the larger sociohistorical context of that debate.

[132] Thibaut, *Besitz und Verjährung*, 113.

[133] Ibid., 113–14.

[134] Ibid., 115.

[135] Ibid., 115.

[136] Ibid., 155.

[137] Ibid., 157. In this Thibaut agreed with a long-established tradition. Cf. above n. 107.

manipulation of legal doctrine too far. But in the context of the rapidly and radically changing legal world described by Klein, the message of Thibaut's handbook was clear: the new learned law might not achieve all an agrarian reformer could hope for, but it would serve only to end existing feudal obligations, not to create new ones.

A year later the young Savigny weighed in with his own book on property law, the *Recht des Besitzes*, which made him instantly famous in the German scholarly world.[138] Savigny's book was a model for all subsequent works the Historical School produced, an attempt to explicate an entire area of Roman law by reference to one single *Grundgedanke*, one fundamental thought, that both explained the ancient texts and put them in the service of current German legal needs.[139] It was also a model of unpolitical political writing, of legal analysis intended to achieve— through revivification and extension of the usus modernus—scholarly rather than legislative reform.

In this as in most things, Savigny was both politically more timid and conceptually more subtle than Thibaut. Current German legal needs in property law were determined by the conceptual revolution in the countryside, where lords had ceased to be owners of their peasants' land and received instead protectable possessory interests in old feudal duties. Savigny's Grundgedanke reintegrated these possessory interests into an ownership system. Savigny declared that careful analysis of the Roman texts showed that Roman law protected possession for only one reason: in order to protect, in accordance with the intent of the parties, possible *usucapio*, acquisition though the law of prescription.[140] In the context of Germany's agrarian legal struggles, this was a highly significant contention. Savigny had in effect asserted that Roman law was designed for the new uses to which it was being put in the coutryside, was conceptually structured for a feudal order in which rights and duties were subject to decay from year to year. Indeed, he made the point explicitly. At the end of his book, Savigny addressed the modifications of Roman law and its extension into new areas. He noted that the influence of Canon law had led Romanists to apply the law of possession to feudal relations. He endorsed this development as analytically proper and the stuff of good pol-

---

[138] Savigny had, it should be noted, already concerned himself extensively with problems of prescription and Verjahrung in the unpublished *Methodenlehre* of 1802. See Cappellini, *Systema Iuris*, 1:620–22, 626.

[139] On Savigny's method, with its roots in romantic organicism, see Stühler, *Erneuerung der Rechtswissenschaft*, 26ff. For W. G. Tafinger as a precursor of Savigny, see Neusüss, *Gesunde Vernunft und Natur der Sache*, 112.

[140] Savigny, *Recht des Besitzes*, 29 and often. Savigny's book was also, it should be noted, important for its care in emphasizing intent over acts—an emphasis characteristic, as I have explained, of Romanists in contrast to Germanists. For the "animus possidendi" in Savigny's book, see Brutti, "Proprietà nella sistema di Savigny," 80.

icy: what was true of Canon law, he noted, was "equally true of the feudal burdens [*Reallasten*] that derive from German law, such as land duties, tithes, and corvée."[141] To apply Roman rules to these feudal duties was not to be unfaithful to Roman law, he wrote; it was simply applying Roman rules "as the Romans themselves might have applied them, if they had been familiar with the institutions in question."[142] Thus Savigny, unlike Thibaut, was willing to allow lords to acquire feudal duties through prescription. But could those duties be lost through prescription? They could indeed: *non usus* could potentially destroy possession.[143]

This was, in some ways, a more timid approach to legal reform on behalf of the peasants than what Thibaut proposed: Savigny never went so far as to suggest that no new feudal obligations could be created by prescription. It was surely a more timid approach than his friend Niebuhr would advocate four years later in Berlin: Savigny would not countenance direct legislative action.[144] On the other hand, Savigny did little to qualify the implications of his acceptance of extinguishing prescription, and he had clearly declared his allegiance to the process of profoundly disruptive social change that had grown out of a century of the application of learned law in the countryside. If what Savigny wrote fell far short of *Babouvisme*, it was enough to establish his own gradualist reformism, with its roots deep in the early modern period. This was a reformism, to be sure, inhospitable to instantaneous abolition of the feudal order. But it was equally a reformism inhospitable to the sort of timeless feudal order that appealed to the reactionaries of Savigny's day. Indeed, Savigny's conservative reformism might best be characterized as a determination to subject the feudal world to the flux of time. In Savigny's mind, the world of property relations was a world in which rights, far from possessing any eternal validity, regularly accrued and decayed. The world was a place in which change, if very slow, was unremitting, and the law of prescription was accordingly central to Savigny's legal thought.[145]

The young Savigny's willingness to countenance extinctive prescription[146] continued in later years. Thus, when decades later he published his

[141] Savigny, *Recht des Besitzes*, 505; cf. ibid., 518. Noted in Brutti, "Proprietà nella sistema di Savigny," 88.

[142] Ibid., 506.

[143] Ibid., 474–75.

[144] For a discussion of Savigny's views in the immediate postwar years, see the discussion of Savigny's manuscript *Nachlaß* in H. Hammen, *Die Bedeutung Friedrich Carl von Savignys für die allgemeinen dogmatischen Grundlagen des Deutschen Bürgerlichen Gesetzbuches*, Schriften zur Rechtsgeschichte, Heft 29 (Berlin, 1983), 164–65.

[145] Cf. K. W. Nörr, "Das Aktionenrecht bei Savigny," *Ius Commune* 8 (1979): 112ff. I must pass over the subtle questions raised by the distinction between prescriptive loss of an action (Prof. Nörr's subject) and prescriptive loss of a right. Cf. below, n. 171.

[146] Cf. Savigny, *System des heutigen Römischen Rechts*, 4:565; 7:186. Cf. Matthiae, *Controversen-Lexikon*, vol. 1, pt. 2, 328–29.

summa, the *System des heutigen Römischen Rechts*, Savigny set himself apart from most lawyers of the day by insisting that the category of *unvordenkliche Zeit*, "immemorial time," had no place in analyzing feudal obligations.[147] Paying close attention to the work of the Hessian courts as described by the liberal reformer Burchard Wilhelm Pfeiffer of Cassel, whose *Practische Ausführungen aus allen Theilen der Rechtswissenschaft*[148] he repeatedly cited, Savigny made it clear that in "pure" Roman law, "immemorial time" could not be used to create a Servitut, and explicitly drew out the implications for the feudal order:

> But the most important consequence for practical law is a negative one, in that according to the proof I have presented, the doctrine of Servituten is entirely freed from any application of immemorial prescription. Indeed, this gain is not limited to Servituten, but rather operates to the benefit of Germanic feudal obligations [*germanische Reallasten*—an ordinary term for feudal obligations owed by the peasant to his lord] whose Verjährung is in large part to be adjudicated according to the Roman rules on Servituten.[149]

Savigny was notoriously not in the habit of alluding to "consequences for practical law"; the fact that he did so testifies to the interest in agrarian relations he shared with his contemporaries, and to his readiness to let the Roman-law transformation continue to undermine the feudal order as it had done for a century.

To be sure, Savigny's pronouncements hardly seem radical. After all, he did little more than repeat what scholars like Boehmer and Leyser had said a century earlier; his politics were the politics of the usus modernus, of the age when natural-law thinking had firmly established itself but codificationist experimentation had not yet begun. And, to be sure, Savigny had at best a mixed success in practice. He faced an uphill battle in the courts, which had long applied "immemorial time" to disputes over feudal services. In line with his belief that scholars, not judges, should make law, he informed the courts that they were simply mistaken about their source of authority. Rules of Roman law, he said, derived their authority not from their customary invocation by the courts, but rather from the

---

[147] For Savigny's comparatively isolated position in this regard, see Matthiae, *Controversen-Lexikon*, vol. 1, pt. 2, 317, and the literature cited there.

[148] F.C. v. Savigny, *System des heutigen Römischen Rechts*, e.g, 4:498 n.(u), 504 n.(bb), and 505 n.(dd). On Pfeiffer, see Nolte, *Pfeiffer*; C. W. Wippermann, *Kurhessen seit dem Freiheitskriege* (Cassel, 1850), index s.v. "Pfeiffer"; idem, "Pfeiffer," in *Allgemeine Deutsche Biographie* (Leipzig, 1887) 25:633–34. For Savigny's approval of Pfeiffer's 1806 dissertation, see Rückert, *Savigny*, 13.

[149] Savigny, *System des heutigen Römischen Rechts*, 4:504. Noted in Brutti, "Proprietà nel Sistema di Savigny," 88. In discussing Savigny's analysis of *Reallasten*, I omit the passage in his *Obligationenrecht*, 2 vols. (Berlin, 1851), 1:134 n. (d). That passage, dating as it does to 1851, is difficult to analyze in terms of pre-March politics.

textual exegeses and systematizations of scholars.[150] The high court in Jena, for one, was not persuaded.[151]

Yet if all this leads one to say that Savigny was a failed conservative reformer, thoroughly rooted in the precodificationist usus modernus of the early eighteenth century, that is hardly to say that he was a reactionary. For the early eighteenth century, as we have seen, had been a time of ever-deepening disruptions. The pre-French-Revolutionary order that Savigny wished to restore was an order marked by the progressive legal decay of feudalism. (Indeed, as we shall see, the possibility of extinctive prescription had, by Savigny's time, become a greater threat to the feudal order than in the time of E. F. Klein simply because the French occupation had interrupted many feudal relationships.) What Savigny wished to see continue was a process as old as the revival of the study of the *Digest*, a process by which learned law had slowly eaten away the conceptual foundations of feudalism.

Puchta too must be seen in the same light. Unlike Savigny, Puchta was skeptical of the propriety of analogizing feudal obligations to servitudes.[152] Yet the intended effect of his *Gewohnheitsrecht*, like that of Savigny's *Recht des Besitzes*, is only clear when seen against the background of the property-law revolution of the period after 1790. As discussed above, the *Gewohnheitsrecht* announced the sleep of customary law and its replacement by a *Juristenrecht*, a scholar's law developed through the systematic elaboration of legal principles. The *Gewohnheitsrecht* furthermore made it clear that Übungen, the performance of feudal services, did not themselves give rise to binding obligations. Rather, such Übungen were merely evidence that a court could consider in determining whether or not a binding obligation existed.[153] In so arguing, Puchta was describing the same feudal world as Savigny, and from a similar point of view. The Übungen whose binding legal effect Puchta wished to limit were precisely these acts whose performance, in Savigny's view, could give rise to acquisitive prescription, and whose non-performance could give rise to extinctive prescription. And, indeed, Puchta was, like Savigny, eager to banish arguments from "immemorial time." Judges, he warned, would often be confronted with litigants who claimed spurious "customs" as

[150] Savigny, *System des heutigen Römischen Rechts*, 4:504–5.

[151] See Matthiae, *Controversen-Lexikon*, vol. 1, pt. 2, 317. But see also below, nn. 162 and 163.

[152] See Puchta, *Cursus der Institutionen*, 6th ed., 2 vols. (Leipzig, 1866), 2:652 n.(d); idem, *Vorlesungen über das heutige römische Recht*, 6th ed., edited by A.A.F. Rudorff (Leipzig, 1873), 75: "Die Praktiker wollten häufig die Analogie der Servituten allgemein anwenden. . . . Dies ist doch ganz unpassend und undurchführbar." See generally ibid., 75–77.

[153] See above, pp. 122–24.

confirming their rights through "immemorial time"; the judges must, however, be sceptical: these rights often would not be justified by customary law at all.[154] The practical difference in Puchta's teaching lay in the fact that it was potentially even more disruptive than Savigny's: Puchta was prepared to deny that feudal obligations existed even in cases where the performance of Übungen would presumably have required Savigny to acknowledge that a prescriptive right to a given service had arisen.

We can trace the intended effect of Romanist thought in Puchta's teaching. Puchta, as I have said, was the *praeceptor Germaniae*—the teacher of [all] Germany—of his time: his texts were standard for the teaching of Roman law, and he was in a position to disseminate his teachings throughout the German states. And indeed, the practice texts that accompanied his treatises did not neglect the law of the transformed countryside. Girtanner's *Rechtsfälle zu Puchtas Pandekten*, a textbook of cases for the Romanist student, included many examples of peasants who were protecting their rights by appealing to the subtle doctrines of the Romanist lawyers. These cases involved all aspects of Roman law doctrine, including the Gewohnheitsrecht and the law of Servituten. In one case from Girtanner, a peasant-commune had turned Roman prescription doctrine to its advantage. Here (as very frequently) special complications had arisen as a result of the French occupation:

The Freiherr von O., as owner [*Eigentümer*] of the estate [*Gut*] O., has the right to pasture his sheep in the grazing green of the commune [*Gemeinde*] E. in Hannover. In the year 1808, when the estate and the village E. belonged to the Kingdom of Westphalia, the Westphalian mayor of the commune E. ... came to the Freiherr von O, and informed him that the commune E. wished to plough up the grazing green that was encumbered with this right of pasturage ... —a step to which von O., as title-holder of the Servitut, might be willing to consent. Von O. gave his permission—though only provisionally and for an indeterminate time—on the condition that the commune E. pay him 2 ½ Thalers per annum.

In the year 1829, von O. started an action with reference to the events narrated and with the allegation that the commune E., although it had ploughed up a part of its green in the years 1808–1810 and put that part in use as a garden, had not paid the promised sum of money. He asked that the commune be required: 1.) to pay him the promised and owed sum at least for the years 1810–1829, as well as 2.) to allow the ploughed section of the meadow in question to lie for pasturage.

The commune E. admitted that a section of the named field had been ploughed up in the year 1809 and used as a garden on the basis of the permission given in the year 1808. But it refused to let the land lie for pasturage

---

[154] Ibid., 2:118. Like Savigny, Puchta cited Pfeiffer.

or to pay the sum demanded. It was true that the sum had been promised by
the communal mayor and never paid; but this promise could not bind the
commune under Westphalian law then in force. . . . Moreover, the commune
claimed that the Servitut of the complainant had been extinguished by nonuse since 1810.[155]

With this case, Girtanner touched on one of the most heatedly debated
questions of Roman law for the countryside. For if the lords' Servituten
could be extinguished by nonuse—as Savigny among others had suggested they could—feudal obligations could lapse simply because they
had not been demanded for as short a time as nineteen years. This doctrine on Servituten was not the only element of Romanist doctrine that
promised to further peasant interests. Another case in Girtanner's textbook showed a peasant protecting his rights through claims based directly on Puchtian teachings on customary law:

The farmer Aumann of Bernsdorf in Württemberg initiated a court action
against the royal department of the treasury for the necessary wood to build
a building he planned. He demanded this wood in return for a third of the
forest tax. He claimed the authority of a contract of the year 1558, according
to which all inhabitants of Bernsdorf were given the right to collect the wood
they required for their buildings from the neighboring royal forest in return
for the aforementioned lower tax. In violation of this contract, half of the
ordinary tax had been demanded from him. The defendant admitted that a
contract with the stated provision had been formed in 1558, but claimed an
alteration of that contract through custom [Herkommen—emphasis in the
original], since inhabitants of the village Bernsdorf had paid for their wood
at the rate of half the ordinary tax on various occasions since 1813. To prove
the existence of this custom, the defendant immediately presented more than
twelve examples of such cases. In response, the plaintiff objected that the
customary law [Gewohnheitsrecht] that had been claimed could not be demonstrated by the proof that the contract was departed from in those cases.
For to prove such a customary law, it was necessary to show that it was
viewed as law by all persons to whom it applied, not merely by a majority;
and that moreover, the cases presented rested on an error, because in the year
1813, as a result of the French invasion, the contract of 1558 had been mis-
laid, and that contract had only recently been rediscovered. Against the first
of these objections, the defendant remarked that it would be sufficient to
establish a customary law if it had been observed only in *many* cases (c. i
Cod. VIII. 53: *quae in oppido* frequenter *servata sunt*).

[155] Girtanner, *Rechtsfälle zu Puchtas Pandekten*, 4th ed. (Jena, 1869), 159–60. Discussed
in E. Pagenstecher, *Pandekten-Praktikum* (Heidelberg, 1860), 275–77.

Does the decision of this case involve the doctrine of Gewohnheitsrecht and its origin?[156]

This question touched on some of the subtlest points in Puchta's Gewohnheitsrecht.[157] As I have discussed above,[158] Puchta insisted that Übungen—the sort of acts of which the defendant in the case had produced his twelve examples—did not create customary law. Rather, Übungen were merely evidence of the existence of a customary gemeinsame Überzeugung, a shared conviction. The twelve cited instances in this case were thus not adequate to defeat farmer Aumann's claim—though the burden remained on farmer Aumann to offer contrary evidence. Behind Puchta's Gewohnheitsrecht, too, stood practical questions of social conflict in the German courts.[159]

The Practical Impact of the New Property Law

But if the romantics of the universities addressed themselves to practical questions, did their answers have any practical effect?

There is no doubt that the new property law had a direct impact. Doctrinal fights over prescription law took place everywhere in early nineteenth-century Germany—including Prussia, where the problems of property law that occupied lawyers elsewhere proved unsolvable according to the plain text of the *Allgemeines Landrecht*.[160] The legal order based on prescription seems to have been widely accepted in the German lands by the early 1830s, at the same time that the revolutionary peasant unrest of 1830–31 forced the promulgation of the first German reform statutes: the High Appellate Court in Cassel declared that Verjährung, not *Herkommen*, was the test of the validity of legally protectable rights in 1834;[161] similarly, the High Appellate Court of Darmstadt declared explicitly in 1833 that the legal principles of Roman law governing Ver-

---

[156] Girtanner, *Rechtsfalle*, 2–3.

[157] Complicated in this case by the existence of the contract, as well as by some subtle differences between *Herkommen* and *Gewohnheit*. For a discussion of the case, see Pagenstecher, *Pandekten-Praktikum*, 3–4.

[158] Above, pp. 122–24. See also below, p. 206.

[159] Scheuermann does not recognize this social significance of the "rapid and complete" acceptance of Puchta's doctrine that he discovers in court records. *Einflüße der historischen Rechtsschule*, 85.

[160] Compare the doctrinal difficulties expressed in, e.g., "Berechnung der Verjährungsfrist bei Erwerbung des juris decimandi," *Jahrbücher für die Preußische Gesetzgebung, Rechtswissenschaft und Rechtsverwaltung* 1 (1814): 129; "Ein auf den Besitz vom Jahre 1740 sich gründendes Recht gehet nicht allein durch Nichtgebrauch . . . verloren," *Allgemeine Juristische Monatsschrift für die Preußischen Staaten* 6, no. 1 (1808): 11.

[161] *Seufferts Archiv für Entscheidungen der obersten Gerichte in den deutschen Staaten* 1, no. 3 (1847): 4–5.

jährung of Servituten were to be applied to "Germanic property rights."[162] A Hannoverian high-court and justice ministry agreed in 1832 in applying Savigny's doctrine on possession in cases of contested Servituten;[163] the Leipzig high court also cited Savigny in reaching the same conclusion in the same year.[164] Romanist treatment of Reallasten had thoroughly established itself by the 1830s, and there was room for lawyers to make use of the doctrine on behalf of the peasants.

The Case of Hannover

There is every evidence that practical lawyers did indeed attempt to realize a transformation of agrarian life through legal doctrinal change. The impact of the new property law shows in the records from the Kingdom of Hannover. These records include both collections of essays and cases published by individual lawyers eager to promote their own viewpoints[165] and the valuable *Juristische Zeitung für das Königreich Hannover*. Hannover offered a testing ground most favorable to the chances of reform by rule of Roman law. Reform legislation never played the prominent role in Hannover that it did east of the Elbe.[166] In any case, eighteenth-century Hannoverian reforms had aimed, for the most part, only at converting feudal obligations into cash rents; and the reform legislation that followed the uprisings of 1830–31 had aimed, not at wholesale abolition, but rather at allowing peasants to buy their freedom at a single capitalized sum.[167] Thus, feudal obligations survived in Hannover, and survived in a legal culture peculiarly suited to the Savignyan idea of nonlegislative reform. Moreover, Hannoverian feudal obligations survived in a peculiar

---

[162] Ibid., 3, no. 192 (1849): 422. Decisions accepting the doctrine continue to be reported as late as 1849 (OAG Munich, in ibid., 3, no. 3 [1849]: 343–44. Cf. also, e.g., ibid., 1, no. 317 [1840]: 122.) (Citing the treatment of Savigny, *Rechts des Besitzes*, discussed above pp. 183–84.)

[163] *Juristische Zeitung* 7, no. 1 (1832): 78–79.

[164] Quoted in P. L. Kritz, *Sammlung von Rechtsfällen und Entscheidungen derselben* (Leipzig, 1833), 1:183–84.

[165] Bülow, *Practische Erörterungen*; G. W. [erroneously "W. G." on the first volume of the series and so catalogued in the collection of Harvard Law Library] Struckmann, *Practische Beiträge zur Kenntniß des Osnabrückischen Eigentumsrechts*, 14 vols. (Lüneburg, 1826–31).

[166] For the comparative unimportance of legislative reform in Hannover, where most legislation simply ratified doctrinal developments, see Wittich, *Grundherrschaft*, viii. For the tendency of Hannoverian legislation to leave existing law in place, see also Buchholz, "Quellen des deutschen Immobiliarrechts," 275.

[167] See Wittich, *Grundherrschaft*, 417–20, 435–45. Apart from the conversion of service obligations into cash obligations, the other principle object of the reform legislation was subdivision of commons. See idem, 423, for the Lüneburgische Gemeinheitsteilungsordnung of 1802, "das Muster für alle späteren Teilungsgesetze."

form: Hannoverian peasants, unlike Prussian ones, tended to owe their obligations to a number of lords, often distant ones.[168] Hannoverian feudalism was thus a legal system, rather than a network of personal relationships, and talk of the beauties of the bond between peasant and lord could play little role in Hannoverian reform debates. Hannover was strong, too, in the pre-nineteenth-century traditions of romantic idealization of the peasantry: it was in Osnabrück that Möser had composed his *Patriotische Phantasien*. Hannover was the type of the uncodified state in which reform of legal practice by itself could have a direct impact.

The new property law had a fairly long history in Hannover. Attempts to end split property dated back to the mid-eighteenth century, sixty years before Thibaut's seminal essay, and Theodor Hagemann, one of the leading lawyers of Hannover, was already promoting the use of Roman rules on behalf of the peasants when Savigny appeared on the scene.[169] But if the reform doctrines were old, they were still quite actively opposed in Hannover in the late 1820s; indeed, the high court in Celle could continue to apply feudal law of Obereigentum for one Hannoverian region as late as 1845.[170] Support for the new property law was far from universal: the violence with which this innovation was met in the countryside shows in one of the longest pieces published in the *Juristische Zeitung für das Königreich Hannover*, an 1827 essay written in response to the question raised by a contributor to the journal, "In welcher Zeit erlöschen die Gutsherrlichen Frohndienste," "How Long Does It Take Before a Lord's Right to Services Is Extinguished?" The author used learned Roman-law reasoning (as well as occasional sarcasm) to counter the anti-feudal arguments for the loss of Servituten through Verjährung: "The right of the lord of an estate to demand unpaid labor can, according to the principles I have discussed, *not* be extinguished by Verjährung, or (rather) nonuse."[171]

Nevertheless, as elsewhere, Hannoverian courts widely declared their acceptance of the law of "Servituten nach prätorischem Rechte," "Servitudes according to Praetorian [i.e., classical Roman] Law," from the late 1820s and through the 1830s, though they puzzled over the exact rules

---

[168] See Wittich, *Grundherrschaft*, 2 and often.

[169] E.g., T. Hagemann, "Erörterung von dem Mithutungsrechte des Eigenthümers," in *Practische Erörterungen*, 6:75–76.

[170] The decision applied to the Duchies of Bremen and Verden. *Juristische Zeitung* 20, no. 1 (1845), 51.

[171] Dr. Valett of Gottingen, "Antwort auf die Frage: in welcher Zeit erlöschen die Gutsherrlichen Frohndienste? Praescriptio qualificata?" *Juristische Zeitung* 2, no. 1 (1827), 94–96, 100–110, 106. Dr. Valett was, however, enough of a Romanist to allow *Klagenverjährung*—the prescriptive loss of a given individual's right to bring an action, without destruction of the underlying right itself, should a later action be brought by a transferee—until such time as a new owner should come into possession of the dominant property.

of the doctrine.[172] Indeed, it is clear that in the atmosphere of the late
1820s, at the period of the height of Savigny's reputation, lawyers felt a
sense of excitement about the possiblities of reform through Romanism,
through reconceptualizing property relations in terms of Servituten. One
anonymous lawyer, for example, reported in 1827 his success in convinc-
ing the Justice Ministry of Celle to apply the Roman law of Servituten in
a case involving a man on one of the lowest rungs of country life in Hannover, a "Häusling": "Cases are not uncommon among the country people in which a Häusling lacks sufficent means to buy a property of his
own but possesses a small capital that however, seems considerable
enough that some property-owner takes him in as a lifetime boarder."
Häuslinge were peasants' peasants, men who turned what little they
owned over to men only somewhat less poor than they.[173] What hap-
pened to such a Häusling if the peasant from whom he rented became
insolvent? In that case "it is bad" for the Häusling, whose claim on his
"small capital" was legally weak. But application of Roman law could
change that: "But if one conceives the contract as a *servitus habitationis
et usufructus* [a servitude carrying the right to dwell in, and use without
impairing, another's property] constituted by the owner of the farm, then
the matter comes out very differently for the lodger." By recasting the
tenant's situation in Roman-law terms, the law could protect his interests,
as indeed the Justice Ministry in Celle had done.[174] Here we see Roman-
law reconceptualization actively benefiting the peasants in the late 1820s.
In another case, the Spruchkollegium of Jena lent its authority to the application of the Roman law of Servituten in the interest of Hannoverian
peasants. This case involved an innovating nobleman, who mounted an
experiment in forestry on feudalized land.[175] Peasants with entitlements
on the same land had first taken matters into their own hands:

> The inhabitants of the village of T. . . . have the right of pasturage [*Hut und
> Weide*] and of half-forage [*halbe Mast*] in the C——berholz; they are also
> entitled to take half their necessary building wood from the same forest. . . .
> For reasons of forestry, the lord of the forest, G.R.v.S. auf B.S., decided to
> seal off a place in this forest—and, indeed, only a surface area of about six
> *Morgen* [approximately 4–5 acres]—which had grown bare through gradual
> felling, in order to train conifers.
>   The Servitut-holders disrupted this undertaking.

[172] E.g., *Juristische Zeitung* 2, no. 1 (1827), 153ff.; 2, no. 2, 100ff., 146ff.
[173] On *Häuslinge*, see Wittich, *Grundherrschaft*, 108–11.
[174] *Juristische Zeitung* 2, no. 2 (1827), 100–104, quoted passages on 100–101.
[175] For the central importance of innovation in agriculture, forestry and husbandry in
Hannover, see generally Wittich, *Grundherrschaft*.

It was the peasants' claim that the project of the lord of the forest interfered with their pasturing and forage. The legal question in this case was a common one: did the burden of proof (*Beweislast*) fall on the peasants to prove that the actions of the lord of the forest had interfered with their enjoyment of their rights, or did the burden fall on the lord? Upon Aktenversendung, the Jena faculty found for the peasants; a royal rescript, however, overturned the faculty's finding.[176] Despite the ultimately unfavorable outcome, it is clear enough that by the late 1820s learned jurisprudence could do service for the peasants. Local lawyers could use learned reasoning themselves: One contributed a long legal-philological essay to the *Juristische Zeitung* demonstrating that all Servituten could be acquired by ten years of Verjährung, with two exceptions, one of which was Reallasten. The latter burdens, not coincidentally of special interest to the peasant, could only be created after thirty years of Verjährung.[177] Scholars were laboring for the peasants on the local level.

But if the last-cited essay is evidence of sincere Romanist reform, it is also evidence of the limits on that reform. The author could not cite court or ministry decisions that supported his program; his program, in any case, would have only mitigated, not ended the peasant's burdens. There were Romanists in the countryside who believed they could free the peasants without violating property rights, reformers in the Niebuhrian spirit who believed that by subjecting Germany to classical Roman law they could build a free Niebuhrian state. But how much did they ultimately achieve?

Their success was inevitably limited. The property law that Romanists introduced into the countryside was supple and varied, well able to preserve old peasant rights and to allow peasants to contest old burdens. But, by the same token, Romanist property law was supple and varied enough to preserve the rights of lords and allow them to contest their burdens. The application of pure rules of Roman property law favored the lords at least as often as it did the peasantry. For example, in the following Hannoverian case of 1839, a variety of sophisticated Romanist doctrines went to support the claims of a lord against a neighboring peasant. One of the most insistent claims of "pure" Roman doctrine on contract law was that there could be no *exceptio jure tertii*—that is, no defense could be based on the rights of a third party. The lord in question made use of that doctrine as well as of that of Verjährung:

---

[176] Dr. Jäger in Zeven, "Ueber die Schuldigkeit zur Uebernahme des Beweises bei Contestationen zwischen Forstherrschaft und Servitut-Berechtigten . . ." *Juristische Zeitung* 3, no. 1 (1828): 141–44, 150–51.

[177] G.P., "Ueber die Verjährung der Servituten und Reallasten," in *Juristische Zeitung* 6, no. 1 (1831), 132–42. G.P. viewed extinction, however, differently. See idem, 142.

The owner of the estate [*Gut*] of Leer bei Melle filed a complaint in 1837 with the royal office at Grönenberg against the peasant [*colonus*] Giesker of Altenmelle, demanding the recognition of an alleged right of way belonging to his estate, allowing him to cart hay away from a meadow of the estate through a meadow belonging to the defendant; he based his complaint on Verjährung.

The "colon" (as he was still called in 1837) responded that his farm had until very recently been enfeofed to the royal domain, and that such lands were not subject by law to Servituten through Verjährung. But the justice ministry in Osnabrück found against the peasant in 1838 on the best of Roman-law grounds: appealing to the interest of any third party was the unacceptable *exceptio jure tertii*.[178] Many other cases could be cited to prove this self-evident point[179]: Roman doctrine could do a great deal of good for the peasants, but it could also do a great deal of good for their lords. Indeed, in a world so recently feudal, "neutral principles" could in practice probably only favor the powerful.

To test the possibilities and limits of Romanist reform in pre-1848 Germany, let us see what use an undoubted Hannoverian champion of the peasantry made of the doctrines of Romanism. This is Gustav Struckmann of Osnabrück (1796–1840), the lawyer who communicated the case of the *exceptio iure tertii* to the *Juristische Zeitung*. The record of Struckmann's contacts with the law of Savigny will serve as an ideal measure of its usefulness for coutryside reform.

Osnabrück remained the home of a number of important figures faithful to the Möserian-Niebuhrian tradition: J.C.B. Stüve, the author of Hannover's legislation freeing its peasants in the early 1830s,[180] lived there along with Struckmann, whose use of Romanist doctrine I wish to examine. Struckmann was precisely the kind of person on whom the fortunes of the Savignyan program depended. He was of the generation of Puchta, having been born in 1796 the son of a highly placed lawyer who maintained a cultivated household. He received a classical education at the Rats-Gymnasium in Osnabrück before arriving at the Göttingen of Hugo and K. F. Eichhorn in 1814. After three years at Göttingen he moved on to Berlin, where he experienced the German cultural transformation at first hand. He diligently attended August Boeckh's lectures on Greek antiquity and art history, and "he was especially enthralled by

---

[178] "Präjudiz . . . mitgetheilt von Dr. Struckmann in Osnabrück," *Juristische Zeitung* 14, no. 3 (1839): 29–31.

[179] Cf., e.g., the 1847 finding of the OAG Munich against a Landgemeinde on considerations of Verjährung, citing Puchta, in *Seufferts Archiv* 1, no. 408 (1847): 164.

[180] Cf. A. F. Ventker, *Stüve und die Hannöversche Bauernbefreiung*, Wirtschaftswissenschaftliche Gesellschaft zum Studium Niedersachsens, Reihe A, Heft 28 (Oldenbourg, 1935).

Savigny's lectures on the Pandects."[181] A beneficiary of romantic scholarship as the romantics believed it should be communicated, through personal contact with the great teachers of his time, Struckmann returned to Osnabrück as a fervent devotee of ancient culture and of Aeschylus in particular.[182] He also returned as a devotee of that great object of love for romantic scholars, the peasants. He studied Möser together with Stüve, and cited all of Möser's writings regularly.[183] Specializing in land law, he published with energy and scholarly acumen various works on peasant relations in his native region.[184] In 1833 he consummated his involvement with the peasants of Osnabrück by buying a so-called colonate—a piece of property that gave him the right to sit and vote with the peasantry.[185] Indeed, as a friend of Stüve, he maintained an intimate connection with the movement for the liberation of the peasants on all levels, scholarly and political, in Hannover.

No one could better claim to embody the hopes of Romanist peasant reform than this representative of romantic classicism in Germany. How did this man use the Roman law he had learned from Savigny to advance the interests of the peasants for whom he labored? The answer shows both the possibilities and the grave limitations of the Romanist program. The peasants of Osnabrück were not personally enserfed, but their land carried with it many obligations, including those of personal service. They were empowered to a varying extent to acquire property and form contracts in their own right, though generally only with the consent of their lord. The exact extent of the rights and obligations of these *Eigenbehörige* ("dependent persons"—the term used in Osnabrück as in some other regions[186]) was a matter of constant litigation. The legal status of the Eigenbehörige of Osnabrück was governed by the *Osnabrückische Eigentums-Ordnung* (Osnabrück Property Ordinance) of 1722. This was a typical piece of pre-absolutist princely legislation, for it carefully deferred to prevailing custom and private will. Thus the *Eigentums-Ordnung* refused to specify the obligations of all Osnabrück Eigenbehörige as a class: "Whereas the obligations of Eigenbehörige vary, in part accord-

---

[181] H. Struckmann, *Geschichte der Familie Struckmann aus Osnabrück* (Berlin, 1909), 163–67, here 167.

[182] Cf. J.C.B. Stüve, *Briefe*, Veröffentlichungen der Niedersächsischen Archivverwaltung, vols. 10 & 11 (Göttingen, 1959), 1:29–30, on Struckmann's "Kultivierwut"; cf. ibid., 1:63, for Struckmann and Stüve's common work on Möser.

[183] E.g., Struckmann, *Practische Beiträge*, 6 (1828): 13; ibid., 10 (1830): 5.

[184] Alongside the *Practische Beiträge*, Struckmann published *Fälle und Entscheidungen aus dem Gebiete des Eigentumsrechts* (Lüneburg, 1828) and numerous contributions to the *Juristische Zeitung*.

[185] H. Struckmann, *Geschichte der Familie Struckmann*, 180.

[186] For discussions of the type and terminology of peasant obligations in two regions of Hannover, see Wittich, *Grundherrschaft*, 220ff.

ing to custom, in part according to the conditions to which the estates are subjected, so shall [the law] take its course according to such customary or conditional obligations, when they are proven."[187] Thus the reigning pre-absolutist legislation potentially left room for the Puchtian and Savignyan innovations of romantic Roman scholarship: the *Eigentums-Ordnung* envisioned nothing other than legal fights over the proof of the existence of custom or of contractual obligations. There were large areas of law that the prince had refused to legislate, areas in which a Romanistically minded lawyer had ample opportunity to introduce his doctrine.

Like so many Germans, Struckmann shared the ideals of the university Romanists, seeking to confer on the peasants of Osnabrück freedom of property and contract. Thus, he was eager to discredit a principle of law enunciated by the drafter of the *Eigentums-Ordnung*, J.J.C. Vincke, but not incorporated into the text of the law: "what the Eigenbehörige acquires, he acquires for the benefit of his lord [*Gutsherr*] and his colonate."[188] In 1833 Struckmann attacked this principle as the product of a misunderstanding of Roman law. If Vincke's principle were correct, wrote Struckmann,

> there could be no question of the Eigenbehöriger having any ability to form contracts either with respect to his movable or his real property, but rather the property- or estate-lord [*Eigentums- oder Gutsherr*] would have to be viewed as the sole owner of these possessions and goods, reserving to the Eigenbehöriger the *usufruct*. . . . But this proposition and the corresponding expressions of the legislation itself obviously contain nothing other than a doctrinal view of the drafter based on a false application of Roman law.[189]

Here Struckmann, like liberal lawyers all throughout Germany, was attempting to reserve sole ownership to the peasant and using Roman learning to do it. But the real test of the usefulness of the new law to him as a practical lawyer lay in whether he was able to make use of the new doctrines. Could the new Roman law make its way into the practice of a reforming Osnabrück lawyer?

In mixed and amended fashion, yes. Struckmann's activity shows, first of all, that romantic Romanism existed somewhat at odds with itself: Struckmann's interest in the peasants, and the example set him by Möser, inevitably led him to concentrate his efforts more and more on local Os-

---

[187] *Osnabrückische Eigentums-Ordnung*, Cap. I, §2. Cited by Struckmann in "Kann nach Osnabrückischem Rechte der Gutsherr von seinem Eigenbehörigen statt des bisher errichteten Dienstgeldes Naturaldienste fordern?" *Juristische Zeitung*, 7, no. 2 (1832): 140–41.

[188] Vincke himself did not claim force of law for his pronouncements, as the title of his commentary to the *Eigentums-Ordnung* witnesses: J. J. Vincke, *Ohnmaaßgebliche Gedancken zu der Eigentums-Ordnung Osnabrücks* (Lemgo, 1721).

[189] Struckmann in *Juristische Zeitung* 8, no. 2 (1833): 50.

nabrück law, rather than on Roman doctrine. Indeed, while there is no evidence of that he ever became violently hostile to Roman law, it is clear enough that his life among the peasants of Osnabrück tended to make him increasingly into a Germanist, an advocate of a "common German, pure German private law. . . ."[190] By the mid-1830s his attention had decisively turned away from Roman law. This is particularly true of inheritance law, which dominated Hannoverian litigation. Inheritance law, whose reform was a major element of the Romanist program, remained firmly governed by local-law principles in the work of Struckmann as in the work of other Hannoverian lawyers. In this respect, the case of Hannover confirms historical research demonstrating that Romanist inheritance law made only limited inroads into German practice.[191]

Nevertheless, in earlier years Struckmann made use of Roman doctrine. He could, for example, cite a principle of interpretation from the *Digest* in an attempt to lift from some peasants the obligation to send their children to serve in the house of their lord.[192] But on crucial doctrinal points the use of Romanist doctrine could be both limited and ill-advised. As we have seen, Struckmann felt obliged to deny, for example, that feudal obligations should be analyzed as Romanist usufructs, as some Romanist lawyers had said they should.[193] Even in the many areas where justice officials left room for the application of Roman doctrine, the case of Struckmann shows that Romanism could seem impractical or undesirable to a lover of the peasantry. Savigny's doctrine on Verjährung, and Puchta's on Gewohnheitsrecht, were impossible to reconcile with the express terms of the *Osnabrückische Eigentums-Ordnung*. By the terms of the *Eigentums-Ordnung*, Übungen created binding obligations. Citations to Puchta were unavailing in such a statutory climate.[194] If Struckmann, a lawyer most favorably placed to put Historical School doctrine into practice, found that its doctrines could sometimes only complicate his task, we must presume that the program could not enjoy more than partial success anywhere in Germany.

The Limits of Reform in Germany

This presumption a fortiori, that if the program of Savigny brought only mixed benefits to the peasants of Hannover it can have brought no better

---

[190] For Struckmann's desire for "ein gemeines deutsches, echt deutsches Privatrecht," see H. Struckmann, *Geschichte der Familie Struckmann*, 179.

[191] E.g., Struckmann, *Practische Beiträge*, vol. 7 (1829), "Von der Abtretung des Anerbenrechts." On the fate of learned reasoning about inheritance law in the courts, see Hedemann, *Fortschritte des Zivilrechts*, vol. 2, pt. 1, 47.

[192] *Juristische Zeitung* 6, no. 2 (1831): 53–62, 67–74, here 69.

[193] *Practische Beiträge* 6 (1828): 14.

[194] *Practische Beiträge* 12 (1831): 6–7, 10–11.

than mixed benefits elsewhere, is supported by evidence from other states. Romanist doctrine could be used by any party to further its legal interests. If in one decision the High Appellate Court of Munich could put the burden of proof to demonstrate the extent of a Servitut on its possessor in the name of "the presumption in favor of freedom from Lasten," in another it could quite as easily cite Puchta's *Pandekten* in finding against a commune that wished to rid itself of the Servituten burdening its land.[195] The principles of Savignyan doctrine were equally available to all litigants, and one must assume that the wealth and influence of the lords enabled them to take better advantage of those principles than peasants could. Even if wealth and influence played no part in a decision, the application of the "neutral principles" of classical Roman law certainly favored the lords as least as often as it favored the peasants. In the last analysis, Savigny's practical program was not much more likely to effect fundamental reform than was his essay on the Roman colonate.

CONCLUSION

Nevertheless, it is important to recognize that the Romanists believed they had resurrected a Roman property law subtle and varied enough to be the basis of the free and just order they envisioned as slowly emerging in the German countryside. The "bourgeois" society Savigny and his followers hoped to establish was not a commercial one. Their Bürger were free in a Kantian, not a Lockeian way. And their bourgeois society was Möser's society of free peasants, as Romanized by Niebuhr.[196] The Romanism embodied in the great textbooks of Savigny, Puchta, and Wächter was the echo in legal doctrine of Niebuhrianism in the universities, an attempt to put an end to feudal Germany not by revolution, but by reconceptualization. High culture would alter Germany. German justice was to become Roman justice, and, by forensic methods, German peasants were to become plebeians. What the Niebuhrian historians saw in Rome—strength without frenzy, freedom without convulsion—they thought they could recreate in Germany. And their counterparts in law thought they

---

[195] *Seufferts Archiv* 1, no. 18 (1847): 11; ibid., 1, no. 408 (1847): 164.

[196] There were, to be sure, critical issues in German land law more precisely analogous to the issues involved in Niebuhr's *ager publicus*. The ownership of abandoned land, for example, was regularly litigated. But in Hannover at least, debates over the law of this land ignored Niebuhr's *Römische Geschichte*. Thus Hagemann, writing in the *Juristische Zeitung* in 1827 ("Ueber die rechtliche Ansprüche auf das Eigenthum uncultivierter Gemeinheiten und verlaßener Aecker und Wiesen," *Juristische Zeitung* 2, no. 1 [1827]: 2–7), cited Hanoverian monographs of 1803 and 1798, but not Niebuhr. For the crucial importance of Gemeinheitsteilungen, see, e.g., Mooser, *Ländliche Klassengesellschaft*, 105ff., 122ff.; Wittich, *Grundherrschaft*, 423ff.

could do the same, by conferring on the peasant legal rights, legally defensible.

Whatever their hopes, however, these historians and lawyers failed. Romanist law reform may have been a doomed cause from its first years in the 1790s. Certainly by the 1840s political conflict had grown too violent to allow any space for a peaceful and "impartial" rule of law under the tutelage of law professors. Accordingly, in the end it was not romantic law reform but the Revolution of 1848 that freed the peasants. In the following chapter I will trace the consequences of the collapse of Savigny's program under the pressure of politics.

Chapter VI

CULTURAL CRISIS AND LEGAL CHANGE AFTER 1840

THE PROGRAM of Savigny did not survive midcentury unaltered. After 1840 the strength of Roman tradition as Savigny conceived it was shaken by two successive cultural countermovements: in the 1840s, romantic Germanists mounted a bitter attack on Roman law and on public respect for Rome. This Germanist challenge faded—if only for a time—after the Revolution of 1848. But Roman tradition was undermined in new ways during the 1850s. The 1850s were the decade of materialism, of a kind of cult of the natural sciences and of commerce that seemed fundamentally incompatible with the cult of the classics. The program of Savigny was not destroyed by materialism. But it was changed. In this last chapter I wish to trace the events of these two difficult decades, the decade of decline in the 1840s and the decade of what could be called stabilized decline in the 1850s. Cultural and legal history remained intimately linked during these decades. But civilization, as the Romanist lawyers understood it, had lost a kind of vigor.

Savigny's program began to crumble in the 1830s, under the pressure of the same events that wrecked the constitutionalism of the south. Hannover and Hesse were his laboratories. When these central German states were shaken by attempts to exercise legislative power, the romantic idea of rule of law lost its cogency. Reform legislation, if of a timid kind, arrived, in the central German states, in the aftermath of 1830.[1] This damaged the program of Savigny, as did the notorious affair of the Göttingen Seven—all leading professors and all discharged for their liberal constitutionalist convictions. The prominence of these liberal professors threatened, inevitably, to diminish the reputation of the professoriate in general for suprapolitical impartiality.[2] After the sudden dismissal of the Seven, Savigny did his best to calm the professorial waters. He wrote his friend Jakob Grimm, asking that Grimm take care to preserve the traditional claim of the professoriate to impartiality. He counseled Grimm not to accept the money that had been raised for him by sympathizers all over Germany:

---

[1] For the reform legisation of Hannover, which left the old order theoretically intact, see Wittich, *Grundherrschaft*, 435–45.

[2] On the affair, see, most recently, Husung, *Protest und Repression*, 95–96.

Anyone would gratefully recognize the good will [embodied in these collections], even if the principle motive of many of those involved may have been the instinctive need to play party politics. But it unavoidably gives the whole event a tinge of partisanship, as false as it is undesired [*eine so unwahre als unerwünschte Parteyfarbe*], and in particular it leads to a personal connection with people one is not in a position to select, a connection with the air of having accepted patronage about it, through which the complete independence of one's position can be uncomfortably endangered later on.[3]

But Savigny's plea only offended Grimm.[4] Within a few years, far from hewing to the old "impartial" Romanist line, Grimm became a vocal enemy of the whole Roman-law tradition: he flatly declared in 1846 that "the use of Roman law has, in practice, brought no advantage to constitutionalism and freedom."[5] In this he was following the lead of other specialists in German law, who, as a class, stood well to the left of the Romanists. Germanists had long accused their Romanist colleagues of being crypto-reactionaries: thus A. L. Reyscher of Tübingen denounced Zachariä's "seeming impartiality" in 1836.[6] Once such charges had begun to fly, politicization had progressed too far; it would soon be impossible for professors to make any plausible claim to "impartiality."

As the Germanists became more and more closely identified with revolutionary liberalism in the late 1830s and after, the Romanists—and classicists in general—tried to dissociate themselves from the politicized Germanist movement and maintain their old reputation for impartiality. Classicists worked hard, in the pronouncements they made after the

[3] Savigny, letter to J. Grimm, December 21, 1837. In A. Stoll, ed., *Friedrich Karl von Savigny*, 2 vols. (Berlin, 1929), 2:501.
[4] See Savigny, letter to Grimm, February 2, 1838, in ibid., 502; cf. ibid., 503 n. 2. For disagreement between Savigny and Grimm over 1830, still fundamentally friendly, see Rückert, *Savigny*, 216. For intellectual/scholarly reactions to the affair more generally, see Fioravanti, *Giuristi e Costituzione Politica*, 99ff.
[5] Quoted in Bender, *Rezeption des Römischen Rechts*, 66. On the political content of Grimm's *Volksgeisttheorie*, see, e.g., R. Feldmann, *Jakob Grimm und die Politik* (Kassel, n.d.), 53. For the connection between Grimm's philological and legal-historical work, see J. Strippel, "Zum Verhältnis von Deutscher Rechtsgeschichte und Deutscher Philologie," in J. J. Muller, ed., *Germanistik und deutsche Nation 1806–1848: Zur Konstitution bürgerlichen Bewußtseins*, Literaturwissenschaft und Sozialwissenschaften, vol. 2 (Stuttgart, 1974), 135–66. For the Germanists at Frankfurt, see W. Siemann, *Die Frankfurter Nationalversammlung 1848/9 zwischen demokratischem Liberalismus and konservativer Reform: Die Bedeutung der Juristendominanz in den Verfassungsverhandlungen des Paulskirchenparlaments* (Bern, 1976), 24 and often (though cf. G. Dilcher and B. Kern, "Die juristische Germanistik und die Fachtradition der deutschen Rechtsgeschichte," ZSS (G) 100 [1984]: 24ff.); J. J. Müller, "Die ersten Germanistentage," in idem, ed., *Germanistik und deutsche Nation*, 316–18; Fioravanti, *Giuristi e Costituzione Politica*, 130.
[6] Reyscher, *Die Grundherrlichen Rechte des Wurttemburgischen Adels* (Tübingen, 1836), 1. On Reyscher, see Rückert, *Reyschers Leben und Rechtstheorie*.

founding of the Congresses of Philologists and Schoolteachers in 1838, to convince the German public that they still stood for neutral, high cultural values, above politics[7]—as one of their leaders put it, "yes, all philologists are born rationalists, but in the good sense, like Reuchlin and Melanchthon."[8] The Hannoverian legal world saw similar efforts. In the same year, 1838, an anonymous essay appeared in the *Juristische Zeitung* that attempted to use Romanist scholarship to defuse the constitutional conflict that had struck the state. A peasant of the duchies of Bremen and Verden refused to pay a tithe required of him by ducal legislation dating to 1743. Like litigants in many cases, the peasant maintained that the law was contrary to the custom of his region and therefore invalid. The anonymous contributor gave the peasant support from Roman law interpreted according to the mode of the Historical School:

> In L. 2. C. "what is long-standing custom" the Emperor Constantine gave the following rescript:
>
> *Consuetudinis ususque longaevi non vilis auctoritas est: verum non usque adeo sui valitura momento, ut aut rationem vincat, aut legem.*
>
> [Custom and long-standing usage are of no mean authority, but they do not carry such weight as to defeat either reason or special enactments.]
>
> Through a misunderstanding of this locus, some legal scholars have derived the principle that written laws cannot be invalidated by custom in monarchical states.
>
> Cf. Voet, Comment. ad. Pand. L. I. T. 3. §37.
> Cocceji, *jus controvers.* L. I. T. 3, qu. 13.

The question was thus laid out as one of sovereignty, with Volksgewohnheit on the one side opposed by princely legislation on the other. This was a delicate topic immediately after the coup d'état, but the author marshalled his tools of scholarship to show what Hannoverian lawyers had believed for so long—that there was no necessary conflict between prince and people:

> But this rescript does not in the least decide the question whether an older law can be invalidated by a more recent custom, but whether an old custom can be set aside by a new law; it is the latter which is affirmed. For the rescript, as its title shows, is addressed "ad Proculum" [to Proculus], and therefore contains, without any doubt, an answer to his prior inquiry; and it is supposed, probably not incorrectly, that this Proculus, proconsul in Africa,

---

[7] Cf. R. Hinton Thomas, *Liberalism, Nationalism and the German Intellectuals (1822–1847)* (Cambridge, 1951), 51–80, esp. 69ff.

[8] Thiersch, quoted in ibid., 70; cf. also Paulsen, *Geschichte des gelehrten Unterrichts,* 2:462.

on the occasion of receiving several mandata from Constantine in which the latter reforms a great deal of the old religion—the people meanwhile appealing to old custom and mores [*Herkommen und Gebrauch*]—sent a report about his situation to the Emperor, and received the rescript in answer.

Gothofredus, Comment. ad. L. unc. Cod. Theodos. de longa consuet.

Averan, interpr. libr. 2. Cap. 1

G. Noodt, ad pand. tit. de legibus

Glück, Commentar, vol. 1, p. 517.

But that a legal custom can invalidate an older law follows not only from the fact that the former has force and consequence equal to that of a written law

L. 32. 33. 35. and 38. D. de legibus (1. 3.)

in that it is irrelevant, whether the legislator makes his will known expressly or tacitly; but is also established by express and clear passages in the text of the law.

The author went on to cite the provisions to the contrary of the *Allgemeines Landrecht*, as though pointedly to emphasize the difference between Prussia and Hannover.[9] There were still lawyers who hoped that the old traditions of Roman law could preserve the old unpolitical ways.

But there was not much hope—especially for a program whose attractiveness depended on the ancient reputation of the professoriate for impartiality. Savigny himself moved increasingly to the right after 1830,[10] and the reputation of the professoriate as impartial was wounded by his role as minister of legislation in the increasingly reactionary government of Friedrich Wilhelm IV.[11] The old unpolitical conservatism was being transformed into monarchical reaction. In 1837 the Hannoverian royal chanceries began to enforce neglected limitations on Aktenversendung[12] as part of a large-scale effort by the new regime to extend its power into the countryside.[13] A crackdown was underway. Most telling was an 1840 item in the *Juristische Zeitung*, wholly out of keeping with the tone of the journal in previous decades. It was entitled "Warum sprechen in monarchischen staaten die Gerichte in Namen des Königs?"—"Why do the Courts in Monarchical States Speak in the Name of the King?"—and contained only an excerpt of positivist legal philosophy by P.J.A. Feuer-

---

[9] *Juristische Zeitung* 13, no. 2 (1838): 92–94.

[10] See Rückert, *Savigny*, 219ff.

[11] For the unexpectedly illiberal character of Friedrich Wilhelm's regime, see, e.g., Rürup, *Deutschland im Neunzehnten Jahrhundert*, 168.

[12] *Juristische Zeitung*, 12, no. 2 (1837): 93–95, noting that an old provision forbidding Aktenversendung in cases in which "the dispute turned on local laws, constitutions and customs difficult for foreign judges to interpret," regularly ignored in the 1820s, was now being invoked against peasants seeking appeal from an administrative decision.

[13] See Husung, *Protest und Repression*, 103–4.

bach.[14] The item was, perhaps, intended ironically. But if so, the irony was one that spoke to a perceived political crisis of the day. The old world of coexistence of ordinance and custom, a world in which professors were a last resort of justice and courts spoke at least as often in the name of the Volk as in the name of the king was gone.

Meanwhile, in the ever more politicized atmosphere of the time, the tenacity of Savigny's commitment to one of the principle points of his program—opposition to the judiciary—wavered. As the royal reaction gathered force, Savigny's constitutionalist colleagues turned decidedly to the judiciary. From the mid-1830s on, the judges became the focus of the constitutionalist program.[15] Savigny and Puchta, with their determination that professors be the leaders of the legal world, had long opposed the legal force of precedent,[16] and by the early 1840s they were viewed as the great enemies of the claims of the judiciary and therefore of the constitutionalist program.[17] But from the late 1830s onward, Savigny had let his old determination to oppose the rule of precedent slip. Gradually he began citing precedent and acknowledging the propriety of judicial power.[18] In part he may simply have been responding to public pressure: scholars, impatient with his resistance to the principal plank in the constitutionalist platform, had begun to publish long attacks on him for his opposition to the judges.[19] In part he was, no doubt, responding to the

[14] "Warum sprechen in monarchischen Staaten die Gerichte im Namen des Königs?" in *Juristische Zeitung*, 15, no. 3 (1840): 31–32, quoting Feuerbach, *Kleine Schriften* (Nuremberg, 1833), 224n.

[15] Typical examples of the large literature over judicial independence in this period are C. v. Pfizer, *Über die Grenzen zwischen Verwaltungs- und Civil-Justiz* (Stuttgart, 1828); and (a response to Pfizer) L. Minnigerode, *Beitrag zur Beantwortung der Frage: Was ist Justiz- und was ist Administrativ-Sache?* (Darmstadt, 1835). On these controversies, see esp. Plathner, *Kampf um die Richterliche Unabhängigkeit*, 73ff. See also E. Kern, *Der Gesetzliche Richter* (Berlin, 1927), 102ff.

[16] Weller, *Bedeutung der Präjudizien*, 95ff.; Mohnhaupt, "Richter und Rechtsprechung im Werk Savignys," 258ff.; Hübner, *Kodifikation und Entscheidungsfreiheit*, 47. See also above, pp. 129–30.

[17] Thus, for example, F.G.L. Strippelmann, as he initiated publication of the decisions of the Hessian High Appellate Court in Cassel, was at particular pains to defend judicial authority against Savigny and Puchta. Strippelmann, "Einleitende Bemerkungen über die Bedeutung der O.A. Gerichts-Entscheidungen als Präjudicien," in idem, ed., *Neue Sammlung bemerkenswerther Entscheidungen des Ober-Appellations-Gerichts zu Cassel* (Cassel, 1842ff.), 1:6–7.

[18] Mohnhaupt, "Richter und Rechtsprechung," 261ff.; Hübner, *Kodifikation*, 47; Plathner, *Richterliche Unabhängigkeit*, 86. Cf. Savigny's "Ministerprogramm," Anlage to A. Stölzel, *Brandenburg-Preußens Rechtsverwaltung und Rechtsverfassung*, 2 vols. (Berlin, 1888), 2:731–50, esp. 738ff., for Savigny's friendlier attitude toward "richterliche Thätigkeit."

[19] Paul Ludolph Kritz, *Sammlung von Rechtsfällen und Entscheidungen derselben*, vol. 4,

growing success of his followers in receiving appointments to the bench, especially to the high court of the four Free Cities in Lübeck, a kind of ideological center of legal liberalism.[20] And in part, perhaps, he was recognizing the fact that the courts had begun to alter the doctrine of the Historical School in spite of the intentions of its leaders: courts began to cite Puchta's *Gewohnheitsrecht* as a justification for the rule of precedent, under the guise of making the same "scholarly" judgment every single time they were forced to examine the state of the customary law of the people.[21] But whether it was harsh attacks, unexpected or unwanted victories, or simply a desire to make peace with constitutionalism, Savigny was clearly defeated in the 1840s: even he could no longer stand by the citadel of pure professorial law making. By the mid-1850s, the defeat was such that J. E. Kuntze, one of the leading Romanist lawyers of the younger generation (though one who resisted many of the innovative tendencies of the period), could write a book entitled *Das ius respondendi in unserer Zeit* (The ius respondendi in Our Time)—entrusting the ius respondendi, not to the professors, its historic trustees, but to the judges.[22]

Revolutionary Germanism

As Roman law "impartiality" and the exclusive claims of the professoriate evanesced, the cult of German law, closely associated with the nationalist politics of the left, gained ground. With the cult of German law came a cult of German history, a kind of *Gegenantike*, a counter-Antiquity.

I have already traced much of the long history of the idea of a "German" law, stretching back to Conring and the Reichspublizisten. As I have noted, "Germanism" had already emerged as a strong force on the intellectual scene in the first years after the Napoleonic occupation, when Thibaut had charged that the *Corpus Iuris* was an alien intrusion into the internal system of the German Volksgeist. But the hostility expressed by Thibaut and others (among them, as I have suggested, Hegel) was not yet the stuff of open war. Savigny always declared his equal interest in German and in Roman sources, and he coedited his journal, the *Zeitschrift für Geschichtliche Rechtswissenschaft*, with a Germanist, K. F. Eich-

---

Uber den Gerichtsgebrauch. Hardeck, "Über das Justizwesen im Königreich Hannover," *Juristische Zeitung* 19, no. 2 (1844): 12.

[20] Prominent scholars on the bench included Martin, Heise, Wächter, Kierulff (an anti-Savignyan), Bluhme, and others. Savigny's avowed preference for the justice of free cities (noted in Mohnhaupt, "Richter und Rechtsprechung im Werk Savignys," 253; Schubert, "Savigny und die Rheinisch-Französische Gerichtsverfassung," 158) should be viewed in light of the ideological associations of the Lübeck court and of the free cities in general.

[21] Weller, *Die Bedeutung der Präjudizien*, 95–96. On the widespread citation of Puchta's book by the courts, see Scheuermann, *Einflüße der historischen Rechtsschule*, 85.

[22] J. E. Kuntze, *Das ius respondendi in unserer Zeit* (Leipzig, 1858), esp. 22ff.

horn.[23] Still, trouble loomed. In practice Savigny gave his energies to the
pandects, and the Germanists began to drift away from Savigny early on:
Jakob Grimm, initially a supporter of Savigny, became a passionate advocate of a revived German law within a few years of liberation.[24] By the
late 1820s, Germanism took on an unrelentingly bitter anti-Roman tone.
Savigny had promoted Roman law while proclaiming law to be the "organic product of the Volksgeist"; was not Roman law to be viewed instead as an infection? So indeed did exponents of a revived and newly
elaborated German law soon contend.[25]

Serious controversy was sparked by the publication in 1828 of the first
volume of Puchta's *Gewohnheitsrecht*.[26] Puchta's book, as I have already
recounted, argued that customary Übungen were to be viewed as evidence
of an understanding shared by lord and peasant, not as law-creating acts
of the parties. This argument, with its strong implication that customary
law was embodied by the jurists and by the jurists alone, might have been
calculated to inflame the sentiments of Germanists; for the latter, led by
Grimm, had embarked on a cult of the Volk that was to mark romantic
scholarship throughout the century. Germanists were convinced that the
Volk continued to create its own law, and accordingly they argued stren-
uously that Übungen were living legal sources. The political issue was
joined as soon as Puchta published his book, and from 1828 onward the
Germanists began to see a grand political significance in the idea of the
restoration of a legal order like that of the Middle Ages, a legal order
founded on "public," "solemn," law-creating acts. The philologist
W. Menzel made the point sharply by declaring that the Germanists, in
favoring the "publicity" of a reformed legal order, were "inclining
themselves toward democracy."[27] Meanwhile A. L. Reyscher responded
to Puchta by proposing a congress of Germanists to develop an alternative to Roman law.[28] The landmarks in the emergence of a Germanist

[23] In this, Savigny was typical of the consensus of 1814. Scholars of the immediate post-
liberation era—preeminently Lachmann and the young Grimm—saw no difficulty in dividing their attention between Germany and Antiquity.

[24] Cf. Bender, *Rezeption des Römischen Rechts*, 64ff.

[25] Cf. Koschaker, *Europa und das Römische Recht*, 147f.

[26] For the dating of the controversy to the late 1820s, cf. Bender, *Rezeption des Römischen Rechts*, 67. Koschaker, *Europa und das Römische Recht*, 151–52, dates hostilities
somewhat later, to the end of the 1830s, and associates them with "das Anschwellen der
nationalen Bewegung." See also the discussion by B. Kern in Dilcher and Kern, "Die juristische Germanistik," 11ff.

[27] "Sofern die Germanisten das Gewissen zum Rechtsprinzip erheben, und die Öffentlich-
keit zur Rechtsform, neigen sie sich zur Demokratie." Quoted in J. J. Müller, "Germanistik—eine Form bürgerlicher Opposition," in idem, ed., *Germanistik und Deutsche Nation*,
57.

[28] Hinton Thomas, *Liberalism, Nationalism, and the German Intellectuals*, 80.

competitor to Roman law came in quick succession. In 1835 a new leader among the Germanist lawyers, Georg Beseler, gave an address that served as a call to arms. In 1839 Reyscher and Wilda began publication of their *Zeitschrift für Deutsches Recht und Deutsche Rechtswissenschaft*.[29] Beseler's influential statement of the Germanist case, *Volksrecht und Juristenrecht* (the latter, of course, Roman law, the former German) appeared in 1843.[30] And in 1846 and 1847 the first Congresses of Germanists met, the great focuses of opposition to Roman law—focuses also of ferment leading to the Revolution of 1848.[31] When it came, this revolution was largely led by Germanists, who believed themselves, despite the skepticism of at least one peasant,[32] to express the aspirations of the German nation.

Indeed, the political and intellectual momentum was wholly with the Germanists in the 1830s and 1840s. The waning of the spirit of the Roman-law world shows, perhaps, in the inability of Roman law to hold the allegiance of one talented student: Karl Marx. Marx began his university career in 1835–36 at Bonn, where he received extensive Roman-law training.[33] He moved thereafter to Berlin, where he heard the lectures of Savigny.[34] These Roman-law studies left their mark. In particular, the

---

[29] See Jakobs, *Wissenschaft und Gesetzgebung*, 77ff.

[30] On Beseler, see Kern, *Beseler*.

[31] For the chronology of emerging opposition, see Bender, *Rezeption des Römischen Rechts*, 78–119; Wieacker, *Privatrechtsgeschichte*, 407 n. 94; Koschaker, *Europa und das Römische Recht*, 151–52; Stintzing-Landsberg, *Geschichte*, vol. 3, pt. 2, 495ff.; Dilcher and Kern, "Die juristische Germanistik," 11ff.; M. G. Losano, *Studien zu Jhering und Gerber*, Abhandlungen zur Rechtswissenschaftlichen Grundlagenforschung, vol. 55, pt. 2 (Ebelsbach, 1984), 33–45. On the *Germanistentage* of 1846 and 1847, see Müller, "Germanistentage"; cf. also Nipperdey, *Deutsche Geschichte, 1800–1866* (Munich, 1984), 312.

[32] Or so we may judge from the following rhyme, inscribed over the lintel of a Paderborn peasant dwelling in 1848 and quoted by Mooser, *Ländliche Klassengesellschaft*, 137:

> Willst du sein ein frommer Christ,
> Bauer bleib auf deinem Mist;
> Laß die Narren Freiheit singen,
> düngen geht vor allen Dingen.

> Jesus loves no man so deep
> As the peasant at his compost heap.
> Let fools cry freedom and end up hung—
> You stay home and spread your dung.

[33] For Marx's Roman-law studies at Bonn, see M. Duichin, *Il Primo Marx: Momenti di un Itinerario Intelletuale* (1835–41) (Rome, 1982), 83–84; and generally D. Kelley, "The Metaphysics of Law: An Essay on the Very Young Marx," *American Historical Review* 83 (1978): 350–67.

[34] Duichin, *Il Primo Marx*, 88–89.

analysis of Roman property relations of Savigny and Niebuhr did much
to shape the understanding of property and society expressed in *The German Ideology*.[35] But on the whole, Marx was shaped more by his rejection of Roman law than by his acceptance of it.[36] Indeed, early in the
1840s he had moved unmistakably into the Germanist camp, going so far
as to attack, in his early essay on wood theft, the Roman lawyers' rejection of split property. Speaking in the tones of romantic Germanism, he
praised the "instinctive legal sensibility" behind long-standing Germanic
customs, which safeguarded the well-being of the poor Volk.[37] The best
young minds were no longer with Savigny.

Nor was Marx the only renegade. As the decade of attacks and defec-
tions progressed, the classics suffered. J. G. Droysen, the leading German
historian of Greece, began to turn his interest to Prussia. Meanwhile, anti-
classical Germanism on the left was matched by anti-classical Germanism
on the right: in the 1840s, in the medievalizing atmosphere of the reign
of Friedrich Wilhelm IV of Prussia, the classics were attacked as "hea-
then."[38] To be sure, the classics were still vigorous: it was during the
1830s and 1840s that Niebuhr's influence began to stimulate a whole
school of Roman historians.[39] But among some young lawyers, this vigor
was intellectual more than political, as J. G. Bachofen's famous autobi-
ography suggests. Bachofen, who came from Switzerland to Berlin to
study with Savigny in 1834, later described his love of Roman law in a
letter to Savigny:

> Roman law has always struck me as a branch of classical and particularly of
> Latin philology, hence as part of a vast field encompassing the whole of An-
> tiquity. What interested me was the ancient world itself and not the applica-
> bility of its lessons to present-day needs; it was ancient and not modern Ro-
> man law that I really wanted to study. With these attitudes taken over from
> philology, I often found myself in a painful opposition to the instructors and
> books I had chosen as my guides.[40]

---

[35] See N. Levine, "The German Historical School of Law and the Origins of Historical
Materialism," *Journal of the History of Ideas* 48 (1987): 431–51. For Savigny and Niebuhr
on Roman property relations, see above, pp. 156–58.

[36] See generally Kelley, "The Metaphysics of Law."

[37] Marx, "Verhandlungen des 6. Rheinischen Landtags, Dritter Artikel: Debatten über
das Holzdiebstahlsgesetz," in *Karl Marx/Friedrich Engels Gesamtausgabe* (Berlin, 1975),
vol. 1, pt. 1, 208–9.

[38] Paulsen, *Geschichte des gelehrten Unterrichts*, 2:460 and ff. For the political beliefs of
the Germanists, see generally Müller, "Germanistik—eine Form bürgerlicher Opposition,"
5–112.

[39] E.g., Drumann, Nitzsch, Peter. Cf. Christ, *Römische Geschichte und Deutsche Geschichtswissenschaft*, 43–48.

[40] J. J. Bachofen, "My Life in Retrospect," in *Bachofen: Myth, Religion and Mother Right*,
translated by G. Boas (Princeton, N.J., 1974), 3–4.

If Bachofen was still an enthusiast for ancient Rome, he had entirely lost, in the atmosphere of political crisis in Germany, the Romanist lawyers' old sense of mission in contemporary society. Roman-law civilization began to reveal a tendency to become solely a thing of high culture, to lose its political meaning. A philologists' Roman law would hardly be law at all.

THE IMPACT OF 1848 AND THE NEW WORLD OF THE 1850s

The year eighteen forty-eight was both a blow and a boon to Romanist followers of Savigny. On the one hand, the Revolution finally made it clear that it was legislation that would free the peasants. The decades of Romanist theorizing about property law, about servitudes and prescription—all this was for naught. Events made the program of cautious scholarly reform through doctrinal manipulation of Roman law look both pointless and timid. Insofar as the Romanist lawyers of the pre-1848 world derived their sense of mission from the promise of Niebuhrian reform, their sense of mission was lost.

Eighteen forty-eight had another damaging consequence for the old Romanist program. With the collapse of the hopes of the Frankfurt parliament, Germany's lawyers at last embraced Thibaut's substitute for national unification: codification. Stimulated in part by a famous 1848 pamphlet mounting a direct attack on the idea that scholarship could provide the source of law,[41] lawyers came to view codification as inevitable. It was no longer possible to claim that the Volksgeist had somehow endorsed the monopoly of the Romanist jurists, and some leading Romanists drew the conclusion that codification could no longer be resisted. In 1852 L. Arndts, publishing one of the leading Roman-law compendia, became the first in the Romanist community not to mention the Volksgeist; he conceded that codification was inevitable.[42] The professors of Roman law widely accepted the inevitability of codification in the 1850s.[43] The scholars of the 1850s would have to work in the presence

---

[41] Kirchmann, *Die Werthlosigkeit der Jurisprudenz als Wissenschaft* (Berlin, 1848). For the changing conceptions of *Wissenschaft* that underlay this pamphlet, see M. Herberger, "Beziehungen zwischen Naturwissenschaft und Jurisprudenz in der ersten Hälfte des neunzehnten Jahrhunderts," in *Berichte zur Wissenschaftsgeschichte* 6 (1983): 79–88. For the significance of the pamphlet, see generally Jakobs, *Wissenschaft und Gesetzgebung*, 59–63.

[42] Polay, *Ursprung, Entwicklung und Untergang*, 62.

[43] Cf. Walter Wilhelm, "Das Recht im Römischen Recht," in F. Wieacker and C. Wollschläger, eds., *Jherings Erbe*, Abhandlungen der Akademie der Wissenschaften in Göttingen. Philosophisch-Historische Klasse. 3d Series, vol. 75 (Göttingen, 1970), 228 and n. 2. For the more or less universal acceptance of codification in the 1860s, see M. L. John, "The Politics of Legal Unity in Germany, 1870–1896," in *The Historical Journal* 28, no. 2 (1985): 342.

of imminent codification. Moreover, according to the jurisprudential wisdom of the day, acceptance of codification entailed acceptance of judicial interpretive authority—a point that was established in the debates surrounding the drafting of the *Allgemeines deutsches Handelsgesetzbuch* (the General German Commercial Code).[44] The great issues in the organization of justice had been decided unequivocally against Savigny.

On the other hand, the revolution contributed to a Savignyan resurgence—simply by failing. For, indeed, from the point of view of law professors whatever their politics, the measure of any successful revolution would have been its establishment of English forms of government in a unified national state.[45] In these goals revolutionary politics had suffered a clear defeat; as a result, the old, less assertive political language of the post-Napoleonic professoriate could enjoy a resurgence. Germanism lost most of its force. Conflicts would resume later, but in the immediate aftermath of the revolution Romanist and Germanist lawyers settled down to scholarly collaboration; the two civilizations no longer seemed so bitterly antagonistic.[46] A kind of reciprocal emulation continued between the two factions over which law, Roman or German, would form the basis for codification.[47] But violent denunciation of Roman law ceased, for a time, to be heard from the Germanists. The classicists, too, were reconciled to their antagonists. August Boeckh, Rector of the University of Berlin and spiritual leader of the classicists of the day, began, after 1848, to give his yearly rectoral address at the University of Berlin in German, not Latin; he also began to play on the newly established Indo-European relationship between the Germans and the Greeks, speaking of the classical civilizations as "our ancestors."[48] A new Aryan quasi-civilization seemed to offer a third way between German and classical tradition.

Meanwhile the old "rule of law" slogans and the philosophy of the

[44] This important point is made by Hübner, *Kodifikation und Entscheidungsfreiheit*, 51. This acceptance of judicial authority in turn entailed a rejection of Puchta: lawyers in the 1850s increasingly acknowledged, in Germanist fashion, the *rechtsbildende Kraft* of Übungen—a shift which put much greater emphasis on the judge's evaluation of the evidence he considered, as opposed to learned treatises. Cf. Weller, *Bedeutung der Präjudizien*, 102.

[45] D. Blackbourn and G. Eley, *The Peculiarities of German History* (Oxford, 1984) have mounted a well-known attack on the standard interpretation of the Revolution of 1848 as a failure because of the failure of Germans to establish English forms of government. This does not adequately address the desire of Germans themselves to imitate English models. The English comparison is not an artificial imposition on German history of latter-day historians. The Germans themselves wished to become English.

[46] The reconciliation was marked by the founding of the *Zeitschrift für Rechtsgeschichte* in 1861. Cf. Bender, *Rezeption des Römischen Rechts*, 12, 57.

[47] See below, pp. 220–21.

[48] Cf. Boeckh, *Kleine Schriften* (Leipzig, 1859), 2:117.

representative authority of Roman-law professors again became prominent. "Who should rule?" asked the liberal politician Schulze-Delitzsch in 1850: "Legality, the law, and the King as the law's guardian and fulfillment."[49] Such language could have been heard from any Romanist law professor in 1825. Moreover, rule of law and rule of law professors still went hand in hand: as law professors took up the great collective task of codification, they renewed the Puchtian justifications for their own influence. A Puchtian revival was possible because codification, despite Savigny's violent opposition to it, did not mean instant death for Roman-law scholarship. Indeed, it gave one last life to Roman-law scholarship, for Roman law was to become the basis for most of the codes. Interpreters of the Roman texts, accordingly, had a wholly undiminished role to play—until codification should become a reality. The decade of the 1850s was thus potentially the beginning of a last flush of enthusiasm and prestige for specialists in ancient law, and they resurrected the old pride. The psychological mark of the decade was the strange coexistence in lawyers' minds of enthusiasm with intimations of a coming end.

Enthusiasm sometimes seemed predominant. A new generation of Savigny students came to the fore in the 1850s, young lawyers who had seen him lecture and who had absorbed some of his fervor. J. C. Bluntschli, the leading public lawyer, remembered Savigny as "the beautiful and imposing man [who] stepped to his lectern like a priest of scholarship"; Rudolf von Jhering, the most brilliant Romanist lawyer of the generation, though he had doubts about Savigny's scholarly judgment,[50] thought of him as "an evangelist."[51] With this revival of the apostolic succession came the theoretical revival of Puchta. As one prominent jurist declared in 1860, the community of lawyers had a right to speak for the legal needs of the whole nation; they embodied *die allgemeine Überzeugung*—the general conviction.[52] Jhering declared himself a follower of Puchta: there had been jurists in Rome, said Jhering, as long as there had been law; indeed, the exemplary virtue of Roman law lay precisely in the fact that it *was* jurists' law.[53] Such Puchtian statements were often heard:

[49] Quoted in Sheehan, *German Liberalism*, 116.

[50] For Jhering's qualms about the doctrines of Savigny, see, e.g., Rückert, *Savigny*, 43 and n. 165.

[51] Jhering and Bluntschli are quoted in H. Vonessen, "Friedrich Karl von Savigny und Jakob Grimm," 53–54.

[52] Graf von Wartensleben in *Verhandlungen des Deutschen Juristentages* 1 (1860): 178: "Man wende gegen die Thätigkeit des Juristentages nicht ein, daß demselben keine Macht zu Gebote stehe, um seinen Vorschlägen in den einzelnen Staaten Deutschlands Geltung zu verschaffen. Es steht ihm allerdings eine Macht zu Gebote: es ist die Macht der allgemeinen Überzeugung!"

[53] Cf., e.g., Jhering, *Der Geist des Römischen Rechts auf den verschiedenen Stufen seiner Entwicklung*, 3 vols. in 4, 5th ed. (Leipzig, 1891–1906), vol. 2, pt. 2, 391, 421.

Bluntschli, for example, upon assuming the presidency of the Congress of Jurists in 1861—the year of Savigny's death as well as of the promulgation of the *Handelsgesetzbuch*, the first of the German codes—acknowledged that many Germans had doubts about the right of the jurists to legislate for the nation as a whole:

> I believe the question has been raised in the standing committee, what legal authority [*Competenz*] we have to speak about these things [i.e., codification]. I have never encountered a stranger question. In my opinion, we claim no legal authority at all, not even in juridical matters. We are not officials who arrive at decisions with binding legal force; we are simply an assembly that expresses opinions—opinions which, however, represent our best convictions. We claim only a *moral* and *scholarly* authority.[54]

Under the banner of "*moral* and *scholarly* authority" the professors could hold to the conviction of their own importance in society throughout the decade. Professors could claim that codification represented the triumph, and not the collapse, of Savigny's program; that the Volksgeist had roused itself in the era of unification, that the professors had only returned the scepter of their rule to the sovereign nation.[55]

But Savigny himself could hardly have agreed, and Roman-law codification was hardly the equivalent of Roman-law rule. If the courts were no longer to use the *Corpus Iuris*—and they clearly were not[56]—scholarship no longer had the mission Savigny believed it to have, and university professors could no longer effect unpolitical change in society by the quiet elaboration of doctrinal principles. For all their fervor, the professors of the decade of the 1850s were thus the first to stand under the shadow of eventual obsolesence. Their sense of their own impending end could be clearly read in their writings and clearly discerned in their legal reasoning and their classical scholarship.

Legal Antiquity in the Age of Codification

A new Antiquity appeared as the professors faced, at a distance, their own eclipse. The Roman-law professors of the 1850s had a kind of in-between status: they were still immensely influential, but they were destined to give way to the judiciary as leaders of the legal world. Their Antiquity fit their place in the world. Antiquity still inspired love and pride, but the feeling had grown widespread that the dignity of the classics had somehow been fundamentally wounded.

---

[54] Bluntschli, *Denkwürdiges aus Meinem Leben* (Nördlingen, 1884), 2:293–94.
[55] Cf. Koschaker, *Europa and das Römische Recht*, 290–91.
[56] Cf. Wieacker, *Privatrechtsgeschichte*, 429.

Materialism

The new Antiquity was the creation of the new public philosophy of the 1850s: materialism. Materialism was formed from an amalgamation of science and industry and was deeply colored by its association with the physical sciences and with a consistent and ostentatious practicality. Materialists flaunted a kind of hard-headedness that grew out of the idealization of engineers and a determination to cultivate a calloused attitude to the world—the attitude Saul Bellow, writing of a different decade of mixed disappointment and fervor, called "hardboileddom."[57] It is a familiar fact that the Germans of the 1850s were marked by their fear of and admiration for this materialist attitude; Marx is the best-remembered "materialist" of the era, but he was hardly alone. Law and classical scholarship were transformed in these years: materialism made the 1850s the era of a new kind of cultural crisis, in many ways much more unsettling to classicists than the challenge of Germanism in the 1840s.[58] The new alternative to Rome was not another, German, past, but the modern world, framed as an alternative to all pasts.

The main elements of materialism for the lawyers were commerce and hard science. Both seemed difficult to reconcile with high morality and the classical tradition. All the leading law professors had a particularly burning belief in the truth of science. Bluntschli, a Swiss student of Savigny who became one of the intellectual leaders of German codificationism, was a passionate disciple of Friedrich Rohmer, the so-called "materialist Messiah."[59] The Zeitgeist expressed itself more mystically in Bluntschli than in others, but all were materialists. Professors now claimed to dissect Roman law, to preserve and display its parts for the purposes of legal-anatomical education. Leist set up his "Naturstudium des Rechts"—naturalist's law—against the "naturwissenschaftliche Methode"—natural-scientific method—of Jhering and Gerber[60] as the

---

[57] S. Bellow, *Danglıng Man* (New York, 1944), 1.

[58] Cf. J. Whıtman, "From Phılology to Anthropology in Mid-Nineteenth-Century Germany," ın *History of Anthropology* 2 (1984): 214–29; "Nıetzsche in the Magısterial Tradıtıon of German Classıcal Philology," ın *Journal of the Hıstory of Ideas* 47, no. 3 (1986): 453–68; Losano, *Studıen,* 21–23. See also the dıscussion of W. Pleıster, *Persönlıchkeıt, Wılle und Freıheıt ım Werke Jherıngs,* Abhandlungen zur Rechtswissenschaftlıchen Grundlagenforschung, vol. 51 (Ebelsbach, 1982), 1–12.

[59] Cf. Bluntschli, *Denkwürdıges aus Meınem Leben,* 2:146ff, 298ff., and often.

[60] For Leıst agaınst Jherıng, see Stıntzıng-Landsberg, *Geschichte,* vol. 3, no. 2, 837. For the theory of Jhering and Gerber, cf. Jherıng, *Geist des Römischen Rechts,* vol. 1, 29ff., 40; vol. 2, pt. 1, 357ff.; "Unsere Aufgabe" ın *Gesammelte Aufsätze aus den Jahrbüchern für dıe Dogmatık des heutıgen römischen und deutschen Prıvatrechts* (Jena, 1881–86) 1:1–46. See generally W. Wertenbruch, *Versuch eıner krıtıschen Analyse der Rechtslehre Rudolf von Jherıngs,* Neue Kölner Rechtswıssenschaftlıche Abhandlungen, Heft 4 (Berlin, 1955), 19–20.

language of the natural sciences became nearly universal among the younger generation of scholars. Kuntze compared his work to that of an "anatomist,"[61] even as, in reaction, E. I. Bekker studied natural science in order to study Roman law as an "Anti-Materialist."[62]

The careers of Rudolf von Jhering and Theodor Mommsen, two of the dominant figures of scholarship in the 1850s, show how legal scholarship took shape under the contrary pressures of materialism and classical tradition. Jhering was born in 1817. He received his training between 1836 and 1842, just as the old professorial hopes were falling apart. He himself was by no means ready to abandon Roman law in those years. But because the great textbooks of Savigny and Puchta had not appeared in their entirety until 1849[63] and 1847,[64] respectively, he never felt that he had been exposed to the real glory of the ancient law: "How I thirsted, as a student, for an exciting work on Roman law," he wrote fifteen years later.[65] Even as it seemed to die, Roman-law romanticism was in a state of unfulfilled yearning. Jhering made his career as the crisis worsened: first as a *Dozent* at Berlin in 1843, then as *Ordinarius* in quick succession at Basel (1845), Rostock (1846), and Kiel (1849). When he arrived at Giessen in 1852, the university where most of his Roman-law scholarship was done, the revival of the old Savignyan language was underway. Like his contemporaries, Jhering was a devotee of Puchta[66] as well as a borrower from Hegel[67]—at least in some moments—and a believer in the antipolitics of neutrality: Jhering declared in 1851 that he had not concerned himself with politics since 1849,[68] and he praised jurisprudence as "neutral, international ground."[69]

---

[61] Kuntze, *Die Obligationen und die Singularsuccession des Römischen und Heutigen Rechts* (Leipzig, 1856), 395.

[62] Cf. Stintzing-Landsberg, *Geschichte*, vol. 3, pt. 2, 847–48.

[63] Savigny, *System des Heutigen Römischen Rechts* (1840–49).

[64] Puchta, *Cursus der Institutionen* (1841–47).

[65] Letter to Windscheid, January 29, 1853, in *Rudolf von Jhering in Briefen an seine Freunde* (Leipzig, 1913), 26.

[66] See the discussion of Pleister, *Jhering*, 170–80. The first volume of the *Geist des Römischen Rechts* was dedicated to Puchta.

[67] For Jhering's reputation for Hegelianism, see H. Lange, *Die Wandlungen Jherings in seiner Auffassung vom Recht* (Berlin-Grunewald, 1927), 32. Losano, *Studien*, 54, however, sees Jhering's Hegelianism as superficial, and Pleister, *Jhering*, 151, sees at most "Hegelreminiszenzen."

[68] Letter to Gerber, August 8, 1851, in *Jhering in Briefen an seine Freunde*, 11; also in M. Losano, ed., *Der Briefwechsel zwischen Jhering und Gerber*. Abhandlungen zur rechtswissenschaftlichen Grundlagenforschung, vol. 55, pt. 1 (Ebelsbach, 1984), 31. As a Jhering scholar has put it, the "productive" jurisprudence of the age represented a "comfortable flight in face of the political decisions of the time." D. Pasini, *Saggio sul Jhering* (Milan, 1959), 179. Cf. Wilhelm, *Zur Juristischen Methodenlehre*, 123ff. For a charming portrayal of Jhering's reactions to the events of 1848, see Losano, *Studien*, 16–19.

[69] Jhering, *Geist des Römischen Rechts*, vol. 2, pt. 2, 315.

But if Jhering was like his contemporaries in putting his hopes in a revival of Savignyan tradition, he was also like them in believing that the materialism of the day had somehow ended the proud era of the professoriate. As the natural-scientific method spread in law, Roman-law scholarship felt deeply the decline in the "honor and dignity" of Rome. Dignity—*Würde*—was the fighting word of the day. In 1852 Jhering wrote to a supporter, "You have converted to a cause anathematized by the bearers of high dignity [*Hochwürdenträger*]."[70] Jhering felt a kind of mischievous pleasure as he undermined the *Würde* of his tribe, a mischievous pleasure that showed in a manuscript that he left among his papers, an unpublished essay fragment entitled, in the natural-scientific style of the day, "Legal Scholarship Considered from the Point of View of Pathology." The essay was a mock confession, addressed to an imaginary interlocutor: "I do not know if you will blame materialism, if I confess to you, that, as in the history of the disciplines in general, so also in jurisprudence, I do not observe [only] the work of spiritual causes and forces, but rather believe in the influence of decidedly materialistic causes as well."[71]

Jhering, engaged in dialogues both imaginary and real with the "bearers of high dignity" of his time, worked to put an end to the dignity of Rome as he and his colleagues sensed the approaching indignity of powerlessness. Full of the hardboiled spirit, he set out to reinterpret Roman history in ways that would show the Romans as the paragons, not of morality, but of practicality, of utility-minded commercial energy and acumen. Jhering declared, in his *Geist des Römischen Rechts*, that the fundamental principle of Roman law was egotism: law, he wrote was "the religion of self-promotion," and that which elevated the Romans above other peoples was a "virtuosity of self-promotion," that transcended the individual and became national.[72] This was too much for his colleague J. E. Kuntze, a man who shared some of Jhering's modernist convictions, despite their scholarly conflicts. Kuntze wrote that Jhering

---

[70] Letter to Stintzing, December 26, 1852, in *Rudolf von Jhering in Briefen an seine Freunde*, 19–20. Losano, *Studien*, 21–22, in describing materialism as representing an intellectual shift from Schellingianism to Darwinianism, misses the intermediate, immoralist phase of materialism that marked so much of the young Jhering's work.

[71] "Ich weiß nicht, ob Sie auch das [*sic*] Materialismus beschuldigen werden, wenn ich Ihnen gestehe, daß ich, wie in der Geschichte der Wissenschaften uberhaupt, so auch in der Jurisprudenz, nicht das Werk von geistigen Kräften und Ursachen erblicke, sondern auch an dem Einfluß höchst materieller Ursachen glaube." Quoted from Nachlaß Rudolf von Jhering, Handschriftenabteilung, Niedersächsische Staats- und Universitätsbibliothek Göttingen, Kasten 7, Mappe 1. My thanks to the Handschriftenabteilung for permission to quote this passage.

[72] Cf. *Geist des Römischen Rechts*, 1:328 and generally 318ff., on Roman "nationale Selbstsucht"; cf. letter to Windscheid, January 1, 1853, in *Rudolf von Jhering in Briefen an seine Freunde*, 28. For this aspect of Jhering's thought, cf. also Pleister, *Jhering*, 49–52.

had misunderstood the Romans: "a higher holy aura hovers over the genius of the Roman character: . . . nobility of soul."[73] Jhering and his followers, irrationally overcome with the desire to scientize, had failed to "steel their faith in the spirit of Roman law."[74] Jhering was undeterred, and continued in subsequent volumes of his work to analyze the practical purposes of Roman law with hardly a mention of ethics. Worse yet, Jhering used the crassest commercial terms. The Romans had begun, he wrote, with the "enterprise capital" of the common human store of legal precepts; this they had returned "with richly accrued interest."[75] Niebuhr, (even though he was a banker by trade) had never spoken of Roman history in this way.

Niebuhr's great successor as leading historian of Rome, the child of the age of revolution Theodor Mommsen,[76] adopted the same style as Jhering: Mommsen's history was full of references to the "capitalists" of early Roman history.[77] Mommsen was never visited by the urges that caused Jhering to "confess," in the quiet of his study, to unspiritual tendencies. But Mommsen's readers were not slow to accuse him of being as much an enemy of Würde as Jhering. K. W. Nitzsch, a follower of Niebuhr who in 1846 had felt able to put his faith in Rome as a bulwark against "encroaching materialism,"[78] declared that Mommsen had "damaged or indeed destroyed the honor and dignity" of Roman history.[79] Mommsen made himself the target of these reproaches by his own, thoroughly materialist, recasting of Roman history, which had all the scientistic color favored by the age. Mommsen was a professor of Roman law himself—though he was a student, not of Savigny, but of the non-Savignyan of Kiel, Kierulff.[80] Like so many others, he was attracted to the

[73] Kuntze, "Das römische und das deutsche Recht in der Gegenwart," review of Jhering, Geist des Römischen Rechts, vol. 1, in Kritische Überschau der Deutschen Gesetzgebung und Rechtswissenschaft 2 (1854): 204.

[74] Ibid., 228 (referring in particular to Esmarch, Windscheid, Kirchmann, and "our most modern sceptic, Brinz").

[75] Jhering, Geist des Römischen Rechts, 1:81.

[76] For the centrality of the intellectual experience of revolution in the formation of Mommsen's work, see J. McGlew, "Revolution and Freedom in Theodor Mommsen's Römische Geschichte," Phoenix 40 (1986): 424–45.

[77] E.g., T. Mommsen, Römische Geschichte, 7th ed. (Berlin, 1881), 1:445f.; 2:395f., and often.

[78] Quoted in Yavetz, "Why Rome?" 294.

[79] Nitzsch, review of Mommsen, Römische Geschichte (erster Artikel), in Neue Jahrbücher für Philologie und Pädagogik 73 (1856): 718.

[80] Mommsen was influenced by Rubino (cf. A. Momigliano, "Interim Report on the Origins of Rome," in Terzo Contributo alla Storia degli Studi Classici e del Mondo Antico, 2:551) as well as by several members of the older historical school (cf. Heuss, Theodor Mommsen und das Neunzehnte Jahrhundert [Kiel, 1956], 34–57). The importance of Kierulff, as an influence on Jhering and Gerber as well on Mommsen, should be mentioned

thought of Puchta.[81] Contemporary reaction to this modernist Roman-lawyer-turned—(like his methodological adversary Bachofen[82])—Roman-historian, shows clearly how the growth of chemical and biologistic metaphors threatened the whole humanistic order of Savigny's era. Mommsen opposed a plain declaration to Niebuhr's exemplaristic Rome of "heroes and patriots": "Just as the greatness of the Roman Republic was not the work of leading individuals, but of a well-organized civic order, the decline of the mighty structure took place, not as a result of the perishable genius of individuals, but from general disorganization."[83] Roman history was the history of a large organism, the "state organism"[84] of the Roman nation. This organism could be traumatized by an encounter with another organism (the Celtic nation);[85] it could suffer from an ultimately fatal cancer (slavery).[86] But its individual cells were of themselves insignificant—even Caesar merely completed what organic development had prepared.[87] "Even the most insightful statesman was in the position of a doctor faced with two equally painful options: to shorten or to prolong the agony" of the Republic.[88] This treatment of Rome thrilled Mommsen's contemporaries, but it also shocked them.[89] Mommsen's use of the "chemical and physical" method, declared Nitzsch, presented "a mortal dilemma [Lebensfrage] for humanism."[90] Carl Peter, another Roman historian, made it his task to shield the secondary schools from Mommsen's influence.[91] Materialistic thought seemed to gnaw at the very root of Romanism.

The materialism of Jhering and Mommsen was bound up, in the legal politics of the time, with codificationism. In part, the connection was direct: their commercialization of Rome made Roman law seem more suitable to form the basis of a commercial code, as I shall discuss below. But in part the connection between codificationism and materialism was much more indirect and vague, a product of the sense that both movements had somehow left an old morality behind.

here. Cf. Wilhelm, Zur Juristischen Methodenlehre, 119–20. For Kierulff against Savigny, see Cappellini, Systema Iuris, 2:136–37.

[81] Cf. Heuss, "Niebuhr und Mommsen," 12–13; Theodor Mommsen und das Neunzehnte Jahrhundert, 34.

[82] Cf. L. Gossman, Orpheus Philologus (Philadelphia, 1983); Christ, Römische Geschichte und deutsche Geschichtswissenschaft, 49–54.

[83] Mommsen, Römische Geschichte, 3:92.

[84] Ibid., 3:341.

[85] Ibid., 1:333.

[86] Ibid., 3:82.

[87] Ibid., 3:476ff.

[88] Ibid., 2:380.

[89] Cf. Christ, Römische Geschichte und Deutsche Geschichtswissenschaft, 61.

[90] Nitzsch, review of Mommsen, Romische Geschichte, 717.

[91] Cf. Christ, Römische Geschichte und Deutsche Geschichtswissenschaft, 76.

Materialism was always a loose congeries of ideas and tendencies all somehow "modern." Within this ill-defined collection of things that were new, codification and materialism seemed to go together. Typical of the time, for example, was Gustav Lenz. Like many contemporaries of Marx, Lenz was a Hegelian, a Romanist lawyer, and a materialist: he thought that he had found the truth of history in a scientistic treatment of Roman law, a treatment whose imperative conclusion was the need for codification. In his *Über die Geschichtliche Entstehung des Rechts*, which was much read in the 1850s, Lenz declared Roman law to be "absolute law"—Hegelian terminology to which he gave a simultaneously Puchtian and materialist content: Roman law, understood by reference to the natural history of the races, was absolute, and was inevitably the law of jurists. This materialism, in Lenz's mind as in the minds of many of his contemporaries, implied an end to morality as pre-1848 Germans had understood it. Roman law was to be seen not as part of the "circle of morality," but as part of the power of human will. Finally, Lenz's programmatic conclusion: this jurists' law, removed from the circle of morality, must be made the basis of a new German code.[92]

This was the tenor of the time: Roman law must be removed from the "circle of morality," Rome must be vulgarized if it was to survive in the new legal world of codes and commerce. The link between vulgarization of Rome and encroaching codification played its part in the controversy that brought fame to Bernhard Windscheid. Windscheid (1818–92), the architect of the German Civil Code,[93] was born one year after Jhering, and like Jhering he experienced as a student and young scholar the great crisis of Roman law in the 1840s. The crisis, indeed, may have hit Windscheid harder than it did Jhering: Windscheid began his career as a specialist in French civil law. Only after 1848 did he turn to the Roman-law studies that would make him influential everywhere where the German Civil Code was influential. Like other Romanist lawyers of the period, he had already accepted the inevitability of codification.[94] Indeed, Windscheid made his fame with a book that bore indirectly on codification, a book about civil procedure in Rome.

Civil procedure was an issue of growing importance; as the decade wore on, lawyers increasingly demanded codification. Indeed, the case of

[92] I have not been able to see a copy of Lenz's book. For this summary I have relied on B. Delbrück, review of Lenz, *Über die Geschichtliche Entstehung des Rechts*, in *Kritische Überschau* 2 (1854–55): 115–32, esp. 120–21, and Stintzing-Landsberg, *Geschichte*, vol. 3, pt. 2, 748–50.

[93] For Windscheid's role in the drafting of the Bürgerliches Gesetzbuch, see Jakobs, *Wissenschaft und Gesetzgebung*, 101ff.

[94] Polay, *Ursprung, Entwicklung und Untergang*, 64. Cf. also Polay's comments on Dernburg in ibid., 65.

civil procedure was considered object proof of the failure of Savignyan ideas of professorial law making as an alternative to codification. The Roman-law professors had preached a national civil procedure based on their texts; meanwhile, the practicing lawyers had been obliged to use the local procedure of the various states. The result, one scholar wrote, was that "scholarship is neglected and held in contempt, and legal practice turns into a kind of plodding."[95] In an effort to make scholarship less contemptible, Windscheid turned his pen against the traditional view of Rome. Germans had erred, he wrote, in submitting scholarship so slavishly to Roman law. Roman law's status as sole master of Germany must be "put aside. It must be put aside in the same way as the entirety of ancient culture must be put aside"—that is, the ancient world must not be allowed to hinder native German development.[96] His work on the Roman *actio* was a capital instance of this project of *impietas*. Windscheid's tactic was Lenz's: Windscheid denied that Roman civil procedure was the product of a moral sensibility. In the Roman Republic, not all complaints were triable. At the beginning of his year-long term of office, the chief juridical official, a *praetor*, would publish a list of cases of which he was willing to take judicial cognizance. If a praetor was willing to accept a complaint for trial, that was called "giving an action." To Savigny, it seemed clear that actions were given in order to provide a legal means for vindicating rights, i.e., subjectively understood claims to justice.[97] Windscheid's book, entitled *Die Actio des Römischen Rechts*, interpreted praetorian procedure as follows: modern scholars, said Windscheid, are wrong in supposing that the praetor gave an action because litigants were thought to have a *right* to an action. The Romans believed that a man had an action if the state had given him an action. Higher notions of right played no part.[98] His assertion, which provoked a notable controversy[99] and paved the way for a new willingness to see procedure and substance as distinct[100] was characteristic of the age of indignity for Rome. Morality

[95] Dr. [J. J.?] Lauk, "Die neuere deutsche Gesetzgebung über den Civilproceß," in *Kritische Überschau* 1 (1854): 300. Dr. Lauk was here echoing common laments about the divorce between theory and practice in German law—laments to be heard even from Savigny.

[96] Windscheid, *Die Actio des Römischen Rechts* (Düsseldorf, 1856), 167.

[97] For Savigny's views as contrasted with Windscheid's, see W. Simshäuser, *Zur Entwicklung des Verhältnisses von materiellem Recht und Prozeßrecht seit Savigny*, Schriften zum deutschen und europäischen Zivil-, Handels- und Prozeßrecht, vol. 32 (Bielefeld, 1965). See also the discussion in Nörr, "Aktionenrecht bei Savigny."

[98] Ibid., 3–4.

[99] Windscheid was attacked by T. Muther, *Zur Lehre von der römischen Actio* (Erlangen, 1857).

[100] See Simshäuser, *Zur Entwicklung*, 79; K. W. Nörr, "Wissenschaft und Schrifttum zum deutschen Zivilprozeß im 19. Jahrhundert," *Ius Commune* 10 (1983): 152, 156.

and right were to be banished from Roman law. And the "specifically Roman" was to be "put aside."

If civil procedure was important, it was not, however, the dominant codificationist issue of the day, nor the issue that had the most important implications for the flourishing of materialist attitudes. The great issue, rather, was the coming of the first of the German codes, the General Commercial Code of 1861.

For many reasons, the Commercial Code would have been an impossible project before the 1850s. Periodic agitation for a commercial code had occurred since 1818, but without effect.[101] The Germanists had made the cause their own, demanding codification at their Congresses in 1846 and 1847.[102] Savigny's influence had, of course, done much to prevent the promulgation of any code before 1848. Moreover, commercial law had been historically customary until the mid-nineteenth century.[103] The idea of state commercial legislation was quite new in the Western world.[104] But after 1848—when a commission convened to draft a code[105]—codification was clearly inevitable, and commercial-law studies began to dominate legal academic literature.

The German Commercial Code emerged under the sponsorship of a figure who would never have been able to exercize much influence before this time: Levin Goldschmidt, a Jew, a man whom many Germans would have considered too crass by birth in any decade when Germans considered themselves less crass. The Commercial Code created by Goldschmidt was not a Roman-law code. Goldschmidt based his work on the old customary commercial law that he had devoted his life to preserving, and the final version of his work gave Roman law a distinctly subordinate place.[106] But during the 1850s it was very unclear what body of law

---

[101] See G. Köbler, "Die Wissenschaft des gemeinen deutschen Handelsrechts," in Coing and Wilhelm, eds., *Wissenschaft und Kodifikation des Privatrechts im Neunzehnten Jahrhundert*, 1:289ff.

[102] Hübner, *Kodifikation*, 52.

[103] Commercial law, customary in the Middle Ages, had lost some of its customary character in the early modern period. See O. Scherner, "Die Wissenschaft des Handelsrechts," in *Coing Handbuch*, 2:799–800.

[104] This new idea made headway in the mid-nineteenth century not only in Germany, but also in the United States. For the idea of commercial law as positive rather than customary law in the United States, see the fine discussion of R. Bridwell and R. Whitten, *The Constitution and the Common Law* (Lexington, 1977).

[105] Köbler, "Gemeines deutsches Handelsrecht," 278.

[106] Article 1 directed judges, in cases in for which the code provided no clear resolution, to draw first on "Handelsgebräuche" and second on "das allgemeine bürgerliche Recht." Quoted in Hübner, *Kodifikation*, 51 n. 229. On Goldschmidt, see esp. M. Pappenheim, "Goldschmidt," in *Zeitschrift für das gesamte Handelsrecht* 47 (1898): 1–49; Stintzing/ Landsberg, *Geschichte der deutschen Rechtswissenschaft*, vol. 3, pt. 2, 938–49; H. Sinzheimer, *Jüdische Klassiker der deutschen Rechtswissenschaft*, Frankfurter Wissen-

would form the basis of the new code, and Romanist lawyers still hoped that the law of the coming commercial age would be based on their ancient texts.[107] Accordingly, their efforts in the 1850s were spent disproportionately in the very difficult attempt to fashion usable commercial doctrine out of Roman law.

Their methodological guide in this attempt was Puchta. Puchta had argued for a "productive" jurisprudence for an age in which scholars had to make law in order to hold the line against codification. The watchword of the 1850s, codificationist though the decade was, was still "production": "Up to now, we have been receptive," wrote J. E. Kuntze in an influential 1856 pamphlet, "The time has come to be productive."[108] Jhering, the most famous scholar of the time as a champion of "productive" (or, as the case might be, "constructive") jurisprudence,[109] saw production as opposed to reception just as Kuntze did: he wrote to his principle collaborator, Gerber, that Roman law must free itself from the received authority of Paulus and Ulpian just as biology had freed itself from Aristotle and Pliny.[110] In making such pronouncements, Jhering claimed the authority not only of Puchta, but also of Savigny: his natural-scientific method, he declared, aimed only to purge Rome of its irrelevant elements, to identify "the specifically Roman, in order to send to its grave what has not already been buried"[111]—a phrase he had borrowed directly from Savigny.[112] But in practice, contemporaries could not mistake the profound change in tone of Roman-law scholarship.

For in the effort to "produce" a new commercial law Jhering and his

schaftliche Beiträge, Rechts- und Wirtschaftswissenschaftliche Reihe, vol. 7 (Frankfurt a.M., 1953), 51–72.

[107] Köbler, "Gemeines deutsches Handelsrecht," 292.

[108] Kuntze, *Der Wendepunkt der Rechtswissenschaft* (Leipzig, 1856), 21. On this pamphlet, see Herberger, "Beziehungen zwischen Naturwissenschaft und Jurisprudenz," 86. The emphasis on "production" as opposed to "reception" was, it should be noted, complicated by the practice of referring to the sixteenth-century introduction of Roman law as the "Reception." It is noteworthy that introductions to *Pandektenlehrbucher* began regularly to concede, in this period, that the Reception of Roman law had in some respects been to Germany's disadvantage. Cf. Bender, *Rezeption des Römischen Rechts*, 75.

[109] E.g., Jhering, "Unsere Aufgabe," in *Gesammelte Aufsätze*, 1:3. For Jhering's theories of "construction," see Losano, *Studien*, 120–29.

[110] Jhering, letter to Gerber, July 17, 1852, in *Rudolf von Jhering in Briefen an seine Freunde*, 14; also in Losano, ed., *Briefwechsel zwischen Jhering und Gerber*, 51. Cf. Jhering, "Unsere Aufgabe," 3.

[111] *Jhering in Briefen an seine Freunde*, 26. This was what Jhering later called "Ausscheidung des Krankheitsstoffs" (*Geist des Römischen Rechts* 4:241). Compare Mommsen's belief that historical knowledge showed the uselessness of obsolete legal principles (Heuss, *Theodor Mommsen*, 39.)

[112] Savigny, *System des heutigen Römischen Rechts*, 1:xv. On the theoretical resemblance between the method of Jhering and that of Savigny, see Wilhelm, *Zur Juristischen Methodenlehre*, 121.

contemporaries were opening up a whole new terrain for Romanism. Roman law had never been used by merchants, and it was not well suited to
the needs of commercial life: as Kuntze put it, "in modern commercial
life . . . we do not have the good fortune to be able to wander shepherded
by the Roman jurists."[113] Romanist lawyers had made some tentative efforts to develop a Roman commercial law since the 1830s.[114] But Roman
law did not lend itself to such projects. Commercial affairs involved op-
erations—negotiable instruments, transfers of title to goods in transit—
that could not be readily analyzed within the ambit of Roman doctrine.
Faced with this problematic misfit between Roman law and nineteenth-
century commerce, Jhering and his contemporaries responded by attempting to extract usable legal principles from the ancient law, legal
principles that would seem sensible and serviceable to German business-
men. This was legal "construction," as Jhering called it, designed for an
age in which industrial production was the world's new force.

Sometimes Jhering's method brought him great success.[115] But it was
not an easy task to portray Roman law as an instrument of commercial
utility. In his struggle to cast Rome as a modern commercial society, Jhering often resorted to speculation which had no foundation in the ancient
texts; he was occasionally guilty of forced interpretation and circular
logic, and his studies accordingly stirred up controversy. The first two
essays he published in the journal he founded in 1857, the *Jahrbücher für
die Dogmatik des heutigen römischen und deutschen Privatrechts*, exemplified his aspirations and his methods. Both essays were intended to
distill from Roman law principles that could be made to conform to modern commerce; both essays were forced to confront the void of commercial history and of suitable commercial doctrine in the ancient texts.

Of course there *was* commercial doctrine to be found in the Roman
texts. But it offered few answers to the problems posed by a modern commercial life full of multiparty transactions. Modern commerce required a
doctrinal flexibility that Roman law—like Anglo-American law—was
hard pressed to provide. Indeed, Jhering's first essay, entitled "Übertragung der *reivindicatio* auf Nichteigentümer," (Transfer of reivindicatio to
Non-Owners), attempted to extract from Roman law some doctrinal ba-

---

[113] Kuntze, *Wendepunkt*, 35. For the unsuitability of Roman law to industrial society
generally, see F. Wieacker, "Pandektenwissenschaft und Industrielle Revolution," in idem,
Industriegesellschaft und Privatrechtsordnung (Frankfurt a.M., 1974), 55–78.

[114] Esp. K. Einert, *Das Wechselrecht nach dem Bedürfniss des Wechselgeschäfts im Neunzehnten Jahrhundert* (Leipzig, 1839), and various works of H. Thöl, later an ally of Jhering.
For the importance of Einert and Thöl, see the discussion of Kuntze, *Wendepunkt*, 15 and
ff.

[115] See esp. Jhering's famous essay, "Culpa in contrahendo, oder Schadensersatz bei nichtigen oder nicht zur Perfection gelangten Verträgen," in *Gesammelte Aufsätze*, 1:327–425.

sis for types of commercial transactions whose legal intractability would still trouble American lawyers a century later as they worked to create the Uniform Commercial Code: the type that involved the transfer of title to goods exemplified by traffic in bills of lading. Jhering's problem took, typically, the following form: a middleman in nineteenth-century commerce ordinarily received a bill of lading for wares before the wares actually arrived. The middleman might sign over the bill of lading to some third party, who, in turn, might sign over the bill of lading to yet another third party. It was settled commercial law that whichever party held the bill of lading, with an appropriate endorsement, had a legally enforceable claim to the goods.

This circulation of bills of lading is perfectly comprehensible to us. But to mid-nineteenth-century Romanist lawyers, such bills (like negotiable instruments[116]) seemed to escape all effort at legal analysis. There was very little in Roman law that was at all analogous to the modern negotiable document that represents a claim cognizable in court.[117] Romanist lawyers tended to think of legal claims as nontransferable—as the glossators had put it, a title "inhered in the bones and innards" of its holder and could not be passed on.[118] Moreover, Romanist lawyers—like most pre-nineteenth-century lawyers—thought either in terms of personal obligations created by direct relations between two individuals or in terms of property rights created by direct relations between an individual and a thing. These two kinds of rights—*in personam* and *in rem* rights—exhausted the vocabulary of Roman legal thought. But by what kind of right could the holder of a bill of lading claim goods that he had never seen from a person he had never met? The holder of the bill of lading had what can only be thought of as an owner's *in rem* action for the goods, a *reivindicatio*—a claim that one be awarded a particular thing by right of ownership. But it was good Roman law that only owners or possessors could claim any *in rem* action, and no effort of legal analysis could make nineteenth-century transshippers into either owners or possessors. Accordingly, Roman law did not, by and large, influence German commerce. German courts simply enforced the rights of the bill's holder as a matter of customary commercial law and ignored Roman law as thoroughly irrelevant to this sort of transaction. As Jhering put it: "Com-

---

[116] For an account of the first coherent analysis of negotiable instruments in Germany—an analysis that astounded lawyers, see C. Bergfeld, "Die Papiergeldtheorie Karl Einerts und ihre Bedeutung für das Wechselrecht," in *Aspekte europäischer Rechtsgeschichte: Festgabe für Helmut Coing*, Ius Commune Sonderheft 17 (Frankfurt a.M., 1982), 1–28.

[117] See K. Luig, *Zur Geschichte der Zessionslehre* (Cologne/Graz, 1966), 2ff. The medieval Roman lawyers had more difficulty in analyzing this problem than did the late antique Roman lawyers themselves. See ibid., 11ff.

[118] Luig, *Zessionslehre*, 12 and often.

merce manages to satisfy its needs without bothering itself about the question of whether its institutions and legal principles, which enrich our law, fit the ideas of the jurists or confuse them."[119] But jurisprudence, too, had to remain faithful to its own systematic doctrinal instinct, and lawyers had to "construct" satisfactory doctrine even if their efforts went wholly unappreciated by the merchants whose needs they served.[120] This was Jhering's project (as it was a number of his contemporaries'): to uncover, somehow, doctrine both faithful to the tenor of Roman law and serviceable for the needs of modern title-transfers.

It was a project that already had a long history of failure. Lawyers had attempted unsuccessfully to deal with this problem for centuries.[121] Usus modernus lawyers had, for example, proposed classic usus modernus solutions: that "natural law" justified title transfers or that the Roman rules had "never been received."[122] In the first half of the nineteenth century lawyers invested a great deal of energy in finding a Roman-law solution to the problem.[123] Nevertheless, midcentury lawyers were unhappy with existing doctrine, and many solutions were proposed. Windscheid's *Actio*, for example, was intended, in part, to offer a solution to this very problem: by detaching the "action" from the right, Windscheid hoped to ease the transferability of title.[124] Of the many solutions proposed, Jhering's was neither the most original nor the most successful. Nevertheless it is worth tracing the steps of Jhering's reasoning (which by and large merely repeated the orthodoxy of the day[125]) in order to gain a better understanding of the mental world of "constructive" Roman lawyers of the mid-nineteenth century.

Jhering presented his analysis in his essay "Transfer of reivindicatio to Non-Owners." Such a transfer of reivindicatio did not exist, as such, in the Roman sources. Rather, Jhering abstracted the concept of "transfer of reivindicatio" from a variety of procedures discussed by the ancient jurists. Reivindicatio was a Roman-law action (i.e., a right to sue) given to owners who wished to recover a *res*, a thing, which was in the possession of someone else. Ordinarily an action, a right to sue, could not be transferred to a third party—if A had a right to an action of reivindicatio in order to recover his wheelbarrow from B, A could *not* transfer that right to C; in Anglo-American terms, choses in action were not alienable. This nontransferability of the right to sue presented grave difficulties for

[119] Ibid., 176–77.
[120] Ibid.
[121] See generally Luig, *Zessionslehre*.
[122] Ibid., 37ff.
[123] The most successful of these was Mühlenbruch. See ibid., 77.
[124] See the discussion of Windscheid's book in ibid., 90ff.
[125] Ibid., 89.

commerce. It meant that the problem of bills of lading was very nearly insoluble. Any third party who failed to receive clear title to the goods from his middleman would have no legally enforceable right to those goods. The middleman, if he could not transfer the goods, had to be able to transfer a legal right to the goods, or he could not do business. "In practical terms," wrote Jhering, "the document of title [*das Cessionsdocument*] serves commerce as a legal surrogate of the goods, that is to say, he [i.e., the middleman] transfers the surrogate instead of the wares."[126] However, Jhering had to concede that Roman law could provide no basis for such a transfer of the right to sue. Thus, if one was to make any use of Roman law at all, one had to "construct" transferability of right to sue: "Thus a theory of the transfer of *vindicatio* is, in fact, a practical necessity. Roman law never expressly established such a theory, but it provides the necessary starting points [*Anhaltspunkte*] for constructing a theory through analysis."[127] "Through Roman law, beyond Roman law!" as he had declared in his statement of purpose in the first number of his journal.[128] Jhering would break Roman law down into its constitutent doctrinal pieces and then reassemble those pieces into a modern machine.

Jhering's act of analysis and construction in the essay was a tour de force, if only because Jhering was able to find so few examples of transferred right to sue in the Roman texts—altogether, he identified no more than fifteen or twenty cases in all of the *Corpus Iuris*, *none* of them involving commerce. First he identified six or seven types of *cessio* of reivindicatio. These were cases like that of a bailee who had lost the thing entrusted to him without fraud or fault. Roman lawyers required the unfortunate bailee to pay a money judgment to the owner. In compensation, they awarded the bailee a partial reivindicatio. The bailee could claim the thing, if it should turn up—but with a critical proviso: the owner himself must neither claim the thing nor renounce his right to it. By asserting or renouncing his own right, the owner would destroy the bailee's merely derivative right.[129] Obviously this sort of derivative right, destroyable by the owner, was *not in itself* an adequate foundation for a Roman law of bills of lading. Roman law did, to be sure, offer a kind of potential escape. Suppose A had a claim on goods held by party B. Suppose further that party A attempted to transfer his claim to party C. Party C's right was, under the law I have just described, destructible—with, however, an exception. If party A formally gave notice of the transfer of title, through a so-called *denuntiatio*, the claim to the goods would inhere in party C. Jhering laid great weight on *denuntiatio* as offering a salvation

---

[126] Jhering, "Übertragung der *reivindicatio*," 108.
[127] Ibid.
[128] Jhering, "Unsere Aufgabe," 45.
[129] See Jhering's discussion at ibid., 104ff.

for the use of Roman law.[130] Clearly, however, a commercial law that
required such regular *denuntiationes* would hardly allow smooth func-
tioning of commerce. But Jhering added to his analysis another, complementary type of transferred reivindicatio that appeared in later centuries
in the history of Roman law, a type of transferred reivindicatio good only
against the owner. This was *reivindicatio utilis*. Later antique Roman
lawyers awarded a reivindicatio utilis, a kind of equitable reivindicatio,
to parties who had been deprived of their ownership of a thing through
unjust operation of the law. Thus, for example, a party to a broken marriage engagement would be awarded a reivindicatio for the marriage gifts
he had given his betrothed.[131] In this and similar cases, the lawful owner
would be forced to yield the thing owned in the name of equity. The doctrine of reivindicatio utilis seemed to supply the defect in cessio of vindicatio: Reivindicatio utilis showed that Roman jurists were capable of
contemplating transferred actions good against the legal owner. Together,
these complementary doctrines offered an adequate foundation for the
construction of a theory of bills of lading. The original sender of the
goods, through his bill of lading, gave the holder in due course a cessio of
vindicatio; the holder in due course could in turn make a further cessio.[132]
This conceptualization, if alien to the Roman texts themselves, was comparatively true to the spirit of Roman law, and it would make it possible
for "we modern jurists" to serve the needs of "the commercial class."[133]

One might well ask whether Jhering, in this essay, had not pointlessly
expended a great deal of energy. Indeed, Jhering would undergo a conversion, some five years later, after which he would himself denounce
these sort of "constructive" essays in a burst of public self-mockery.[134]
What, after all, had Jhering done in his "Übertragung der reivindicatio
auf Nichteigentümer"? He had begun his research knowing what doctrine he wanted to find. His immense learning and diligence had produced
only a sparse few prefigurings of that doctrine in Roman law, none of
them really on point, since none of them involved commerce. He had then
bridged the wide gap between Roman sources and modern necessities by
declaring his activity to be "constructive." But why bother? If Jhering
knew from the beginning that modern life required transferability of

---

[130] Luig, *Zessionslehre*, 89. For doubts about the exact reach of this doctrine in ancient
law, see ibid., 6ff.

[131] See Jhering, "Übertragung des *reivindicatio*," 124.

[132] Ibid., 182–83.

[133] Ibid., 187.

[134] See Jhering's famous satire (in part, of course, a self-satire), "Im juristischen Begriffs-
himmel," in *Scherz und Ernst in der Jurisprudenz*, 13th ed. (Leipzig, 1924), 245–333. Cf.
H. Kantorowicz, "Jherings Bekehrung," *Deutsche Richterzeitung* 6, no. 2 (1914): cols. 84–
87.

rights to sue for goods, why not simply campaign for transferability of rights to sue for goods? Why not dispense with the palpably unsatisfactory Roman-law underpinnings?

Jhering could not dispense with the Roman-law underpinnings, because he was constrained by two related intellectual forces. On the one hand, there was the strength of legal tradition, which disposed him to work within Roman law just as American lawyers work within precedent. Limited by legal tradition, Jhering was moving with caution and gravity, just as most lawyers in most times and places move with caution and gravity. But Jhering was not by temperament a cautious or a grave man, and the pious love of legal tradition would not of itself explain his faithfulness to Roman law. There was another urge at work in his desire to revivify Rome for modern commerce: the cultural love of Rome, thoroughly inculcated in Jhering as in all German university-bound schoolchildren. He was, like most educated Germans, an honest admirer of Antiquity, and he wanted to make it live in an alien modern world.

Attacks by other scholars could force him to admit that admiration for the beauty of Antiquity, and the desire to command support among traditionally minded lawyers were, in the end, his motivation. The second of his essays in the *Jahrbücher für die Dogmatik des heutigen römischen und deutschen Privatrechts*, for example, came out in two parts, the second a response to the many critics who found his interpretations of Roman law forced and twisted. Jhering admitted that he had gone searching through the ancient texts for passages that could fit his preconceived scheme. But he needed Roman law, both for its beauty and for the authority of tradition it represented:

> As for the passages in question, I gladly admit that I only looked for them and found them after I had already independently constructed the [legal theory of this essay], and that I added them more as a decoration, and to soothe the sort of personalities who think a proposition of law ought to have some textual support [*zur Decoration und zur Beruhigung zeugnißbedürftiger Gemüther*], than because they served as indispensable support for my position.[135]

To make Roman law serve as decoration and documentation, however, Jhering was forced to rewrite the history of ancient life, to find commercial or commercializable features in ancient Rome—in this the second essay was very much like the first.[136] This same codificationist imperative lay behind his *Geist des Römischen Rechts*, as behind the relevant pro-

---

[135] Jhering, "Mitwirkung für fremde Rechtsgeschäfte (Fortsetzung)," in *Gesammelte Aufsätze*, 1:249.

[136] Jhering, in this essay, relied occasionally on undefended assertions that Roman lawyers *must* have been conscious of the imperatives of commerce. See esp. ibid., 226.

nouncements in Mommsen's *Römische Geschichte*: without a commercial Antiquity, there would be no future for Roman law.

CONCLUSION

In the end, of course, there *was* no future for Roman law. Roman law was fated to become what it already was for Bachofen in the 1830s: a branch of classical philology, a "decoration," to use Jhering's word. Once Roman law became philology, Roman-law professors would mean little in German society. In 1858 Windscheid read a kind of eulogy for professorial lawmaking, as codification came to seem inevitable and Roman law was displaced from the curriculum. He no longer made the claims Savigny had once made for the authority of jurists. Jurists, said Windscheid, represented, not the Volksgeist, but the classics [*klassische Bildung*]; and the classics, in turn, represented only a kind of other-worldly beauty. Germany was to become a united fatherland, with a single code, and the call went out to every man to cultivate the national well-being,

> not least to the teacher of Roman law. He too should contribute his labor to the cathedral of national magnificence; he should help to prepare a German law for the German people. . . . And when this work is achieved the science of Roman law shall not perish, but shall bloom in a new glory. For our discipline shall have the opportunity to give itself wholly to the contemplation of Roman law as such, of pure Roman law, without any extraneous thoughts; the opportunity to immerse itself in the vision of that greatness and beauty. And this too will be a practical task, the most practical of tasks, the task of education. When the authority of the *Corpus Iuris* is put aside in Germany, then, for the first time, the lecture halls of the teachers of Roman law shall truly fill; and the rising generations shall sit at their feet, to learn, not contempt for national law, not the foolish exaltation that bends all law to the measure of Roman concepts—but what one learns from Antiquity, what beauty is. They shall learn what a law worthy of the name should be. . . . [T]hey shall learn that the true jurist is a man about whom stand ranged the concepts of his law, like marble statues, sharp and cold, and yet familiar figures, awaiting only the wave of his hand to set themselves in motion and accomplish his work.[137]

This was the charming future picture of pride and impotence among the professors of Roman law a half century after Savigny had declared the vocation of his time for legal science. Their stuff was now to be the art, and not the rule, of law.

[137] Windscheid, "Das Römische Recht in Deutschland," in *Gesammelte Reden und Abhandlungen* (Leipzig, 1904), 48. For Windscheid on the need to "germanize" Roman law, see Cappellini, *Systema Iuris*, 2:170ff.

CONCLUSION

I CLOSE this study in 1861. This was the year of Savigny's death. It was also the year of the completion of the Commercial Code, after which the process of codification irreversibly began, and the displacement of the ancient texts inevitably loomed. After the Commercial Code, codes for other areas of law followed at intervals until 1900, when the great *Bürgerliches Gesetzbuch* came into force, at last completely displacing the *Corpus Iuris* from the German legal order. With codification, interpretive authority passed to the class of the judges, against whose authority Savigny and Puchta had struggled so hard and so long. The post-1861 world would be one of very different issues.

Nevertheless, my closing date may seem artificial. For it is true that the history of Roman law in Germany did not end in 1861, despite the triumph of codification. Centuries of Romanist scholarship had produced a body of systematic argument and fine reasoning that could survive as a basis for codification, even in a legal world in which the study of ancient Roman law as such was losing its centrality. Indeed, Windscheid succeeded so well in associating himself with the codificationist cause that his voice became the dominant one in the first drafting committee for the *Bürgerliches Gesetzbuch*.[1] The *Bürgerliches Gesetzbuch* that became the law of the German Empire on January 1, 1900, embodied a wide range of Romanist doctrine and adopted the systematic structure developed by the Romanist lawyers over centuries and consecrated by Savigny's *System des Heutigen Römischen Rechts*.[2] Thus the Romanist lawyers, in some sense, won out.

And yet, after 1861, all had changed. For the type of Roman lawyer familiar throughout the early modern period, the scholar both learned in the remains of classical antiquity and deeply engaged in the legal political battles of his own time, was vanishing. In consequence, the ideological

---

[1] For the place of Windscheid and the influence of *Pandektistik* in the drafting of the *Bürgerliches Gesetzbuch*, see Wieacker, *Privatrechtsgeschichte*, 473; Jakobs, *Wissenschaft und Gesetzgebung*, 101ff.

[2] For the reliance on the Romanist system in the *Burgerliches Gesetzbuch*, see B. Dölemeyer, "Kodifikationen und Projekte," in *Coing Handbuch*, vol. 3, pt. 2, 1610–11; see also the excellent doctrinal survey of H. Coing, "Einleitung," in *J. von Staudingers Kommentar zum Bürgerlichen Gesetzbuch*, 12th ed. (1978), 1:30–40. For the Germanist elements, see H. Krause, "Der deutschrechtliche Anteil an der heutigen Privatrechtsordnung," in *Juristische Schulung* 10 (1970): 313–21.

history that has been my concern in this study, the long history of the link in German minds between Roman law and the changing idea of Rome itself, was at an end in 1861. The study of Roman history and the understanding of Roman law diverged. Scholars of ancient Roman law began to take a different attitude toward their texts. No longer searching for usable legal principles, they began studying the text-history of the *Corpus Iuris*.[3] Historians of Rome, too, moved in new directions, no longer seeking to make Rome somehow relevant to the work of lawyers in their own day. Ancient Roman law had become, as Ernst Fuchs, a champion of the cause of judicial authority, triumphantly declared in 1912, "mere philology."[4]

To be sure, the ideological battles of the 1850s had left their traces in the understanding of Roman law. The idea of Roman law promoted by the young Jhering and Mommsen—the idea of Roman law as commercial, capitalist, materialist—hung on in German legal debate after 1861. Particularly in the eyes of its detractors, Roman law became what it had never been before the generation of the 1850s set to work on it: "bourgeois" law, with all the ugly connotations "bourgeois" acquired in the last decades of the century. Jhering and Mommsen had, indeed, unintentionally put a kind of mark of Cain on Roman law, visible to its enemies on both the left and the right in succeeding generations. The new antibourgeois, anti-Roman rhetoric made its appearance in 1888, when the first draft of the *Bürgerliches Gesetzbuch*, heavily Romanist in structure and content, was published. The draft provoked an immediate outcry, most notably from the great Germanist of the later nineteenth century, Beseler's student Otto von Gierke. To Gierke, the draft was "un-German, out of touch with the Volk, remote from the wellsprings of creativity."[5] He conceded that the Romanists had "sent to its grave" that which was "specifically Roman."[6] But left behind was a thing of lifeless abstrac-

---

[3] One of the most telling pieces of evidence for the connection between codification and the philologization, so to speak, of Roman law, is the history of *Interpolationenforschung*. Despite F. Blu(h)me's discovery of the so-called "masses" in the *Corpus Iuris* in 1820 (F. Blu[h]me, "Die Ordnung der Fragmente in den Pandectentiteln," in *Zeitschrift für Geschichtliche Rechtswissenschaft* 4 [1820]: 257–472), the great works of *Interpolationenforschung* date only from the 1880s, "eben als das BGB in Sicht kam" (Wieacker, *Privatrechtsgeschichte*, 420; cf. Koschaker, *Europa und das Römische Recht*, 294–96; Bender, *Rezeption des Römischen Rechts*, 79; Polay, *Ursprung, Entwicklung und Untergang*, 60; Heuss, *Mommsen und das Neunzehnte Jahrhundert*, 40.)

[4] Fuchs was anticipating the elimination of Roman law as a required examination subject. Quoted in Bender, *Rezeption des Römischen Rechts*, 91.

[5] Gierke, *Der Entwurf des Bürgerlichen Gesetzbuches und das deutsche Recht* (Leipzig, 1889), 2: "nicht deutsch . . . nicht volkstümlich . . . nicht schöpferisch."

[6] Gierke, *Entwurf*, 2: "mit Weglassung vieler noch vegetierender römischer Institute." Gierke's phrase clearly echoed the similar phrases of Jhering and Windscheid, and indeed of Savigny.

tions—though lifeless abstractions that betrayed a "hidden social agenda": "the individualistic and exclusively capitalistic agenda of the purest Manchesterism . . . that hostility to the communal impulse in man, that program of fortifying the strong in their struggle against the weak, that frankly anti-social tendency."[7] In mounting this attack, Gierke joined forces with the socialist Anton Menger[8]; Germanism had abandoned its old emphasis on "public, solemn acts," and become a communitarian legal ideology, deeply akin to socialism.[9] Roman law, for its part, had become, in the eyes of its critics at least, bourgeois individualist law, and it was to remain bourgeois individualist law in the eyes of its critics—among them, chillingly, the Nazis; Point 19 of the Nazi Party Program of 1920 demanded "the replacement of Roman law, which serves the materialist world order, with a German common law."[10] The 1850s view of Roman law became, indeed, definitive: to contemporary historians, too, the Roman law of Windscheid has remained unmistakeably bourgeois.

But to Romanist lawyers themselves, Roman law had become something other after 1861. To Romanist lawyers, Roman law had lost its historical and ideological associations and become a gorgeous analytical vocabulary—Windscheid's "concepts . . . like marble statues, sharp and

[7] Gierke, Entwurf, 3–4: "Wohnt ihm [dem Entwurf] dennoch etwa eine verborgene sociale Tendenz inne? Aber dann wäre dies die individualistische und einseitig kapitalistische Tendenz des reinsten Manchestertums, es wäre jene gemeinschaftsfeindliche, auf die Starkung des Starken gegen den Schwachen zielende, in Wahrheit antisociale Richtung, mit der im übrigen unsere neue deutsche Gesetzgebung so entschieden gebrochen hat!"

[8] Menger, Das bürgerliche Recht und die besitzlosen Volksklassen: Eine kritik des Entwurfs eines burgerlichen Gesetzbuches für das Deutsche Reich, 2d ed. (Tübingen, 1890). For a bibliography of reactions to the draft, see G. Maas, "Bibliographie des bürgerlichen Rechts: Verzeichnis von Einzelschriften und Aufsätzen uber das im Bürgerlichen Gesetzbuche für das Deutsche Reich vereinigte Recht, 1888–1898," in Archiv für Bugerliches Recht, 16 (1899): 36–56.

[9] Gierke's seminal contribution to this "communalization" of German law was, of course, his Das deutsche Genossenschaftsrecht, 4 vols. (Berlin, 1868–1913). The beginnings of the new emphasis on communal existence among the Germanists dated to 1831, the date of Wilda's Das Gildenwesen im Mittelalter. See G. Dilcher, "Zur Geschichte und Aufgabe des Begriffs Genossenschaft," in G. Dilcher and B. Diestelkamp, eds., Recht, Gericht, Genossenschaft und Policey: Studien zu Grundbegriffen der germanistischen Rechtshistorie (Berlin, 1986), 114. For an earlier stage in the development of this new emphasis in Germanist legal thought, dating to an 1835 work by Beseler, see J. Schröder, "Zur Älteren Genossenschaftstheorie: Die Begründung des modernen Körperschaftsbegriffs durch Georg Beseler," Q. Fior. 11/12 (1982–83): 399–459. On Gierke, see further, G. Dilcher, "Genossenschaftstheorie und Sozialrecht: Ein 'Juristensozialismus' Otto von Gierkes?" Q. Fior. 3/4 (1974–75): 319–65; S. Pfeiffer-Munz, Soziales Recht ist deutsches Recht: Otto von Gierkes Theorie des sozialen Rechts untersucht anhand seiner Stellungnahmen zur deutschen und zur schweizerischen Privatrechtskodifikation, Zürcher Studien zur Rechtsgeschichte, 2 (Zürich, 1979), and the literature cited there. On the drafting of the Bürgerliches Gesetzbuch, see now John, Politics and the Law.

[10] See the discussion of Koschaker, Europa und das Römische Recht, 311–15.

cold, and yet familiar figures, awaiting only the wave of [the jurist's] hand to set themselves in motion and accomplish his work." Visions of a revivified past had ceased to move Romanist lawyers later in the nineteenth century. What moved them was no longer the idea of a materialist Rome, nor attachment to the constitution of the Holy Roman Empire. What moved them was no idea of Rome or Roman tradition at all. As the historian of the politics of the *Bürgerliches Gesetzbuch* has observed, what moved the Romanist lawyers of the later nineteenth century was "systematic precision and consistency."[11] Love of their conceptual vocabulary marked the Romanist lawyers after 1861, not any vision of society. Indeed, the Romanist lawyer who did have a vision of society, Jhering, simply abandoned Roman law. Jhering, the great Romanist, discarded his Puchtian "jurisprudence of concepts" in the years around 1860, turning from the professorial elaboration of Roman concepts, first to Darwinianism,[12] then to the judicial balancing of individual, class, and social interests.[13] Among the Romanist lawyers whom the apostate Jhering left behind in 1861, Roman law became the Roman law that Weber knew, the Roman law of rationalization, of the calculus of concepts.

Indeed, past the milestone of 1861, we are on the threshold of the age of Weber, whose view of German Roman law has dominated most twentieth-century scholarship. And it is with Weber that I would like to close, contrasting his analysis of the history of German Roman law with my own. It has not been my desire, in this study, to argue that Weber's assessment of the ultimate significance of the German history of Roman law was wrong. Quite the contrary. Viewed from Weber's vantage point in the Wilhelmine Reich, the four-century history of Roman law in Germany *was*, perhaps, best understood as a part of the history of the rise of the German administrative state. Perhaps German Roman law *was* best described as a vector of rationalization, as the legal instrument by which German bureaucrats perfected their rule.[14] The great systematic tradition that extended back to Melanchthonian neoscholasticism, through Wolffianism and into the *System* of Savigny, had shown itself, in Weber's time, to possess a life of its own, independent of all the historical associations

---

[11] M. John, "The Politics of Legal Unity in Germany, 350. Cf. also John, "The Peculiarities of the German State: Bourgeois Law and Society in the Imperial Era," *Past and Present* 119 (1988): 126: "jurisprudential imperatives involving technical systematization and legal 'certainty' were the principal forces determining the content of the German civil code."

[12] Jhering, *Der Kampf ums Recht* (Vienna, 1872).

[13] For a survey of of Jhering's intellectual development, see Lange, *Die Wandlungen Jherings*. See also, F. Wieacker, *Rudolf von Jhering*, 2d ed. (Stuttgart, 1968).

[14] See the discussion of B. Vogel, "Beamtenkonservatismus: Sozial- und verfassungsgeschichtliche Voraussetzungen der Parteien in Preußen im frühen 19. Jahrhundert," in D. Stegmann et al., eds., *Deutscher Konservatismus im 19. und 20. Jahrhundert: Festschrift für Fritz Fischer* (Bonn, 1983), esp. 27ff.

of Roman law with Roman civilization. In the end, it was the systematic tradition, in its Pandectist incarnation, that had survived in Germany, while the *Corpus Iuris* and visions of the Roman past had been displaced. Whatever the intentions of Romanist lawyers before 1861, those intentions had ceased to matter.

But in this study I have written from a vantage point earlier in the nineteenth century, when the intentions and visions of Romanist lawyers still seemed to matter, when the strength of Roman law still lay in its grand association with ancient Rome. I have attempted to describe the aspirations of romantic Romanist lawyers who never wished to erect a bureaucratic state in Germany. I have tried to show that during the romantic era Roman law was the focus of a kind of visionary political activity that, if it is to be described in Weberian terms at all, would have to be called charismatic. As Roman law reestablished its rule after two generations of decline, the great Romanist lawyers were guided, not by any bureaucratizing impulse, but by an unshakeable conviction that they were the living representatives of an ancient Roman order. Whatever the ultimate effect of their work on the rise of the German bureaucracy, the great Romanist lawyers did not promote the use of Roman law because they believed it was "rational." They promoted the use of Roman law because they believed it carried within it the seeds of a rebirth of Rome.

Of course, intentions fail, and it may well have been the end-result of the Romanist lawyers' work that Germany became a grey, bureaucratic, illiberal, administrative state. The Romanist lawyers provided, intentionally or not, a highly rationalized educational matter very well suited to the training of bureaucrats. They also cultivated a kind of corporate spirit, and a sense of independence that later provided the basis for the corporate spirit of the judges of the Wilhelmine era. Perhaps that same lawyers' spirit also helped provide the basis for the corporate spirit of the Wilhelmine bureaucrats. Nevertheless, Savigny, his followers, and his students were not of a grey or bureaucratic mentality, and no proper description of them can be written until we forget, for a moment, the world of the Wilhelmine Reich. From the last years of Kant's life into the time of Hegel and that of Marx, German law was made by charismatics, and true historical accuracy means bringing those charismatics to life.

That has been my purpose in this study: I have attempted to describe, accurately, the aspirations of the romantic Romanist lawyers. As I hope I have shown, the charismatic lawyers of Savigny's Berlin have always been poorly understood by those who believed them to be reactionaries. They are better described as visionary constitutionalist reformers. They believed that the key to reform lay in the three centuries of tradition that bound together Roman law with the Holy Roman Empire. They believed that reviving those three centuries of tradition could end feudalism in

Germany, without either revolution or what they viewed as the excessive economic freedom of the English kind. Through these beliefs they made romantic philosophy an active political force in German life. Their program of reform provided the closest link between the life of the German countryside and the life of the German intellectual centers. It was as lawyers' conceptualizations that the details of the German social order were introduced into the calculations of the intellectual leaders in Berlin and Heidelberg, and it was in the courts of law that the intellectual fervor of the capitals brushed the lives of the German peasants. The program of the generation of Savigny failed, as I have shown, in practice. Nevertheless, the charismatic sense that they represented Rome survived among Romanist lawyers for a few years more. After 1848 new great Romanist lawyers—Jhering, Windscheid, and their contemporaries—began presenting themselves to their compatriots as the representatives of a very different Rome, of Rome as commercial empire. A modern Germany governed by a commercial law based on Roman principles would, they implied, be a kind of Rome, and not some new, grey European state. But Jhering and his contemporaries were no more successful than Savigny and his had been. The Germany that emerged was neither Savigny's free Rome, nor Jhering's commercial Rome. The Germany that emerged was indeed Weber's Wilhelmine Reich, in which the schemes of Savigny and Jhering counted for naught.

Between the intention and the act, in short, fell the shadow. For better or for worse, the history of Roman law in Germany proved to be a history of unrealized hopes and miscalculated programs—as, sadly, has so much of modern legal history.

GLOSSARY OF TERMS AND PHRASES

Agrarfrage — The "agrarian question." The debate over agrarian reform in nineteenth-century Germany.

Aktenversendung — "Dispatching the record." The practice of referring a decision to a law faculty.

Allgemeines Landrecht (ALR) — The General Territorial Law of Prussia, promulgated in 1794.

Bauer — "Peasant."

Bauernbefreiung — The "liberation of the peasants." The nineteenth-century abolition of feudal and quasi-feudal obligations imposed on German peasants.

Bund — The Federation of German States established after the end of the Napoleonic Wars.

Bürger — "Citizen." The adjective form, "bürgerlich," can carry the connotation "bourgeois."

Bürgerliches Gesetzbuch (BGB) — The Civil Code of Germany, in force from January 1, 1900.

Colon, colonus — "Serf" or "peasant" in legal Latin.

"Communis opinio doctorum habet vim consuetudinis" — The "shared opinion of the learned has the force of custom." Under this medieval doctrine, an interpretation of learned law prevailing among learned lawyers had force of law in the same way that an understanding of customary law prevailing among those subject to the custom in question had force of law.

Code — See *Corpus Iuris Civilis.*

Corpus Iuris Civilis — The "Corpus of the Civil Law." The authoritative collection of Roman legal texts, compiled on the order of the emperor Justinian in the sixth century A.D. and including the "Institutes" (an introductory textbook); the "Digest" or "Pandects" (a bulky collection of opinions on legal matters by jurists of the classical period in Roman law); the "Code" and the "Novels" (collections of decrees by the emperors). Often referred to by the shorthand "Corpus Iuris," but not to be confused with the "Corpus Iuris Canonici," the collection of Canon legal texts.

Digest — See *Corpus Iuris Civilis.*

Dominium directum, dominium utile — "Direct ownership" and "equitable ownership." Medieval and early modern lawyers distinguished between these two types of ownership, in order to attribute some form

of ownership to both the lord of a given piece of land and to the person
who held of that lord. See also *Obereigentum* and *Untereigentum*.

Eigenbehörige — Personal dependents. The term used in some parts of
Germany for peasants subject to the obligation to perform services or
render payments in return for the right to hold land.

Epieikeia — The Aristotelean idea of justice or equity.

Fürst — "Prince."

Fürstendiener — "Servant of the prince." The ideal of the government
official as personal servant of his prince, rather than as "Staatsdiener,"
"servant of the [impersonal] state."

Gemeinsame Überzeugung — "Common conviction." A shorthand
phrase for the doctrine, found especially in the theory of Puchta, that a
given custom can claim force of law only if all affected parties are inwardly convinced that that custom has binding force.

Gericht — "Court."

Gesetz — Positive law, law created through the process of statute-mak-
ing, rather than through force of custom or by scholarly interpretation
of preexisting sources.

Gutachten — Formal legal opinion.

Iudex, iudices (pl) — Ancient Roman lay judges. Cases were ordinarily
disposed of by such lay judges, acting under the instructions of a magistrate.

Ius commune — "Common law," or "shared law." Under the system of
the ius commune as it prevailed in later medieval and early modern
Europe, some form of written law was used to supplement customary
or local law when the applicability of the latter form of law could not
be proven. Ius commune can refer either to the supplementary written
law or to the system of the ius commune taken as a whole.

Ius honorarium — Law made by Roman magistrates with the authority
to interpret, correct, and supplement the traditional rules of Roman
law.

Ius scriptum — "Written law."

Ius scripturae — "The law of scripture," i.e., of the bible.

Juristenrecht — A law made by jurists.

Kammergericht — "Cameral court." A name for a high appellate court
in early modern German states.

Land — A German territory, sovereign in most matters but theoretically
subject in certain ways to the authority of the Holy Roman Empire
(before 1806) or the Federation of German States (after 1815).

Landfriede — A Public Peace, under which violent acts in a given territory were subject to the jurisdiction of public courts.

Mos Gallicus — The "French Style" of Roman-law scholarship, which emphasized understanding the original meaning of the legal texts of the Corpus Iuris.

Mos Italicus — The "Italian Style" of Roman-law scholarship, which emphasized the practical contemporary application of the legal texts of the Corpus Iuris.

"Nec vi, nec clam, nec precario" — "Not by force, nor by stealth, nor by permission." Three conditions, under Roman law, for the prescriptive acquisition or loss of a right.

Obereigentum — "Over-property." The German term for *dominium directum*, characterizing the lord's rights in a piece of feudal property. See also *Untereigentum*.

Pandects — The Digest of Justinian.

Pandektistik — "The systematic study of the Pandects"; a name given to nineteenth-century Roman-law scholarship in Germany.

Possessio — Actual, physical control, as opposed to ownership, of a thing.

Reception (or Rezeption)—The introduction of Roman law into German legal practice, especially in the sixteenth century.

Recht — Law.

Rechtsstaat — Literally, "the state [governed by] law"; the peculiarly German idea of rule of law.

Reich — Empire, especially Holy Roman Empire.

Reichskammergericht — The "Imperial Cameral Court." One of two high appellate courts in the early modern Holy Roman Empire (the other being the *Reichshofrat*, or "Imperial Aulic Council").

Reichspatriotismus — Late eighteenth-century enthusiasm for the institutions and traditions of the Holy Roman Empire.

Reichspublizist — A scholarly specialist in the institutional structure and history of the Holy Roman Empire.

Reichspublizistik — The scholarly study of the institutional structure and history of the Holy Roman Empire.

Reichsstand — An "estate," or semi-sovereign constituent unit, of the Holy Roman Empire, with the right to participate in the governing institutions of the Empire.

Schöffen or Schöppen — German lay judges, without any formal legal training but regularly sitting to decide cases.

Schöppenstuhl — A traditional German lay court, staffed by Schöppen.

Servitus — "Servitude." A legal right to use someone else's property.

Spruchkollegium — Members of a law faculty sitting as a court to decide cases sent to them by Aktenversendung. Judgments of a Spruchkollegium were ordinarily authored by one professor, but were issued as the decision of the entire Spruchkollegium.

Staatsdiener — "Servant of the State." As opposed to "Fürstendiener," a

Staatsdiener is a government official who views himself as a representative of the impersonal state, rather than as the personal servant of the prince.

Stand — "Estate." A status group in society; also (as "*Reichsstand*") a constituent unit of the Holy Roman Empire.

Übungen — Actions that could potentially give rise to an obligation under customary law.

Untereigentum — "Under-property." The German term for *dominium utile*, characterizing the vassal's or serf's rights in a piece of feudal property. See also *Obereigentum*.

Usus modernus pandectarum, usus modernus — "The modern application of the Pandects." The characteristic type of German legal scholarship of the late seventeenth and eighteenth centuries, marked by its practical bent and its willingness to draw eclectically on a wide variety of legal sources.

Verjährung — "Prescription." The acquisition or loss of a right by virtue of a lapse of time.

Volk — A "people" or a "nation," conceived of, in the romantic era, as a unit, with a shared history and a shared spirit or soul.

Volksgeist — The "soul of a nation or people" or the "spirit of a nation or people."

WORKS CITED

ARCHIVAL MATERIAL

Nachlaß Rudolf von Jhering. Handschriftenabteilung, Niedersächsische Staats- und Universitätsbibliothek Göttingen.

STATUTES, DECREES, OFFICIAL ACTS

Chur-Braunschweig-Lüneburgische Landesordnungen und Gesetze. 5 vols. Göttingen: Universitätsbuchhandlung, 1739–40.
Deutsche Reichstagsakten. Göttingen: Vandenhoeck und Ruprecht, 1956ff.
Monumenta Germaniae Historica.
Peinliche Gerichtsordnung Karls V. von 1532. Edited by G. Radbruch. Leipzig: Reclam, n.d.
Sammlung der verordnungen und ausschreiben welche für sämmtliche provinzen des Hannoverschen staats, jedoch was den Calenbergischen, Lüneburgischen und Bremen- und Verdenschen theil betrifft, seit dem schlusse der in denselben vorhandenen gesetzsammlungen bis zur zeit der feindlichen usurpation ergangen sind. Edited by E.P.J. Spangenberg, Hannover: Hahn, 1819–25.
Staatsarchiv des teutschen Bundes. Edited by J. L. Klüber. 2 vols. Erlangen: Palme und Enke, 1816–17.
Statuta und Gewohnheiten der Chur und Marcke Brandenburg. Edited by L. Distelmeier. Jena: Henning Gross, 1607.
Verhandlungen des Deutschen Juristentages. Tübingen: Mohr, 1860.

COLLECTIONS OF DECISIONS AND LEGAL OPINIONS

Fälle und Entscheidungen aus dem Gebiete des Eigentumsrechts. Edited by G. Struckmann. Lüneburg: Herold und Wahlstab, 1828.
Gutachten der Juristen-Fakultäten in Heidelberg, Jena und Tübingen, die hannoversche Verfassungsfrage betreffend. Edited by F. C. Dahlmann. 2d ed. Jena: Fromann, 1839.
Neue Sammlung Bemerkenswerther Entscheidungen des Oberappellationsgerichts zu Cassel. Edited by B. W. Pfeiffer. 5 vols. Hannover: Hahn, 1818–20.
Neue Sammlung bemerkenswerther Entscheidungen des Ober-Appellations-Gerichts zu Cassel. Edited by F.G.L. Strippelmann. Cassel: T. Fischer, 1842ff.
Rechtsgutachten und Entscheidungen des Spruchcollegii der Universität Heidelberg. Edited by C. Martin. Heidelberg: Mohr und Zimmer, 1808.
Sammlung von Rechtsfällen und Entscheidungen derselben. Edited by P. L. Kritz. 5 vols. in 3. Leipzig: Barth, 1833–45.
Selectae Decisiones et Resolutiones Tubingenses, ex Jure Publico, Feudali, Canonico, Criminali, Civili & Statutario, Nomine Inclutae Facultatis Juridicae Conscriptae. Edited by W. A. Schoepff. 2 pts. Tübingen: Cotta, 1726–30.

Seufferts Archiv für Entscheidungen der obersten Gerichte in den deutschen Staaten. Edited by J. A. Seuffert. Munich: Cotta, 1847ff.

Staats-Archiv. Edited by C. F. Häberlin. 60 pts. in 16 vols. Helmstedt/Leipzig: n.p., 1796–1808.

Wetzlarische Nebenstunden: Auserlesene beym Höchstprießlichen Cammergericht entschiedene Rechtshändel. Edited by J. U. Freiherr von Cramer. 128 pts. in 32 vols. Ulm: Wohler, 1755–73.

PERIODICAL LITERATURE

Allgemeine Juristische Monatsschrift für die Preußischen Staaten. Edited by Mathis. Berlin: n.p., 1805ff.

Jahrbücher für die Preußische Rechtswissenschaft und Rechtsverwaltung. Edited by K. A. v. Kamptz. Berlin: Hitzig, 1814ff.

Juristische Zeitung für das Königreich Hannover. Lüneburg: Herold und Wahlstab, 1826ff.

Kleins Annalen der Gesetzgebung und Rechtsgelehrsamkeit in den Preussischen Staaten. Edited by E. F. Klein, Berlin/Stettin: Nicolai, 1801ff.

Kritische Überschau der deutschen Gesetzgebung und Rechtswissenschaft. Edited by L. Arndts, J. C. Bluntschli, L. Pözl. Munich: Verlag der Literarisch-artistschen Anstalt, 1853–59.

OTHER WORKS CITED

Abel, G. *Stoizismus und Frühe Neuzeit.* Berlin: de Gruyter, 1977.

Achenwall, G. *Staatsverfassung der Europäischen Reiche.* 3d ed. Göttingen: Vandenhoeck, 1756.

Angermeier, H. "Introduction" to *Deutsche Reichstagsakten unter Maximilian I.* In idem, ed. *Deutsche Reichstagsakten.* Mitllere Reihe, Band 5, Band 1 [*sic*], Teil 1. Göttingen: Vandenhoeck und Ruprecht, 1981, 23–86.

———. *Königtum und Landfriede im deutschen Spätmittelalter.* Munich: Beck, 1966.

———. *Die Reichsreform, 1410–1555: Die Staatsproblematik in Deutschland zwischen Mittelalter und Gegenwart.* Munich: Beck, 1984.

———. "Die Reichsregimenter und ihre Staatsidee." *Historische Zeitschrift* 211 (1970): 265–315.

Apel, Johannes. *Isagoge per Dialogum in Quatuor Libros Institutionum.* Bratislava: Erasmus Poherl, 1540.

Aretin, K. O. von. *Heiliges Römisches Reich.* Veröffentlichungen des Instituts für Europäische Geschichte, Mainz, Abt. Universalgeschichte, no. 38. 2 vols. Wiesbaden: Steiner, 1967.

Armstrong, E. *Emperor Charles V.* 2 vols. London: Macmillan, 1910.

Arnaud, A.-J. *Les origines doctrinales du Code Civil Français.* Bibliothèque de philosophie du droit, vol. 9. Paris: Librairie Générale de Droit et de Jurisprudence, 1969.

Bachofen, J. J. *Bachofen: Myth, Religion and Mother Right.* Translated by G. Boas. Princeton, N.J.: Bollingen, 1974.

Bader, K. S. "Arbiter, arbitrator seu amicabilis compositor: Zur Verbreitung einer Canonistischen Formel in Gebieten nördlich der Alpen." *ZZS (K)* 46 (1960): 239–76.

Bader, K. S. "Approaches to Imperial Reform at the End of the Fifteenth Century." In Strauss, ed., *Pre-Reformation Germany*, 136–161.

Bähr, O. *Der Rechtsstaat.* Cassel/Göttingen: Wigand, 1864.

Bailyn, B. *Ideological Origins of the American Revolution.* Cambridge, Mass.: Harvard University Press, 1967.

Baker, K. M. "A Script for the French Revolution." *Eighteenth-Century Studies* 14 (1981): 235–63.

Baumgärtel, G. *Die Gutachter- und Urteilstätigkeit der Erlanger Juristenfakultät in dem ersten Jahrhundert ihres Bestehens.* Erlanger Forschungen. Reihe A: Geisteswissenschaften, vol. 14. Erlangen: Universitätsbund Erlangen, 1962.

Becker, H.-J. "Kommentier- und Auslegungsverbot." *Handwörterbuch zur deutschen Rechtsgeschichte* (1978) 2: cols. 963–74.

———. "Diplomatik und Rechtsgeschichte: Conrings Tätigkeit in den Bella Diplomatica um das Recht der Königskrönung, um die Reichsfreiheit der Stadt Köln und um die Jurisdiktion über die Stadt Lindau." In Stolleis, ed., *Conring* 335–53.

Behmer, F. E. (praeside J. J. Moser). *De Transmissione Actorum.* Frankfurt a. Oder: Schwarz, 1739.

Behrendts, W. *Reformbestrebungen in Kursachsen im Zeitalter der französischen Revolution.* Leipziger Historische Abhandlungen, Heft 38. Leipzig: Quelle und Meyer, 1914.

Behrens, C.B.A. *Society, Government and the Enlightenment: The Experience of Eighteenth-Century France and Prussia.* New York: Harper and Row, 1985.

Bellow, Saul. *Dangling Man.* New York: Vanguard, 1944.

Below, G. *Die Ursachen der Rezeption des Römischen Rechts.* Munich/Berlin: Oldenbourg, 1905.

Bender, P. *Die Rezeption des Römischen Rechts im Urteil der Deutschen Rechtswissenschaft.* Rechtshistorische Reihe, vol. 8. Frankfurt a.M./Bern: Peter Lang, 1979.

Benson, R. L. "Political *Renovatio*: Two Models from Roman Antiquity." In Benson and Constable, eds., *Renaissance and Renewal*, 339–86.

Benson, R. L., and G. Constable, eds. *Renaissance and Renewal in the Twelfth Century.* Cambridge, Mass.: Harvard University Press, 1982.

Bergfeld, C. "Die Papiergeldtheorie Karl Einerts und ihre Bedeutung für das Wechselrecht." In *Aspekte europäischer Rechtsgeschichte: Festgabe für Helmut Coing.* Ius Commune Sonderheft 17. Frankfurt a.M.: Klostermann, 1982, 1–28.

Beseler, G. *Volksrecht und Juristenrecht.* Leipzig: Weidmann, 1843.

Bethmann-Hollweg, M. A. von. "Erinnerung an Friedrich Karl von Savigny als Rechtslehrer." *Zeitschrift für Rechtsgeschichte* 6 (1867): 42–81.

———. *Der Civilprozeß des gemeinen Rechts in geschichtlicher Entwicklung.* 6 vols. in 7. Bonn: Marcus, 1864–74.

Birtsch, G. "Freiheit und Eigentum: Zur Erörterung von Verfassungsfragen in der deutschen Publizistik im Zeichen der Französischen Revolution." In R. Vierhaus, ed., *Eigentum und Verfassung: Zur Eigentumsdiskussion im ausgehenden achtzehnten Jahrhundert.* Veröffentlichungen des Max-Planck-Instituts für Geschichte, vol. 37. Göttingen: Vandenhoeck und Ruprecht, 1972, 179–92.

Blackbourn, D., and G. Eley. *The Peculiarities of German History.* Oxford: Oxford University Press, 1984.

Bleek, W. *Von der Kameralausbildung zum Juristenprivileg.* Berlin: Colloquium Verlag, 1972.

Blickle, P. *The Revolution of 1525.* Translated by T. Brady and H. Midelfort. Baltimore: Johns Hopkins University Press, 1982.

Blu(h)me, F. "Die Ordnung der Fragmente in den Pandectentiteln." *Zeitschrift für Geschichtliche Rechtswissenschaft* 4 (1820): 257–472.

Bluntschli, J. G. *Denkwürdiges aus Meinem Leben.* 2 vols. Nördlingen: Beck, 1884.

Böckenförde, E.-W. "Der deutsche Typ der konstitutionellen Monarchie im neunzehnten Jahrhundert." In idem, *Staat, Gesellschaft und Freiheit,* 112–45.

———. "Entstehung und Wandel des Rechtsstaatsbegriffs." In idem, *Staat, Gesellschaft und Freiheit,* 65–92. Originally in *Festschrift für A. Arndt.* Frankfurt a.M.: Europäische Verlagsanstalt, 1969.

———. *Staat, Gesellschaft und Freiheit.* Frankfurt a.M.: Suhrkamp, 1976.

Boeckh, A. *Gesammelte Kleine Schriften.* 7 vols. Leipzig: Teubner, 1858–74.

Boehmer, J. H. *Introductio in Ius Publicum Universale ex Genuinis Iuris Naturae Principiis deductum.* Frankfurt/Leipzig: In Officinis Trattnerianis, 1758.

———. *Ius ecclesiasticum Protestantium, usum modernum iuris canonici iuxta seriem decretalium ostendens et ipsis rerum argumentis illustrans adiecto triplice indice.* 5 vols. in 4. Halle: Litteris et impensis Orphanotrophei, 1727–36.

Bohnert, J. "Beiträge zu einer Biographie Georg Friedrich Puchtas." *Zeitschrift der Savigny Stiftung für Rechtsgeschichte, Germanistische Abteilung* 96 (1979): 229–42.

———. *Über die Rechtslehre Georg Friedrich Puchtas.* Freiburger rechts- und staatswissenschaftliche Abhandlungen, vol. 41. Karlsruhe: C. F. Müller, 1975.

Boldt, H. *Die Deutsche Staatsrechtslehre im Vormärz.* Beiträge zur Geschichte des Parlamentarismus und der politischen Parteien, vol. 56. Düsseldorf: Droste, 1975.

Bornhak, C. "J. J. Moser als Professor in Frankfurt/Oder." *Forschungen zur Brandenburgischen und Preußischen Geschichte* 11 (1898): 329–39.

Brandt, H. *Landständische Repräsentation im deutschen Vormärz: Politisches Denken im Einflußfeld des monarchischen Prinzips.* Politica, vol. 31. Neuwied/Berlin: Luchterhand, 1968.

Bravo, B. *Philologie, histoire, philosophie de l'histoire: Étude sur Droysen.* Zaklad Narodowy Imienia Ossolinskich. Wroclaw: Polska Akademia Nauk, 1968.

Bretschneider, C. G. Preface to *Chronicon Carionis.* In Melanchthon, *Opera,* 12:707–10.

Bridwell, R. and R. Whitten. *The Constitution and the Common Law.* Lexington: Lexington Books, 1977.

Brie, S. "Die Stellung der deutschen Rechtsgelehrten der Rezeptionszeit zum Gewohnheitsrecht." In *Festgabe für F. Dahn*, 3 vols. in 1. Breslau: M. and H. Marcus, 1905, 1:129–64.

———. *Der Volksgeist bei Hegel und in der Historischen Schule.* Berlin/Leipzig: Rothschild, 1909.

Brocher, C. K. S. *Zachariä, sa vie et ses oeuvres.* Paris: A. Durand et Pedone-Laurel, 1869.

Brunschwig, H. *Enlightenment and Romanticism in Eighteenth-Century Prussia.* Translated by F. Jellinek. Chicago: University of Chicago Press, 1974.

Brutti, M. "L'intuizione della proprietà nel sistema di Savigny." *Q.Fior.* 5/6 (1976–77): 41–103.

Buchda, G. "Die Spruchtätigkeit der Hallischen Juristenfakultät." *ZZS (R)* 62 (1942): 210–94; 63 (1943): 251–318; 64 (1944): 223–75; 68 (1948): 308–47.

Buchholz, S. *Abstraktionsprinzip und Immobiliarrecht: Zur Geschichte der Auflassung und der Grundschuld.* Ius Commune Sonderheft 8. Frankfurt a.M.: Klostermann, 1978.

———. "Einzelgesetzgebung." In *Coing Handbuch*, vol. 3, pt. 2, 1626–1773.

———. "Die Quellen des deutschen Immobiliarrechts im 19. Jahrhundert." *Ius Commune* 7 (1978): 250–325.

Bülow, F. von (continued first by T. Hagemann, then by E. P. J. Spangenberg). *Practische Erörterungen aus allen Theilen der Rechtsgelehrsamkeit.* 10 vols. Hannover: Hahn, 1798–1837.

Bülow, O. *Das Ende des Aktenversendungsrechts.* Freiburg i.B.: Mohr, 1881.

Burmeister, K. *Das Studium der Rechte im Zeitalter des Humanismus im deutschen Sprachbereich.* Wiesbaden: Guido Pressler Verlag, 1974.

Buschmann, A. "Ursprung und Grundlagen der geschichtlichen Rechtswissenschaft: Untersuchungen und Interpretationen zur Rechtslehre Gustav Hugos." Diss., Munich, 1963.

Buss, B. "Die historische Schule und die Beseitigung des geteilten Eigentums in Deutschland." Diss., Munich, 1966.

Bussi, E. *Il Diritto Publico del Sacro Romano Impero alla fine del XVIII Secolo.* 2 vols. Milan: Giuffrè, 1957.

Buszello, H. "Gemeinde, Territorium und Reich in dem politischen Programm des deutschen Bauernkrieges." In *Der Deutsche Bauernkrieg, 1524–1526.* Edited by U. Wehler. Geschichte und Gesellschaft, Sonderheft 1. Göttingen: Vandenhoeck und Ruprecht, 1975, 105–28.

———. *Der deutsche Bauernkrieg von 1525 als politische Bewegung.* Berlin: Colloquium Verlag, 1969.

Canning, J. *The Political Thought of Baldus de Ubaldis.* Cambridge Studies in Medieval Life and Thought, Fourth Series, vol. 6. Cambridge: Cambridge University Press, 1987.

Cappellini, P. *Systema Iuris.* Per la Storia del Pensiero Moderno Giuridico, vols. 17 and 19. Milan: Giuffrè, 1984–85.

Cargill Thompson, W.D.J. *The Political Thought of Martin Luther.* Edited by P. Broadhead. Sussex: Harvester Press, and Totowa, N.J.: Barnes & Noble, 1984.

Carion, J. *Chronicon Carionis.* Edited by P. Melanchthon. In Melanchthon, *Opera*, 12: 707–1094.

———. *Chronica durch Magistrum Johan Carion/ Vleissig zusammen gezogen/ meniglich nützlich zu lesen.* Wittenberg: Rhau, 1532.

Caroni, P. "La Cifra Codificatoria nell'opera di Savigny." *Q. Fior.* 9 (1980): 69–111.

———. "Savigny und die Kodifikation." *ZSS(G)* 86 (1969): 97–176.

Carsten, F. L. *Princes and Parliaments in Germany.* Oxford: Oxford University Press, 1959.

Cassirer, E. *The Philosophy of the Enlightenment.* Translated by F. Koelln and J. Pettegrove. Princeton N.J.: Princeton University Press, 1951.

Cenci, L. *Tractatus de censibus, totam materiam constituendi, conservandi, & extinguendi annuos census juxta formam, & stylum etiam in Romana curia adhiberi solitum, theoricè, & practicè explicatam continens: Cui accesserunt non modo additiones, & Sacrae Rotae romanae decisiones jam separatim impressae, sed & aliae pleraeque ab ipso authore manuscriptae suis locis repositae sunt; necnon Joannis Baptistae Leonelij, & Ludovici Molinae commentaria ad bullam Pij v. De censibus.* Lyons: Sumptibus Arnaud, Petri Borde, Ioannis & Petri Arnaud, 1676.

Christ, K. *Römische Geschichte und Deutsche Geschichtswissenschaft.* Munich: Beck, 1982.

———. *Römische Geschichte und Wissenschaftsgeschichte.* 3 vols. Darmstadt: Wissenschaftliche Buchgesellschaft, 1983.

———. *Von Gibbon zu Rostovtzeff.* Darmstadt: Wissenschaftliche Buchgesellschaft, 1972.

Clarke, M. L. *Classical Education in Britain, 1500–1900.* Cambridge: Cambridge University Press, 1959.

Coing, H. "Einleitung." In *J. von Staudingers Kommentar zum Bürgerlichen Gesetzbuch.* 12th ed. Berlin: Staudinger, 1980, 1–123.

———. "L'Influence de la France sur le Droit Allemand." In *Gesammelte Aufsätze.* Frankfurt a.M.: Klostermann, 1982, 1:263–76.

———. *Die Rezeption in Frankfurt.* Frankfurt a.M.: Klostermann, 1939.

———. *Römisches Recht in Deutschland.* Ius Romanum Medii Aevi, pt. 5, subpt. 6. Milan: Gluffrè, 1964.

———. "Das Verhältniß der positiven Rechtswissenschaft zur Ethik im Neunzehnten Jahrhundert." In *Recht und Ethik.* Studien zur Philosophie und Literatur des neunzehnten Jahrhunderts, vol. 9. Edited by J. Blühdorn and J. Ritter. Frankfurt a. M.: Klostermann, 1970, 11–28.

———. ed., *Handbuch der Quellen und Literatur der neueren Europäischen Rechtsgeschichte.* Munich: Beck, 1973ff.

Coing, H. and W. Wilhelm, eds. *Wissenschaft und Kodifikation des Privatrechts im Neunzehnten Jahrhundert.* Studien zur Rechtswissenschaft des neunzehnten Jahrhunderts. Frankfurt a.M.: Klostermann, 1974ff.

Conrad, H. *Deutsche Rechtsgeschichte.* 2d ed. 2 vols. Karlsruhe: C. F. Müller, 1966.

———. *Die Geistigen Grundlagen des Allgemeinen Landrechts.* Arbeitsgemeinschaft für Forschung des Landes Nordrhein-Westfalen, Abt. Geisteswissenschaft, Heft 77. Cologne: Westdeutscher Verlag, 1958.

———. *Rechtsstaatliche Bestrebungen im Absolutismus.* Arbeitsgemeinschaft für Forschung des Landes Nordrhein-Westfalen, Abt. Geisteswissenschaft, Heft 95 Cologne: Westdeutscher Verlag, 1961.

Conring, H. *De Origine Iuris Germanici.* In Conring, *Opera*, 7 vols. Edited by J. W. Göbel. Reprint. Aalen: Scientia, 1970–73, 6:75–188.

Conze, W. *Die liberalen Agrarreformen Hannovers.* Hannover: Landbuch-Verlag, n.d.

Coquille, G. *La Coutume de Nivernais.* Edited by M. Dupin. Paris: Henri Plon, 1864.

Curzon, A. de. "L'Enseignement du Droit Français dans les Universités aux XVIIᵉ et XVIIIᵉ siècles." *Nouvelle Revue Historique de Droit Français et Étranger* 43 (1919): 209–69, 305–64.

D.S.N.H.P. *Observatio Juris Practica de Academiis Germaniae in Transmittendis Actis.* Leiden: Ultrajecti Sumptibus, 1722.

Dahm, G. "On the Reception of Roman and Italian Law in Germany." In Strauss, ed., *Pre-Reformation Germany*, 282–315.

Dany, P. "Grundeigentum und Freiheit: Liberalisierung der preußischen Agrarverfassung in der Zeit von 1794 bis 1850." Diss., Kiel, 1970.

Danz, W.A.F. *Grundsäze des gemeinen, ordentlichen, bürgerlichen prozesses.* 3d ed. Stuttgart: Erhard, 1800.

Dawson, J. P. *The Oracles of the Law.* Ann Arbor, Mich.: University of Michigan Law School, 1968.

Delbrück, B. Review of Lenz, *Über die Geschichtliche Entstehung des Rechts. Kritische Überschau* 2 (1854–55): 115–32.

Diestelkamp, B. "Zur Krise des Reichsrechts im 16. Jht." In *Säkulare Aspekte der Reformationszeit.* Edited by H. Angermeier. Munich/Vienna: Oldenbourg, 1983, 49–64.

———. "Das Reichskammergericht im Rechtsleben des 16. Jht." In *Rechtsgeschichte als Kulturgeschichte: Festschrift für A. Erler.* Aalen: Scientia, 1976, 435–80.

———, ed. *Forschungen aus Akten des Reichskammergerichts.* Quellen und Forschungen zur höchsten Gerichtsbarkeit im Alten Reich, vol. 14. Cologne/Vienna: Böhlau, 1984.

The Digest of Justinian. Edited by T. Mommsen, P. Krueger, and A. Watson. 4 vols. Philadelphia: University of Pennsylvania Press, 1985.

Dilcher, G. "Genossenschaftstheorie und Sozialrecht: Ein 'Juristensozialismus' Otto von Gierkes?" *Q. Fior.* 3/4 (1974–75): 319–65.

———. "Zur Geschichte und Aufgabe des Begriffs Genossenschaft." In *Recht, Gericht, Genossenschaft und Policey: Studien zu Grundbegriffen der germanistischen Rechtshistorie.* Edited by G. Dilcher and B. Diestelkamp. Berlin: Erich Schmidt Verlag, 1986.

Dilcher, G., and B. Kern. "Die juristische Germanistik und die Fachtradition der deutschen Rechtsgeschichte." *ZSS (G)* 100 (1984): 1–46.

Dilthey, W. "Das Allgemeine Landrecht." in *Gesammelte Schriften*. 19 vols. Leipzig: Teubner, 1914–58, 12:131–207.

Dippel, H. *Germany and the American Revolution, 1770–1800: A Sociohistorical Investigation of Late Eighteenth-Century Political Thinking*. Veröffentlichungen des Instituts für Europäische Geschichte Mainz, Band 90 (Abteilung Universalgeschichte). Wiesbaden: Steiner, 1978.

Dipper, C. *Die Bauernbefreiung in Deutschland*. Stuttgart: Kohlhammer, 1980.

Dölemeyer, B. "Kodifikationen und Projekte." In *Coing Handbuch*, vol. 3, pt. 2, 1440–1625.

Dotzauer, W. "Deutsches Studium und deutsche Studenten an europäischen Hochschulen (Frankreich, Italien)." In *Stadt und Universität im Mittelalter und in der früheren Neuzeit*. Stadt in der Geschichte, Veröffentlichungen der Südwestdeutschen Arbeitskreises für Stadtgeschichtsforschung, vol. 3. Edited by Maschke. Sigmaringen: Thonbecke, 1977, 112–41.

Dreitzel, H. "Hermann Conring und die politische Wissenschaft." In Stolleis, ed., *Conring*, 135–72.

Du Boulay, F.R.H. *Germany in the Later Middle Ages*. London: Athlone, 1983.

Duichin, M. *Il Primo Marx: Momenti di un Itinerario Intellectualle (1835–41)*. Rome: Cadmo, 1982.

Duncker, L. *Die Lehre von den Reallasten*. Marburg: Elwert, 1837.

Einert, K. *Das Wechselrecht nach dem Bedürfniss des Wechselgeschäfts im neunzehnten Jahrhundert*. Leipzig: F.C.W. Vogel, 1839.

Ekelöf, P. O. "Zur Naturhistorichen Methode Jherings." In Wieacker and Wollschläger, eds., *Jherings Erbe*, 27–28.

Eley, G. See D. Blackbourn.

Ellis, H. A. "Genealogy, History and Aristocratic Reaction in Eighteenth-Century France." *Journal of Modern History* 58, no. 2 (1986): 414–51.

Elsässer. "Über den Geschäftsgang der Acten an Rechtscollegien." Appendix to W.A.F. Danz, *Grundsäze des gemeinen, ordentlichen, bürgerlichen Prozesses*. 3rd ed. Stuttgart: Erhard, 1800.

Engelmann, W. *Die Wiedergeburt der Rechtskultur in Italien*. Leipzig: Koehler, 1938.

Engels, W. *Ablösungen und Gemeinheitsteilungen in der Rheinprovinz*. Rheinisches Archiv, Veröffentlichungen des Instituts für geschichtliche Landeskunde der Rheinlands, vol. 51. Bonn: Röhrscheid, 1957.

Erhard, C. D. "Vorrede zur deutschen Ausgabe." In Sidney, *Betrachtungen über die Regierungsformen*, I–XXXIV.

Evans, R.J.W. "Culture and Anarchy in the Empire." *Central European History* 18 (March 1985): 14–29.

Faber, K.-G. *Die Rheinlande zwischen Restauration und Revolution*. Wiesbaden: Steiner, 1966.

Fehrenbach, E. *Traditionale Gesellschaft und revolutionäres Recht: Die Einführung des Code Napoléon in den Rheinbundstaaten*. Kritische Studien zur Geschichtswissenschaft, vol. 13. Göttingen: Vandenhoeck und Ruprecht, 1974.

———. "Zur sozialen Problematık des rheinischen Rechts im Vormärz." In *Vom Staat des Ancıen Regime zum Modernen Parteienstaat: Festschrift für Theodore Schieder.* Edited by H. Berdıng et al. Munich/Vienna: Oldenbourg, 1978, 195–212.

Feldmann, R. *Jakob Grimm und die Polıtik.* Kassel: Bärenreıter-Verlag, n.d. [1970].

Felgentraeger, W. *Friedrıch Karl von Savignys Einfluß auf die Übereignungslehre.* Leıpzig: A. Deichert, 1927.

Feuerbach, P.J.A. *Kleine Schrıften.* Nuremberg: T. Otto, 1833.

Fioravantı, M. *Giuristı e Costituzione Politica nell'Ottocento Tedesco.* Per la Storia del Pensiero Moderno Gıuridico, vol. 8. Milan: Giuffrè, 1979.

Forbes, D. *Hume's Philosophıcal Politics.* Cambridge: Cambridge Universıty Press, 1975.

Franklin, J. *Jean Bodin and the Sixteenth-Century Revolutıon in the Methodology of Law and Hıstory.* New York: Columbia University Press, 1963.

Franklin, O. *Das Reichshofgericht im Mittelalter.* 2 vols. Weimar: Böhlau, 1869.

Franz, G., ed. *Quellen zur Geschichte des Bauernkrieges.* Munich: Oldenbourg, 1963.

Friedlieb, E. *Dıe Rechtstheorie der Reallasten.* Jena: Mauke, 1860.

Friedrich, C. J. "The Continental Tradıtion of Training Admınıstrators in Law and Jurisprudence." *Journal of Modern History* 11 (1939): 129–48.

Frier, B. *The Rise of the Roman Jurısts.* Princeton, N.J.: Princeton University Press, 1985.

Fueter, E. *Geschichte der neueren Historiographie.* Munich/Berlin: Oldenbourg, 1911.

Gagliardo, J. G. *Reich and Nation.* Bloomington, Ind.: Indıana University Press, 1980.

Gall, L. *Der Liberalismus als regıerende Partei.* Wiesbaden: Steiner, 1968.

Gangl, H. "Der deutsche Weg zum Verfassungsstaat im neunzehnten Jahrhundert." In *Probleme des Konstitutionalismus im Neunzehnten Jahrhudert.* Edıted by Böckenförde et al. Berlin: Duncker und Humblot, 1975, 46ff.

Gaudemet, J. "Tendances à l'Unification de droit en France." In *Formazione Storıca del Diritto Moderno in Europa.* Atti del Terzo Congresso Internazionale della Società Italiana di Storia del Dırıtto, 3 vols. (1977), 1:157–94.

Gesenius, K. *Das Meyerrecht.* 2 vols. Wolfenbüttel: H. G. Albrecht, 1801–3.

Gibbon, E. *Declıne and Fall of the Roman Empıre.* The Modern Library. 3 vols. New York: Random House, n.d.

Gierke, O. von. *Das deutsche Genossenschaftsrecht.* 4 vols. Berlin: Weidmann, 1868–1913.

———. *Deutsches Privatrecht,* 3 vols. Systematisches Handbuch der deutschen Rechtswissenschaft, Abteilung 2, Teil 3. Leıpzig: Duncker und Humblot, 1905.

———. *Der Entwurf eines Bürgerlichen Gesetzbuches und das deutsche Recht.* 2d ed. Leipzig: Duncker und Humblot, 1889.

Girtanner, W. *Rechtsfälle zu Puchtas Pandekten.* 4th ed. Jena: Mauke, 1869.

Glück, C. F. *Ausführliche Erläuterungen der Pandekten.* 2d ed. 68 vols. Erlangen: Palm, 1797.

Gobler, J. *Interpretatio Constitutionis Criminalis Carolinae.* Edited by J.F.H. Abegg. Heidelberg: Mohr, 1837 (orig. 1543).

Gönner, N. T. *Handbuch des deutschen gemeinen Prozeßes.* 2d ed., 2 vols. Erlangen: Palm, 1804.

Goez, W. *Translatio Imperii.* Tübingen: Mohr, 1958.

Goldschmidt, L. *Handbuch des Handelsrechts.* 2d ed., 2 vols. Erlangen: Enke, 1864.

Gooch, G. P. *History and Historians in the Nineteenth Century.* London: Longmans Green, 1952.

Gossman, L. *Orpheus Philologus.* Philadelphia: American Philosophical Society, 1983.

Gouron, A. "Le rôle sociale des juristes dans les villes méridionales au Moyen Age." In *Annales de la Faculté des Lettres et Sciences de Nice* 9–10 (1969): 55–67. Also in idem, *La Science du droit dans le Midi de la France au Moyen Age.* London: Variorum, 1984.

Grafton, A. "Prolegomena to F. A. Wolf." *Journal of the Warburg and Courtauld Institutes* 44 (1981): 101–29.

———. "The World of the Polyhistors." *Central European History* 18 (March 1985): 31–47.

Greve, F. *Die Ministerialverantwortlichkeit im Konstitutionellen Staat.* Schriftenreihe zur Verfassungsgeschichte, Heft 26. Berlin: Duncker und Humblot, 1977.

Grimm, J., and W. Grimm, eds. *Deutsches Wörterbuch.* 15 vols. Leipzig: Hirzel, 1854–1919.

Gros, C. H. *Geschichte der Verjährung nach römischem Rechte.* Göttingen: Dieterich, 1795.

Gross, R. *Die bürgerliche Agrarreform in Sachsen in der ersten Hälfte des neunzehten Jahrhunderts.* Weimar: Böhlau, 1968.

Grossi, P. *Le Situazioni Reali nell'Esperienza Giuridica Medievale.* Padua: Cedam, 1968.

Grossmann, F. *Über die gutsherrlich-bäuerlichen Rechtsverhältnisse in der Mark Brandenburg vom 16. bis 18. Jahrhundert.* Staats- und socialwissenschaftliche Forschungen, vol. 9, Heft 4. Leipzig: Duncker und Humblot, 1890.

Günter, W. *Martin Luthers Vorstellung von der Reichsverfassung.* Münster: Aschendorff, 1976.

Guizzi, V. "Il Diritto Commune in Francia nel XVII secolo." In *Tijdschrift voor Rechtsgeschiednis* 37 (1969): 1–46.

Gutman, R. *Richard Wagner: The Man, his Mind and his Music.* New York: Harcourt, Brace & World, 1968.

A. Guzmán, A. *Ratio Scripta.* Ius Commune Sonderheft 14. Frankfurt a.M.: Klostermann, 1981.

Häberlin, C. F. "Darf der Ausdruck: Unveräusserliche Menschenrechte in Satzschriften bey dem Reichskammergericht nicht gebraucht werden?" *Staats-Archiv* 3 (1797): 365–68.

———. "Justizrath Kober wider den Fürsten von Hohenloh-Schillingsfürst." *Staats-Archiv.* 3 (1797): 102–5.

———. *Pragmatische Geschichte der neuesten kaiserlichen Wahlkapitulation and der an kaiserlichen Majestät erlassenen kurfürstlichen Collegialschreiben.* Leipzig: Weidmann, 1792.

———. "Teutsche Reichsjustiz." *Staats-Archiv* 1 (1796): 83–90.

———. Über die Güte der deutschen Staatsverfassung." *Deutsche Monatsschrift*, n.s. 1 (1793): 3–33.

Hagemann, T. See F. Bülow.

Haikala, S. *"Britische Freiheit" und das Englandbild in der öffentlichen deutschen Diskussion im ausgehenden 18. Jahrhundert.* Studia historica Jyväskyläensia, vol. 32. Jyväskylä: Jyväskylän yliopisto, 1985.

Hamerow, T. *Restoration, Revolution, Reaction.* Princeton, N.J.: Princeton University Press, 1958.

Hammen, H. *Die Bedeutung Friedrich Carl von Savignys für die allgemeinen dogmatischen Grundlagen des Deutschen Bürgerlichen Gesetzbuches.* Schriften zur Rechtsgeschichte, Heft 29. Berlin: Duncker und Humblot, 1983.

Hammerstein, N. "Die Historie bei Conring." In Stolleis, ed., *Conring*, 217–36.

———. *Jus und Historie.* Göttingen: Vandenhoeck und Ruprecht, 1972.

———. "Das Römische am Heiligen Römischen Reich Deutscher Nation." *ZSS(G)* 100 (1983): 119–144.

———. "Zur Geschichte und Bedeutung der Universitäten im Heiligen Römischen Reich." *Historische Zeitschrift* 241 (1985): 287–328.

Hartung, F. "Imperial Reform, 1485–1495." In Strauss, ed., *Pre-Reformation Germany*, 73–135.

Hasselwander, N. *Aus der Gutachter- und Urteilstätigkeit an der alten Mainzer Juristenfakultät.* Beiträge zur Geschichte der Universität Mainz, vol. 3. Wiesbaden: Steiner, 1956.

Hattenhauer, H. "Burchard Wilhelm Pfeiffer und die Bauernbefreiung in Kurhessen." in *Festschrift für Hermann Krause.* Cologne/Vienna: Böhlau, 1975, 188–209.

———. "Einleitung." In idem, ed., *Thibaut und Savigny: ihre Programmatischen Schriften.* Munich: Vahlen, 1973, 9–51.

———. *Geschichte des Beamtentums.* Cologne: Heymann, 1980.

Haubold, C. G. *De Consistorio Principum, Specimina II.* 2 vols. in 1. Leipzig: Saalbach, 1788–89.

Hedemann, J. W. *Die Fortschritte des Zivilrechts im Neunzehnten Jahrhundert.* 2 vols. in 3. Berlin: Carl Heymann, 1910–34.

Heffter, H. *Die Deutsche Selbstverwaltung im neunzehnten Jahrhundert: Geschichte der Ideen und Institutionen.* Stuttgart: Koehler, 1950.

Hegel, G.F.W. *Vorlesungen über die Aesthetik.* 2 vols. Frankfurt a.M.: Suhrkamp, 1970.

Hegendorffinus, Christophorus. *Oratio de Rationibus Restaurandi Collapsas Academias Publicas.* Rostock: Ludwig Dyetz, 1540.

Heger, G. *Johann Eberlin von Günzburg und seine Vorstellungen über Reform in Reich und Kirche.* Schriften zur Rechtsgeschichte, 35. Berlin: Duncker und Humblot, 1985.

Hegewisch, D. H. *Geschichte der Gracchischen Unruhen in der Römischen Republik.* Hamburg: Friedrich Perthes, 1801.

Hegewisch, D. H. *Über die für die Menschheit glücklichste Epoche in der Römischen Geschichte.* Hamburg: Friedrich Perthes, 1800.

Heine, H. *Die Romantische Schule.* Stuttgart: Reclam, 1976.

Heineccius, J. G. *Antiquitatum Romanarum Jurisprudentiam Illustrantium Syntagma.* Strasbourg: Dulssecker, 1741 (orig. 1719).

———. *Elementa Juris Civilis.* Utrecht: Schoonhoven, 1772.

———. *Historia Juris Civilis Romani et Germanici.* Edited by Ritter. Strasbourg: J. G. Bauer, 1751.

Hellmuth, E. *Naturrechtsphilosophie und bürokratischer Werthorizont.* Veröffentlichungen des Max-Planck-Instituts für Geschichte, vol. 78. Göttingen: Vandenhoeck und Ruprecht, 1985.

Henning, F.-W. *Dienste und Abgaben der Bauern im Achtzehnten Jahrhundert.* Quellen und Forschungen zur Agrargeschichte, vol. 21. Stuttgart: G. Fischer, 1969.

Herberger, M. "Beziehungen zwischen Naturwissenschaft und Jurisprudenz in der ersten Hälfte des neunzehnten Jahrhunderts." *Berichte zur Wissenschaftsgeschichte* 6 (1983): 79–88.

Hertz, F. "Die Rechtsprechung der höchsten Reichsgerichte im römisch-deutschen Reich und ihre politische Bedeutung." *Mitteilungen des Instituts für Österreichische Geschichtsforschung* 69 (1961): 331–58.

Heuss, A. "Niebuhr und Mommsen." *Antike und Abendland* 14, no. 1 (1968): 1–18.

———. *Niebuhrs Wissenschaftliche Anfänge.* Abhandlungen der Akademie der Wissenschaften in Göttingen, vol. 114. Göttingen: Vandenhoeck und Ruprecht, 1981.

———. *Theodor Mommsen und das Neunzehnte Jahrhundert.* Kiel: F. Hirt, 1956.

Heyne, C. G. "Herr Hofrath Heyne über die Ehrenbezeugungen welche den Römischen Rechtsgelehrten unter den Kaisern wiederfuhren." *Hugos Civilistisches Magazin* 1, no. 4 (1791): 477–89.

———. "Honores Iurisconsultis habiti ab Impp. Romanis." In *Opuscula Academica.* Göttingen: J. C. Dieterich, 1796, 4:211–30 (orig. 1790).

———. "Über Freyheits-Revolutionen." *Deutsche Monatsschrift* (August 1790): 311–25.

Hintze, O. "Der Beamtenstand." In *Gesammelte Abhandlungen.* Vol. 2, *Soziologie und Geschichte.* 2d ed. Göttingen: Vandenhoeck und Ruprecht, 1964, 66–125.

———. "Preußens Entwicklung zum Rechtsstaat." In *Gesammelte Abhandlungen.* Vol. 3, *Regierung und Verwaltung.* 2d ed. Göttingen: Vandenhoeck und Ruprecht, 1967, 97–163.

Hölzle, E. *Das Alte Recht and die Revolution: Eine politische Geschichte Württembergs in der Revolutionszeit, 1789–1805.* Munich/Berlin: Oldenbourg, 1931.

———. *Die Idee einer altdeutschen Freiheit vor Montesquieu.* Historische Zeitschrift, Beiheft 5. Munich/Berlin: Oldenbourg, 1925.

Hoffmann, M. *August Boeckh.* Leipzig: Teubner, 1901.

Honoré, A. *Emperors and Lawyers*. London: Duckworth, 1981.

Huber, U. "Oratio Exhibens Historiam Juris Romani, & ex ejus argumento continuam probationem, literas humaniores cum jurisprudentia esse conjungendas." In idem, *Opera Minora*. Edited by A. Wieling. Trier: Vonk van Lynden, 1746, 101–23.

Hübner, H. *Kodifikation und Entscheidungsfreiheit des Richters in der Geschichte des Privatrechts*. Königstein: Peter Hanstein, 1980.

Hugo, G. *Beyträge zur Civilistischen Bücherkenntniß*. 4th ed. Reprint. Berlin: Mylius, 1823.

———. "Über die Institutionen des heutigen römischen Recht." *Hugos Civilistisches Magazin* 1 (1791): 305–75.

———. "Juristische Nachrichten von der Leydenschen Universität. 1790." *Hugos Civilistisches Magazin* 2 (4th. ed., 1823): 225–38.

———. *Lehrbuch der Rechtsgeschichte bis auf unsere Zeiten*. Berlin: Mylius, 1790.

———. "Über den Plan dieses Journals." *Hugos Civilistisches Magazin* 1 (1791): 1–22.

Hume, D. *History of England*. 6 vols. London: A. Millar, 1762–63.

Husung, H.-G. *Protest und Repression im Vormärz: Norddeutschland zwischen Restauration und Revolution*. Kritische Studien zur Geschichtswissenschaft, vol. 54. Göttingen: Vandenhoeck & Ruprecht, 1983.

Iggers, G. *The German Conception of History*. 2d ed. Middletown, Conn.: Wesleyan University Press, 1982.

Ilse, L. F. *Geschichte der politischen Untersuchungen, welche durch die neben der Bundesversammlung errichteten Commissionen, der Central Untersuchungs-Commission zu Mainz und der Bundes-Central-Behörde zu Frankfurt in den Jahren 1819 bis 1827 und 1833 bis 1842 geführt sind*. Frankfurt a.M.: Meidinger, 1860.

Immel, G. "Typologie der Gesetzgebung des Privatrechts und Prozessrechts." In *Coing Handbuch*, vol. 2, pt. 2, 3–96.

Jakobs, H. H. *Wissenschaft und Gesetzgebung im bürgerlichen Recht nach der Rechtsquellenlehre des neunzehnten Jahrhunderts*. Rechts- und Staatswissenschaftliche Veröffentlichungen der Görres-Gesellschaft, n.s., Heft 38. Paderborn: Schöningh, 1983.

Jammers, A. *Die Heidelberger Juristenfakultät im Neunzehnten Jahrhundert als Spruchkollegium*. Heidelberg: Carl Winter, 1964.

Jellinek, G. "Die Staatsrechtslehre und ihre Vertreter." In *Ausgewählte Schriften und Reden*, 2 vols. Berlin: Häring, 1911, 1:314–43. Originally in *Heidelberger Professoren aus dem neunzehnten Jahrhundert*. 2 vols. Heidelberg: Carl Winter, 1903.

Jeserich, K.G.A. "Die Entstehung des öffentlichen Dienstes." In Jeserich, et al., *Deutsche Verwaltungsgeschichte*, 2:302–32.

Jeserich, K.G.A., H. Pohl, G.-C. Unruh, eds. *Deutsche Verwaltungsgeschichte*. 3 vols. Stuttgart: Deutsche Verlagsantalt, 1983.

Jhering, R. *Briefe und Erinnerungen*. Edited by Biermann. Berlin: H. W. Müller, 1907.

Jhering, R. "Culpa in contrahendo, oder Schadensersatz bei nichtigen oder nicht zur Perfection gelangten Verträgen." *Jahrbücher für die Dogmatik des römischen und deutschen Rechts* 4 (1861): 1–112. Also in *Gesammelte Aufsätze*, 1: 327–425.

———. *Der Geist des Römischen Rechts auf den verschiedenen Stufen seiner Entwicklung*. 3 vols. in 4. 5th ed. Leipzig: Breitkopf und Härtel, 1891–1906.

———. *Gesammelte Aufsätze aus den Jahrbüchern für die Dogmatik des heutigen römischen und deutschen Privatrechts*. 3 vols. Jena: Mauke, 1881–86.

———. "Mitwirkung für fremde Rechtsgeschäfte." *Jahrbücher für die Dogmatik des römischen und deutschen Rechts* 1 (1857): 273–305; 2 (1858): 67–180. Also in *Gesammelte Aufsätze*, 1:122–290.

———. *Rudolf von Jhering in Briefen an seine Freunde*. Leipzig: Breitkopf und Härtel, 1913.

———. *Scherz und Ernst in der Jurisprudenz*. 2d ed. Leipzig: Breitkopf und Härtel, 1885.

———. "Uebertragung der Reivindicatio auf Nichteigentümer (Cession derselben, reiv. utilis, Connossement)." *Jahrbücher für die Dogmatik des römischen und deutschen Rechts* 1 (1857): 101–88. Also in *Gesammelte Aufsätze*, 1: 47–121.

———. "Unsere Aufgabe." *Jahrbücher für die Dogmatik des römischen und deutschen Rechts* 1 (1857): 1–46.

John, M. "The Peculiarities of the German State: Bourgeois Law and Society in the Imperial Era." *Past and Present* 119 (1988): 105–31.

———. *Politics and the Law in Late Nineteenth-Century Germany: The Origins of the Civil Code*. Oxford: Clarendon Press, 1989.

———. "The Politics of Legal Unity in Germany, 1870-1896." *The Historical Journal* 28, no. 2 (1985): 341–55.

Judeich, A. *Die Grundentlastungen in Deutschland*. Leipzig: Brockhaus, 1863.

Junghans, H., ed. *Leben und Werk Martin Luthers*. Göttingen: Vandenhoeck und Ruprecht, 1983.

Kantorowicz, H. "Jherings Bekehrung." *Deutsche Richterzeitung* 6, no. 2 (January 15, 1914): cols. 84–87.

———. *Rechtshistorische Schriften*. Edited by H. Coing and G. Immel. Freiburger Rechts- und Staatswissenschaftliche Abhandlungen, vol. 30. Karlsruhe: C. F. Müller, 1970.

———. "Savigny and the Historical School of Law." *Law Quarterly Review* 53 (1937): 326–43. Also in *Rechtshistorische Schriften*, 419–34.

———. *Was ist uns Savigny?* Berlin: Heymann, 1912. Also in *Rechtshistorische Schriften*, 397–419.

Kaser, M. *Römische Rechtsgeschichte*. 2d ed. Göttingen: Vandenhoeck und Ruprecht, 1982.

Kawakami, R. "Die Begründung des 'neuen' gelehrten Rechts durch Savigny." *ZSS(R)* 98 (1981): 303–37.

Kehr, E. "Zur Genesis der preußischen Bürokratie." In *Primat der Innenpolitik*. Veröffentlichungen der historischen Commission zu Berlin, vol. 19. Berlin: de Gruyter, 1965, 31–52.

Kelley, D. R. "Civil Science in the Renaissance: Jurisprudence in the French Manner." *History of European Ideas* 2 (1981): 261–76. Also in idem, *History, Law and the Human Sciences: Medieval and Renaissance Perspectives.* London: Variorum Reprints, 1984.

———. *Foundations of Modern Historical Scholarship.* New York: Columbia University Press, 1970.

———. *Historians and the Law in France.* Princeton, N.J.: Princeton University Press, 1984.

———. "The Metaphysics of Law: An Essay on the Very Young Marx." *American Historical Review* 83 (1978): 350–67.

Kelley, D. R., and B. Smith. "What Was Property? Legal Dimensions of the Social Question in France (1789–1848)." *Proceedings of the American Philosophical Society* 128 (1984): 200–230.

Keohane, N. *Philosophy and the State in France.* Princeton, N.J.: Princeton University Press, 1980.

Kern, B.-R. *See* Dilcher, G.

Kern, B.-R. *Georg Beseler.* Schriften zur Rechtsgeschichte, Heft 26. Berlin: Duncker und Humblot, 1982.

Kern, E. *Geschichte des Gerichtsverfassungsrechts.* Munich: Beck, 1954.

———. *Der Gesetzliche Richter.* Berlin: Liebmann, 1927.

Kiefner, H. "Rezeption (privatrechtlich)." *Handwörterbuch zur deutschen Rechtsgeschichte* 4:970–84.

Kirchmann, J. H. von. *Die Werthlosigkeit der Jurisprudenz als Wissenschaft.* Berlin: Springer, 1848.

Kisch, G. *Erasmus und die Jurisprudenz seiner Zeit: Studien zum humanistischen Rechtsdenken.* Basler Studien zur Rechtswissenschaft, Heft 56. Basel: Helbing & Lichtenhahn, 1960.

———. *Melanchthons Rechts- und Soziallehre.* Berlin: de Gruyter, 1967.

Klein, E. F. "Ueber die gesetzliche und richterliche Begünstigung des Bauernstandes." *Annalen der Gesetzgebung und Rechtsgelehrsamkeit in den Preussischen Staaten [Kleins Annalen]* 24 (1806): 167–80.

Klemm, P. C. *Eigentum und Eigentumsbeschränkungen in der Doktrin des usus modernus pandectarum.* Basler Studien zur Rechtswissenschaft, Reihe A: Privatrecht, vol. 10. Basel/Frankfurt a.M.: Helbing & Lichtenhahn, 1984.

Klempt, A. *Die Säkularisierung der Universalhistorischen Geschichtsauffassung.* Göttingen: Musterschmidt-Verlag, 1960.

Klenner, H. "Anmerkungen zu 'Savigny,' " In *Studien zu einer Geschichte der Gesellschaftswissenschaften.* Edited by J. Kuczynski. vols. Berlin (E): 1977, 6:158–73.

Klugkist, E. "Die Aktenversendung an Juristenfakultäten." *Juristenzeitung* 22 (1967): 155–58.

———. *Die Göttinger Juristenfakultät als Spruchkollegium.* Göttinger Rechtswissenschaftliche Studien, Heft 5. Göttingen: Schwartz, 1952.

Knapp, G. F. *Die Bauern-Befreiung und der Ursprung der Landarbeiter in den älteren Teilen Preußens.* 2 vols. Munich/Leipzig: Duncker und Humblot, 1887.

Köbler, G. "Die Wissenschaft des gemeinen deutschen Handelsrechts." In Coing and Wilhelm, eds., *Wissenschaft und Kodification des Privatrechts im Neunzehnten Jahrhundert*, 289ff.

König, R. *Vom Wesen der Deutschen Universitäten*. Berlin: Verlag die Runde, 1935.

Koschaker, P. *Europa und das Römische Recht*. Munich/Berlin: Beck, 1947.

Koselleck, R. *Preußen zwischen Reform und Revolution*. Stuttgart: Klett, 1967.

Kramnick, I. *Bolingbroke and his Circle*. Cambridge, Mass.: Harvard University Press, 1968.

Kraul, M. *Gymnasium und Gesellschaft im Vormärz*. Studien zum Wandel von Gesellschaft und Bildung im Neunzehnten Jahrhundert, vol. 18. Göttingen: Vandenhoeck und Ruprecht, 1980.

Krause, H. "Der deutschrechtliche Anteil an der heutigen Privatrechtsordnung." In *Juristische Schulung* 10 (1970): 313–21.

———. *Die Geschichtliche Entwicklung des Schiedsgerichtswesens in Deutschland*. Berlin: Heymann, 1930.

———. *Kaiserrecht und Rezeption*. Abhandlungen der Heidelberger Akademie der Wissenschaften (Philosophisch-historische klasse), vol. 1. Heidelberg: Winter, 1952.

Krause, O. W. *Naturrechtler des Sechzehnten Jahrhunderts*. Rechtshistorische Reihe, vol. 5. Frankfurt a.M./Bern: Lang, 1982.

Krieger, L. *The German Idea of Freedom*. Chicago: University of Chicago Press, 1957.

Kritz, P. L. *Sammlung von Rechtsfällen und Entscheidungen derselben*. 5 vols. Leipzig: Barth, 1833–45.

Kroeschell, K. "Bauernbefreiung." In *Handwörterbuch des Agrarrechts*. Edited by V. Götz, K. Kroeschell, and W. Winkler. Berlin: E. Schmidt, 1981.

———. "Zur Lehre vom 'germanischen Eigentumsbegriff.' " In *Rechtshistorische Studien Hans Thieme zum 70. Geburtstag zugeeignet*. Cologne: Böhlau, 1977, 34–71.

Kuczynski, J. "Savigny—Glanzvolle Jugend eines reaktionären Gelehrten von einstigem Weltruf." In idem, ed., *Studien zu einer Geschichte der Gesellschaftswissenschaften*, 10 vols. Berlin (E): 1977, 6:125–57.

Kühlmann, W. *Gelehrtenrepublik und Fürstenstaat*. Studien und Texte zur Sozialgeschichte der Literatur, vol. 31. Tübingen: Niemeyer, 1982.

Kunder, L. "Die Deutsche Ruinenpoesie." Diss. Heidelberg, 1933.

Kunisch, J. "Hermann Conrings Mächtepolitisches Weltbild." In Stolleis, ed. *Conring*, 237–54.

Kunkel, W. "The Reception of Roman Law in Germany." In Strauss, ed., *Pre-Reformation Germany*, 263–81.

———. *Römische Rechtsgeschichte*. Cologne/Vienna: Bohlau, 1972.

Kuntze, J. E. *Das ius respondendi in unserer Zeit*. Leipzig: Hinrichs, 1858.

———. *Die Obligationen und die Singularsuccession des Römischen und Heutigen Rechts*. Leipzig: H. Mendelssohn, 1856.

———. "Das römische und das deutsche Recht in der Gegenwart," review of, inter alia, Jhering, *Geist des Römischen Rechts*, vol. 1. *Krıtısche Überschau der Deutschen Gesetzgebung und Rechtswissenschaft* 2 (1854): 173–228.

———. *Der Wendepunkt der Rechtswissenschaft*. Leipzig: Hinrıchs, 1856.

Kuttner, S. "The Revival of Jurısprudence." In Benson and Constable, eds., *Renaissance and Renewal ın the Twelfth Century*, 299–323.

Landau, P. "Hegels Begründung des Vertragsrechts," In *Materıalien zu Hegels Rechtsphilosophie*. Edited by M. Riedel. 2 vols. Frankfurt a.M.: Suhrkamp, 1975, 2:176–97.

———. "Schwurgerichte und Schöffengerichte in Deutschland im 19. Jahrhundert bıs 1870." In *The Trıal Jury in England, France, and Germany, 1700–1900*. Edited by A. Padoa Schıoppa. Comparative Studies in Continental and Anglo-American Legal History. Berlin: Duncker und Humblot, 1987, 241–304.

Landsberg, E. See R. Stıntzing.

Langbein, J. "The Constitutio Criminalis Carolina in Comparative Perspective." in *Strafrecht, Strafprozess und Rezeptıon*. Edited by P. Landau and F.-G. Schroeder. Frankfurt a.M.: Klostermann, 1984, 215–25.

———. *Torture and the Law of Proof*. Chicago: University of Chıcago Press, 1977.

Lange, H. *Die Wandlungen Jherings ın seiner Auffassung vom Recht*. Berlin-Grunewald: Rothschild, 1927.

Lange, M. *De Actorum Transmissione secundum Usum Fori hodıerni praecipue saxonici*. Leipzig: Immanuel Titus, 1708.

Lentulus, C. *Augustus, sıve de convertenda ın Monarchiam Republica*. Amsterdam: Elzevir, 1645.

Lenz, M. *Geschıchte der Königlichen Friedrich-Wilhelms-Universität zu Berlin*. 4 vols. in 5. Halle: Buchhandlung des Waisenhauses, 1910–18.

Leotardus, H. *Liber Singularis de Usuris*. Venice: Savioni, 1761.

Levine, N. "The German Historical School of Law and the Origins of Historical Materialism." *Journal of the History of Ideas* 48 (1987): 431–51.

Levy, E. *West Roman Vulgar Law: The Law of Property*. Philadelphia: Amerıcan Philosophical Society, 1951.

Leyser, A. *Meditationes ad Pandectas*. 13 vols. in 11. Leipzig: Meisner, 1741–80.

Löning, G. A. "Spätes Lob der Aktenversendung." *ZSS(G)* 63 (1943): 333–44.

Loisel, A. *Instıtutes Coustumieres, ou Manuel de plusieurs & diverses Regles, Sentences & Proverbes, tant anciens que modernes, du droict Coustumier & plus ordinaire de la France*. Paris: Michel Bobın & Nicolas le Gras, 1665.

Losano, M. G., ed. *Der Briefwechsel zwischen Jhering und Gerber*. Abhandlungen zur rechtswissenschaftlichen Grundlagenforschung, vol. 55, pt. 1. Ebelsbach: Gremer, 1984.

———. *Studien zu Jherıng und Gerber*. Abhandlungen zur Rechtswissenschaftlichen Grundlagenforschung, vol. 55, pt. 2. Ebelsbach: Gremer, 1984.

Lütge, F. *Geschichte der deutschen Agrarverfassung vom frühen Mittelalter bis zum 19. Jahrhundert*. Stuttgart: Verlag Ulmer, 1963.

———. *Mitteldeutsche Grundherrschaft*. Quellen und Forschungen zur Agrargeschichte, vol. 4. Stuttgart: G. Fischer, 1957.

Luig, K. "Conring, das deutsche Recht, und die Rechtsgeschichte." In Stolleis, ed., *Conring*, 355–95.

———. "The Institutes of National Law in the Seventeenth- and Eighteenth-Centuries." *Juridical Review* 17 (1972): 193–226.

———. "Universales Recht und Partikulares Recht in den 'Meditationes ad Pandectas' von Augustin Leyser." In *Diritto Commune e Diritti Locali nella Storia dell'Europa*. Atti del Convegno di Varenna. Milan: Giuffrè, 1980.

———. "Zession und Abstraktionsprinzip." In Coing and Wilhelm, eds., *Wissenschaft und Kodifikation des Privatrechts im 19. Jahrhundert*, 2:112–43.

———. *Zur Geschichte der Zessionslehre*. Cologne/Graz: Böhlau, 1966.

Lukács, G. *Die Zerstörung der Vernunft*. Berlin: Aufbau-Verlag, 1954.

Lundgreen, P. "Bildung und Besitz." *Geschichte und Gesellschaft* 7 (1981): 262–75.

Luther, M. Letter to Melanchthon, dated July 13, 1521. In Lehmann, ed., *Works*, 48:256–63.

———. "Predigt, daß man kinder zur Schule halten solle." In *Werke*, vol. 30, pt. 2, 508–88.

———. "Von Ehesachen." In *Werke*, vol. 30, pt. 3, 198–248.

———. "Vorrede zu Spenglers Auszug aus den päpstlichen Rechten." In *Werke*, vol. 30, pt. 2, 215–19.

———. *Werke: Kritische Gesammtausgabe*. 58 vols. Weimar: Böhlau, 1883–.

———. *Works*. 55 vols. Vols. 1–30 edited by J. Pelikan; vols. 31–55 edited by H. T. Lehmann. St. Louis: Concordia Publishing House; Philadelphia: Fortress Press (formerly Muhlenberg Press), 1957–67.

Maas, G. "Bibliographie des bürgerlichen Rechts: Verzeichnis von Einzelschriften und Aufsätzen über das im Bürgerlichen Gesetzbuche für das Deutsche Reich vereinigte Recht, 1888–1898." *Archiv für Bürgerliches Recht* 16 (1899).

McGlew, J. "Revolution and Freedom in Theodor Mommsen's *Römische Geschichte*." *Phoenix* 40 (1986): 424–45.

Maffei, D. *Gli Inizi dell'Umanesimo Giuridico*. Milan: Giuffrè, 1956.

Mannheim, K. "Conservative Thought." In idem, *Essays on Sociology and Social Psychology*. New York: Oxford University Press, 1953, 74–164.

Marini, G. *Friedrich Carl von Savigny*. Naples: Guida, 1978.

———. *L'Opera di Gustav Hugo nella Crisi del Giusnaturalismo Tedesco*. Milan: Giuffrè, 1969.

Marquardt, H. "Ein unbekannter Aufsatz F. C. von Savignys." *Die Sammlung: Zeitschrift für Kultur und Erziehung* 6 (1951): 321–36.

Marx, K. "Das philosophische Manifest der historischen Rechtsschule." In idem, *Gesamtausgabe*, vol. 1, pt. 1, 191–98. Translated as "The Philosophical Manifesto of the Historical School of Law," in Marx and Engels, *Collected Works*, 1:203–10.

———. "Verhandlungen des 6. Rheinischen Landtags: Dritter Artikel, Debatten über das Holzdiebstahlsgesetz," in Marx and Engels, *Gesamtausgabe*, vol. 1, pt. 1, 199–236. Translated as "Proceedings of the Sixth Rhine Province Assembly: *Third Article*, Debates on the Law on Thefts of Wood," in Marx and Engels, *Collected Works*, 1:224–63.

Marx, K., and F. Engels, *Collected Works*. New York: International Publishers, 1975–88.

———. *Gesamtausgabe*. 47 vols. Berlin: Dietz, 1975–.

Matthiae, C. *Controversen-Lexikon des römischen Rechts*. 3 vols. Leipzig: Wigand, 1856–64.

Maurer, W. *Der Junge Melanchthon*. 2 vols. Göttingen: Vandenhoeck und Ruprecht, 1967.

———. "Reste des kanonischen Rechts im Frühprotestantismus." *ZSS(K)* 51 (1965): 190–253.

Meinecke, F. *Erlebtes, 1862–1901*. In *Werke*, 9 vols. Stuttgart: Koehler, 1969, vol. 8.

———. *Historism*. Translated by J. E. Anderson. London: Routledge and Kegan Paul, 1972.

———. *Machiavellism*. Translated by D. Scott. London: Routledge and Kegan Paul, 1957.

Meiners, C. "Geschichte der Sitten der Römer in den beyden ersten Jahrhunderten nach Christi geburt." *Göttingisches Historisches Magazin* 5 (1789): 369–417.

Melanchthon, P. *Chronicon Carionis*. In Bretschneider, ed., *Opera*, 12:704–1094.

———. "Commentarii in aliquot Politicos Libros Aristotelis." In Bretschneider, ed., *Opera*, 16:416–51.

———. "De dignitate legum oratio." In Kisch, *Melanchthon*, 221–27.

———. "De scripto iure et de dignitate veterum interpretum iuris." In Bretschneider, ed., *Opera*, 9:218–23.

———. "Estne iudicandum iuxta scriptum ius an secundum aequitatem." In Bretschneider, ed., *Opera*, 16:78–81.

———. *Opera quae supersunt*. Corpus Reformatorum, vols. 1–28. Edited by C. G. Bretschneider. Halle/Braunschweig: Schwetschke und Sohn, 1834–60.

———. "Oratio de dignitate legum." In Kisch, *Melanchthon*, 234–40.

———. "Oratio de Inerio et Bartolo." In Kisch, *Melanchthon*, 214–20.

Menger, A. *Das bürgerliche Recht und die besitzlosen Volksklassen: Eine kritik des Entwurfs eines bürgerlichen Gesetzbuches für das Deutsche Reich*. 2d ed. Tübingen: Laupp, 1890.

Merten, D. "Rechtsstaatliche Anfänge im Preußischen Absolutismus." *Deutsches Verwaltungsblatt* 96 (1981): 701–9.

Middendorp, J. *Academiarum Orbis Christiani Libri Duo*. Cologne: apud Maternum Cholinum, 1572.

Minnigerode, L. *Beitrag zur Beantwortung der Frage: Was ist Justiz- und was ist Administrativ-Sache?* Darmstadt: J. W. Meyer, 1835.

Mitteis, H. *Vom Lebenswert der Rechtsgeschichte*. Weimar: Böhlaus Nachfolger, 1947.

Möser, J. *Sämmtliche Werke: Historisch-kritische Ausgabe*. 14 vols. in 16. Oldenburg/Berlin: G. Stalling, 1944–81.

Mohl, R. von. *Lebenserinnerungen*. 2 vols. Stuttgart and Leipzig: Deutsche Verlags-Anstalt, 1902.

Mohl, R. von. *Geschichte und Literatur der Staatswissenschaften.* 3 vols. Erlangen: Enke, 1855–58.

Mohnhaupt, H. "Potestas Legislatoria und Gesetzesbegriff im Ancien Régime." *Ius Commune* 4 (1972): 188–239.

——. "Richter und Rechtsprechung im Werk Savignys." In *Studien zur Europäischen Rechtsgeschichte.* Edited by W. Wilhelm. Frankfurt a.M.: Klostermann, 1972, 243–64.

Momigliano, A. D. "Alle origini dell'interesse su Roma arcaica: Niebuhr e l'India." *Rivista Storica Italiana* 92 (1980): 561–71.

——. "La Formazione della moderna storiografia sull'impero Romano." In *Contributo alla Storia degli Studi Classici.* Roma: Edizioni di Storia e Letteratura, 1955, 107–64.

——. "Interim Report on the Origins of Rome." In *Terzo Contributo alla Storia degli Studi Classici e del Mondo Antico.* 2 vols. Roma: Edizioni di Storia e Letteratura, 1966, 2:545–98.

——. "The Introduction of the Teaching of History as an Academic Subject." *Minerva* 21, no. 1 (Spring 1983): 1–15.

——. "Niebuhr and the Agrarian Problems of Rome." In idem, *New Paths of Classicism in the Nineteenth Century.* History and Theory, Beiheft 21. Middletown, Conn.: Wesleyan University Press, 1982, 3–15.

Mommsen, T. *Römische Gechichte.* 2d ed., 5 vols. Berlin: Weidmann, 1857.

Mooser, J. *Ländliche Klassengesellschaft, 1770–1848: Bauern und Unterschichten, Landwirtschaft und Gewerbe im östlichen Westfalen.* Kritische Studien zur Geschichtswissenschaft, vol. 64. Göttingen: Vandenhoeck und Ruprecht, 1984.

——. "Property and Woodtheft: Agrarian Capitalism and Social Conflict in Rural Society, 1800–1850, A Westphalian Case Study." In *Peasants and Lords in Modern Germany.* Edited by R. G. Moeller. Boston: Allen and Unwin, 1986, 52–80.

Moser, F. C. *Patriotische Briefe.* N.p. [Frankfurt a.M.]: n.p., 1767.

——. *Politische Wahrheiten.* 2 vols. Zürich: Orell, Gessner, Füssli, 1796.

Moser, J. J. "Freye, aber wohlgemeinte und auf die Erfahrung gegründete Gedancken, wie Universitäten, Besonders in der Juridischen Facultät, sowohl in einen guten Ruf und Aufnahm zu bringen und darinnen zu erhalten, als auch recht nützlich und brauchbar zu machen seyn möchten?" In *Opuscula Academica.* Jena: J.F. Ritter, 1744, 432–55.

——. *Lebensgeschichte.* N.p. [Offenbach]: n.p., 1768.

——. *Von der Landeshoheit derer Teutschen Reichsstände überhaupt.* 10 vols. Frankfurt/Leipzig: Mezler, 1773.

Mühlmann, S. "Luther und das Corpus Iuris Canonici bis zum Jahre 1530." *ZSS(K)* 58 (1972): 235–305.

Müller, G. "Luthers Beziehungen zu Rom." In *Leben und Werk Martin Luthers.* Edited by H. Junghans. 2 vols. 1:369–401.

Müller, J. J. "Die ersten Germanistentage." In idem, ed., *Germanistik und deutsche Nation,* 297–318.

——. "Germanistik—eine Form bürgerlicher Opposition." In idem, ed., *Germanistik und deutsche Nation,* 5–112.

————, ed. *Germanistik und deutsche Nation, 1806–1848: Zur Konstitution bürgerlichen Bewußtseins.* Literaturwissenschaft und Sozialwissenschaften 2. Stuttgart: Metzler, 1974.

Müller-Dietz, H. *Das Leben des Rechtslehrers und Politikers Karl Theodor Welcker.* Beiträge zur Freiburger Wissenschafts- und Universitätsgeschichte, Heft 34. Freiburg i.B.: Eberhard Albert Universitätsbuchhandlung, 1968.

Müller-Kinet, H. *Die Höchste Gerichtsbarkeit im deutschen Staatenbund, 1806–1866.* Bern: Lang, 1975.

Muther, T. *Zur Lehre von der römischen Actio.* Erlangen: Deichert, 1857.

Neuber, C. L. *Die Juristischen Classiker: Ein Beitrag zur Civilistischen Biographie.* Berlin: G. A. Lange, 1806.

Neumeyer, K. *Die Entwicklung des Internationalen Privat- und Strafrechts bis Bartolus.* 2 vols. Munich: Schweitzer, 1901–16.

Neusüss, W. *Gesunde Vernunft und Natur der Sache: Studien zur Juristischen Argumentation im Achtzehnten Jahrhundert.* Schriften zur Rechtsgeschichte, Heft 2. Berlin: Duncker und Humblot, 1970.

Niebuhr, B. G. *Römische Geschichte.* 3 vols. Berlin: G. Reimer, 1853.

Nipperdey, T. *Deutsche Geschichte, 1800-1866.* Munich: Beck, 1984.

Nitzsch, K. W. Review of Mommsen, *Römische Geschichte* (erster Artikel). *Neue Jahrbücher für Philologie und Pädagogik* 73 (1856): 716–45.

Nörr, K. W. "Das Aktionenrecht bei Savigny." *Ius Commune* 8 (1979): 110–19.

————. "Institutional Foundations of the New Jurisprudence." In Benson and Constable, eds., *Renaissance and Renewal*, 324–38.

————. "Wissenschaft und Schrifttum zum deutschen Zivilprozeß im 19. Jahrhundert." *Ius Commune* 10 (1983): 141–99.

Nolte, J. *Burchard Wilhelm Pfeiffer: Gedanken zur Reform des Zivilrechts. Ein Beitrag zur Geschichte der deutschen Zivilgesetzgebung.* Göttinger Studien zur Rechtsgeschichte, vol. 1. Göttingen: Musterschmidt-Verlag, 1969.

Noonan, J. T. *The Scholastic Analysis of Usury.* Cambridge, Mass.: Harvard University Press, 1957.

Oberschelp, R. *Niedersachsen, 1760–1820: Wirtschaft, Gesellschaft, Kultur im Land Hannover und Nachbargebieten.* 2 vols. Veröffentlichungen der Historischen Kommission für Niedersachsen und Bremen, vol. 35; Quellen und Untersuchungen zur allgemeinen Geschichte Niedersachsens in der Neuzeit, vol. 4. Hildesheim: Lax, 1982.

O'Boyle, L. "Klassische Bildung und Soziale Struktur in Deutschland zwischen 1800 und 1848." *Historische Zeitschrift* 207 (1968): 584–608.

Oestreich, G. *Neo-Stoicism and the Early Modern State.* Cambridge: Cambridge University Press, 1982.

Olivier-Martin, F. *Histoire du droit français.* Montchréstien: Éditions Domat, 1948.

Osler, D. "Budaeus and Roman Law." *Ius Commune* 13 (1985): 195–212.

Overfield, J. *Humanism and Scholasticism in Late Medieval Germany.* Princeton, N.J.: Princeton University Press, 1984.

Ozment, S. *The Reformation in the Cities.* New Haven, Conn.: Yale University Press, 1975.

Pagenstecher, E. *Pandekten-Praktikum*. Heidelberg: Bangel und Schmitt, 1860.

Palmer, R. R. "Foreword" to H. Dippel, *Germany and the American Revolution, 1770–1800: A Sociohistorical Investigation of Late Eighteenth-Century Political Thinking*. Veröffentlichungen des Instituts für Europäische Geschichte Mainz, Band 90 (Abteilung Universalgeschichte). Wiesbaden: Steiner, 1978.

Pappenheim, M. "Levin Goldschmidt." *Zeitschrift für das gesammte Handelsrecht* 47 (1898): 1–49.

Pasini, D. *Saggio sul Jhering*. Milan: Giuffrè, 1959.

Paulsen, F. *Geschichte des Gelehrten Unterrichts in Deutschland*. 3d ed., 2 vols. Berlin/Leipzig: Veit/Vereinigung wissenschaftlicher Verleger, 1919–21.

Pfeiffer, B. W. "Einleitung" to idem, ed., *Neue Sammlung Bemerkenswerther Entscheidungen des Oberappellationsgerichts zu Cassel*. Hannover: Hahn, 1818–20.

———. *Ideen zu einer neuen Civil-Gesetzgebung für Teutsche Staaten*. Göttingen: Dieterich, 1815.

———. *Practische Ausführungen aus allen Theilen der Rechtswissenschaft*. 8 vols. in 7. Hannover: Hahn, 1825–46.

———. *Vermischte Aufsätze über Gegenstände des deutschen und des römischen Rechts*. Marburg: Akademische Buchhandlung, 1803.

———. "Ueber den wesentlichen Unterschied der adquisitiven und extinctiven Verjährung." In *Vermischte Aufsätze*, 272–341.

Pfeiffer-Munz, S. *Soziales Recht ist deutsches Recht: Otto von Gierkes Theorie des sozialen Rechts untersucht anhand seiner Stellungnahmen zur deutschen und zur schweizerischen Privatrechtskodifikation*. Zürcher Studien zur Rechtsgeschichte, vol. 2. Zürich: Schultheiss Polygraphischer Verlag, 1979.

Pfizer, C. von. *Über die Grenzen zwischen Verwaltungs- und Civil-Justiz*. Stuttgart: Cotta, 1828.

Pflanze, O. "Juridical and Political Responsibility in Nineteenth-Century Germany." In *The Responsibility of Power*. Edited by L. Krieger and F. Stern. Garden City, N.Y.: Doubleday, 1967, 162–82.

Piano Mortari, V. *Diritto Romano e Diritto Nazionale in Francia nel Secolo XVI*. Milan: Giuffrè, 1962.

Pirenne, H. *Medieval Cities*. Translated by F. Halsey. Princeton, N.J.: Princeton University Press, 1952.

Plathner, G. *Der Kampf um die Richterliche Unabhängigikeit bis zum Jahre 1848*. Abhandlungen aus dem Staats- und Verwaltungsrecht, Heft 51. Breslau: M. and H. Marcus, 1935.

Pleister, W. *Persönlichkeit, Wille und Freiheit im Werke Jherings*. Abhandlungen zur Rechtswissenschaftlichen Grundlagenforschung, vol. 51. Ebelsbach: Gremer, 1982.

Pocock, J.G.A. *The Ancient Constitution and the Feudal Law*. 2d ed. Cambridge: Cambridge University Press, 1987.

———. *Virtue, Commerce and History*. Cambridge: Cambridge University Press, 1985.

Polay, E. *Ursprung, Entwicklung, und Untergang der Pandektistik*. Acta Universitatis Szegediensis. Acta Juridica et Politica, Tomus 28, Fasc. 10 (1981).

Polley, R. *Anton Friedrich Justus Thibaut (A.D. 1772–1840) in seinen Selbstzeugnissen und Briefen*. Rechtshistorische Reihe, no. 13. 3 vols. Frankfurt a.M./ Bern: Lang, 1982.

Puchta, G. F. *Cursus der Institutionen*. 2d ed. Leipzig: Breitkopf und Härtel, 1845.

———. *Das Gewohnheitsrecht*. 2 vols. Reprint. Darmstadt: Wissenschaftliche Buchgesellschaft, 1965.

———. *Kleine civilistische Schriften*. Edited by A.A.F. Rudorff. Leipzig: Breitkopf und Härtel, 1851.

———. *Vorlesungen über das heutige römische Recht*. Edited by A.A.F. Rudorff. 6th ed. Leipzig: Bernhard Tauchnitz, 1873.

Pütter, J. S. *Nova Epitome Processus Imperii Amborum Tribunalium Supremorum*. 4th ed. Göttingen: Vandenhoeck und Ruprecht, 1786.

Pufendorf, F. E. *Friedrich Esaias Pufendorfs Entwurf eines hannoverschen Landrechts (vom Jahre 1772)*. Quellen und Darstellungen zur Geschichte Niedersachsens, vol. 78. Edited by W. Ebel. Hildesheim: Lax, 1970.

———. *Observationes Iuris Universi*. 4 vols. Hannover: Foerster, 1744–70.

Radbruch, G. *Paul Anselm Johann Feuerbach: Ein Juristenleben*. Reprint. Göttingen: Vandenhoeck und Ruprecht, 1969.

Radding, C. *The Origins of Medieval Jurisprudence*. New Haven, Conn.: Yale University Press, 1988.

Ranieri, F. "Diritto Commune e Diritto Locale nei primi decenni della Giurisprudenza del Reichskammergericht." In *Diritto Commune e Diritti Locali nella Storia dell'Europa*. Atti del Convegno di Varenna. Milan: Giuffrè, 1980.

———. *Recht und Gesellschaft im Zeitalter der Rezeption*. 2 vols. Quellen und Forschungen zur höchsten Gerichtsbarkeit im Alten Reich, vol. 17, pts. 1 and 2. Cologne/Vienna: Böhlau, 1985.

———. "Die Tätigkeit des Reichskammergerichts und seine Inanspruchnahme während des 16. Jahrhunderts." In *Forschungen aus Akten des Reichskammergerichts*. Quellen und Forschungen zur höchsten Gerichtsbarkeit im Alten Reich, vol. 14. Edited by B. Diestelkamp. Cologne/Vienna: Böhlau, 1984.

Redfield, R. *Peasant Society and Culture*. Chicago: University of Chicago Press, 1956.

Rehberg, A. W. *Die Erwartungen der Deutschen von dem Bund ihrer Fürsten*. Jena: Friedrich Bran, 1835.

Reineccius, R. *Methodus Legendi Cognoscendique Historiam tam Sacram quam Profanam*. Helmstedt: Transylvanus, 1583.

Remer, J. A. *Darstellung der historischen Welt durch alle Jahrhunderte*. Berlin/ Stettin: Nicolai, 1801.

Remus, *Nemesia Carulina*. Edited by J.F.H. Abegg. Heidelberg: Mohr, 1837 (orig. 1600).

Reyscher, A. L. *Die Grundherrlichen Rechte des Württembergischen Adels*. Tübingen: L. F. Fues, 1836.

Rheinhardt, D.T.J. *Dissertatio Juridica de Transmissionis Actorum Jure, ejusve abusu*. Erfurt: J. H. Grosch, 1716.

Ridder-Symoens, H. de. "Deutsche Studenten an Italienischen Rechtsfakultäten." *Ius Commune* 12 (1984): 287–315.

Riehl, W. H. *Land und Leute.* 6th ed. Stuttgart: Cotta, 1867.

Ringer, F. "Bestimmung und Messung von Segmentierung: Eine Teilantwort an Lundgreen." *Geschichte und Gesellschaft* 8 (1982): 280–85.

———. *Decline of the German Mandarins.* Cambridge, Mass.: Harvard University Press, 1969.

———. *Education and Society in Modern Europe.* Bloomington, Ind.: University of Indiana Press, 1979.

Ritter, G. *Stein: Eine Politische Biographie.* 2 vols. Stuttgart/Berlin: Deutsche Verlagsanstalt, 1931.

Robbins, C. *The Eighteenth-Century Commonwealthman.* Cambridge, Mass.: Harvard University Press, 1959.

Rowan, S. *Ulrich Zasius: A Jurist in the German Renaissance.* Ius Commune Sonderheft 31. Frankfurt a.M.: Klastermann, 1987.

Rückert, J. *A. L. Reyschers Leben und Rechtstheorie.* Abhandlungen zur Rechtswissenschaftlichen Grundlagenforschung, vol. 13. Berlin: Schweitzer, 1974.

———. "Heidelberg um 1804, oder: Die erfolgreiche Modernisierung der Jurisprudenz durch Thibaut, Savigny, Heise, Martin, Zachariä, u.a." In *Heidelberg im säkularen Umbruch: Traditionsbewußtsein und Kulturpolitik um 1800.* Edited by F. Strack. Stuttgart: Klett-Cotta, 1987, 83–116.

———. *Idealismus, Jurisprudenz und Politik bei Friedrich Carl von Savigny.* Abhandlungen zur Rechtswissenschaftlichen Grundlagenforschung, vol. 58. Ebelsbach: Gremer, 1984.

———. Review of Polley, *Thibaut.* ZSS(R) 101 (1984): 435–47.

Rüfner, W. *Verwaltungsrechtsschutz in Preußen, 1749–1842.* Bonner Rechtswissenschaftliche Abhandlungen, vol. 53. Bonn: Röhrscheid, 1962.

Rürup, R. *Deutschland im Neunzehnten Jahrhundert, 1815-1871.* Göttingen: Vandenhoeck und Ruprecht, 1984.

———. *J. J. Moser: Pietismus und Reform.* Wiesbaden: Steiner, 1965.

Ruge, A. "Die Wahre Romantik." In idem, *Gesammelte Schriften.* 3 vols. Mannheim: Grohe, 1846, 3:117–34.

Ruhberg, U. "Die Rechte des Grundeigentümers: Entwicklung des Eigentumsbegriffes in Preußen zwischen ALR und BGB im agrarischen Bodenrecht." Diss. Kiel, 1972.

Sakai, E. *Der Kurhessische Bauer im Neunzehnten Jahrhundert und die Grundlastenablösung.* Hessische Forschungen zur Geschichtlichen Landes- und Volkskunde, Heft 7. Melsungen: A. Bernecker-Verlag, 1967.

Sartorius, J. B. "Revision der Lehre von der Aktenversendung." *Zeitschrift für Civilrecht und Prozess* 14 (1840): 219–56.

Savigny, F. C. von. *Friedrich Karl von Savigny.* Edited by Stoll. 2 vols. Berlin: Heymann, 1929.

———. *Geschichte des Römischen Rechts im Mittelalter.* 6 vols. Heidelberg: Mohr, 1815.

———. "Ministerprogramm." Anlage to A. Stölzel, *Brandenburg-Preußens*

Rechtsverwaltung und Rechtsverfassung. 2 vols. Berling: Vahlen, 1888, 2:731–50.

——. "Nachträge" to "Vom Beruf unserer Zeit für Gesetzgebung und Rechtswissenschaft (1828 ed.)." In *Thibaut und Savigny.* Edited by H. Hattenhauer. Munich: Vahlen, 1973, 228–60.

——. "Niebuhrs Wesen und Wirken." In *Vermischte Schriften.* 6 vols. Reprint. Darmstadt: Wissenschaftliche Buchgesellschaft, 1968, 4:220–24.

——. *Das Obligationenrecht.* 2 vols. Berlin: Veit, 1851.

——. "On the Present State of the German Universities." Quoted in R. Wellek, "Ein unbekannter Artikel Savignys über die deutschen Universitäten." *ZSS(R)* 51 (1931): 529–37; German version in H. Marquardt, "Ein unbekannter Aufsatz F. C. von Savignys," in *Die Sammlung: Zeitschrift für Kultur und Erziehung* 6 (1951): 321–36.

——. *Das Recht des Besitzes.* Edited by A. F. Rudorff. 7th ed. Vienna: Carl Gerolds Sohn, 1865.

——. Review of Schleiermacher, *Gelegentliche Gedanken über Universitäten in deutschem Sinn.* In *Vermischte Schriften,* 4:255–69.

——. *System des heutigen Römischen Rechts.* 8 vols. Berlin: Veit, 1840–49.

——. "Ueber den Römischen Colonat" and "Nachtrag 1859." In *Vermischte Schriften,* 2:1–66.

——. "Ueber den Zweck der Zeitschrift für geschichtliche Rechtswissenschaft." In *Vermischte Schriften,* 1:105–26.

——. *Vermischte Schriften.* 6 vols. Reprint. Darmstadt: Wissenschaftliche Buchgesellschaft, 1968.

——. "Vom Beruf unserer Zeit für Gesetzgebung und Rechtswissenschaft." In *Thibaut und Savigny.* Edited by H. Hattenhauer. Munich: Vahlen, 1973, 95–192.

——. "Wesen und Wert der deutschen Universistäten." In *Vermischte Schriften,* 4:255–69.

Scala, P. *De Consilio Sapientis in Forensibus Causis Adhibendo Libri IIII.* Venice: Aldus Manutius, 1560.

Schelsky, H. *Einsamkeit und Freiheit.* 2d ed. Düsseldorf: Bertelsmann Universitätsverlag, n.d. [1971].

Scherer, E. C. *Geschichte und Kirchengeschichte an den deutschen Universitäten.* Frieburg i.B.: Herder & Co., 1927.

Scheuermann, R. *Einflüße der historischen Rechtsschule auf die oberstrichterliche gemeinrechtliche Zivilrechtspraxis bis zum Jahre 1861.* Münsterische Beiträge zur Rechts- und Staatswissenschaft, Heft 17. Berlin: de Gruyter, 1972.

Scheuner, U. *Der Beitrag der deutschen Romantik zur politischen Theorie.* Rheinisch-Westfälische Akademie der Wissenschaften (Geisteswissenschaften), Vorträge G 248. Opladen: Westdeutscher Verlag, 1980.

——. "Die neuere Entwicklung des Rechtsstaats in Deutschland." In *Staatstheorie und Staatsrecht.* Berlin: Duncker und Humblot, 1978, 185–222. Originally in *Hundert Jahre Deutsches Rechtsleben.* Edited by E. v. Caemmerer et al. Karlsruhe: C. F. Müller, 1960, 229–62.

Schieder, W. "Probleme einer Sozialgeschichte des frühen Liberalismus in Deutschland." In idem, ed., *Liberalismus in der Gesellschaft des deutschen Vormärz. Geschichte und Gesellschaft, Sonderheft 9.* Göttingen: Vandenhoeck und Ruprecht, 1983, 9–21.

Schildt, B. "Die Rechtsprüche deutscher Juristenfakultäten als Quelle rechtshistorischer Forschung." *Staat und Recht* 32 (1983): 470–77.

Schlözer, A. L. von. "Deutsche Reichsjustiz." In *Stats-Anzeigen.* 18 vols. Göttingen: Vandenhoeck, 1782–93, Heft 43, Band 11, 270–71.

Schlosser, J. G. *Briefe über die Gesezgebung überhaupt, und den Entwurf des preußischen Gesezbuchs insbesondere.* Frankfurt: J. G. Fleischer, 1789.

———. "Über das Studium des Reinen Römischen Rechts." *Hugos Civilistisches Magazin* (4th ed., 1823): 20–55.

Schmid, K. E. *Deutschlands Wiedergeburt.* Jena: Fromann, 1814.

Schmitt, C. *Politische Romantik.* 3d ed. Berlin: Duncker und Humblot, 1968.

Schnabel, F. *Deutsche Geschichte im Neunzehnten Jahrhundert.* 3d ed. 4 vols. Freiburg i.B.: Herder, 1949.

———. "Geschichte der Ministerialverantwortlichkeit in Baden." *Zeitschrift für die Geschichte des Oberrheins* 75 (1921): 87–110, 171–91, 303–31.

Schnapper, B. "Les rentes chez les théologiens et les canonistes du XIIIᵉ au XVIᵉ siècle." In *Études d'histoire du droit canonique dédiées à Gabriel Le Bras,* 2 vols. Paris: Sirey, 1965, 2:965–95.

Schnur, R., ed. *Der Beitrag der Juristen für die Ausbildung der frühmodernen Staaten.* Berlin: Duncker und Humblot, 1987.

Schrader, E. *Die Prätorischen Edicte der Römer auf unsere Verhältnisse übertragen, ein Hauptmittel unser Recht allmälich gut and volksmäßig zu bilden.* Weimar: im Verlage des G.H.S. priv. Landes-Industrie-Comptoirs, 1815. Also reprinted in idem, *Civilistische Abhandlungen.* Weimar: Im Verlage des G.H.S. priv. Landes-Industrie-Comptoirs, 1816.

Schröder, H. *Friedrich Karl von Savigny: Geschichte und Rechtsdenken beim Übergang vom Feudalismus zum Kapitalismus in Deutschland.* Frankfurt a.M.: Lang, 1984.

Schröder, J. *Wissenschaftstheorie und Lehre der "Praktischen Jurisprudenz" auf deutsche Universitäten an der Wende zum neunzehnten Jahrhundert.* Ius Commune Sonderheft 11. Frankfurt a.M.: Klostermann, 1979.

———. "Zur Älteren Genossenschaftstheorie: Die Begründung des modernen Körperschaftsbegriffs durch Georg Beseler." *Q. Fior.* 11/12 (1982–83): 399–459.

Schubert, W. *Das Französische Recht in Deutschland.* Cologne/Vienna: Böhlau, 1977.

———. "Das französische Recht in Deutschland zu Beginn der Restaurationszeit." *ZSS(G)* 94 (1977): 129–84.

———. "Savigny und die rheinisch-französische Gerichtsverfassung." *ZSS(G)* 95 (1978): 158–69.

Schulz, F. *Classical Roman Law.* Oxford: Oxford University Press, 1951.

———. *Geschichte der Römischen Rechtswissenschaft.* Weimar: Böhlau, 1961.

Schweitzer, C. W. "Ein Rechtsfall, hauptsächlich als Beitrag zur Bestimmung des

Verhältnisses zwischen der richterlichen und der gesetzgebenden Gewalt." *Jahrbücher der Gesetzgebung und Rechtspflege in Sachsen* 1 (1829): 297–321.

Schwinge, E. *Der Kampf um die Schwurgerichte bis zur Frankfurter Nationalversammlung.* Strafrechtliche Abhandlungen, Heft 213. Breslau: Schletter, 1926.

Scriptores Historiae Augustae. Translated by W.H.D. Rouse. The Loeb Library, 3 vols. Reprint. Cambridge, Mass.: Harvard University Press, 1975.

Seckel, E. "Geschichte der Berliner Juristenfakultät als Spruchkollegium." In Lenz, ed., *Geschichte der Königlichen Friedrich-Wilhelms-Universität zu Berlin,* 3:447–79.

Selchow, J.H.C. von. *Elementa Antiquitatum Juris Romani Publici et Privati.* Göttingen: Vandenhoeck, 1757.

Seneca. *Apocolocyntosis.* Translated by D. Magie. The Loeb Library. Reprint. Cambridge, Mass: Harvard University Press, 1982.

Sheehan, J. *German Liberalism in the Nineteenth Century.* Chicago: University of Chicago Press, 1977.

Siblewski, K. *Ritterlicher Patriotismus und Romantischer Nationalismus in der deutschen Literatur, 1770–1830.* Munich: W. Falk, 1981.

Sidney, A. *Betrachtungen über die Regierungsformen.* Translated by C. D. Erhard, 2 vols. Leipzig: Weygand, 1793.

Siemann, W. *Die Frankfurter Nationalversammlung 1848/9 zwischen demokratischem Liberalismus und konservativer Reform: Die Bedeutung der Juristendominanz in den Verfassungsverhandlungen des Paulskirchenparlaments.* Bern: Lang, 1976.

Simon, D. *Die Unabhängigkeit des Richters.* Darmstadt: Wissenschaftliche Buchgesellschaft, 1975.

Simshäuser, W. *Zur Entwicklung des Verhältnisses von materiellem Recht und Prozeßrecht seit Savigny.* Schriften zum deutschen und europäischen Zivil-, Handels- und Prozeßrecht, vol. 32. Bielefeld: Ernst und Werner Gieseking, 1965.

Sinzheimer, H. *Jüdische Klassiker der deutschen Rechtswissenschaft.* Frankfurter Wissenschaftliche Beiträge, Rechts- und Wirtschaftswissenschaftliche Reihe, vol. 7. Frankfurt a.M.: Klostermann, 1953, 51–72 (originally Amsterdam: Menno Hertzberger & Co., 1938).

Sjöholm, E. *Rechtsgeschichte als Wissenschaft und Politik: Studien zur germanistischen Theorie des neunzehnten Jahrhunderts.* Abhandlungen zur rechtswissenschaftlichen Grundlagenforschung, vol. 10. Berlin: Schweitzer, 1972.

Skinner, Q. *Foundations of Modern Political Thought.* 2 vols. Cambridge: Cambridge University Press, 1978.

Smend, R. *Das Reichskammergericht.* Pt. 1, *Geschichte und Verfassung* (no more appeared). Quellen und Studien zur Verfassungsgeschichte des Deutschen Reiches im Mittelalter und Neuzeit, vol. 1, Heft 3. Weimar: Böhlau, 1911.

Spangenberg, K.F.W. von. *Versuch einer systematischen Darstellung der Lehre vom Besitz.* Leipzig: Dyk, 1794.

Sprengler-Ruppenthal, A. "Zur Rezeption des Römischen Rechts im Eherecht der Reformatoren." *ZSS(K)* 68 (1982): 363–418.

Srbik, H. Ritter von. *Geist und Geschichte des deutschen Humanismus*. 2 vols. Munich: F. Bruckmann, 1950–51.

Stadelmann, R. "Das Zeitalter der Reformation." In *Handbuch der deutschen Geschichte*. Edited by L. Just. 6 vols. Konstanz: Dr. Albert Hochfeld, 1956, 2:1–132.

Stahl, F. J. *Philosophie des Rechts*. 3 vols. in 2. 2d ed. Heidelberg: Mohr, 1846.

Stammler, R. *Deutsches Rechtsleben*. 2 vols. Charlottenburg: Pan-Verlag, 1928–32.

Stein, A. "Luther über Eherecht und Juristen." In Junghans, ed., *Leben und Werk Martin Luthers*, 1:171–85.

Stein, L. v. *Verwaltungslehre*. 8 vols in 4. Stuttgart: Cotta, 1866–84.

Stein, P. *Legal Evolution*. Cambridge: Cambridge University Press, 1980.

Stern, A. "Das Römische Recht und der deutsche Bauernkrieg." *Zeitschrift für Schweizerische Geschichte* 14 (1934): 20–29.

Stintzing R. (continued by E. Landsberg). *Geschichte der deutschen Rechtswissenschaft*. 3 vols. in 5. Munich/Berlin: Oldenbourg, 1910.

Stobbe, O. *Geschichte der deutschen Rechtsquellen*. 2 vols. Leipzig: Duncker und Humblot, 1860–64.

Stölzel, A. "Die Berliner Mitwochgesellschaft über Aufhebung oder Reform der Universitäten." *Forschungen zur Brandenburgischen und Preußischen Geschichte* 2 (1889): 201–22.

———. *Brandenburg-Preußens Rechtsverwaltung und Rechtsverfassung*. 2 vols. Berlin: Vahlen, 1888.

———. *Die Entwicklung der gelehrten Rechtsprechung*. 2 vols. Berlin: Vahlen, 1901–10.

———. *Die Entwicklung des gelehrten Richtertums*. 2 vols. Stuttgart: Cotta, 1872.

Stolleis, M. "Grundzüge der Beamtenethik." *Die Verwaltung* 13 (1980): 447–75.

———, ed. *Hermann Conring (1606–1681): Beiträge zu Leben und Werk*. Historische Forschungen, vol. 23. Berlin: Duncker und Humblot, 1983.

———. "Verwaltungslehre und Verwaltungswissenschaft." In Jeserich et al. *Deutsche Verwaltungsgeschichte*, 2:56–94.

Strack, F., ed. *Heidelberg im säkularen Umbruch: Traditionsbewußtsein und Kulturpolitik um 1800*. Stuttgart: Klett-Cotta, 1987.

Strauch, D. "F. C. von Savignys Landrechtsvorlesungen vom Sommer 1824." In *Staat-Recht-Kultur: Festgabe für E. v. Hippel*. Bonn: Röhrscheid, 1965, 245–64.

Strauss, G. *Law, Resistance and the State: The Opposition to Roman Law in Reformation Germany*. Princeton, N.J.: Princeton University Press, 1986.

———, ed. *Pre-Reformation Germany*. New York: Harper and Row, 1972.

Strippel, J. "Zum Verhältnis von Deutscher Rechtsgeschichte und Deutscher Philologie." In Müller, ed., *Germanistik und deutsche Nation*, 113–66.

Struben [sometimes Strube], D. G. *Rechtliche Bedenken*. 3 vols. 2d ed. Hannover: J. W. Schmidt, 1787.

Struckmann, G. W. *Fälle und Entscheidungen aus dem Gebiete des Eigentumsrechts*. Lüneburg: Herold und Wahlstab, 1828.

———. *Practische Beiträge zur Kenntniß des Osnabrückischen Eigentumsrechts.* 14 vols. Lüneburg: Herold und Wahlstab, 1826–33.

Struckmann, H. *Geschichte der Familie Struckmann aus Osnabrück.* Berlin: Norddeutsche Buchdruckerei und Verlagsanstalt, 1909.

Struve, G. A. *Syntagma Juris Feudalis.* 8th ed. Frankfurt a.M.: Oehrling, 1703.

Stryk, S. *Specimen Usus Moderni Pandectarum.* 14 vols. Florence: Giuseppe Celli, 1841.

Stühler, H.-U. *Die Diskussion um die Erneuerung der Rechtswissenschaft von 1780–1815.* Schriften zur Rechtsgeschichte, Heft 15. Berlin: Duncker und Humblot, 1978.

Stüve, J.C.B. *Briefe.* Veröffentlichungen der Niedersächsischen Archivverwaltung, nos. 10 and 11. 2 vols. Göttingen: 1959.

Tarello, G. *Le Ideologie della Codificazione nel secolo XVIII.* Università di Genova. Facoltà di Giurisprudenza. Corso di Filosofia di Diritto, Parte 1. Genoa: Cooperativa Libraria Universitaria, n.d.

Der Teutsche Justinianus. Augsburg: Kühtzen, 1718.

Thibaut, A.F.J. "Besprechung des Einleitungssatzes der *Zeitschrift für Geschichtliche Rechtswissenschaft.*" In Hattenhauer, ed., *Thibaut und Savigny,* 269–73.

———. *Über Besitz und Verjährung.* Jena: Mauke, 1802.

———. "Über die Notwendigkeit eines allgemeinen bürgerlichen Rechts für Deutschland." In Hattenhauer, ed., *Thibaut und Savigny,* 61–94.

Thibaut und Savigny: Ihre Programmatische Schriften. Edited by H. Hattenhauer. Munich: Vahlen, 1973.

Thieme, H. "Die Zeit des Späten Naturrechts," *ZSS(G)* 56 (1936): 202–63.

Thireau, J.-L. *Charles Du Moulin.* Travaux d'humanisme et renaissance, no. 176. Genèva: Droz, 1980.

Thomas, R. Hinton. *Liberalism, Nationalism and the German Intellectuals (1822–1847).* Cambridge: Heffer, 1951.

Thomas, H. *Deutsche Geschichte des Spätmittelalters.* Stuttgart: Kohlhammer, 1983.

Thomasius, C. *Naevorum Jurisprudentiae Romanae Antejustinianeae Libri Duo.* 2d ed. Halle: Christopher Salfeld, 1707.

Treitschke, H. von. *History of Germany.* 7 vols. Translated by E. and C. Paul. New York: AMS Press, 1968.

Treutler, H. *Selectarum disputationum ad jus civile Justinianeum quinquaginta libris Pandectarum comprehensum, volumina duo.* Marburg: Paulus Egenolphus, 1606.

Troeltsch, E. "The Idea of Natural Law." Appendix to O. Gierke, *Natural Law and the Theory of Society.* Translated by E. Barker. 2 vols. Cambridge: Cambridge University Press, 1934.

Troje, H. E. "Die Literatur des gemeinen Rechts unter dem Einfluß des Humanismus." In *Coing Handbuch,* vol. 2, pt. 1, 615–795.

Trusen, W. *Die Anfänge des gelehrten Rechts in Deutschland.* Recht und Geschichte, vol. 1. Wiesbaden: Steiner, 1962.

Tuck, R. *Natural Rights Theories: Their Origin and Development.* Cambridge: Cambridge University Press, 1979.

Turner, R. S. "University Reformers and Professorial Scholarship in Germany, 1760–1806." In *The University in Society*. Edited by Stone. 2 vols. Princeton, N.J.: Princeton University Press, 1974, 2:495–531.

Unterholzner, K.A.D. *Ausführliche Entwicklung der Gesammten Verjährungslehre*. 2 vols. Leipzig: Barth, 1828.

———. *Lehre von der Verjährung durch fortgesetzten Besitz*. Breslau: J. F. Korn, 1815.

Vahlen, A., ed. *Savigny und Unterholzner: Vierundzwanzig Briefe F. K. v. Savignys aus dem Nachlass von K.A.D. Unterholzner, mit einem Lebensabriss Unterholzners*. Verhandlungen der Akademie der Wissenschaften zu Berlin (1941), no. 3.

Valjavec, F. *Die Entstehung der politischen Strömungen in Deutschland, 1770–1815*. Munich: Oldenbourg, 1951.

van Hall, W. "Savigny als Praktiker: Die Staatsratsgutachten (1817–1842)." Diss., Kiel, 1981.

———. "Savigny als Praktiker: Die Staatsratsgutachten (1817–1842)." Summarized in article form. *ZSS(G) 99* (1982): 287–97.

Ventker, A. F. *Stüve und die Hannöversche Bauernbefreiung*. Wirtschaftswissenschaftliche Gesellschaft zum Studium Niedersachsens, Series A, Heft 28. Oldenbourg: G. Stalling, 1935.

Vierhaus, R. "Montesquieu in Deutschland: Zur Geschichte seiner Wirkung als politischer Schriftsteller im 18. Jahrhundert." In *Collegium Philosophicum: Studien Joachim Ritter zum 60. Geburtstag*. Basel/Stuttgart: Schwabe, 1965, 403–37.

Vincke, J. J. *Ohnmaaßgebliche Gedancken zu der Eigentums-Ordnung Osnabrücks*. Lemgo: H. W. Meyer, 1721.

Virck, H. "Melanchthons Politische Stellung auf dem Reichstag zu Augsburg 1530." *Zeitschrift für Kirchengeschichte* (1888): 67–104, 293–340.

Vogel, B. "Beamtenkonservatismus: Sozial- und verfassungsgeschichtliche Voraussetzungen der Parteien in Preußen im frühen 19. Jahrhundert." In *Deutscher Konservatismus im 19. und 20. Jahrhundert: Festschrift für Fritz Fischer*. Edited by D. Stegman et al. Bonn: Verlag Neue Gesellschaft, 1983, 1–31.

Vonessen, H. "Friedrich Karl von Savigny und Jakob Grimm." Diss., Munich:1958

Wächter, C. G. *Gemeines Recht Deutschlands*. Leipzig: Weidmann, 1844.

Wagner, H. *Das geteilte Eigentum im Naturrecht und Postivismus*. Breslau: G. Märtin, 1938.

Wagner, H. *Die Politische Pandektistik*. Berlin: Berlin Verlag Arno Spitz, 1985.

Walker, M. *The German Home Towns*. Ithaca, N.Y.: Cornell University Press, 1971.

———. *J. J. Moser and the Holy Roman Empire of the German Nation*. Chapel Hill, N.C.: University of North Carolina Press, 1981.

Walter, G. *Der Zusammenbruch des Heiligen Römischen Reichs deutscher Nation und die Problematik seiner Restauration in den Jahren 1814/1815*. Studien und Quellen zur Geschichte des deutschen Verfassungsrechts, Series A, vol. 12. Heidelberg/Karlsruhe: Müller Juristischer Verlag, 1980.

Watson, A. *The Evolution of Law*. Baltimore, Md., Johns Hopkins Press, 1985.

———. *The Making of the Civil Law*. Cambridge, Mass.: Harvard University Press, 1981.

Weber, M. *Economy and Society*. Edited by G. Roth and C. Wittich, translated by E. Shils. 2 vols. Berkeley, Calif.: University of California Press, 1968.

———. *Die Römische Agrargeschichte in ihrer Bedeutung für das Staats- und Privatrecht*. Stuttgart: Enke, 1891.

———. *Wirtschaft und Gesellschaft*. 5th ed., 2 vols. Tübingen: Mohr, 1975.

Weitzel, J. *Der Kampf um die Appellation ans Reichskammergericht*. Quellen und Forschungen zur höchsten Gerichtsbarkeit im alten Reich, vol. 4. Cologne/Vienna: Böhlau, 1976.

Welcker, K. T. Review of *Gutachten der (Königl. Preußischen) Immediat-Justiz-Commission (zu Köln) über das Geschworenengericht*. *Heidelberger Jahrbücher der Litteratur* 11 (1818): 785–822.

———. *Die Vervollkommnung der organischen Entwicklung des deutschen Bundes*. Karlsruhe: C. T. Groos, 1831.

———, ed. *Neuer Beitrag zur Lehre von den Injurien und der Preßfreiheit durch die Rechtsgutachten der Spruchkollegien von Heidelberg, Kiel und Tübingen über den Preßprozeß des Hofrath [sic] Welcker und durch die Prüfung der hofgerichtlichen Entscheidungsgründe in den Appellationsschriften des Geheimraths Duttlinger und des Hofraths Welcker*. Freiburg: Gebrüder Groos, 1833.

Welcker, K. T., and K.W.R. von Rotteck, eds., *Staats-Lexikon*. 2d. ed. Altona: Hammerich, 1845.

Wellek, R. "Ein unbekannter Artikel Savignys über die deutschen Universitäten." *ZSS(G)* 51 (1931): 529–37.

Weller, H. *Die Bedeutung der Präjudizien im Verständnis der deutschen Rechtswissenschaft*. Schriften zur Rechtstheorie, vol. 77. Berlin: Duncker und Humblot, 1979.

Wertenbruch, W. *Versuch einer kritischen Analyse der Rechtslehre Rudolf von Jherings*. Neue Kölner Rechtswissenschaftliche Abhandlungen, Heft 4. Berlin: de Gruyter, 1955.

Westphal, E. C. *System des Römischen Rechts über die Arten der Sachen, Besitz, Eigentum und Verjährung*. Leipzig: Weygand, 1788.

Whitman, J. "Commercial Law and the American *Volk*: A Note on Llewellyn's German Sources for the Uniform Commercial Code." *Yale Law Journal* 97, no. 1 (November 1987): 156–175.

———. "From Philology to Anthropology in Mid-Nineteenth-Century Germany." In *History of Anthropology*, vol. 2. Edited by G. Stocking. Madison, Wis.: University of Wisconsin Press, 1984, 214–29.

———. "Nietzsche in the Magisterial Tradition of German Classical Philology." *Journal of the History of Ideas* 47 (1986): 453–68.

Wickert, L. *Theodor Mommsen*. 4 vols. Frankfurt a.M.: Klostermann, 1969.

Wieacker, F. "Einflüsse des Humanismus auf die Rezeption: Eine Studie zu Johann Apels 'Dialogus.' " *Zeitschrift für die gesamte Staatswissenschaft* 100 (1939): 423–56.

Wieacker, F. "Pandektenwissenschaft und Industrielle Revolution." In idem, *Industriegesellschaft und Privatrechtsordnung*. Frankfurt a.M.: Athenäum-Fischer-Taschenbuch-Verlag, 1974, 55–78.

———. *Privatrechtsgeschichte der Neuzeit*. 2d ed. Göttingen: Vandenhoeck und Ruprecht, 1967.

———. *Rudolf Von Jhering*. 2d ed. Stuttgart: Koehler, 1968.

Wieacker, F., and C. Wollschläger, eds. *Jherings Erbe*. Abhandlungen der Akademie der Wissenschaften in Göttingen. Philosophisch-Historische Klasse. Folge 3, vol. 75. Göttingen: Vandenhoeck und Ruprecht, 1970.

Wiegand, W. *Studien zur Rechtsanwendungslehre der Rezeptionszeit*. Abhandlungen zur Rechtswissenschaftlichen Grundlagenforschung, vol. 27. Ebelsbach: Gremer, 1977.

———. "Zur Herkunft und Ausbreitung der Formel, 'Habere Fundatam Intentionem.' " In *Festschrift für Hermann Krause*. Cologne/Vienna: Böhlau, 1975, 126–70.

———. "Zur Theoretischen Begründung der Bodenmobilisierung in der Rechtswissenschaft: Der abstrakte Eigentumsbegriff." In Coing and Wilhelm, eds. *Wissenschaft und Kodifikation des Privatrechts im Neunzehnten Jahrhundert*, 3:118–55.

Wiggenhorn, H. "Das Reichskammergerichtsprozeß am Ende des alten Reichs." Diss., Munich: 1966.

Wilhelm, W. "Das Recht im Römischen Recht." In Wieacker and Wollschläger, eds., *Jherings Erbe*, 228–39.

———. *Zur Juristischen Methodenlehre im Neunzehnten Jahrhundert*. Frankfurter Wissenschaftliche Beiträge. Rechts- und Wirtschaftswissenschaftliche Reihe, vol. 14. Frankfurt a.M.: Klostermann, 1958.

Willoweit, D. "Dominium und Proprietas: Zur Entwicklung des Eigentumsbegriffs in der mittelalterlichen und neuzeitlichen Rechtswissenschaft." *Historisches Jahrbuch* 94 (1974): 131–56.

———. "Kaiser, Reich und Reichsstände bei Hermann Conring." In Stolleis, ed., *Conring*, 321–34.

Windscheid, B. *Die Actio des Römischen Rechts*. Düsseldorf: J. Buddeus, 1856.

———. "Das römische Recht in Deutschland." In *Gesammelte Reden und Abhandlungen*. Leipzig: Duncker und Humblot, 1904, 25–49.

Wippermann, C. W. "B. W. Pfeiffer." In *Allgemeine Deutsche Biographie*. 56 vols. Leipzig: Duncker und Humblot, 1875–1912, 25:633–34.

———. *Kurhessen seit dem Freiheitskriege*. Cassel: T. Fischer, 1850.

Wittich, W. *Der Grundherrschaft in Nordwestdeutschland*. Leipzig: Duncker und Humblot, 1896.

Wohlhaupter, E. "Die Spruchtätigkeit der Kieler Fakultät." *ZSS(G)* 58 (1938): 752ff.

Wolf, E. *Grosse Rechtsdenker der Deutschen Geistesgeschichte*. 4th ed. Tübingen: Mohr, 1963.

Wolter, U. *Ius Canonicum in Iure Civili*. Forschungen zur neueren Privatrechtsgeschichte, vol. 23. Cologne/Vienna: Böhlau, 1975.

[Wurmb, F. L.] *Das Grabmal des Leonidas*. N.p. [Dresden]: n.p., 1798.

Yavetz, Z. "Why Rome?" *American Journal of Philology* 97 (1976): 276–96.

Zachariä, K. S. *Biographischer und Juristischer Nachlaß.* Tübingen: Cotta, 1843.

———. "Erstreckt sich das richterliche Entscheidungsrecht auf die Frage, ob die Regierung eine Verordnung, auf welche sich in einer Streitsache die Partheyen beziehen, zu erlassen berechtigt gewesen sey?" *Archiv für die civilistische Praxis* 16 (1832): 145–82.

———. *Der Kampf des Grundeigenthumes gegen die Grundherrlichkeit.* Heidelberg: Osswald, 1832.

———. *Lucius Cornelius Sulla, genannt der Glückliche, als Ordner des Römischen Freystaates.* 2 vols. Heidelberg: Osswald, 1834.

———. "Die Nationaleinheit der Teutschen und die teutschen Universitäten." *Jahrbücher der Geschichte und Politik* 10, no. 2 (1837): 385–420.

———. *De Originibus Juris Romani ex Jure Germanico Repetendis.* N.p. [prize pamphlet, faculty of law, Ruperto-Carola University, Heidelberg], 1817.

———. *Vierzig Bücher vom Staate.* 7 vols. in 5. Stuttgart/Tübingen: Cotta, 1820–32.

———. "Wissenschaftliche Entwicklung der Lehre des römischen Rechts von den dinglichen Servituten." *Hugos Civilistisches Magazin* 2 (1795): 320–49.

Zagorin, P. *Rebels and Rulers, 1500–1660.* 2 vols. Cambridge: Cambridge University Press, 1982.

Zeumer, K. *Heiliges Römisches Reich Deutscher Nation.* Quellen und Studien zur Verfassungsgeschichte des deutschen Reichs, vol. 4, pt. 2. Weimar: Böhlaus Nachfolger, 1910.

Ziegler, K.-H. "Arbiter, arbitrator, et amicabilis compositor." *ZSS(R)* 84 (1967): 376–81.

INDEX

Absolutism, 42, 54, 56, 58, 74, 137; opposition to, 66, 73, 76, 95
Accursian Gloss, 15
Achenwall, G., 72
actio, 219, 224
Aeschylus, 195
ager privatus, 164
ager publicus, 156, 198n.196
Agrarfrage. *See* agrarian reform
agrarian laws. *See* leges agrariae
agrarian reform, xv, 79, 151, 153, 154, 155, 160, 161, 178, 180
Aktenversendung, 34–36, 51–54, 55, 77, 79, 91, 98, 100, 109, 118n.108, 119, 132, 135–50, 192–93, 203; defined, 235. *See also* Spruchkollegien
Albrecht, W.E.A., 180–81n.123
Allgemeines Burgerliches Gesetzbuch (General Civil Code of Austria, 1811), 55, 103, 108
Allgemeines deutsches Handelsgesetzbuch (1861), 210, 211, 220, 229
Allgemeines Landrecht (General Territorial Law of Prussia, 1794), 55, 103, 108, 113, 167, 170n.120, 189, 203; defined, 235
America, 98
American Revolution, 69, 71–72, 73
ancient constitutionalism. *See* constitutionalism
Antonines (Roman emperors), 81–90, 155. *See also* Hadrian
Aristotle, 25–26, 37, 45, 48, 221
Arndts, L., 209
Aryans, 210
auctoritas, 163
Augsburger Allgemeine Zeitung, 144
Augustus (Roman emperor), 57, 58–65, 85, 89, 128
Austria, 92

Babeuf, Gracchus, 156
Babouvisme, 156, 184
Bachofen, J. G., 208, 217, 228

Baden (German state), 132, 133, 143, 159, 168
Badisches Landrecht (Territorial Law of Baden, 1809), 168
Baldus de Ubaldis, 30
Bartolus of Sassoferrato, 27, 36, 167, 180
Basel, University of, 214
Bauer. *See* peasants
Bauernbefreiung (liberation of the peasants), 152, 156, 167, 178, 209; defined, 235
Bavaria, 74, 167
Bekker, E. I., 214
Bellow, Saul, 213
Berlin, 98, 156, 184
Berlin, University of, 99, 100, 113, 131, 135, 147, 148, 150, 194, 207, 214, 233, 234
Beseler, G., 207
Besitz. *See* possession
Bible, 17
Bildung, 126
bills of lading, 223, 225, 226
Bismarck, O. v., 94, 140
Bluntschli, J. C., 107n.66, 211, 212–13
Bodin, Jean, 70
Boeckh, August, 194, 210
Boehmer, Just Henning, 48, 173, 185
Bologna, University of, 6
Bonn, University of, 207
Boulainvilliers, Henri de, 71
Brandenburg, 172–73
Braunschweig, 79, 86, 115, 116, 173
Bremen (Free City), 135
Bremen and Verden, 116, 117n.102, 119, 191n.170, 202
Brenz, Johannes, 24
Breslau, University of, 147
Bund (Federation of German States, German Federation), 100, 101, 135, 137, 143; defined, 235
Bundesacte of 1815, 100, 135–36, 145
Bundesbeschlüsse of 1834 and 1835, 143, 147
Bundesversammlung, 92

systematicity: as legal ideal in Germany, 37, 48–49, 80, 121, 232–33

Taciteanism, 59
Territorial governments, 52
theology, 80
Thibaut, Anton Friedrich Justus, 104–5, 106, 108, 109, 110, 112n.90, 114, 132, 136–39, 140, 141, 148, 180–81, 182, 205, 209; "conversion" of in 1819, 139n.202; and B. G. Niebuhr, 159; on split property, 180, 191
Thirty Years' War, 39, 41, 59
Thomasius, Christian, 62, 63, 84
Tories, 147
translatio imperii, 4–5, 22, 24, 26, 28
Treutler, Hieronymus, 38, 60
Troeltsch, E., 70n.11
Tübingen, University of, 47, 98, 100, 104, 131, 140, 147, 148, 201
Twelve Tables, 127, 128, 130, 164

Übungen, 122–24, 186–87, 189, 206; defined, 238
Ulpian (Roman jurist), 221
unification, German, 95
Uniform Commercial Code, 223
universities, 64, 139; German, 80, 92, 99, 144, 147; Savigny on, 106–7, 109
Untereigentum, 167–68; defined, 238. See also dominium utile; split property
Unterholzner, K.A.D., 169n.75
urbaria, 177
usury, 168
usus fori, 117n.102
usus modernus pandectarum, 49, 55–56, 60, 85, 109, 119, 171, 173, 183, 185, 186, 224; defined, 238

Verjahrung, 171, 182, 185, 189–90, 191, 193, 194, 197; defined, 238
Vincke, J.J.C., 196
Volk, 96, 105, 109, 116, 117, 120, 121, 122, 125, 126, 127, 128, 129, 137, 204, 206, 208; defined, 238

Volksgeist, 112, 122, 123–24, 126, 127, 130, 205, 206, 209, 212; defined, 238

Wachter, C. G., 143, 198, 205n.20
Wagner, Richard, 24n.85
Weber, A. D., 64
Weber, Max, xi, 77n.46, 133, 162, 232, 234
Weisse, C. E., 74
Welcker, K. T., 101, 137–39, 145, 146, 148, 149–50; as Germanist, 137
Westphalia, 72, 154
Westphalia, kingdom of, 187
Westphalia, Peace of, 88
Whigs, 69, 71
Wiener Schlußakte. See Final Act of Vienna
Wilamowitz-Moellendorff, Ulrich von, 106n.59
Wilda, W. E., 207
Wilhelmine Reich, 232–34
Winckelmann, J. J., 82
Windscheid, Bernhard, 218–20, 224, 228, 229, 230, 234
Wittenberg, University of, 81
Wolf, F. A., 86, 99
Wolff, Christian, 48–49, 51, 63–64, 75, 78, 88, 232
written law, 7, 25, 28
Württemberg (German state), 76, 133, 138, 188

yeomanry, 157
Young England Movement, 71

Zacharia, K. S., 81, 95, 101, 140, 141–43, 144, 146, 147–48, 149–50, 159–60, 178, 181–82, 201
Zamindar, 157
Zeitschrift für Deutsches Recht und Deutsche Rechtswissenschaft, 207
Zeitschrift für geschichtliche Rechtswissenschaft, 205–6
Zimmern, S. W., 139n.200
Zopfl, H., 140

Lightning Source UK Ltd.
Milton Keynes UK
UKOW03f2232290814

237736UK00007B/356/P